HARDY OF WESSEX

HARDY AT EIGHTY-THREE
see page vi

HARDY OF WESSEX

WESSEX

His Life and Literary Career

by

CARL J. WEBER

NEW YORK: COLUMBIA UNIVERSITY PRESS
LONDON: ROUTLEDGE & KEGAN PAUL

First edition 1940
Revised edition published 1965
by Columbia University Press
New York
and Routledge & Kegan Paul Ltd
London

Copyright © Routledge & Kegan Paul Ltd, 1965

Library of Congress Catalog Card Number 65–20474

Printed in Great Britain
by Western Printing Services Ltd, Bristol

Contents

Contents

ILLUSTRATIONS

PORTRAIT OF THOMAS HARDY *Frontispiece*

The original portrait was painted by Augustus John in 1923 when Hardy was eighty-three. It was presented by T. H. Riches, Esq., to the Fitzwilliam Museum, Cambridge, England, where it now hangs. On seeing the portrait Hardy remarked: 'I don't know whether that is how I look or not, but that is how I feel.' The portrait is here reproduced by special permission of the Director of the Fitzwilliam Museum.

THE MANUSCRIPT OF HARDY'S POEM 'TO SHAKESPEARE AFTER THREE HUNDRED YEARS' *pages* 267 and 268

Hardy wrote this poem on February 14, 1916. It was first published in *A Book of Homage to Shakespeare* in April 1916 on the three hundredth anniversary of Shakespeare's death. It was reprinted in June 1916 in the *Fortnightly Review* and was again reprinted at the Chiswick Press (London) in July 1916 in an edition limited to fifty copies for private distribution by Mrs. Hardy. In 1917 Hardy 'collected' this poem in *Moments of Vision*. The manuscript was given to Magdalene College, Cambridge, and is now in the Pepysian Library of that college, which had made Hardy an Honorary Fellow in 1913. The manuscript is here reproduced through the kindness of, and with the permission of, the late Mrs. Florence Hardy.

Preface

WHEN the first edition of this biography was published in 1940, its preface began with the statement that 'the birth of Thomas Hardy on June 2, 1840, is easily the most significant event calling for centennial commemoration in the year 1940'. Since then, twenty-five years have passed—a quarter-century that has seen the awarding of the Nobel Prize to William Faulkner, the revival of enthusiastic interest in Henry James, and the emergence of a large and vigorous company of younger writers. Interest in Hardy and his writings might quite conceivably have been dimmed if not wholly obliterated by this passage of time and this rise of energetic competitors. Such has, however, not been the case, for the public has continued to show a lively interest in Hardy's work, and since his death in 1928 there has been an unremitting tide of volumes and essays about him.

The eighteenth day of March 1965 marked the one hundredth anniversary of Hardy's first publication in London. The present revised edition of this biography can therefore continue to be regarded as a centennial commemorative volume and can invite readers for exactly the same reason as in 1940: 'No author born within the last hundred years has made so deep an impression upon the minds and hearts of his readers. Hardy has been the most voluminously discussed writer of modern times, and a memorial publication might easily be justified if it did no more than offer a synthesis of the thousands of books, articles, dissertations, studies, critiques, and annotations which testify to the important position he holds in the modern world.'

In every author's heart there doubtless is, as there was in Hamlet's, a kind of fighting that will not let him sleep; but in Hardy's case the 'fighting' arose from certain radical discords which are not always easy to detect. Hardy himself rarely gives much help to anyone attempting to discover the causes of his particular adjustment, or maladjustment, to his world. 'Ache deep, but make no moans' was the formula by which he guided his conduct; and in the two volumes which he prepared in the last decade of his life—*The Early Life* and *The Later Years of Thomas Hardy*, published in 1928 and 1930 as the work of his second wife but now known to be largely his own work—Hardy had little to say about the psychological complexity and unrest that found release in his writings.

The biographer, however, cannot rest satisfied with the sort of information that Hardy himself often gives us, that he once caught one of Lady Malmsbury's green linnets or that he once heard Lottie Collins sing 'Ta-ra-ra boom-de-ay'. The biographer must try to penetrate into the *inner* life of the man; he must learn what Hardy read and what he thought; he must inspect his secret desires and ambitions, study his rebuffs and disappointments, and analyse his frustrations. In the 1940 edition of this work I stated: 'Until recently it has been impossible to penetrate far into the inner life of Thomas Hardy, but the time has now come when the attempt can be made. Access to hundreds of his unpublished letters has facilitated the present study and has often permitted the turning of surmise into dogmatic statement or categorical denial.' In the present revision, the 'hundreds' of letters referred to in 1940 have been greatly multiplied. Three volumes of Hardy's letters have been edited by the present biographer, and access has been had to many more as yet unpublished, some in libraries and museums, some in private hands. These letters make it possible to trace Hardy's literary career from Higher Bockhampton to the grave in Poets' Corner, Westminster Abbey, with an assurance that has hitherto been impossible. It is now reasonable to believe that we know quite accurately why Thomas Hardy wrote, why he chose the subjects on which he wrote, and how his books grew from ideas and emotions and experiences to the printed volumes that have delighted the world.

Guided by his letters, we are often able to avoid being led astray by Hardy's own statements when they were based on faulty memory. One illustration of this point may serve. In *Later Years* (p. 164) Hardy stated that his 'volume of verses entitled *Satires of Circumstance, Lyrics and Reveries*', published in 1914, containing fifteen satires, included these poems which (he said) were 'caustically humorous productions' of a sort 'he would readily have suppressed' in 1914, because 'he was in no mood now to publish humour or irony'. The satires had, so he said, been originally 'issued with a light heart before the war'. That is the way Hardy remembered it in 1920 when he was eighty years old and his eyes were dim. Fortunately, his letters enable us to see the 1914 situation with clearer vision. That the satires were *not* 'humorous productions' and had *not* 'been issued with a light heart' is made clear by a letter which Hardy wrote to his friend Edmund Gosse: 'The little group of satires cost me much sadness. . . .' And the assertion that Hardy 'would readily have suppressed' them in 1914 is disproved by a letter he wrote to Sydney Cockerell on August 28, 1914: 'What I care most about just now is that the poems entitled *Satires of Circumstance* (they are by no means all satires, but the title seems as good as any) should be brought out by the Macmillans at some time or other. The manuscript is already in their hands.'

Cardinal Newman once remarked: 'Biographers varnish, they assign motives, they conjecture feelings, they interpret Lord Burleigh's nod, but contemporary letters are facts.' In the present revision of *Hardy of Wessex* the use of letters, published and unpublished, has made it possible to reduce conjecture to a minimum.

This revised edition has also provided a welcome opportunity to correct errors in the 1940 edition. Some were trivial though annoying misprints; a few were more serious scars—errors from which the present edition is, I hope, free. In revising the book I have also eliminated a lot of the bibliographical detail which, in 1940, I thought desirable and important, but which, since the publication of Professor Richard Little Purdy's *Thomas Hardy: A Bibliographical Study* in 1954 is no longer needed.

Before her death in 1937 the second Mrs. Hardy granted me certain permissions and performed certain acts of assistance by which *Hardy of Wessex* was benefited and enriched. I regretted that she did not live to see the results of her help. Since her death, permission has been granted me by the Trustees of the Hardy copyrights (Lloyds Bank Ltd., London, and Miss I. Cooper Willis) to quote from Hardy's *Collected Poems*, and from *The Early Life* and *The Later Years*. I am happy to have the opportunity here to acknowledge once again the help of Miss Willis and to place on record my gratitude for all the kindness and encouragement which she has crowded into the past twenty-five years. My wife, Clara Carter Weber, has also continued to toil in the Hardy vineyard throughout this quarter-century, and this book would not be what it is without having had the benefit of her eyes, her hand, and her critical taste and judgment. It is now fifty years since I began the study of Hardy, and since this is probably my last appearance upon the Wessex stage I make a grateful valedictory bow to all the friends of Thomas Hardy who have been kind enough to aid me in one way or another in the preparation of this book.

C. J. W.

Waterville, Maine.

'And one was Lord of the Wessex Coast
and all the lands thereby.'

—Rudyard Kipling,
in 'The Three Captains'

I

Birth and Boyhood
at Bockhampton

THE year 1840 in England was a memorable one in a number of ways. On the tenth of January Sir Rowland Hill's great benefaction—penny postage—began its ministrations to mankind and the world's first postage stamps were issued. Every stamp-collector is familiar with the girlish portrait of Queen Victoria on that new postal device which Hill called 'a bit of paper just large enough to bear the stamp and covered at the back with a glutinous wash'. Queen Victoria herself remembered the year 1840 less for her appearance upon the first postage stamp than for her appearance before the altar on February 10 to marry Albert. And before spring tripped north again that year, Victoria and her husband were happily looking forward to the birth of their first child—the Princess Royal who arrived punctually on November 10.

Two other English households remembered the year 1840 for the same reason. In a house a hundred miles or so to the west of London, and also in another dwelling seventy-five miles beyond the first, there were expectant parents—one pair in Dorset, the other in Devon. The Dorset baby proved to be a boy, born five months before the royal princess. The Devon baby proved to be a girl, born two weeks after the princess.

The humble parents of the Dorset baby occupied a small but comfortable brick house which stood in a secluded spot on the western edge of Puddletown Heath. 'It was a spot which returned upon the memory of those who loved it with an aspect

1

of peculiar and kindly congruity. The vast tract of unenclosed wild known as Egdon Heath wore the appearance of a thing majestic without severity, impressive without showiness, emphatic in its admonitions, grand in its simplicity. The qualifications which frequently invest the façade of a prison with far more dignity than is found in the façade of a palace double its size lent to this heath a sublimity in which spots renowned for beauty of the accepted kind are utterly wanting. Haggard Egdon was a place perfectly accordant with man's nature—neither ghastly, hateful, nor ugly: neither commonplace, unmeaning, nor tame; but, like man, slighted and enduring; and withal singularly colossal and mysterious in its swarthy monotony. As with some persons who have long lived apart, solitude seemed to look out of its countenance. It had a lonely face, suggesting tragical possibilities.'

On the edge of this heath there stood in 1840 a few dwellings known as the hamlet of Higher Bockhampton, in the parish of Stinsford, Dorset. Stinsford lies about a mile east of Dorchester, and Higher Bockhampton is about two miles east of Stinsford. The houses of this hamlet lined either side of a narrow lane shaded by cherry trees, and in the easternmost thatched-roofed dwelling lived Mr. and Mrs. Thomas Hardy, twenty-nine and twenty-seven years of age. Hardy was a master mason and building-contractor. He and his wife Jemima (*née* Hand) were occupying the house built in 1801 by Thomas's grandfather, John Hardy of Puddletown—built for his son, the first Thomas Hardy of Higher Bockhampton, upon the occasion of Thomas's marriage. Thomas Hardy the First had died in 1837, three years before Thomas the Second handed the name on to the future novelist and poet, Thomas the Third. Here, then, on the edge of Egdon heath, with its 'lonely face suggesting tragical possibilities', Mr. and Mrs. Hardy went about their humble activities, watching the signs of the return of spring, and awaiting like their Queen the arrival of their first-born child.

The baby, born on June 2, 1840, was so frail as to be at first supposed to be dead. Rescued, however, by the attendant nurse, the child survived and lived to make famous a name that, eighty-eight years later, was carved into a stone in Westminster Abbey. In spite of obscurity of birth, of deficiency of education, of discouragement and misrepresentation, by sheer imaginative

2

genius and by the power of his pen, that frail infant born on the edge of Egdon Heath gained for himself a final resting place among England's greatest. He is the subject of this book.

When that June baby was almost six months old, the third of the 1840 births here singled out for notice took place in the historic Devon town of Plymouth.

> Ah, that is the place
> Where chanced, in the hollow of years ago, . . .
> The birth of a little girl of grace—
> The sweetest the house saw, first or last; . . .
> There, there she lay
> In a room by the Hoe, like the bud of a flower.

The house in Plymouth stood on York Street. There, on November 24, a solicitor named John Attersoll Gifford and his wife Emma (*née* Farman) welcomed into the world the 'little girl of grace' whom they named Emma Lavinia. Thirty years later she was destined to see for the first time the baby boy born on the edge of Egdon Heath, and years after that meeting he was to write about her the poem 'Places' from which the lines just quoted are taken.

Several points call for notice in connection with the birth of Thomas Hardy in 1840. First of all, 'Egdon Heath' became one of the earliest, and remained one of the most powerful, influences upon his mind. He celebrated its austere dignity, not only in *The Return of the Native*, from which the description quoted above is taken, but also in book after book. He learned to love 'the enormous Egdon Waste', and when, later on, he came to the creation of Clym Yeobright in *The Return of the Native*, he had only to look into his own heart and write of what he found there.

If any one knew the heath well it was Clym. He was permeated with its scenes, with its substance, and with its odours. He might be said to be its product. His eyes had first opened thereon; with its appearance all the first images of his memory were mingled; his estimate of life had been coloured by it; his toys had been the flint knives and arrow-heads which he found there . . . ; his flowers, the purple bells and yellow furze; his animal kingdom, the snakes and croppers; his society, its human haunters. Take all the varying hates felt by

3

Eutacia Vye towards the heath, and translate them into loves, and you have the heart of Clym.

And you have the heart of Thomas Hardy.

The significance of this fact was grasped by one of Hardy's earliest critics, Lionel Johnson. 'Many novelists,' wrote Johnson in 1894, 'are not at home among the places of their imagination; from first to last, they describe their woods and fields, not as long familiarity makes them appear, but as they appear to unaccustomed eyes: there is no heart in them. But Mr. Hardy has the art of impressing upon us so strong a sense of familiarity with his scenes, that we read of Wessex and we think of our own homes.'

Second, the fact that Hardy's father was a mason and builder placed the future author, in the England of 125 years ago, in a very different social category from that into which Emma Lavinia Gifford was born as the daughter of a Plymouth solicitor. In Chapter VIII of *A Pair of Blue Eyes* there is a revealing conversation between Stephen Smith, a mason's son, and Elfride Swancourt. As we listen to the talk of these two fictional characters, it is hard to resist the suspicion that we are overhearing a conversation that once took place between Hardy and Miss Gifford. Whether the words were ever actually uttered or not, the conversation in the book indicates a sensitiveness to class distinctions on Hardy's part which is rendered unmistakably clear by the frequency with which this sort of observation is found in the Wessex novels:

'Did you ever think what my parents might be, or what society I originally moved in?'
'No, not particularly. I suppose you have moved in the ordinary society of professional people.'
'Supposing I have not—that none of my family have a profession except me?'
'I don't mind.'
'Where do you think I went to school . . . ?'
'Doctor Somebody's academy.'
'No. To a dame school originally, then to a national school.'
'Only to those! . . .'
'What do you think my father . . . does for his living . . . ?'
'He practices some profession or calling, I suppose.'
'No; he is a mason . . . .'
'O, Stephen! . . . I do own that it seems odd . . . .'

4

No precise date can be set for the first dawning of a sense of social 'inferiority' in Hardy's mind, but it was there before he had reached the age of ten; and, once planted in his mind, it never left him. The conditions that confronted him in the England into which he was born and the people whom he met, early and later, made it impossible for him ever to forget his position. When he was a schoolboy of only nine or ten, he went to a harvest-supper—'the only harvest-supper and dance he ever saw', according to *The Early Life*—and there received a pointed lesson in recognizing the distinction between his class as a mason's son and that of 'the Squire' and 'the manor-lady' and others in 'the manor-house party' who graced the harvest-supper occasion for a few minutes 'and then left'. The lesson, once learned, was never forgotten. Hardy's first novel, entitled *The Poor Man and the Lady*, emphasized throughout its action the social disparity announced in the title. In *An Indiscretion in the Life of an Heiress*, 'this perception of their disparity weighed more and more heavily upon him as the days went on'. In *The Woodlanders*, Giles Winterborne 'feared anew that they could never be happy together. . . . She was accomplished; he was unrefined. It was the original difficulty.'

Hardy's early awareness of his social disadvantages is traceable to his mother. His interest in books also came from her. He once called himself 'a born bookworm' and it was clearly his mother to whom he was indebted for this characteristic. 'She read omnivorously,' he remembered, and in this she was like her mother and her grandmother. That grandmother, Maria Childs, had moved in literary circles and was the sister of a newspaper editor. She married a man named Swetman, and their daughter Elizabeth (Hardy's grandmother) eventually came to possess a large library—unusually large for a yeoman's daughter. She read—so Hardy was afterwards told—not only Milton and Bunyan, Richardson and Fielding, but also 'knew the writings of Addison, Steele, and others of the *Spectator* group almost by heart'.[1] Some of Elizabeth Swetman's books descended to her daughter Jemima, and from her to her son, Thomas the novelist, and he in turn used the titles later on to indicate the books owned by Bathsheba and Gabriel Oak in *Far from the Madding Crowd*. Elizabeth Swetman had married 'beneath her', and her daughter Jemima, a girl of unusual ability and judgment, grew up under conditions of such extreme poverty that Hardy remembered how, in later years, she could never speak of her youth without pain.

In the case of William Shakespeare, a gifted mother who traced her ancestry back to the Ardens of Park Hall passed her abilities on to her son. Similarly, in the case of Thomas Hardy, his mother, Jemima Hand, endowed her son with those talented gifts and interests which eventually made him one of England's great authors. Unfortunately, Hardy was also indebted to his mother for his earliest awareness of the fact that, in her eyes, he belonged to a debased class in English society. Before writing his novel about the Durbeyfield family, degenerated from the ancient Turbervilles, Hardy made a note in his journal regarding 'the decline and fall of the Hardys. . . . So we go down, down, down.'

On the day of his birth, then, the stage was already set for moulding and fashioning the mind of the future author. His Dorchester schooling (with its emphasis on the Greek and Latin classics) and his professional life in London are the only major influences not already present at the time of his birth, and even these two were implied. For Hardy's mother's intellectual ambitions for her son made inevitable the sort of schooling the future novelist received; and his father's trade as a mason led directly to Hardy's apprenticeship to an architect, and that in turn took him eventually to London. Arnold Bennett once remarked to Hugh Walpole: 'My dear Hugh, when you're born, you're done for!' Thomas Hardy's birth and all the circumstances attendant upon that second day of June 1840 are an excellent illustration of whatever truth lies in Arnold Bennett's jest.

The house in which Hardy was born is still standing; and, although Egdon Heath beyond it is no longer 'the untameable Ishmaelitish thing' that it seemed to be in Hardy's boyish eyes, the garden and the birthplace behind it have seen so little change that we can easily recognize them when they turn up in the pages of *Under the Greenwood Tree*. 'A little wicket admitted to the garden, and a path led up to the house. It was a long low cottage with a hipped roof of thatch, having dormer windows breaking up into the eaves, a chimney standing in the middle of the ridge and another at the further end. . . . The walls of the

dwelling were for the most part covered with creepers. . . .'
When we enter the house, we still find 'the main room on the
left . . . with a beam bisecting the ceiling'. A still earlier word-
picture of his birthplace is given in Hardy's poem 'Domicilium',
written before he was twenty. This poem, consisting of thirty-
four lines of Wordsworthian blank verse, is not included in
Hardy's *Collected Poems*, but it *is* found in *The Early Life*. Hardy
always objected when his home was called 'a humble cottage'.
It was a low thatched building, but in his eyes it was nevertheless a rambling and spacious house.

Here he spent the first seven years of his life in unhurried
idleness. The time was not wasted, however, for the boy's eyes
and ears were wide open. He learned to know intimately the
birds, the snails, the toads, the spiders, and the sheep. Once he
pretended to be a sheep. Getting down on all fours, he crawled
out into the field and pretended to eat grass. For the rest of his
life he remembered his own surprise when, on looking up, he
found himself encircled by real sheep staring in perplexed
wonder at this new member of the fold. Nor was the animal
world the only part of nature to arouse his interest, for from
his father the boy learned to follow the rotation of the seasons
and to look lovingly upon the mysterious countenance of Egdon
Heath.

To his father Hardy was also indebted for one of his earliest as
well as one of his most persistent interests—music. The father,
Thomas Hardy the Second, had played the violin in Stinsford
Church for nearly twenty years before the birth of the future
novelist, just as *his* father, Thomas Hardy the First, had played
the bass-viol in the same church for thirty-five years. This was
before the days of small church-organs, and for many years the
Hardy musicians were regarded as the best instrumentalists in
any of the parishes of the neighbourhood. When Hardy
(Thomas the Third) was only four years old, his father gave
him a toy accordion with his name and the date, '1844', written
on it. Before long, 'Tommy' was taught how to 'tune the fiddle',
and as soon as his fingers were large enough to function on the
strings of his father's violin, he was given instruction about
fingering. In a short time he was able to play some of the church
music, and soon thereafter he knew and could play 'hundreds of
jigs and country-dances'.[2] This early enthusiasm for music

never left him. When he moved to London, he attended (on October 27, 1865) the funeral of Lord Palmerston (the Prime Minister) in Westminster Abbey. The 'Dead March' from Handel's celebrated oratorio, *Saul*, was played at the close of the service, after which Hardy wrote to his sister Mary: 'I think I was never so much impressed with a ceremony in my life before.' This pleasure in music eventually left its mark in novel after novel. In his very first fictional attempt, *The Poor Man and the Lady*, Hardy wrote about the 'rush' of glorious music in Handel's *Messiah* and described how the 'deafening harmonies' of the Hallelujah Chorus went 'flying from this group and from that' until they 'seemed to absorb all the love and poetry that his life had produced, to pour it upon that one moment' of ecstatic response to the music. The musicians of *Under the Greenwood Tree* were all obviously drawn directly from real life and we can easily recognize the Hardy instrumentalists when we read that 'Old William Dewy, with the violoncello, played the bass; his grandson Dick the treble violin; and Reuben and Michael Mail the tenor and second violins'. In *Far from the Madding Crowd*, Gabriel Oak 'drew out his flute and began to play ... with Arcadian sweetness, and the sound of the well-known notes cheered his heart'. In the fifth chapter of *The Return of the Native* Hardy gives an amusing description of his grandfather (disguised in the novel as 'neighbour Yeobright'), who, when he 'warmed to his work, drove his bow into the strings that glorious grand that he almost sawed the bass-viol into two pieces'. His playing made every window in the church rattle 'as if 'twere a thunderstorm'.

'To be honest,' Hardy wrote to a friend in 1909, 'I am never tired of music.' At the age of seventy-six, when he was writing up an account of himself for the 1916 edition of *Who's Who*, he mentioned 'old church and dance music' among his recreations. When the Hardy Memorial Room, constructed in the Dorset County Museum in Dorchester, was opened on May 10, 1939, by the Poet Laureate, John Masefield, Hardy's violin and 'cello appropriately stood in one corner of the Room, and there they still stand to remind visitors that the novelist and poet was a musician as well.

Music was not the only thing Hardy learned from his father. Like 'Grandfather James' in *Under the Greenwood Tree* who was 'by trade a mason', Hardy's father 'was often engaged to work at buildings far away' from Higher Bockhampton. Young Tommy was sometimes taken along on these trips about the Dorset countryside and was thus given his earliest introduction to geography and local history. The time would eventually come when William Archer could exclaim to Hardy: 'What you don't know about this Wessex of yours isn't knowledge! It seems to me there isn't a contour of the country ... that isn't mapped in your mind.'[3] This familiarity with the Dorset countryside began with rides with his father. One day, when Tom was enjoying a school holiday, Thomas Senior took his son on a business trip to Weymouth. At this date, Edmund Gosse was a boy of four in Weymouth. Years later, after he and Hardy had both become well-known authors and were fellow-members of the Savile Club in London, they amused themselves by trying to figure out how near they had come to seeing each other as boys in Weymouth in 1853.

Hardy's father was the more inclined to take his son along with him because of the boy's obvious need for exercise and fresh air. Tom's physical frailty had, in fact, led his parents to fear that he would never survive or attain to maturity, and he was accordingly not sent to school at the usual age. In 1848, however, when Mrs. Julia Augusta Martin (wife of 'Squire' Francis P. B. Martin, who had bought the manor-house of Kingston-Maurward, near Stinsford, in 1845) built a new school at nearby Bockhampton, Hardy's parents decided that Tom was now, at the age of eight, strong enough to walk to the new school. Here, then, he began his studies. Mrs. Martin herself 'taught him his letters', as she recalled with pleasure in a letter she wrote him forty years later, after he had become a famous author.

From the very start of his schooling, reading, writing, and arithmetic all came so easily to 'Tommy' (as Mrs. Martin called him) that his mother wished for him better instruction than was available in the Bockhampton school. After one year with Mrs. Martin, Hardy was accordingly transferred to a day school in Dorchester conducted by Isaac G. Last. For the next seven years, small and delicate though he was, Hardy had a daily walk of three miles each way, to Dorchester and back. After three years, he began the study of Latin; and when Mr. Last moved to another site in Dorchester and opened an 'Academy for Young Gentlemen', Hardy went with him. In 1853 he was reading Caesar and Eutropius with Isaac Last, and eventually so far outstripped his classmates in the Academy that he was awarded a copy of Beza's Latin *Testament* as a school prize. Forty years later, Hardy transferred this facility in Latin to young Jude Fawley—a facility 'which enabled him with great ease to himself to beguile his lonely walks by imaginary conversations therein'.[4]

While this mastery of Latin was being acquired, Hardy was busily soaking up an amazing acquaintance with the English Bible. Strict and regular attendance at church services at Stinsford on Sundays resulted in his learning the morning and evening services by heart, and no one who leafs through *Jude the Obscure* to note Jude's mastery of Latin will fail to notice the even more complete mastery of the Bible; for there are numerous allusions to or quotations from *Genesis, Exodus, Job*, the *Psalms*, the *Song of Solomon*, and *Daniel*; and from the New Testament, quotations from the *Gospels, Acts, First Corinthians*, and even from the 'uncanonical books'.

What is here said about *Jude the Obscure* is equally true of the other Wessex novels. In *Far from the Madding Crowd*, for example, there are no less than thirty-eight Biblical quotations or allusions, the Old Testament appearing more than twice as often as the New. In this novel (written twenty years before *Jude*), Hardy showed his intimate knowledge of *Genesis, Exodus, Judges, Ruth, II Samuel, I Kings, II Chronicles, Esther, Ecclesiastes, Daniel, Hosea, Jonah, Matthew, Mark, Luke, Galatians, I Thessalonians, II Timothy*, and *Revelation*. At the age of eighty-two he could toss off, in a private letter to Amy Lowell, a quotation like 'I do remember my faults this day'—probably without stopping to wonder whether 'Cousin Amy' (as he called Miss Lowell) would recognize that these were the words of the chief butler to Pharaoh in *Genesis* XLI : 9.

At a surprisingly early date Hardy began not only to know verses like these by heart, but also to have his favourites among them. Many referred to the grimmer side of life, and the 'pessimistic' thoughts of his later years are often traceable to roots in the Bible: 'Man that is born of a woman is of few days and full of trouble': *Job* XIV : 1 (a book Hardy came to know particularly well); 'Man is like to vanity: his days are as a shadow that passeth away': *Psalm* CXLIV : 4 (a verse he later wrote out in one of his notebooks); 'For we know that the whole creation groaneth and travaileth in pain together until now': *Romans* VIII : 22 (eventually quoted by Hardy in the twenty-first chapter of *The Return of the Native*). It is an understatement to say that Hardy knew the Bible as no other author who has written English novels ever knew it.

Not satisfied with what her son was learning in Latin, Mrs. Hardy arranged for him to receive private lessons in French; and with his mother's encouragement he tried to teach himself German by subscribing to Cassell's *Popular Educator*. Mrs. Hardy further extended the boundaries of the school curriculum at Mr. Last's Academy by giving Tom copies of Dryden's *Virgil*, of Johnson's *Rasselas*, and of Bernardin de Saint-Pierre's *Paul and Virginia*. Hardy also began to read Dumas and Shakespeare. When he read *Pilgrim's Progress*, he was so alarmed by the description of Apollyon that for the next seventy-five years he remembered how he had dreaded the solitary walk from Dorchester back to Bockhampton in the dark, because of his fear that Apollyon would spring out at him.

One of Hardy's favourite books in boyhood was *The Scottish Cavalier* (1850), by James Grant, the military novelist. Seventy years later, Hardy still retained—so he told Stewart M. Ellis—vivid memories of the scenes and characters in this now-forgotten romance. The Waverley Novels also received some attention, though they apparently failed to stir in young Hardy as much enthusiasm as had James Grant. *The Early Life* states (p. 64) that Hardy preferred Scott's poetry to his novels, but one is inclined to question this statement on noticing that not a line of Scott's poetry is quoted anywhere by Hardy, whereas he remembered the Waverley Novels he had read as a boy and mentioned or quoted from four of them. *The Antiquary* is quoted in *The Mayor of Casterbridge*, and in that same novel *The Bride of Lammermoor* is referred to and Gurth in *Ivanhoe* is mentioned. In *The Woodlanders* Hardy mentions Amy Robsart (in *Kenilworth*).

G. P. R. James was another author whose books delighted Hardy as a boy, and the Wessex novelist recalled *The Ancient Régime* with particular pleasure. The most powerful literary influence upon his mind in boyhood, however, was William Harrison

Ainsworth, and *Old St. Paul's* was his favourite romance. Later, he liked Ainsworth's *Windsor Castle*, and at the age of seventy-three he acknowledged the gift of an illustrated copy by saying: 'I am carried back to the days of my boyhood.' He remembered temporarily falling in love with a girl just because she came from Windsor! One of the most popular novels of Hardy's youth was Ainsworth's *Rookwood*, and Dick Turpin, the hero of this novel, reappears in a sensational chapter of *Far from the Madding Crowd*. Hardy was particularly impressed with Ainsworth's description of a storm in *Rookwood*, and when he came to describing a similar storm in *Far from the Madding Crowd* he took from the shelf his old copy of *Rookwood* and used Ainsworth's description with results to which we shall give attention in a later chapter.

All these names—Saint-Pierre and Dumas, Scott and James Grant, G. P. R. James and Ainsworth—must be kept in mind, if one is interested in tracing Hardy's predilection for romantic tales of fair ladies and moonlight meetings, mysterious horsemen and secret marriages, Gothic casements and unlucky accidents.

In addition to acquiring these tastes from books, Hardy was learning directly from people. During his leisurely years at Higher Bockhampton he came to know and admire the shepherd whose portrait he later painted as Gabriel Oak in *Far from the Madding Crowd*. Mrs. Hardy's sister, whom young Thomas and his mother visited at Puddletown, appears in the same novel as Bathsheba Everdene. And in these early years he learned to listen attentively to, and to look understandingly upon, the Dorset rustics. Their speech, gait, habits, and ideas became as firmly fixed in his retentive memory as did the tunes he learned to play upon his father's violin.

Those tunes he knew only less well than those which the Wessex winds played upon the trees in the woods through which he walked on his daily tramp between Bockhampton and Dorchester. That walk was often taken in the dark, when the uselessness of eyes increased the keenness of ears. Hardy soon learned that 'almost every species of tree has its voice as well as its feature. At the passing of the breeze the fir trees sob and moan no less distinctly than they rock; the holly whistles as it battles with itself; the ash hisses amid its quaverings; the beech rustles while its flat boughs rise and fall.'[5] No wonder that the time eventually came when James M. Barrie could remark of Hardy: 'He had an intimacy with trees . . . and . . . the trees had a similar knowledge of him. . . . When he passed through their wood, they could tell him from all other men!'

When Hardy was fifteen, he began to teach in the Stinsford Church Sunday School. In this way he not only increased his familiarity with the characters and the phraseology of the Bible, but learned also to know the vicar, and the vicar's sons, and the dairymaids, and the farmers, and the tranters—all of whom were later to appear in the Wessex novels. Marian, in *Tess of the D'Urbervilles*, was one of the dairymaids in Hardy's Sunday School class; and the numerous clergymen who appear in Hardy's writings, from Mr. Maybold in *Under the Greenwood Tree* and Mr. Woodwell in *A Laodicean*, down to the Reverend Mr. Clare and his clerical sons in *Tess of the D'Urbervilles*, are all traceable to actual personalities.

Hardy also learned things from the town of Dorchester. It was no ordinary or average small town but one that possessed unusual features, some of them extremely impressive. There was, for instance, the Ring, 'the local name of one of the finest Roman Amphitheatres . . . remaining in Britain. The Amphitheatre was a huge circular enclosure, with a notch at opposite extremities of its diameter north and south. . . . It was to Casterbridge [Hardy's fictional name for Dorchester] what the ruined Coliseum is to modern Rome, and was nearly of the same magnitude.' There were other marks of age in Dorchester. In one of the little-used alleys of the town was an ancient doorway, the keystone of the arch of which was a mask. 'Originally the mask had exhibited a comic leer, but generations of Casterbridge boys had thrown stones at the mask, aiming at its open mouth; and the blows thereon had chipped off the lips and jaws as if they had been eaten away by disease. The appearance was so ghastly that one could not bear to look at it.' But obviously young Thomas Hardy had looked often and steadily at it.

The boy's daily walk between Bockhampton and Dorchester gave him an opportunity to study faces and to read character. As he approached the town he had to cross two bridges. The first one was built of stone; the second, at the end of High Street, was of weather-stained brick. (Modern visitors to Dorchester can no longer see the weather-stained bricks, for the old bridge was rebuilt in 1954 of stone, and it no longer presents the contrasts which Hardy's observant eyes had noticed.) In his day, it was not the bridges themselves that attracted his attention but the people he learned to associate with them. For 'to this pair of bridges gravitated all the failures of the town. There was a marked difference of quality between the personages who haunted the near bridge of brick, and the personages who haunted the far bridge of stone. Those of lowest character preferred the former . . . ; they did not mind the glare of the public eye. The *misérables* who would pause on the remoter bridge were of a politer stamp. . . . The eyes of this species were mostly over the parapet upon the running water below. While one in straits on the townward bridge did not mind who saw him . . . and kept his back to the parapet to survey the passers-by, one in straits on the stone bridge never faced the road, never turned his head at coming footsteps, but watched the current whenever a stranger approached.'[6] The 'failures of the town' can have little suspected how much a slight boy who passed them every day was observing.

Sometimes these unfortunate Dorset folk were not strangers to the boy. 'As a child,' so Hardy wrote to Sir William Rothenstein on March 11, 1912, 'I personally knew a boy who was starved to death in "the hungry forties". . . . He used to keep sheep near our house.' On another occasion, a Dorchester boy stopped Hardy on the street and asked to borrow his Latin grammar. The boy worked for a widow and had been hired to drive her baker's-cart; but his studious (i.e. absent-minded) habits interfered with his attending to the bakery business. The conflict between the boy's humble occupation and his pathetic ambition for a university education touched a sympathetic chord in Thomas Hardy's make-up; and thirty years later, when a chance event recalled the baker's-cart driver to Hardy's mind, the boy was put (with suitable disguise) into the tragic pages of *Jude the Obscure*.

Fortunately, Hardy's memories of boyhood days were not all associated with poverty or darkened by tragedy. He remembered also Louisa Harding, a farmer's daughter, whose 'gauzy muslin' and whose 'life-lit brow' captured his youthful eye and fancy. As he passed her one day in the lane at Higher Bockhampton, he mustered up enough courage to murmur 'Good

evening' to her. She made no reply, and that 'Good evening' was
the only word Hardy ever addressed to her in real life. Many
years later, after Louisa had died and had been buried in the
Stinsford churchyard, he wrote a poem about her entitled
'Louie', and from it come the words quoted above.

One Wednesday afternoon shortly before Hardy's sixteenth
Christmas, he came home from school with something obviously
on his mind. Whether his brother Henry and his sister Kate were
both on hand to observe him or not, it is now impossible to say;
but many years later it was reported that they had observed
Tom opening the door of the old grandfather's clock which
stood in the home at Higher Bockhampton and had watched
him write something on the back of the door. He wrote a poem
which consisted of three stanzas of twelve lines each. It began:

> Oh the old old clock of the household stock
> Is the brightest thing, and neatest;
> Its hands though old have a touch of gold
> And its chime rings still the sweetest; . . .
> Tick Tick, it said, quick quick to bed
> For of ten I've given warning,
> Up, up and go or else you know
> You'll never rise soon in the morning.

At the end of his writing of the thirty-six lines, Hardy signed
his name and added the date: December 19, 1855. The clock
was later in the possession of Kate Hardy; and after her death
it came into the possession of Dr. E. W. Mann. When he had
copied out the words written on the inside of the clock door, Dr.
Mann supplied a transcript of them to the London *Times
Literary Supplement*,[7] and informed the editor that Hardy's
brother and sister 'recollected that the verses were written by
him one Sunday morning while their parents were at church'.

Unfortunately, we begin to sense something wrong in this
'recollection' when we notice that December 19 was not a
Sunday but a Wednesday. In any case, one week after the publication of 'Hardy's Earliest Verses', the *Times Literary Supplement* had to retract its (and Dr. Mann's) claim, for a reader had
identified the poem as the work of Charles Swain (1801–74),
the versifier who had enjoyed a brief fame as 'the Manchester
poet'.

Swain's name was not signed to the poem on the clock door; Hardy's name *was* signed there, and Kate Hardy had apparently lived all her life under the impression that the verses had been composed by her brother. Whether Hardy had deliberately encouraged members of his family to believe that he had written a poem, or whether he had merely kept silent and had allowed a younger brother and sister to enjoy thinking such a thought, or whether Kate Hardy's own memory many years later was at fault, no one can now say. The few slight departures from Swain's text suggest that Hardy had memorized the poem and wrote it out on the clock door from memory and then signed his name as copyist rather than as composer. He did recall long afterwards that in 1856 'he began writing verses . . . which do not appear to have been printed anywhere'.[8] Readers will have to do their own conjecturing as to what this means, and estimate for themselves the likelihood that fifteen-year-old Tom deliberately misled his sister. If he did, we shall be the less surprised when we find him doing the same sort of thing on a larger scale and before a larger audience twenty years later.

A more charitable hypothesis would be that Hardy, at the age of fifteen, thoughtlessly did the same sort of thing that Edna St. Vincent Millay did at the age of twelve. She copied a poem entitled 'Nest Eggs' and signed her name to it. After Miss Millay's death, her sister Norma discovered the MS. poem, gave it to Mr. Vincent Sheean, who supplied the text to *Vogue* magazine, where it was printed in the issue for August 1951 as a previously unpublished poem by Edna St. Vincent Millay. By August 22 at least ten readers of *Vogue* had written in to the editor to call attention to the fact that the poem was actually by Robert Louis Stevenson and had been published in *A Child's Garden of Verses* before Edna Millay was born. Hardy's copying differed from Miss Millay's chiefly in the fact that he wrote on a clock door rather than in a copybook. His copying is worth emphasizing here because it turns out to be not an isolated or a trivial act but one that heralds a future habit. The seed of plagiarism had been planted.

In later life Hardy remarked that he had remained a child until he was sixteen. While this was doubtless true as far as experience and the development of physical powers and of initiative and resourcefulness are concerned, Hardy's mind and sympathies, like his knowledge and insights, were far from being those of a child when his formal schooling came to an end shortly after his sixteenth birthday. For one who had had only eight years of classroom instruction, he had accomplished amazing things. He may have been timid and retiring—like Wordsworth he had learned to know perhaps too well the self-sufficing power of solitude—but in mental equipment he was much farther along towards maturity than are most boys of sixteen. The seeds which were to grow and blossom in future novels had already been sown. Hardy's knowledge of nature and his observation of Dorset people, his keen interest in music and his proficiency with the violin, his acquaintance with the countryside around Dorchester, his thoroughgoing familiarity with the Bible and the Prayer Book, and his reading of books in English, French, and Latin, all were to flower in the novels he was to begin to write a dozen years after he had left Mr. Last's Academy for Young Gentlemen.

II

In Search of a Profession

IN the last paragraph of *The Mayor of Casterbridge* Hardy tells the reader that his self-effacing heroine Elizabeth-Jane never ceased to wonder at the persistence of the unforeseen. Hardy too never ceased to wonder at the large proportion of a man's life which is determined by pure chance, and he transfers this thought to a great many of the characters in his novels. It is mere chance that makes Clym Yeobright in *The Return of the Native* become the manager of a diamond-shop in Paris. Hardy saw nothing unusual in this dispensation. 'That waggery of fate,' he wrote, 'which started Clive as a writing clerk, Gay as a linen-draper, Keats as a surgeon, and a thousand others in a thousand other odd ways, banished the wild and ascetic heath-lad [Clym] to a trade' which sent him first to Budmouth (Hardy's fictional name for Weymouth). 'Yeobright did not wish to go there, but it was the only feasible opening. Thence he went to London; and thence, shortly after, to Paris.' There is not a little autobiography written into this account of how Clym Yeobright became a diamond merchant.

On leaving school Hardy went into an architect's drafting office. 'He did not wish to go there, but it was the only feasible opening. Thence he went to London,' as we shall see in the next chapter. More than sixty years later, Hardy recalled that he 'had sometimes wished to enter the Church',[1] and this statement has often led to a raising of eyebrows by those acquainted with Hardy's later much-publicized agnostic views. But in 1856 the idea of his entering the Church was not as fantastic as it may seem to readers in 1965. As a boy Hardy had been a regular

attendant at the services in Stinsford Church. He knew all the
responses by heart. He had learned to recite hymns with great
fervency. When, as a little fellow, he had been allowed to stay
at home on a rainy Sunday morning under the tolerant eye of
his grandmother, he would wrap a tablecloth around his little
body, to imitate the vicar's surplice; and then, standing on a
chair, he would 'read' the morning service and even 'preach a
sermon' by repeating some of the well-known admonitions of
the vicar. From one of Hardy's sisters we learn that he had his
favourite passages in the Bible; one of them was: 'and after the
fire a still small voice'. Tom's teaching in the Stinsford Sunday
School and his association there with the vicar's two sons had
likewise contributed to the thought that he might become a
clergyman. But it was not to be.

Entering the Church would have involved him in the pursuit
of a university education—a vague and distant goal for a boy in
a home where there had been no previous experience with
Oxford or Cambridge—and the vision of attaining to such a
goal was further obscured by thoughts of the expense and by
Tom's physical immaturity. Whenever discussions of the boy's
future were held in the Hardy home, his father insisted that he
ought, in some way or other, to equip himself 'to make an
income' by the time he was twenty-one. Hardy himself felt that
this insistence on his father's part was entirely reasonable, since
the son had 'never as yet earned a farthing in his life'.[2]

This positive stand taken by Hardy Senior is likely to surprise
those who are acquainted with the son's frequent references to
his father as an impractical man. The father, we are told, 'did
not possess the art of enriching himself by business'.[3] His preoccupation with the music of the parish church 'did not, to say
the least, assist his building business'.[4] When Mrs. Hardy urged
him to move to a more convenient place 'nearer or in the town',
where there would be better opportunities for the development
of her husband's business, the son tended to agree with his
mother, for 'it must be admitted that a lonely spot between a
heath and a wood . . . was almost unreasonable as a place for
carrying on the building trade. But Thomas Hardy the Second
had not the tradesman's soul.'[5]

Chance, however, 'that waggery of fate', decided the question
of Hardy's future. Thomas Senior, in the course of his building

trade, had often been called upon to carry out the designs of an architect named John Hicks who had an office at 39 South Street in Dorchester. Hicks had observed the quickness and the intelligence shown by young Thomas in occasionally helping his father when the latter was employed on a Hicks project, and in 1856 Hicks suggested that he take young Tom as a pupil and train him to become an architect. Tom had no particular desire to become an architect, 'but it was the only feasible opening'. The boy's parents decided that the proposal made by Hicks was a reasonable one and they promptly accepted it. No one suggested that Tom stick to his own idea of becoming a parson. Tom was no rebellious Samuel Butler. As Hardy's friend of later years, Sir James M. Barrie, once remarked: 'Whatever angel guards the portals of Elysium, he must have had to push Thomas Hardy in!' No angel was on hand to push him into Oxford or into Holy Orders. Instead, in July 1856, fate pushed him into the office of John Hicks, architect.

For the next three years, therefore, the daily walk back and forth between Bockhampton and Dorchester continued, often in the dark. Under John Hicks's tutelage, Hardy began to learn about the technical details of architecture, about stones and brick, about stresses and strains, about drainage and roofing. Without knowing what 'the waggery of fate' had in store for him, Hardy was engaged in equipping himself for creating one of the marked features of the novels of the future. He was learning about the 'small wooden lantern fitted with louvre-boards' of Warren's Malthouse at Puddletown, and about the 'fluted pilasters' and the 'coped gables with finials' of Waterston House, which was to serve the novelist shortly as the residence of Bathsheba Everdene in *Far from the Madding Crowd*. He was learning about the 'lanceolate windows and chamfers' of the Great Barn, 'called for the nonce the Shearing-barn', and about the 'two stone gurgoyles [*sic*] on each of the four faces of the parapet' of the Weatherbury Church tower—'all eight different from each other'. John Hicks was particularly well qualified for teaching Hardy about this church tower, for he was an ecclesiastical architect. His specialty was Gothic churches. Many of them, scattered all over southern England, were sadly in need of repair, and Hicks was often called upon, sometimes from as far away as Cornwall, to design and supervise the repairs. This business was often called 'restoration' but it oftener turned out to be a wanton destruction of Gothic beauty—a procedure which Hardy came later to deplore. (In 1906 he wrote an essay on 'Memories of Church Restoration' which was printed in the *Cornhill Magazine*, August 1906; and in February 1927, at the age of eighty-six, he wrote a brief note on 'The Preservation of Ancient Cottages' which was published a month later by the Royal Society of Arts.) Under Hicks's instruction, young Thomas became familiar with the technical features of St. Peter's, Dorchester, the 'grizzled church' of *The Mayor of Caster-bridge*, and learned to know St. Mary's at Bridport, the 'Port Bredy' of *Fellow Townsmen* and of the dairy where Tess Durbey-field worked for a while. A new church which Hicks built at Athelhampton, a mile east of Puddletown, acquainted Hardy with this village and thus prepared him for writing, later, about the 'new rooms' at Athelhall in an ironical poem entitled 'The Dame of Athelhall'.

But the hours spent in Hicks's office were not all devoted to architecture or to Gothic churches. Hardy found two other young men there. One, named Fippard, five years older than Hardy, was just about to leave at the end of his term with John Hicks; the other, Henry Robert Bastow, two years older than Hardy, was not yet half-way through his period of instruction. Both these young men interested Hardy, but for entirely different reasons.

Fippard, as the end of his training-period approached, made several trips up to London and from one of them he brought back a quadrille tune which he liked to whistle. Hardy long remembered not only the faultless whistling but also the way Fippard would caper about the architect's office while whistling the fascinating tune, with his arm around the waist of an imaginary belle. Hardy's interest in music was keen enough for him to wish to know more about this tune, but Fippard was unable to give it a name or supply any information about it other than the fact that it was a quadrille. Hardy remembered it, however, and later, when he himself was in London, he went to various second-hand music shops and hunted over a lot of dance music, but without finding Fippard's tune. Later still, he went to the British Museum and continued his search, but again to no avail. One day, during the summer of 1878, while he was sitting at his writing-desk near Wandsworth Common, he heard a street barrel-organ begin to play. It was then twenty-two years since he had watched Fippard caper and heard him whistle, but when the barrel-organ began to play, Hardy recognized the tune at once. It was Fippard's quadrille! He threw down his pen, rushed hatless out of doors, ran down the street, turned the corner, and finally caught up with the organ-grinder.

'What's the name of that tune?' asked the panting Hardy.

The frightened grinder could only point to the index on the front of the street-organ. Hardy looked, but 'Quadrille' was the only word there. He never learned the name of the tune and never heard it played again. Fippard soon moved out of Hardy's ken and, except for Tom's memory of the whistled dance-tune, Fippard would doubtless have been soon forgotten. But Hardy's poem, 'Reminiscences of a Dancing Man', and Chapter III of the Fourth Book of *The Return of the Native* with its vivid description of 'the ceaseless glides and whirls' of the dancing enjoyed by Wildeve at East Egdon, are enough to convince us that Hardy had not forgotten his whistling and capering colleague in Hicks's office.

The other young man, Henry Bastow, made a much deeper and more permanent impression upon Hardy, and for two reasons wholly unconnected with either architecture or music. Bastow was much interested in Latin and Greek; and, having been brought up in a Baptist home, he was prepared to question many of the Church of England dogmas which Hardy had come to accept at Stinsford Church without having given them much thought. For both these reasons, Bastow's presence in Hicks's office had important results in the development of Hardy's mind.

Bastow had studied Greek and Latin at a good school in or near London and came to Dorchester equipped with a knowledge of the classics that excelled Hardy's. Tom had done well with Latin under Isaac Last, but he had not gone far enough to reach Virgil, Horace, or Ovid. Of Greek he of course knew nothing. Challenged by Bastow's attainments, Tom set himself to try to catch up. By getting up at five o'clock in the morning, or (in the summer) even as early as four o'clock, he managed to work his way through several books of the *Aeneid*. Then, with a determination that called for even greater fortitude, he set about teaching himself Greek. It is a mark of the quickness of his mind that, in a short while, he and Bastow were able to read Greek together. In later years Hardy was inclined to think that the two pupils 'often gave more time to books than to drawing'. It might have been said of him what he later on made Drusilla Fawley say of her great-nephew Jude: 'The boy is crazy for books, that he is. It runs in our family.'

By the time that Hardy had mastered enough Greek to feel ready to tackle the dialect of the *Iliad*, his fellow-student Bastow introduced another complication into his life. Bastow's Baptist upbringing had led him, upon his arrival in Dorchester, to attend the Baptist Church there, the minister of which was an argumentative Scotsman named Perkins. Before long, Bob Bastow became convinced that he ought to be baptized, and shortly afterward he *was* baptized. His earnestness about the matter made such an impression upon young Hardy that he began to wonder whether he too ought to be baptized again as an adult. When Bastow's arguments about the meaninglessness of infant baptism left Hardy in a quandary, Tom went to the vicar at Stinsford Church for help, but received from him no more enlightenment than Tess Durbeyfield in the novel was later to receive from her 'parson of the parish' to whom she went for help after she had 'mused on the christening a good deal . . . for the child'.[6] When Hardy's replies to some of Bastow's arguments seemed to need demolishing, Bastow called for the help of the two Perkins boys, sons of the Baptist minister. Hardy long remembered them as 'hard-headed Scotch youths fresh from Aberdeen University . . . who could rattle off at a moment's notice the Greek original of any passage in the New Testament'.[7] The immediate result of these arguments about infant-christening was that Hardy dropped Homeric Greek and transferred his attention to Biblical Greek. When the Perkins boys wanted, like George Somerset in Chapter VII of *A Laodicean*, to 'prove the point by reasoning', Hardy obtained a copy of Griesbach's Greek New Testament (just as Jude Fawley does in Chapter I, 7, of *Jude the Obscure*) and soon learned to refer to infant-christening as 'paedo-baptism' and learned too—what is much more important for us to notice—how excited and even violent these Baptist debaters could become in the course of carrying on their arguments. When, later on, Hardy came to write *A Laodicean*, these

23

heated theological debates in Hicks's office came back to him. Their echoes reach us in the pages of the novel: 'I know that passage well—it is the last refuge of the Paedobaptists—I foresee your argument—I have met it dozens of times, and it is not worth that snap of the fingers!'

These vehement debates about church dogma are not likely to have much interest for the modern reader, but they are here made part of the biographical record so that confusing statements elsewhere will not prove misleading. In *The Later Years of Thomas Hardy*, for example, we are told that in *Jude the Obscure* 'there is not a scrap of personal history'.[8] This is simply not true. Jude Fawley's 'earnestly reading from his Griesbach's text' recalls Hardy's own purchase of Griesbach's Greek New Testament in 1859—'his new one, with better type . . . and with variorum readings in the margin'[9]—and the passages which Jude reads in the *Iliad* are the same as those that Hardy read and marked as his favourites in the Clarke edition of Homer (1818) when he was reading the *Iliad* with Robert Bastow.

Nor is *Jude the Obscure* the only Wessex novel in which we hear echoes from the Hicks drafting room. The Reverend Mr. Woodwell would not be present in *A Laodicean* if Thomas Hardy had not become acquainted with the Reverend Mr. Perkins and his argumentative sons.

Henry Robert Bastow remained a lively influence on Hardy as long as he continued a pupil in Hicks's office, and for some years after his departure he and Hardy corresponded. But when Bastow's term with Hicks expired, Hardy dropped his concern over adult baptism, closed his Griesbach, and returned to his interest in the *Iliad*. By 1861 he had got through 'a lot of Homer'.

After Bastow's departure, Hardy's duties in the Hicks office became more exacting. The term of his pupilage had been extended for one or two years longer, 'in consideration of his immaturity', but Hicks was not a harsh task-master and Hardy still found time for Greek. His return to the classical form of the language, instead of the Biblical, was encouraged by Hardy's friendship with another young man in Dorchester, Horace Moule, eight years Hardy's senior. Moule was the son of the Reverend Henry Moule (1801–80) who for over fifty years was the vicar of Fordington Church, Dorchester. Since both father and son were to play more than a minor part in Hardy's story, it will pay us to pause here a moment and identify the various members of the Moule family.

Fordington is a part of Dorchester lying behind the building where Hicks had his office—that is, between South Street and the Froom (or Frome) River—and, in the latter part of his term with John Hicks, when Hardy resided for a while in the Hicks home (upstairs, over the office), Tom got into the habit of attending Mr. Moule's church. He found Henry Moule to be an impressive preacher, and the memory of the vicar's voice long remained vivid in his mind. In William Hazlitt's famous essay 'My First Acquaintance with Poets' there is an account of how, one cold January Sunday in 1798, young Hazlitt went to hear Samuel Taylor Coleridge preach. 'When ... Mr. Coleridge rose and gave out his text ... which he pronounced loud, deep, and distinct, it seemed to me, who was then young, as if the sounds had echoed from the bottom of the human heart and ... might have floated in solemn silence through the universe.' Young Thomas Hardy had a similar experience. One Sunday evening in 1860, he went to Fordington Church and heard the Reverend Henry Moule give out his text: 'All the days of my appointed time will I wait, till my change come.' The words sounded as if they too had echoed from the bottom of the human heart, and they went on echoing, in Hardy's memory, for sixty-five years. In June 1919, when he was reading the fourteenth chapter of the *Book of Job*, Hardy came to the fourteenth verse and then remarked: 'That was the text of the Vicar of Fordington one Sunday evening about 1860. I can hear his voice repeating the text, just as if it were yesterday.' Shortly after this, Hardy wrote his poem 'Waiting Both', published in *Human Shows* in 1925. This use of a boyhood memory two-thirds of a century later is characteristic of the working of his mind.

The vicar had eight sons, three or four of whom were well known to Hardy. (Numbering them may help the reader to get acquainted with this large family.) No. 1, Henry J. Moule (1825–1904), became very much interested in Dorchester anti-quities and could later on inform Hardy about one of the features of the town which the novelist was to use in Chapter XI of *The Mayor of Casterbridge*: 'It looked Roman, bespoke the art of Rome, concealed dead men of Rome.' This ancient aspect of Dorchester became of increasing interest to Hardy in later years; and, while he never became as much of an antiquarian as Henry J. Moule, he did share Moule's interest in Roman remains. In 1885 Hardy wrote a sketch 'Ancient Earthworks and What Two Enthusiastic Scientists Found Therein'.[10] Twenty-three years later, when Hardy was sixty-eight years old, he went on a drenchingly wet day to the old Roman Ring— 'with sticky chalk-mud half way up to our knees', so he told his wife—and watched the excavations then being conducted there. The diggers (so he reported to Mrs. Hardy) 'found very little ... beyond a few coins, bits of pottery, etc. that show the construction to have been Roman.' A week later, however, when the London *Times* solicited an article on the excavations, Hardy promptly complied. His account 'Maumbury Ring' appeared in *The Times*, October 9, 1908.[11] Henry J. Moule eventually became curator of the Dorset County Museum in Dorchester, and in time, after building a house next door to Max Gate, became Hardy's neighbour.

(2) George E. Moule (1828–1912) became a missionary in China. (3) Frederick Moule (1830–1900), ten years Hardy's senior, seems to have had little contact with him, though they were acquainted, and in the summer of 1899 Mrs. Frederick Moule came to a garden party at Max Gate. (4) Horace Moule (1832–73) became Hardy's closest friend, not only among the Moules but also in an even wider circle. He was an excellent Greek scholar, and from him Hardy learned about Aeschylus and Sophocles. Moule went from Dorchester to Queens' College, Cambridge, and after graduation embarked upon a literary career. He and Hardy saw each other from time to time in London. Something went wrong, however, and at the age of forty-one Horace Moule committed suicide. Hardy never forgot the shock of this event in 1873. (5) Arthur E. Moule (b. 1834) became rector of Burwarton in Shropshire. (6) Charles Moule (b. 1836) became a Senior Fellow and eventually President of Corpus Christi College, Cambridge. He served Hardy as a model for Angel Clare in *Tess of the D'Urbervilles*. (7) Christopher Moule (b. 1838) died in infancy. (8) Handley C. G. Moule (b. 1841) also entered the Church and eventually became Bishop of Durham.

When, in reading the second chapter of *Tess of the D'Urbervilles*, we come to the 'three young men of a superior class' whose general likeness to each other 'suggested that they might be, what in fact they were, brothers', we know where Thomas Hardy found them; and when he makes them speak of 'getting through another chapter of *A Counterblast to Agnosticism*', we can feel sure that we are hearing an echo of the theological discussions Horace Moule must have had with his clerical brothers and must have reported to Thomas Hardy. It was Horace Moule who brought to Hardy's attention the notorious *Essays and Reviews* of 1860—that volume by Archbishop Temple, Benjamin Jowett, and others, which led to their being accused of heresy. They were tried and found guilty, as Hardy well remembered when he referred to the authors of the *Essays* as 'The Seven against Christ'.[12] Just what Horace Moule's attitude towards the seven heretics was, it is now very difficult to surmise. One or two of Hardy's notes invite the suggestion that Horace may have been moved by the arguments of the Tractarians at Oxford and was contemplating following John Henry Newman into the Catholic Church. When, in the first week in August 1862, Moule came up to London from Cambridge, he and Hardy went to a Roman Catholic chapel on August 7 and afterwards had supper together. In July 1865 Hardy was reading Newman's *Apologia* and expressed 'a great desire to be convinced by him, because Moule likes him so much'. But Hardy remained unconvinced. He thought Newman's style was charming but that there was 'no first link to his . . . chain of reasoning'. Although the young architect and the Cambridge scholar did not agree about the *Apologia*, Hardy's talks with Moule were as good as a course in philosophy. Under the stimulus of his Dorchester companionship, Hardy's mind expanded, his alertness to logical analysis improved, and his intellectual horizons widened. When Darwin's *Origin of Species* appeared, Hardy was one of the first to read it.

This epoch-making green-backed volume appeared on November 24, 1859. On that day, the little girl born in Plymouth in 1840 was celebrating her nineteenth birthday. She did *not* read Darwin's book.

Next door to Hicks's draughting office in South Street was a school taught by the Reverend William Barnes. Hardy became

27

acquainted with one of Barnes's pupils, a young man named Hooper Tolbort, who (Hardy remembered) 'had an extraordinary facility in the acquisition of languages'. Like Clym Yeobright in *The Return of the Native*, Tolbort could 'talk French as fast as a maid can eat blackberries'. In time, Hardy became acquainted with Tolbort's teacher, William Barnes himself. Barnes was known throughout Dorset as the author of poems in the Dorset dialect. A third collection of them was published in 1862. Barnes was in the habit of contributing a poem once a week to the *Dorset County Chronicle*, published in Dorchester, and there Hardy read many of them as they appeared during his days of apprenticeship under John Hicks. Of some of these poems we shall have more to say when we come to *Under the Greenwood Tree* (1872). One of Barnes's poems, 'Woak Hill', quoted by Hardy in *Far from the Madding Crowd*, appeared in the *Chronicle* on March 6, 1862, only a few weeks before the end of Hardy's time with John Hicks.

When Hardy went up to London, he carried a copy of Barnes's *Poems of Rural Life* with him. On finding that these Dorset poems were unknown in London, he turned publicity-agent for Barnes. He talked of the Dorchester poet, he read from his poems whenever he found a receptive audience, and in this way showed what a deep impression they had made upon his mind. The time would come—in 1879—when Hardy would write an unsigned review of Barnes's *Poems*: it appeared in the *New Quarterly Magazine* for October 1879; and in 1886 he prepared an obituary notice of Barnes for the *Athenaeum*. When, in 1908, the Oxford University Press wished to find an editor for a new edition of Barnes's poems, they knew that Hardy, with his familiarity with the Dorset dialect, was the man to turn to.

Barnes's success as a Dorset poet must have had not a little to do with encouraging Hardy to pursue a course on which he had embarked with somewhat uncertain steps some years before the end of his term with Hicks. For Barnes's weekly contributions to the *Dorset County Chronicle* may have planted in young Hardy's mind the idea that he too might write and be published in the *Chronicle* and thus achieve at least a local fame. As early as March 1856, before he had left Mr. Last's Academy, Hardy had written a satirical sketch and sent it to the paper; and later, after he had begun his studies under John Hicks, he wrote

28

accounts of the 'restorations' of Dorset churches for which Hicks was responsible.[13]

Thus, even before he had ever left Dorset, Hardy had already responded to the itch to write which was to remain with him for the rest of his life. It was not this lure of the pen, however, of which he was most conscious when his apprenticeship ended. By April 1862—he was then twenty-one—he had developed some of those attitudes towards Dorchester which he was later to ascribe to Clym Yeobright; he was ready to adventure out into the place he had so often heard about from Fippard and Bastow and Horace Moule. London beckoned. 'When I first got away from home,' Hardy was later to make Clym Yeobright say, 'I thought this place was not worth troubling about. I thought our life here [in Dorset] was contemptible. To oil your boots instead of blacking them, to dust your coat with a switch instead of with a brush: was there ever anything more ridiculous?'[14] Hardy was ready to turn his back upon Dorchester.

III

London Tried

HARDY arrived in London on Thursday, April 17, 1862. Pink-cheeked, with a small incipient moustache that tried manfully to conceal his youthfulness, he carried a letter of introduction from John Hicks to an architect-friend of his, John Norton. Mr. Norton had no vacancy on his office-staff at this time, but he generously made a place for Hardy until the Dorchester youth could find better employment. Within a week Chance, with that 'waggery of fate' that Hardy was later to write about, presented Norton with an inquiry from another London architect, Arthur Blomfield, who was seeking a young draughtsman who could deal with designs for church and other Gothic 'restorations'. Norton recommended Hardy, and on Monday morning, May 5, Hardy went to work for Arthur Blomfield. For the rest of the year 1862 he worked at 8 St. Martin's Place; in the following year he moved with Blomfield to larger offices on the second floor of 8 Adelphi Terrace, from the windows of which he could look out on the River Thames.

The London to which Hardy had come was not the city with which English residents and American visitors are familiar in 1965. There were of course no automobiles and no electric lights. There was as yet no Charing Cross Railway station. The Victoria Embankment had not yet been built and Cleopatra's Needle would not be set up there until 1878. There was no Tate Art Gallery: it was not opened until 1897. The Victoria and Albert Museum, not to be begun until 1899, would not be opened to the public until 1909. Temple Bar still stood in its place between Fleet Street and the Strand, just as it had stood

in the days of Johnson and Goldsmith. Hardy described the city
to which he had come as 'the London of Dickens and Thackeray',
and both these novelists were still alive. Their London, however,
was already beginning to undergo transformation. The Houses
of Parliament, begun in the year of Hardy's birth, had been
completed in 1857, just five years before his arrival. The famous
Reading Room of the British Museum, with its impressive dome,
had been built in 1857, and a new Westminster Bridge, replacing the one crossed by Wordsworth in 1802, would open its
splendid span to traffic shortly after Hardy's arrival. There can
be no doubt about the fact that, when the young man from
Dorchester stepped out of the London station on to the streets of
London, he knew that he had left more than Dorchester behind.
He had crossed 'an extraordinary chronological frontier'. What
made him particularly aware of this crossing was the London
Exhibition of 1862. He had, in fact, timed his arrival in the
metropolis in order to be present when the Exhibition was
thrown open to the public.

The words 'extraordinary chronological frontier' are quoted
from the beginning of Hardy's story 'The Fiddler of the Reels'.
Although, in writing this story, Hardy made specific mention of
the Great Exhibition of 1851, his words reflect his own feelings
in 1862 and describe accurately enough the part the London
Exhibition of 1862 played in his life.

Talking of Exhibitions, World's Fairs, and what not, I would not go
round the corner to see a dozen of them nowadays. The only exhibition that ever made any impression upon my imagination was the
first of the series, the parent of them all—the Great Exhibition of
1851, in Hyde Park, London. None of the younger generation can
realize the sense of novelty it produced in us who were then in our
prime. For South Wessex, the year formed in many ways an extraordinary chronological frontier or transit-line, at which there occurred what one might call a precipice in Time. As in a geological
'fault', we had presented to us a sudden bringing of ancient and
modern into absolute contact, such as probably in no other single
year since the Conquest was ever witnessed in this part of the
country.[1]

The Great Exhibition of 1851, which had originated in a suggestion of Prince Albert at a meeting of the Society of Arts, had
been a gigantic success. The Crystal Palace, built in Hyde Park

at that time to house the industrial exhibits, survived on another site until some years after Hardy's death. In 1861 Prince Albert proposed an international exhibition in London on an even larger scale, and he was busy with plans for its realization when typhoid fever carried him off. In spite of this loss, the exhibition was held, and on the day of its opening Thomas Hardy was present and experienced that 'sudden bringing of ancient and modern into absolute contact'.

After that first visit, Hardy repeatedly returned, and throughout the summer of 1862 he would 'generally run down to the Exhibition for an hour in the evening two or three times a week'. In August he spent half a day there; even that was not time enough. There was so much to see, so much to store up for future use. For instance, the automatic substitutes for human limbs, designed by a clever Swiss mechanician named Jacques Droz, came to Hardy's mind a dozen years later when he was describing Fanny Robin's painful walk in *Far from the Madding Crowd*. He 'tried the Underground Railway one day', and wrote home that 'everything is excellently arranged'. Everything in London was new to him. After the Exhibition was all over, he continued his visits to what Londoners came to call the 'Brompton Boilers'—the iron sheds used to house the exhibits until the South Kensington Museum had been built. One of his reasons for these repeated visits was the fact that he had decided to compete for a prize offered by the Royal Institute of British Architects.

Hardy was not yet twenty-two when he arrived in London, but within a year of that arrival he had won not only the medal offered by the Royal Institute but a second prize as well. On March 16, 1863, his essay on 'The Application of Coloured Bricks and Terra Cotta to Modern Architecture' was awarded the medal of the Royal Institute. Shortly before this he had written his sister Mary: 'I am now very busy getting up a design for a country mansion for which a small prize is offered' by the Architectural Association. Hardy's design won the prize of two or three pounds. As soon as the prize money was in his hands, he spent it in the purchase of several volumes of Bohn's Classical Series—English versions of Greek and Latin authors made by Theodore A. Buckley and others. In reading Buckley's translation of *Aeschylus* (1849) Hardy came upon the 'Aeschylean phrase' about the President of the Immortals which he was to recall a quarter of a century later and put into *Tess of the D'Urbervilles*, thereby making the phrase famous and himself notorious. In *Horace* (as translated by C. Smart, with notes by T. A. Buckley) Hardy found words which have left their mark in both *Jude the Obscure* and *The Dynasts*. As William R. Rutland remarks: 'No one who has read *Jude the Obscure* is likely to forget the passage in the fifth chapter in which Jude . . . "knelt down on the roadside bank with open book". . . . There are other references to Horace in Hardy's writings, but none so striking as that.'[2] There are marks of Hardy's pencil on dozens of pages in his copy of *Horace*. For example, in one of the 'Epistles', Horace's 'concordia discors' is translated as 'the jarring harmony of things'. Forty-five years later, Hardy recalled this phrase and used it on the last page of *The Dynasts*, where it reappears as 'the chordless chime of Things'.

In this purchase of the Greek and Latin classics, the influence of the fourth son of the Vicar of Fordington may be discerned. Horace Moule was now living in Cambridge, but he came up to London from time to time and saw Hardy, and in August 1862 Tom wrote his sister Mary that Moule was contemplating leaving the university town and coming to settle permanently in London.

The industrial novelties of the London Exhibition were not the only new objects on which Hardy feasted his eyes. London offered him two additional enrichments of a sort for which there had been no opportunity during his life in Dorchester— the theatre and the art gallery. Both these influences made such extensive contributions to his future novels as to demand careful examination here.

The theatre, at the time of Hardy's arrival in London, meant (at least to him) Shakespeare. Charles Kean and his abler wife, Ellen Tree, were performing in Shakespearean rôles at the Princess's Theatre, and Hardy was prompt in seizing the opportunity to see them. Later, he saw every one of the Shakespeare plays acted in by Samuel Phelps at Drury Lane Theatre; he carried a copy of the play with him to the theatre to enable him to follow the action more intelligently. He thought that Phelps was especially good as Falstaff.

In going to see Phelps at Drury Lane, Hardy could not help

recalling the stories he had heard as a boy at Higher Bockhampton about another Shakespearean actor—an Irishman
named William O'Brien—who had performed at Drury Lane a
century and more before. He had played Sir Andrew Aguecheek
in *Twelfth Night* with great success, and Prince Hal in *Henry the
Fourth*. In 1764 O'Brien had eloped with Lady Susan Strang-
ways, daughter of the first Earl of Ilchester, and that ended his
career at Drury Lane. ('I suppose you can mind poor Lady
Elfride and how she ran away with the actor?'[3]) Lady Susan's
scandalized father lent Stinsford House to the runaway couple,
with the result that, for many years, they attended Stinsford
Church. Both of Hardy's grandmothers remembered the handsome Irish actor, and Hardy's grandfather was eventually called
upon to construct the vault in Stinsford Church in which
O'Brien and his wife were at last buried. 'Make it just large
enough for our two selves only,' Lady Susan is said to have
directed Thomas Hardy the First. Thomas the Third had heard
many other stories about her—for instance, that she kept a
cellar at Stinsford House full of home-brewed beer so strong
'that 'twould a'most knock you down' and that her head
gardener was drunk every morning before breakfast. 'There are
no such houses now!' Readers of *A Pair of Blue Eyes* will find in
Chapter XXVI a description of the Stinsford vault built by
Hardy's grandfather, and in two poems published long afterwards readers can find the evidence of how long and how
persistently Hardy's memory of this romantic couple stayed
with him. In 'Friends Beyond' Hardy tells us that 'the Squire,
and Lady Susan, [who] lie in Mellstock churchyard now . . .
have a way of whispering to me'; and in 'The Noble Lady's
Tale' he returns, in a poem of 205 lines, to the story of O'Brien
and his wife who had been 'housed . . . in this nook' at Stinsford
until both died and were laid 'within that hoary last dark mew
in Mellstock Quire'.[4]

Hardy's memory of these stories heard in boyhood came back
to him as he watched Phelps's performance at Drury Lane, but
he had an additional, and doubtless a better, reason for finding
the Shakespeare plays especially appealing. His visits to the
theatre aroused in him a desire to know more about the author
of the plays, and among the books bought by him was Walter
Bagehot's *Estimates of Some Englishmen* (1858), one chapter of

which deals with Shakespeare. The more Hardy learned about the man from Warwickshire, the clearer it became that there was a striking parallelism between his own life and Shakespeare's. Both had been born in or near a small town a little more than a hundred miles from London, in days when that meant comparative isolation in a quiet sheep-raising countryside. Both were born in small thatched houses which are still standing. Both had mothers of marked character and superior minds, and both had fathers who were engaged in business. Both received only a limited schooling and that chiefly in the classics. Neither went on to the university. Both read widely, and both went up to London soon after attaining their majority. There, as we shall shortly see, both began with crude and imitative work as writers; both wrote anonymously; and both brought to their work their fathers' sense of humour.

In order not to have to return to this subject again, let us continue our examination of this striking parallelism beyond the date at which we have arrived. As we shall see, Hardy, like Shakespeare, attained success as an author before he was thirty-five. Both men aroused the jealousy of other writers. Both appealed to ordinary folk, but good critics and royalty also joined in acclaiming the work of both men. The writings of both include some excellent rustic portraits, for both men knew the folklore and the superstitions, the songs and the dances, the accent and the idiom of the rustics. Both were patriotic Englishmen and wrote in celebration of England's heroes, of English wars, and of the English countryside. Both had a tender sympathy for mankind, a hatred of hypocrisy and injustice, and an intense sense of loyalty. Both returned to the place of their birth and built themselves houses in which they died. The hearts of both are buried in or near the parish church of their boyhood, and their names are graved in stone in Westminster Abbey. These names have, in each case, been given to their own sections of England. In 1964 tens of thousands of pilgrims made their way to 'the Shakespeare Country' in commemoration of the four-hundredth anniversary of the birth of the playwright. This year, one hundred years after the publication of Hardy's first London sketch, 'the Hardy Country' will doubtless attract its usual army of interested and admiring visitors. All these similarities between the two men may be nothing more than coincidence, but they may also help to explain the extraordinary interest that Thomas Hardy took in the work of William Shakespeare—an interest which may have begun with nothing more than the memory of stories told about how his grandfather had been called upon to construct a cosy vault in the parish church for a Shakespearean actor, but which certainly did not end with such stories. What did they end with?

For one thing, Hardy's interest in Shakespeare set up many a milestone along his future pathway. In the margin of his copy of *Hamlet*, opposite the passage 'Thou wouldst not think how ill all's here about my heart', Hardy wrote the date 'December 15, 1870'. In his copy of *Macbeth*, beside the passage that runs 'Things at their worst will cease or else climb upward', he wrote 'July 1871'. In February 1882 he took part in some 'readings' of *The Tempest* at Wimborne. On August 14, 1882, he went to see a performance of *Othello* given by a company of strolling players at Dorchester, and afterwards wrote up an amusing account of their performance. On July 9, 1888, he saw Drew and Ada Rehan in *The Taming of the Shrew*, and in 1890 he went to see Miss Rehan again in *As You Like It*. In 1891 he wrote down all the Shakespearean quotations he had heard and had recognized at the dinner table in a London hotel. When Hardy's father died on July 20, 1892, the novelist summarized his life by recalling four lines of *Hamlet*:

> Thou hast been
> As one, in suffering all, that suffers nothing,
> A man that fortune's buffets and rewards
> Hast ta'en with equal thanks.

In December 1895 he saw Forbes-Robertson and Mrs. Patrick Campbell in *Romeo and Juliet*. In 1896 Hardy and his wife not only went to Stratford-on-Avon but took lodgings there for a week, during which he visited all the places associated with Shakespeare and began a careful re-reading of *King Lear*. This reading was finished on September 6, 1896, at Dover, near the famous 'Shakespeare Cliff'. Hardy thereupon wrote out some observations on the play, in which he disagreed with the 'commentators'. In June 1902 he wrote a note on Edmund Kean and had it published in the *Dorset County Chronicle*. On June 26, 1905, he wrote to the Shakespeare Memorial Committee and sent a second letter three years later. In April 1916 he wrote his poem 'To Shakespeare after Three Hundred Years', published in the *Shakespeare Memorial Volume* of that year. When Hardy was seventy-eight, he again recorded his views of Shakespeare. In 1922, at the age of eighty-two, he took pleasure in recalling his early London days when he would carry a text of the Shakespeare play to a performance by Samuel Phelps. In July of that year he attended an outdoor performance of *A Midsummer Night's Dream*. When he was eighty-six years old, Hardy read an editorial in the London *Times*, discussing the 'dram of eale' passage in *Hamlet*, whereupon he sat down and wrote the following letter, which appeared in *The Times* on June 17, 1926:

> Your leading article on the famous passage with which Shakespeare's printers have tantalized the poet's readers for the last 300 years reminds me that in the 1860's I worked at elucidating it and marked in the margin of a copy I used my own conjectural reading. I give it here, since it may pass in the crowd of conjectures on what Shakespeare really did write, as being not much worse than the rest:
>
> > The dram of ill
> > Doth all the noble substance leaven down
> > To his own scandal.

It is clear that, for more than sixty years, Hardy saturated his mind with Shakespearean words, Shakespearean thoughts, Shakespearean characters, Shakespearean attitudes, Shakespearean situations, Shakespearean humour, Shakespearean tragedy.

Knowing this, no one can be surprised to find that lines from the plays frequently appear in his novels; they also appear with similar frequency in his letters, and one can suspect that they appeared also in his conversation. In a letter written on March 13, 1904, Hardy quoted 'Piece out my imperfections with your thoughts', and then added that this was 'a line which often occurs to me'. Does the reader recognize it? It comes from the Prologue of *Henry the Fifth*.

The most easily recognized part of Hardy's debt to Shakespeare is, of course, the direct borrowings from the plays. *Hamlet* is the one most frequently quoted, but Hardy knew them all, from the earliest to the latest. He quotes from twenty-six of the plays. He knew the lines that everyone knows, but he quotes unusual and little-known lines as well. He began to quote

Shakespeare when he was twenty-five and he was still at it sixty years later. It is safe to say that the list of his direct quotations from Shakespeare cannot be paralleled in the work of any other novelist. The Shakespearean trail runs through all fourteen of the Wessex novels, through three of the four books of short stories, and is seen in at least two of the books of Hardy's poetry.[5]

And now, to get back to the year 1862, let us turn our attention to the second of the two sources of enrichment of Hardy's experience in London which we have mentioned on a previous page—the art gallery. Arthur Blomfield's office in Adelphi Terrace was within easy walking distance of the National Gallery, and Hardy soon got into the habit of spending part of his lunch hour in looking at pictures. It was almost as if he were acting upon the advice he had heard in the opening scene of *The Taming of the Shrew*:

> No profit grows where is no pleasure ta'en;
> In brief, sir, study what you most affect.

Hardy soon learned to lavish his affection upon the paintings in the National Gallery, where the Turner Collection had been set up only a few years before Hardy's arrival in London. Day after day he went to the Gallery and came, in time, to know with a fair degree of intimacy the work of several dozen painters, from Giotto in the thirteenth century down to Hardy's contemporaries, Wiertz and Van Beers. (Not all of these painters could be seen in the National Gallery, but the habit of going there in London was continued in other art galleries whenever Hardy had a chance, both at home and abroad, to visit them.)

This study of painting shortly led the young architect to exercise his own pencil in original artistic efforts, and he was eventually able to achieve the drawings used to illustrate his *Wessex Poems* in 1898 and his *Famous Tragedy of the Queen of Cornwall* in 1923. But the visits to the National Gallery had another, more immediate result: they account for one of the marked, sometimes annoying, characteristics of the Wessex novels—that of referring to one or another of the long list of European painters covering six centuries in the history of art. The habit (probably first learned by Hardy from William Harrison Ainsworth) appeared in the very first published Wessex novel, and it remained with Hardy to the end of his career as a writer of fiction. At times this practice undoubtedly helps the reader to gain a more vivid impression of the person or scene Hardy is trying to describe, especially if his reference is to some painter whose work is commonly known—for instance, when we read in *Far from the Madding Crowd* that 'fine autumn afternoons and eves intensified into Rembrandt effects the few yellow sunbeams'. But when, in the same novel, we come upon a reference to the 'effects in the landscapes of Ruysdael and Hobbema', we may question whether the reader's imagination is cleared or clouded by the allusion.

Whatever his success in his use of this wide acquaintance with painting, Hardy's expert and detailed knowledge is unquestioned. The list of artists whose work he knows is an impressive one. Without turning the pages of more than five or six of his novels, we find that he is acquainted with at least thirty-four painters.[6] Critics who do not share Hardy's interest in art have sometimes been inclined to think that his frequent allusions to painters were made as a cheap parade of the novelist's learning. This is not likely. Hardy wrote with a sincere desire to enable his reader to see just as clearly as he himself saw; but it cannot be denied that the references to less well-known painters often seem like annoying intrusions in the narrative.

Hardy's habit of spending part of his lunch hours at the National Gallery and his studious pursuit of Shakespeare in the theatre cannot have made any great contribution to his usefulness in Blomfield's office. As an architect, Hardy did what was asked of him, but it is clear that Blomfield did not ask very much. The office work with T-square and ruler was monotonous rather than challenging. Hardy's duties came, in time, to include the instruction of younger men whom Blomfield had taken as pupils, but the professional atmosphere of the office was informal enough to permit the inclusion of literature with the lessons in architecture. This combination led to Hardy's writing a sketch which he called 'How I Built Myself a House'—he had never built one—and after it had served its purpose in the office, Hardy sent the article to the editor of *Chambers's Journal*. It was accepted, and *Chambers's* thus gained the distinction of printing —in the issue for March 18, 1865— the first words of Hardy's to be published in London. In later years, Hardy placed a low estimate upon this composition, saying 'That was a trifle, done for my pupils'. He called the sketch 'unrepresentative' and said that it 'had no connection with my literary pursuits at the time'. There was a time, however, when it had seemed in his eyes no trifling matter. When the editor of *The Literary World* wrote to Hardy for some biographical facts about the author of *The Return of the Native* (then being serialized in *Harper's Magazine*), Hardy replied by sending a biographical sketch which was published in the Boston magazine in August 1878. In this sketch Hardy reported that 'he sent a first attempt in fiction to a London magazine. It was at once accepted, and his career was determined.' The prompt acceptance of 'How I Built Myself a House' by the editor of *Chambers's Journal* thus 'determined'—so Hardy believed thirteen years later—his choice of career.

When the time came, many years later, for the preparation of *The Early Life*, he had obviously come to believe that his 'literary pursuits' in 1865 were something else. He wrote at least one poem, calling it 'Amabel'. The name Hardy remembered as that of the grocer's daughter, the beautiful heroine of William Harrison Ainsworth's *Old St. Paul's*. The poem is an uninspired lyric of eight short stanzas in which Hardy's success in finding eight rhymes for 'Amabel' does not conceal the mediocrity of the performance. This poem and the sketch in *Chambers's Journal* appear to be the sole products of Hardy's pen in 1865 which have come down to us. The likelihood is that he was spending more time in reading than in writing. In 1864 he had been reading *Childe Harold*, Tom Moore's *Lalla Rookh*, and John Stuart Mill's *On Liberty*.

This last-named treatise made a great impression upon him and remained a potent influence on his mind until the day when Mill and *On Liberty* reappear in the pages of *Jude the Obscure*. Hardy came to regard Mill as 'one of the profoundest thinkers of the century', and when Mill became a candidate for election to Parliament, Hardy went to hear him speak. What he saw and heard can be given in Hardy's own words, for he sent a description of the event to the London *Times*, where it was printed on May 21, 1906:

It was a day in 1865, about three in the afternoon, during Mill's candidature for Westminster. The hustings had been erected in Covent Garden, . . . and when I—a young man living in London—

drew near the spot, Mill was speaking. The appearance of the author of the treatise *On Liberty* (which we students of that date knew almost by heart) was so different from the look of persons who usually address crowds in the open air that it held the attention of people for whom such a gathering in itself had little interest. Yet it was, primarily, that of a man out of place. The religious sincerity of his speech was jarred on by his environment—a group on the hustings who, with few exceptions, did not care to understand him fully, and a crowd below who could not. He stood bareheaded, and his vast pale brow, so thin-skinned as to show the blue veins, sloped back like a stretching upland. . . . The picture of him as personified earnestness surrounded for the most part by careless curiosity derived an added piquancy—if it can be called such—from the fact that the cameo clearness of his face chanced to be in relief against the blue shadow of a church which, on its transcendental side, his doctrines antagonized. But it would not be right to say that the throng was absolutely unimpressed by his words; it felt that they were weighty, though it did not quite know why.

Hardy's statement that he knew Mill's treatise *On Liberty* 'almost by heart' is not to be taken lightly. The thoughts that came from behind that 'vast pale brow' exercised a profound influence upon Hardy's own thoughts and encouraged him in the formation of habits that were destined to make the road rough for him. In his chapter on 'Liberty of Thought' Mill had declared: 'No one can be a great thinker who does not recognize that as a thinker it is his duty to follow his intellect to whatever conclusions it may lead. Truth gains . . . more by the errors of one who . . . thinks for himself, than by the true opinions of those who . . . do not suffer themselves to think.' This was a heady brew for an inexperienced young man of twenty-four, but Hardy resolved nevertheless 'to follow his intellect to whatever conclusions it may lead'. Mill made him wonder whether he had been reading the right sort of books. What had Ovid or Horace or Tom Moore to offer him in planning his life? Thirty years later Hardy transferred these thoughts to another puzzled young man. In the fifth chapter of *Jude the Obscure*, Jude 'began to wonder whether he could be reading quite the right books for his object in life'. The more he thought about it the more convinced he was of his inconsistency. Later on, we can see with what determination Hardy followed up his resolve, when we find him acquainted with Gibbon and Malthus, with Fuller and

Herbert Spencer, with Keble and South, with Arnold and Bacon, with Bede and with Burton. This was obviously a curious programme for a budding architect; but, then, Hardy had never had a strong desire to be an architect. Readings which could hardly be regarded as a valuable preparation for a career as a London architect were, however, to prove useful to the later Wessex novelist. In *Jude the Obscure*, for example, Hardy remembered Gibbon as 'the smoothly shaven historian so ironically civil to Christianity'—the 'sly author' in whose volume Sue Bridehead (in *Jude*) read 'the chapter dealing with the reign of Julian the Apostate'. Jude Fawley, too, in remembering the authors who 'used to look friendly in the old days', mentioned 'particularly Gibbon'.

By the summer of 1865 Hardy had made good progress in his readings but he was still a very disorganized young man. Years later, in a poem called 'The Vatican', he was to rebuke himself for 'inconstancy'. On June 2 he wrote in his notebook: 'My 25th birthday. Not very cheerful. Feel as if I had lived a long time and done very little. Walked about by moonlight in the evening. Wondered what woman, if any, I should be thinking about in five years' time.' He was probably lonely. 'Knowing not a human being here, Jude began to be impressed with the isolation of his own personality.'[7] In his wondering about 'what woman, if any', the emphasis was probably on 'if any' rather than on 'woman'. Hardy still enjoyed solitude. He missed the solitary walks back and forth between Bockhampton and Dorchester. Now and then he got a chance at that sort of thing. On Sunday, July 14, 1865, he walked all the way from his lodgings near Hyde Park to Harrow, a good four-hour hike. He remembered the day, later, because he called at a house in Harrow where everyone was discussing the tragedy that had just befallen three Englishmen on the Matterhorn. Two of the three who had lost their lives were from Harrow. There was only one survivor, a mountaineer named Whymper. Thirty years later Hardy met Whymper at a dinner table and characteristically asked him for a sketch-map of the Matterhorn showing the path taken by the climbers and the exact spot of the accident.

At the end of this summer, Hardy enrolled in an evening course in French under Professor Stièvenard: on October 28, 1865, he wrote his sister Mary that he 'had joined the French class at King's College'. He afterwards remembered his teacher as 'the most charming Frenchman he had ever met'. He remembered also, in all honesty, that he gave 'but a perfunctory attention to his French readings'.[8] The survival of the textbook which Hardy used in this course—*Half-Hours of French Translation* by Alphonse Mariette (London: Williams & Norgate, 1863)—enables us to be more specific about the state of his mind at this time than he himself was able (or willing) to be in the pages of *The Early Life*. The textbook contains no evidence of his mastery of French or even of any serious study of the French language at all. Hardy was busy with other things. When, for example, Professor Stièvenard reached page 212, on which a quotation from Thackeray's novel *The Newcomes* is given: 'Yonder sit forty cherry-cheeked boys, thinking about home . . .', Hardy, instead of asking himself how to say 'cherry-cheeked' in French, paused instead on the words 'thinking about home' and went off on a flying carpet to Wessex. Turning from page 212 to the rear flyleaf, Hardy drew a rough map of the Dorset coast, showing Portland Bill and the town and harbour of Weymouth; then he illustrated his map by making a landscape sketch which shows the rock at Portland as seen from the coast just east of Weymouth. Instead of learning French under the 'charming Frenchman' at King's College, Hardy was sketching and charting the locale he was shortly to make use of in *Desperate Remedies*, in parts of *Under the Greenwood Tree*, in *The Trumpet-Major*, and in *The Well-Beloved*.

Even when he was not 'thinking about home', Hardy's thoughts were directed to other things than French. The marks in the textbook left by Hardy's pencil indicate an eye alert for the striking phrase, the challenging thought, the sententious aphorism, the sage generalization. He marked the phrase 'centenary oaks'. He noted that 'fear is more nimble than gratitude', and that 'a lively imagination and a sensitive heart only promise a stormy life to those who possess them'. In a quotation from Samuel Rogers's *Italy*, Hardy underlined 'The old cares are left clustering round the old objects', and in a quotation from Hallam's translation of Pascal, he noted that 'man has a secret instinct . . . which springs from the sense of his continual misery'. Pascal was destined to turn up—and in French!—in Chapter XVIII of *Tess of the D'Urbervilles*. Hardy was absorbing training in Clym Yeobright's 'view of life as a thing to be put up with, replacing that zest for existence which was so intense in early civilizations'. Sometimes the marked passages are suggestive of more pointed subjective meaning. On page 267 of *Half-Hours*, for example, Hardy underlined William Cobbett's observation that 'men fail much oftener from want of perseverance than from want of talent'. Within a very few years, Hardy was to be writing about 'adherence to a course with persistence sufficient to ensure success'.[9] If he was not learning how to persevere as an architect or as a student of the French language, he *was* learning how to manipulate the English language. He was learning the subleties of idiom and irony. In his copy of *Gibbon* he marked the 'sly author's' description of the conduct of the priests and virgins of the early Church: 'Insulted Nature sometimes vindicated her rights.'

Early in March 1866 Hardy ended his course with Professor Stièvenard and with characteristic 'inconstancy' transferred his attention elsewhere. For when Algernon Charles Swinburne flashed upon the scene, French and Mill and Gibbon and prose aphorisms were all forgotten. Without knowing it, Hardy had arrived at a critical crossroads in his life.

IV

London Found Wanting

'I LOVED *Atalanta*,' Hardy reminisced, years later. 'I used to walk from my lodgings near Hyde Park to the draughting office every morning, and never without a copy of the first edition of the *Poems and Ballads* sticking out of my pocket.' In 1866 Swinburne's *Poems* dropped like a bomb into a social order that was as unprepared for them as the red-haired poet was unprepared for the storm of censure that his book aroused. Young men were delighted. In these prosaic days of 1965, it is hard for us to visualize the effect that Swinburne's book of poetry created a hundred years ago. 'It simply swept us off our legs with rapture,' recalled one eminent critic, then an undergraduate at Oxford. At Cambridge, so Edmund Gosse reported, young men joined hands and marched along the streets shouting the words of 'Dolores' or of 'A Song in Time of Revolution'. The metaphors and similes of water, light, wind, and fire, which seemed to inspire and animate that wonderful poetry, took the whole lettered youth of England by storm with their melody and their audacity.

Thomas Hardy was swept along with the rest. He had no difficulty in recalling, long afterwards,

> that far morning of a summer day
> When, down a terraced street whose pavements lay
> Glassing the sunshine into my bent eyes,
> I walked and read with a quick glad surprise
> New words, in classic guise. . . .
> I still can hear the brabble and the roar
> At those . . . tunes.[1]

45

Hardy never forgot the 'quick glad surprise' of those days. Twenty-five years later he mentioned 'Aholibah' and quoted 'The Garden of Proserpine' and 'Behold, when thy face is made bare' in *Tess of the D'Urbervilles*. In *Jude* he quoted the 'Prelude' to *Songs before Sunrise* and the 'Hymn to Proserpine'. Swinburne's 'Tristram of Lyonnesse' is echoed in Hardy's poems about Lyonnesse as well as in *The Queen of Cornwall*. Up to the date of Swinburne's meteoric flashing upon the literary scene, Hardy's impulse towards poetic composition had apparently been largely in the direction of Shakespearean sonnets and of Spenserian stanzas, but after the spring of 1866 Swinburne's addiction to anapests began to leave its influence in many of Hardy's lines.

What is even more important, Swinburne's success in attracting attention by publishing a volume of poems pushed Hardy's interest in architecture as a career further into the background. Not that he was as yet prepared to turn his back upon his work in Blomfield's office—he needed the income his work there brought him—but from now on he began to give ever more serious consideration to the thought that a literary career might prove more interesting, if not more rewarding financially, than a career as an architect. Swinburne had achieved success by writing poetry. William Barnes had achieved local fame in Dorset by writing several books of poetry. Charles Swain had made a name for himself as 'the Manchester Poet'. Why should not Thomas Hardy be equal to following their example?

Nor were these three men the only ones to encourage Hardy to think of poetry as a possible career. Another name—that of Robert Browning—had just come prominently into public view. Browning had, as we now know, been writing and publishing verse for more than thirty years, but for twenty-five of those years the public had turned him a deaf ear. When, in 1855, Browning published *Men and Women*, the *Athenaeum* denounced the book as giving evidence of 'energy wasted and powers mis-spent'. But after Browning's return as a widower from Italy and after his settling into a London house at 19 Warwick Crescent, not very far away from the site of Hardy's lodgings, the winds of literary popularity began to shift. An edition of Browning's *Collected Poems* in 1863 sold well, and when *Dramatis Personae* was published in 1864, it attracted enough favourable attention to result in the publication of a second edition before the date of

Hardy's twenty-fifth birthday (June 2, 1865). Such a thing had never happened to Robert Browning before. By the time Swinburne flashed upon the scene, Browning had enough of a following to be able to meet the new competition without dismay. Thomas Hardy heard the growing praise of the older poet, and as soon as he had acquired a copy of his poems Hardy found himself much more impressed with Browning's verse than he was with Swinburne's. The author of 'The Garden of Proserpine' could teach Hardy rhythms and techniques—'new words' he called them in 'A Singer Asleep'—but Browning had much more to offer. Swinburne was lyrical but Browning was dramatic. Hardy's response was immediate. He became a Browning enthusiast and never ceased in his allegiance. Not that he shared Browning's roseate views of life—he didn't, and in *Jude the Obscure* he refers to Browning somewhat disparagingly as 'the last of the optimists'—but he learned to admire the originality of the poet's language, the forthright expression of his views, the clarity of his characterizations, and the vigour of the dramatic situations. Even the consonantal cacophony of Browning's verse came to have an appeal for Hardy's ear—a fact which is likely to surprise anyone who remembers that Hardy played the violin. In Browning's 1864 volume, *Dramatis Personae*, the poet had written a line which can be regarded as typical: 'Irks care the crop-full bird? frets doubt the maw-crammed beast?' An earlier poem by Browning had contained the line: 'This low-pulsed forthright craftsman's hand of mine'. Swinburne later wrote an amusing parody of Browning called 'John Jones' in which he caught this element of Browning's verse perfectly:

> Ah, how can fear sit
> And hear as love hears it
> Grief's heart's cracked grate's screech?

Hardy, too, was led to try to capture this sort of rhythmical screeching. In 'Hap' (written in 1866) he followed the verse-form of a Shakespearean sonnet, but the sound is that of Robert Browning's rasping instrument:

> Know . . .
> That thy love's loss is my hate's profiting.
> Crass Casualty obstructs the sun.

Years later, Hardy confessed to Edmund Gosse that he had

come to feel that jewelled lines in poetry—'Jewels five-words-long', as Tennyson had called them in *The Princess*, 'that on the stretched forefinger of all Time sparkle forever'—were effeminate and that in his own compositions he wished to avoid them. He did avoid them. Not many of Hardy's rasping lines will 'sparkle forever', but if their grating cacophony has turned some readers away from him, Robert Browning's influence is to be blamed for this result.

Hardy's reputation as an alleged pessimist long obscured his indebtedness to the great optimist. Hardy and Browning were strikingly different in disposition and personality, and the aggressive faith of the one as contrasted with the nostalgic agnosticism of the other long concealed from critical eyes their true relation. But now that a hundred years have passed since the dawning of 'that far morning of a summer day', we have had time to examine the evidence, and there is no longer any excuse for a failure to recognize the extent and the permanence of Browning's influence on the Wessex author.

Rather than interrupt our biographical narrative on many a future page in order to glance from time to time at Browning's footprints, let us take a quick flight over the next sixty years and note the nature of Hardy's indebtedness to the older poet. In his very first work of fiction, *The Poor Man and the Lady*, written only two years after the date at which we have arrived, Hardy quoted Browning twice: once from 'Instans Tyrannus' and once from 'The Statue and the Bust'. This last-named poem supplied two additional quotations for *Desperate Remedies*, and the fact that it had become one of Hardy's favourite poems becomes clear when, in *Far from the Madding Crowd*, 'The Statue and the Bust' turns up for the fourth time, in a reference to 'the mouldering gentlefolk of the poet's story'.

In the eighteen-eighties Hardy met Browning at the home of Mrs. Anne Procter (wife of 'Barry Cornwall', the poet) in London, and in the following year Browning's lines

> There shall never be one lost good! What was, shall live as before:
> What was good shall be good, with, for evil, so much good more.

reappeared in Hardy's notebook as: 'Conserve the existing good, supplant the existing bad by good.' In the pages of *Two on a Tower* Hardy paraphrased lines from 'Rabbi Ben Ezra'. While writing *The Woodlanders*, Hardy again quoted from 'The Statue and the Bust', and when he went to Italy in 1887, one of the first things he did in Florence was to hunt up the scene of the events in that poem. In writing 'The Waiting Supper' Hardy quoted 'The Statue and the Bust' for the sixth time, nor must the frequent reappearance of this poem in Hardy's prose be taken to mean that the novelist was merely using, over and over again, a single phrase or line or thought. He wasn't, and all six of the passages quoted from 'The Statue' are different. In May 1888, when Hardy's *Wessex Tales* was published, he inscribed a copy 'To Robert Browning, Esq., D.C.L., from Thomas Hardy' and sent it to Browning on the latter's seventy-sixth birthday (May 7, 1888). In the following year, after reading in the newspaper that Browning had died in Venice, Hardy recorded in his notebook Browning's words: 'Incidents in the development of a soul: little else is worth study!'

At this time Hardy was at work on *Tess of the D'Urbervilles*. In it he quoted Browning's 'By the Fireside' and 'Pippa Passes' and paraphrased a passage in 'Rabbi Ben Ezra'. In *Jude the Obscure*, Hardy quoted Browning at least four times—twice from the poem 'Too Late'. Even in his private correspondence Hardy would toss off a line or two from Browning, obviously quoting from ready memory: for example,

> I, never the worse for a touch or two
> On my speckled hide

from 'The Worst of It'.

Much as Hardy liked and admired Browning's poetry, he found it impossible to accept his confident philosophy of life. 'The longer I live,' Hardy wrote to Edmund Gosse on March 6, 1899, 'the more does Browning's character seem *the* literary puzzle of the nineteenth century. How could smug Christian optimism worthy of a dissenting grocer find a place inside a man who was so vast a seer and feeler when on neutral ground?' Two years later he was still puzzled. In a conversation with William Archer, Hardy remarked: 'I believe that a good deal of the robustious, swaggering optimism of recent literature is at bottom cowardly and insincere. My pessimism—if pessimism it be —does not involve the assumption that the world is going to the dogs. On the contrary, my practical philosophy is distinctly

49

meliorist.' On one of the uncertain and depressing days of World
War I, Hardy turned to Browning's *Asolando* and there read
from the famous 'Epilogue': 'Never dreamed though right were
worsted wrong would triumph.' 'Well,' remarked Hardy, 'that
was a lucky dreamlessness for Browning.'

The record of quotations and allusions could be extended, but
this is not the place for attempting a complete list. On the night
before he died, Thomas Hardy asked his wife to read 'Rabbi
Ben Ezra' aloud to him. It is a long poem, but Hardy wanted
none of the thirty-two stanzas skipped. Riddle though Browning
was, he had fascinated Hardy's mind for more than sixty years.
If Hardy had been called upon to express his own sense of
indebtedness to the older poet, he might well have used Browning's own words:

> Yes, I have loved you so, followed you, honoured you,
> Lived in your mild and magnificent eye,
> Learned your great language, caught your clear accents,
> Made you my pattern to live and to die.

For Hardy *had* learned Browning's 'great language' and had
quoted it in half a dozen of the Wessex novels, this half-dozen
including some of the greatest: *The Woodlanders, Tess,* and *Jude.*
He had caught Browning's 'clear accents' and had echoed them
in a dozen or more of his own poems as well as in *The Dynasts.*

One of the poems in the volume of Browning which first came
into Hardy's hand was 'Memorabilia', beginning with the oft-
quoted line: 'Ah, did you once see Shelley plain . . . ?' Hardy's
curiosity about this earlier poet was aroused, and he promptly
acquired Shelley's *Poems*—two dumpy volumes which he could
carry in his pockets as he walked to and from work—and in
them he recorded his reactions to what he read. When Sir
James M. Barrie saw those books many years later, he remarked:
'There are a hundred, a thousand, pencil marks on those two
volumes that look now like love messages from the young poet
of one age to the young poet of a past age.' Hardy had declared
'I loved *Atalanta*.' He loved Shelley, too. He liked to remember
that he had once stayed overnight at a coaching-inn—The
Cross-Keys in London—where Shelley had once stayed, and
enjoyed imagining that he might have occupied the same room
'as that occupied by our most marvellous lyrist'.[2] When Hardy

went to Italy, he visited Shelley's grave and wrote a poem
about it, 'At the Pyramid of Cestius'.[3] When, many years later,
he was in Oxford, and when his hosts expected a man of eighty-
three to have little energy and less zest for sight-seeing, Hardy
insisted upon being shown the Shelley Memorial in University
College. At least six of the Wessex novels contain quotations
from Shelley. 'Laon and Cythna', 'The Revolt of Islam',
'Alastor', 'When the lamp is shattered', 'One word is too often
profaned', the 'Ode to the West Wind', 'Adonais', and 'Prometheus Unbound', have all left their mark in the Wessex
writings. Of the Shelley poems by which Hardy had been
impressed, none was more frequently in his consciousness than
'Epipsychidion'. He quoted it in *An Indiscretion*, in *The Mayor*,
in *The Woodlanders*, and in *Jude the Obscure*. In *The Pursuit of the
Well-Beloved*, Shelley's influence is so extensive, so all-pervasive,
that we shall postpone dealing with it until a later chapter.

In noting the marks of Hardy's indebtedness to Shakespeare,
to Swinburne, to Browning, and to Shelley, we run the risk of
implying that these four poets constituted the sole influence
upon his mind in 1866 and 1867. But if such an idea had been
expressed in Hardy's hearing, he might well have replied by
quoting Wordsworth's *Prelude*:

> Thus far a *scanty* record is deduced
> Of what I owed to Books in early life. . . .
> But let me add at once that . . . *many* books
> Were read in process of this time, devoured,
> Tasted or skimmed, or studiously perused.

Many books, and by many poets, not just by four of them. It is
important to stress this fact, because of erroneous statements
that have appeared in print, and once printed they tend to
spread into popular misconceptions. One recent English writer,
for instance, has described Hardy as 'a great and lonely figure
in our literature'. 'It is possible,' this writer has observed, 'to
trace the descent of almost every other writer, to name the
artistic influences that went to his making, but Hardy is without
literary ancestry.' This statement is strangely naïve. For of all
the authors whose literary ancestry can be traced, Hardy is the
one who supplies the investigator with the most generous guidance. His habits of exactness and accuracy, learned in the

architect's draughting office, resulted in his rarely thinking of an idea merely as an idea, but usually as Somebody's idea; and when a phrase or a sentence or a line of poetry came to his mind, it was not as the words of some indefinite Somebody-or-other, but as 'Coleridge's proof', or 'as Comte argued', or 'in Matthew Arnold's familiar phrase', or 'to use Wordsworth's observation', or 'if one may quote Tennyson'—all of these examples taken from just one piece of Hardy's writing.[4] We are thus greatly helped in tracing his 'literary ancestry' by his habit of naming the books and the authors that had left their imprint upon him.

In the course of his study of the poets, Hardy acquired a copy of Thomas Arnold's *Manual of English Literature* (1862). This textbook by the younger brother of Matthew Arnold provided Hardy with an introduction to a large number of authors previously unknown to him—especially the poets. 'For nearly two years he did not read a word of prose,' he tells us, for the simple reason that he had come to believe that in poetry is 'concentrated the essence of all imaginative and emotional literature' and that 'to read verse and nothing else was the shortest way to the fountain-head of such'.[5] Accordingly he got into the habit of shutting himself up in his room at Westbourne Park Villas night after night and reading poetry there from six p.m. till midnight, 'every evening . . . , reading incessantly'.[6] He does not state what he read, but his own books, published later, show clearly enough what ground he had covered in those evening sessions. It would be a tedious tax on the reader's time to go into details here; let it suffice to say that Hardy came to know the work of at least two dozen other poets besides the four we have already noticed. The two dozen can at least be named:

Burns	Drayton	Milton
Byron	Dryden	Rossetti
Campbell	Dyer	Tennyson
Campion	Gray	Thomson
Chatterton	Herbert	Waller
Coleridge	Herrick	Wordsworth
Cowper	Hood	Wyatt
Crashaw	Keats	Young

Even this impressive list does not indicate the full extent of Hardy's intense attack upon poetry; for, not satisfied with this array of English authors, he managed to include a few American poets as well. Walt Whitman who had begun scandalizing readers in the United States in 1855 is quoted in *Desperate Remedies*. Longfellow's 'Excelsior' is mentioned in *Jude the Obscure*, and in this same novel Poe's 'Raven' is quoted. John Cowper Powys has informed us that in his own youth 'Thomas Hardy pointed out to me, with more passionate appreciation than I ever heard him display for any other author, the power and beauty of Poe's *Ulalume*. . . . Hardy it was, the very first time I saw him, who introduced me to that most startling and characteristic of all Poe's poems.' Nor was this interest in Edgar Allan Poe an early enthusiasm which Hardy later outgrew. When he was nearly seventy, Hardy spoke of Poe as 'that fantastic and romantic genius' who was 'the first to realize to the full the possibilities of the English language in rhyme and alliteration.'

The inevitable outcome of this zealous pursuit of 'the essence of all emotional literature' was a greatly stimulated desire to write poems of his own. Shakespeare had observed that

> The poet's eye, in a fine frenzy rolling,
> Doth glance from heaven to earth, from earth to heaven,

but Hardy's eye, rolling (we may well believe) in an equally fine frenzy as he sat under his midnight lamp, glanced, *not* from heaven to earth, but from this book to that, and from that book to this. He composed Shakespearean sonnets; he tried turning *Ecclesiastes* into Spenserian stanzas; he imitated Swinburnian anapests; he wrote lyrics *à la* Shelley; he echoed the sound of Browning's description of disappointed artists with 'vexed beating stuffed and stopped-up brains'. And when he had achieved a result which seemed to him not unworthy, he took the next step and sent his manuscript to an editor—just as he had done early in 1865 when he sent 'How I Built Myself a House' to the editor of *Chambers's Journal*. But this time the response was different. His manuscript was returned, unwanted. He tried again, and his poem was again rejected. He remembered in later years that he rarely sent the same manuscript out twice, but he also remembered that none of his poems were accepted. Nothing 'got published'. He meditated bitterly about this discouraging fact.

> I sometimes think as here I sit
> Of things I have done,

Which seemed in doing not unfit
To face the sun:
Yet never a soul has paused a whit
On such—not one.

Why was this?

Hardy was never one to blame himself. In this respect he was like Eustacia Vye in *The Return of the Native*, who 'instead of blaming herself . . . laid the fault upon the shoulders of some indistinct colossal Prince of the World who . . . ruled her lot'. Hardy blamed the magazine editors. Though in their positions of authority they ruled his lot, they 'probably did not know good poetry from bad'. He consoled himself with the thought that 'he was not so keenly anxious to get into print as many young men are',[7] but in thinking this thought he was not thinking truthfully. For he *was* eager to get into print. He thought his verses had merit, that they were 'not unfit to face the sun'. He had worked long and hard over them. His evening hours of toil had been spent with joy and gladness, with 'the best hope ever sown' —that of achieving publication and subsequent renown. But nothing 'got published'. His joy was changed to pain, and after telling himself that he was not 'keenly anxious to get into print' he wrote a poem in which he recorded his true feelings:

. . . How arrives it joy lies slain,
And why unblooms the best hope ever sown?
Crass Casualty obstructs the sun and rain,
And dicing Time for gladness casts a moan.[8]

The twenty-six-year-old would-be poet had no one at hand with whom he could talk the situation over. His associates in Blomfield's office were more interested in chattering about Adah Isaacs Menken and 'Skittles' than they were in discussing poetry. Browning had written a poem urging young men to 'welcome each rebuff that turns earth's smoothness rough' and Hardy was well acquainted with those words. But Browning himself had found it difficult to follow his own advice, and after the disappointing reception which *Men and Women* received in 1855 he could hardly bring himself to write more poetry. 'Welcome each rebuff'? In March 1861 Mrs. Browning complained that 'all last summer he did nothing', and 'he was not inclined to write this winter'. Hardy could be even more easily discouraged. After all, Browning had a wife and a son, and an income not dependent upon the sale of his books. Hardy was alone and in a big city where loneliness is more keenly felt than anywhere else. He wrote in his notebook: 'The world does not despise us; it only neglects us.'

In later years when his thoughts went back to these early days of 'neglect', Hardy was inclined to wonder what might have happened if Crass Casualty had *not* obstructed the sun. His lodgings in 1867 were near both Browning and Swinburne. What if they had taken an interest in the young man and had given him encouragement, advice and help? 'Somebody might have come along . . . who would have asked him his trouble and might have cheered him, . . . but nobody did come, because nobody does.'[9] The thought that Browning, in person, 'might have cheered him' suggests the extent of Hardy's youthful *naïveté*, and one may well wonder what would have happened if the red-headed Swinburne had told young Hardy that a word like 'unbloom' would simply not do. But nobody did tell him, and as a result Hardy went on perplexing editors with his use of 'un-' for the rest of his life. We can now see that Hardy did not mean a negative reversal of an action, as in 'tie' and 'untie', but the mere absence of such action. When he asked in 'Hap' 'Why unblooms the best hope', he meant 'Why does the best hope not bloom? Why does it fail to bloom?' But to write this way would fill up the line with five words instead of one, and had not Browning demonstrated what could be done with the tightly packed line? 'Irks care the crop-full bird?' As a result, 'un—' words in Hardy continued to make his readers stumble, and fifty years later readers of *The Dynasts* would be trying to figure out what Hardy meant by 'His projects they unknow, his grin unsee'. In 1866 when he wrote 'Hap', Hardy 'unsaw'.

By the end of his two years' exclusive devotion to poetry, there was no doubt about the fact that, for the young architect, joy lay slain. Gladness had disappeared from his life. His health suffered. He had gone so long without the bodily exercise to which he had become accustomed in Dorset that his pink-cheeked healthy appearance gave way to a pallor which eventually attracted Arthur Blomfield's attention. The work in the draughting room lost none of its distasteful monotony, and Hardy's pallor was soon accompanied by languor, by a lassitude, the depth and intensity of which can be surmised when we learn from Hardy's notebook that he came to write down some 'Cures for despair'. Characteristically enough, his cures were not more exercise, or better hours, or more friendly contacts with his fellows; the 'cures' consisted of more reading! For example, 'Read Wordsworth's *Resolution and Independence*.' As for Hardy's associates in architecture, they were often 'bunglers'. They were, Hardy thought, satisfied with their own ignorance. At twenty-seven he had decided that being satisfied with ignorance on irrelevant subjects is 'more conducive to success in life than the desire for much knowledge'.[10]

Hardy was probably quite incapable, at this date, of looking at himself objectively enough to understand why what he called Crass Casualty obstructed his sun. He was ambitious, he was bright, he had won a prize in Dorchester and two prizes in London, he had worked hard, but—he had not 'succeeded'. If he had been asked to explain why doors that were open to Thackeray (who had died twenty months after Hardy's arrival in London) were closed to him, or why his winning of the medal of the Royal Institute of British Architects was not immediately followed by invitations from the *haute monde*, he would probably have used words he was shortly to put into one of his poems, words about 'hap of birth'. Within a little more than a year, Alexander Macmillan was to comment on 'the utter heartlessness' of all the conversation about the working-classes in Hardy's first attempt at novel-writing, *The Poor Man and the Lady*; and in this comment we can note the evidence that Hardy had become painfully impressed with the fact that, in the eyes of the London people he came into contact with, he was one of 'the working-classes'. By 'hap of birth' he was not a 'gentleman'. He had ability; he was acquiring some polish: a photograph of him, taken in London, shows that he had learned to black his boots instead of oiling them; but he remained an outsider. He recalled his mother's comments on the regrettable way in which she and her mother and her grandmother had all come 'down' in the world.

Hardy's gloomy feelings were not offset by any satisfaction he could take in the environment in which he found himself placed. Now that the first bloom of novelty in London had worn off, visits to the Brompton Boilers and the National Gallery had lost their appeal. Winters were often accompanied by the pea-soup fog of which Hardy complained to his sister Mary—when it would be 'almost pitch dark in the middle of the day'—and in the summer the stench from the mud-banks of the River Thames at low tide offended his nostrils. After five years in the metropolis, Hardy had lost his interest in London. He 'was beginning to feel that he would rather go into the country'[11] and stay there.

Blomfield finally became alarmed at Hardy's loss of vigour and suggested that he take a vacation, at least 'for a time'. Crass Casualty played its part in the game of deciding things for Hardy, for a letter just then came from John Hicks in Dorchester, asking if Hardy could recommend some good assistant accustomed to church 'restorations'. Hardy replied that he would go himself, and at the end of July 1867 he returned to Dorchester. He did not regard this return as a permanent arrangement, but left his books and manuscripts in his lodgings at Westbourne Park Villas.

On page 71 of *The Early Life* Hardy lists some of the poems in manuscript which, at this date of leaving London, he 'thought worth keeping'. Most of them, he says, 'had never been sent anywhere'—i.e., had not been stigmatized for him by editorial rejection. When we look into *Wessex Poems* and into the volumes that followed it, we observe that there are twenty-seven dated poems which Hardy had thus thought were 'worth keeping'. Fifteen of these he eventually published in 1898. Two more followed in 1902. Seven had to wait until 1909. Two more were published in 1922, and one straggler finally appeared in print in 1925. 'Hap' was one of the fifteen published in 1898. Many of the others show the results of Hardy's burning the lamp till midnight. One is written in a modification of the Burns stanza. Two are in couplets reminiscent of Scott's poems. One ballad is written in the dialect of William Barnes, and one is in the anapestic-couplet meter of Browning's 'How They Brought the Good News from Ghent to Aix'. A few of the poems deal with Dorset characters. Many are of a melancholy turn of mind and speak of 'beauty marred', 'bitter knowledge', 'frost', 'chill', and 'visions ghast and grim'. Even Nature is 'racked and wrung'. A sonnet called 'Discouragement' speaks of a whole life's circumstance being dependent 'on hap of birth'. Of the twenty-seven poems, the one which eventually came to win the highest praise from critics is 'Neutral Tones'. Robert W. King called this the best of Hardy's early poems,[12] and John Middleton Murry once declared: 'That is, I think, a fine poem.'

The likelihood is that most readers will conclude that, if all the manuscripts which Hardy left behind in London in 1867 had been destroyed by some London fire during his absence, his future reputation as a poet would not have been greatly affected.

In *The Return of the Native* Clym Yeobright announces: 'I have come home.'[13] Before the end of July 1867, Thomas Hardy enacted a dress-rehearsal of that fictional scene. He walked down 'the lonely lane' at Higher Bockhampton, opened the 'little wicket' that admitted him to the garden, and 'proceeded up the path' to the familiar door.[14] After five years in the big city, the native had returned.

V

'The Poor Man' and the Critics

IN the twenty-first chapter of *The Return of the Native* we read that, after Clym Yeobright's return to the heath where he had grown up, 'he gazed upon the wide prospect . . . and was glad'. Egdon Heath suited him. He would (we may assume) have had no difficulty in understanding Henry David Thoreau's famous exclamation about Concord, Massachusetts: 'I have never got over my surprise that I should have been born into the most estimable place in all the world.'

It would be pleasant if one could record that, upon Thomas Hardy's return to Bockhampton in July 1867, he felt that he had returned to the most estimable place in all the world. He was, of course, glad to have escaped from London and to be able to breathe fresh clean air again; but Egdon Heath, Hardy had in all honesty to admit, was not 'the most estimable place in all the world'. In an unpublished letter which he wrote some years later, he spoke of re-reading *The Return of the Native* and then remarked: 'Although some people say it is my best, I don't feel it interests me like some of the others on returning to it. Perhaps a certain dreariness that there is about the *real* heath affects me . . . , though readers, knowing only the description in the novel, do not feel it.'

The 'certain dreariness' was undoubtedly there; but there were two additional considerations which interfered just now with any possibility that Hardy would feel that he had returned to a bower of perfect bliss. One had to do with the 'neighbouring yeomen'; the other, with his mother. Both were to leave their trace in *the Native*.

59

Hardy knew from his long experience with people in Dorchester just what they would be saying when he turned up once again in Hicks's office. 'Ah, Tom Hardy! What's he doing now?'[1] 'When the instinctive question about a person is "What is he doing?" . . . the devout hope is that he is doing well. The secret faith is that he is making a mess of it. . . . If he were making a tragical figure in the world, so much the better for a narrative.'[1]

With regard to his mother, the situation was even more disturbing. As we listen to Clym Yeobright talk with his mother after his return to the heath, we surmise that we are listening to echoes of a conversation Hardy had with his mother after his return from London. This autobiographical suggestion is strengthened when we remember that Clym's name, Clement, was derived from Hardy's ancestor, Clement le Hardy. The young architect cannot have long concealed from his mother his distaste for what he had been doing in Blomfield's office, his dissatisfaction with London, and his uncertainty about returning thither.

'I am astonished, Clym. How can you want to do better than you've been doing?'

'But I hate that business of mine. . . . I want to do some worthy thing before I die.'

'After all the trouble that has been taken to give you a start, and when there is nothing to do but keep straight on towards affluence, you say you . . . —it disturbs me, Clym, to find that you have come home with such thoughts. . . . I hadn't the least idea that you meant to go backward in the world by your own free choice. . . .'

'I cannot help it,' said Clym, in a troubled tone. . . .

'Why can't you do . . . as well as others?'

'I don't know, except that there are many things other people care for which I don't. . . .'

'And yet you might have been a wealthy man if you had only persevered. . . . I suppose you will be like your father. Like him, you are getting weary of doing well. . . .'

'Mother, what is doing well?'

Mrs. Yeobright [Mrs. Hardy?] was far too thoughtful a woman to be content with ready definitions and, like the 'What is wisdom?' of Plato's Socrates, and the 'What is truth?' of Pontius Pilate, Yeobright's burning question received no answer.[2]

Fortunately, Hardy's promise to assist John Hicks in the work

of 'restoring' Gothic churches provided the much-needed bene-
ficial tonic. Health and equanimity were soon regained. With
the arrival of August 1867, Hardy resumed the three-mile walk
into Dorchester, and enjoyed the luxury of being able to go when
and as he wished. 'His attendances at Mr. Hicks's drawing-
office . . . were not regular.'[3] The walk back and forth from
Bockhampton soon brought the colour back into Hardy's
cheeks; and, as he walked, Nature, which in London had seemed
'racked and wrung', resumed her earlier appeal. The August
morning walks became a delight. 'Fuchsias and dahlias . . .
changed the colour of their sparkle at every movement of the
air. . . . The threads of garden spiders appeared thick and
polished. In the dry and sunny places, dozens of long-legged
crane-flies whizzed off the grass at every step the passer took.'[4]

One day Hicks reported that he would be absent from the
office on the morrow, for he was going to inspect a dilapidated
Gothic church in a remote parish in Cornwall. Hardy thought
that the place had a romantic name—St. Juliot—but just at this
time he had become interested in something other than Gothic
churches and so paid little attention to Hicks's destination.
With characteristic vacillation, and with a total ignoring of his
mother's 'if you had only persevered', he was now going to drop
poetry and try to write a novel. Tom had decided that 'writing
rhymes is a stage people pass through', and had come to the
conclusion that 'poetical days were getting past with him'. And
he 'suddenly became more practical'[5] and subjected himself to a
thoroughgoing act of mental stock-taking. This is what he wrote
in self-appraisal:

'He's a very worthy fellow. There's no nonsense in him.
Though he is not a Public School man, he has read widely and
has a sharp appreciation of what's good in books and art. His
knowledge isn't nearly so exclusive as most professional men's.
That's great deal to say of an architect. This man is rather of
a melancholy turn of mind. Of course he isn't married. He is a
thorough artist, but a man of very humble origin, the son of a
farmer, or something of the kind. He's about six-and-twenty. He
is rather untidy in his waistcoat. He's a thorough bookworm—
despises the pap-and-daisy school of verse—knows Shakespeare
to the very dregs of the footnotes. Indeed, he's a poet himself in
a small way. Architecture is a bewitching profession, but he

won't advance in it. Worldly advantage from an art doesn't depend upon mastering it. He used to think it did; but it doesn't. Those who get rich need have no skill at all as artists. They need a certain kind of energy which men with any fondness for art possess very seldom indeed—an earnestness in making acquaintances, and a love for using them. They give their whole attention to the art of dining out, after mastering a few rudimentary facts to serve up in conversation. When he found all this out, from having already loved verse passionately he went on to read it continually; then he went rhyming himself. If anything on earth ruins a man for useful occupation, and for content with reasonable success in a profession or trade, it is a habit of writing verses on emotional subjects. Poetical days are getting past with him, according to the usual rule. Writing rhymes is a stage people of his sort pass through, as they pass through the stage of shaving for a beard, or thinking they are ill-used, or saying there's nothing in the world worth living for.'

This is a remarkable description, well worth reading over a second time. Hardy applied these words to Edward Springrove, a character in *Desperate Remedies*, and he has explicitly stated that he patterned this character after a young architect's assistant whom he met in Weymouth. In view of this assertion,[6] what justification is there for stating that the description quoted above is an interesting portrait of Hardy himself rather than a thumbnail sketch of G. R. Crickmay's new assistant?

Of course no reader is likely to believe that the young assistant of 'about six-and-twenty' had repeated Hardy's own experience with such amazing, such incredible duplication. The 'melancholy turn of mind', the untidy clothing, the 'poet in a small way', and the interest in Shakespeare, even 'to the very dregs of the footnotes', are all personal features so obviously derived from Hardy himself that we are forced to wonder whether Hardy was blind in thinking that he had found these traits in Crickmay's young assistant, or whether (in the statement about 'Springrove' in *The Early Life*) Hardy was disingenuously trying to conceal the extent of the autobiographical element in his novel. Doubtless neither alternative will wholly serve as an explanation. Hardy of course knew where the dregs of the Shakespeare footnotes came from. They and the 'melancholy turn of mind' did not come from the new assistant at Weymouth. That young man's nature was much more frivolous. He liked dancing and joined a class 'where a good deal of flirtation went on', and after a few months of this young man's company the serious-minded Hardy left him 'and returned to his rural home'. But this examination of Edward Springrove teaches us two things which it will be well to keep in mind: that Hardy's characterizations are composite creations, made up of various elements drawn from various sources, and that his disclaimers about autobiography—disavowals often made by him and often repeated in future years—are only partly to be taken seriously. In creating Edward Springrove's appearance and in inventing his experiences in the novel, Hardy doubtless had Crickmay's assistant in mind; but in equipping Springrove with a background Hardy drew on what he knew best of all—his own personality and his own experience. If the resultant portrait is not wholly consistent, it will not be the last time that we shall find Hardy's photographs to be double-exposures.

Of Clym Yeobright in *the Native*, Hardy was later to remark: 'I think Clym is the nicest of all my heroes, and *not a bit* like me.' Yet, as we have noted on previous pages, a great deal of Hardy's own experience and personality went into the creation of Clym. Hardy could say a thing like 'not a bit like me' because he was aware of elements in Yeobright that had come from sources outside his author's own experience. Hardy as a young man had not had Clym's business experience in Paris, nor did he have Clym's great gift of content. In lacking it, Hardy was more like Eustacia. When we come to deal with *A Laodicean*, we will find a similar pattern in the use of autobiography. And in the creation of Tess Durbeyfield, Hardy has informed us that three models were used. In *Jude the Obscure*, Jude like Edward Springrove was given some of his author's own characteristics; others came from outside. This sort of composite creation began, then, with Hardy's very first attempt at fiction.

In the intervals of his irregular 'attendances at Mr. Hicks's drawing-office', Hardy went to work on a novel which he called *The Poor Man and the Lady*. There was to be little disguising the autobiographical element in it, for its title-page was to announce that it was 'By the Poor Man'. In five months, from August to Christmas 1867, Hardy completed his first draft of the story. In *The Early Life* (p. 75) he remarks: 'Thus it happened that under the stress of necessity he . . . set about a kind of literature in which he had hitherto taken but little interest—prose fiction.' Two statements in this assertion will not stand up under close scrutiny.

The statement that he turned to novel-writing in 1867 'under the stress of necessity' was made by Hardy when he was eighty years old, and that was conceivably the way he remembered it at that advanced age. But he repeated the assertion on various other occasions both before and after the writing of *The Early Life*. When Professor William Lyon Phelps called on Hardy in September 1900, the Yale professor was surprised to discover that Hardy wished to talk only about his verse. (*Wessex Poems* had been published only two years before.) Hardy, so Phelps reported later, 'had ceased to care about his novels; he did not wish to discuss them'.[7] In a letter written in 1923 Hardy stated: 'I never wanted to write prose novels at all. I was forced to manufacture my novels; circumstances compelled me to turn them out.' On February 14, 1926, Hardy asked his wife to write a letter to Professor Phelps, remonstrating with him over the fact that in his published comments on Hardy Phelps had bestowed nearly the whole of his attention on the novels— writings which (said Hardy) 'were dictated by accident and circumstances not under his own control'.

This picture of a young Hardy, uninterested in prose fiction but forced 'under the stress of necessity', by 'circumstances not under his own control', to write novels, is a picture which soon fades when exposed to the bright sunlight of fact. Hardy himself admitted that he was not really 'in want of a means of subsistence' in 1867 and that 'architectural jobs were offered him readily by Blomfield and other London architects'.[8] Hardy mentions working, after 1867, not only for Blomfield and Hicks, but also for G. R. Crickmay, Raphael Brandon, and T. Roget Smith. He could, if he had wished, have easily supported himself without ever writing a novel.

Nor will his assertion that prose fiction was 'a kind of literature in which he had hitherto taken but little interest' bear close examination. He had not forgotten—nor did he ever forget (as future events are to demonstrate)—his early interest in the novels of William Harrison Ainsworth. Shortly after his arrival in London he acquired a copy of Henry Fielding's *Joseph*

Andrews (London, Routledge, 1861) which survives to show, by its pencil markings, Hardy's interest in the 'Moral Reflections' on page 166 and the 'Philosophical Reflections' on pages 219–220. Fielding and Smollett are both mentioned in *Jude the Obscure*, but Defoe has left an even broader trail. He is mentioned in *Far from the Madding Crowd*, is quoted in *A Laodicean*, is referred to in *The Woodlanders*, and is again mentioned in *Jude the Obscure*. Before he had become immersed in poetry, Hardy bought a copy of *Barchester Towers* and in October 1865 sent it to his sister Mary, telling her that 'this novel is considered the best of Trollope's'. Later he told her that he thought 'Wells is the place intended'. Later still, after he had learned that Salisbury was the place, not Wells, Trollope's 'Barchester' became Hardy's 'Melchester', and we are free to conjecture that Trollope's 'Barset'—suggestive of the dialectal pronunciation of 'Darset' for Dorset—may have been the origin of Hardy's idea of creating a fictional Wessex. For a comment on the possibility that Hardy was even more deeply indebted to Trollope, we shall have to wait until we reach the chapter on *The Mayor of Casterbridge*.

Also significant is Hardy's advice to his sister: 'If you can get *Pelham*, read it . . .' for in this novel Hardy had found the sort of dialogue, witty and satirical, which he was shortly to try to create in *The Poor Man and the Lady*. In this attempt he did not succeed, for Hardy's lack of experience with the sort of people who appear in *Pelham* unfitted him for the task. His effort did not fool Alexander Macmillan, for when the publisher wrote Hardy, just a year later, he remarked: 'I don't know what opportunities you have had of seeing the class you deal with. My own experience of fashionables is very small . . . but it is inconceivable to me that any considerable number of human beings . . . should be so bad. . . .' Hardy did not try to explain that he had never been in the drawing-rooms and ball-rooms of the 'fashionables', and that Bulwer Lytton was the mirror into which he had looked. (Published in 1828, *Pelham* was Bulwer Lytton's second novel.)

Hardy seems to have decided at a very early date that Dickens had less to offer him. He did go, however, during his first year in London, to hear Dickens read at the Hanover Square Rooms. There Dickens gave a series of readings from

March until the end of May, and in our lack of knowledge as to the exact date of Hardy's visit, it is pleasant to think that he went on Tuesday, April 28, when Thomas Carlyle sat on the front bench to hear 'The Trial from *Pickwick*'. Another member of the audience on that occasion was James S. Pike, United States Minister to the Netherlands; to him we are indebted for the information that Carlyle 'haw-hawed right out, over and over, till he fairly exhausted himself'. Dickens would read and then would have to stop to give Carlyle time to get over his uproarious haw-hawing. 'I laughed', said Pike, 'till my jaws ached.'[9] If Thomas Hardy was present on that occasion, he ought to have been equally entertained; but the likelihood is that he went on some other date and that Fagin and Sykes and Little Nell were not Hardy's meat. Pike called the Dickens show 'the greatest thing in London'. Hardy, however, had nothing further to say about it.

With Thackeray the case was quite different. Hardy had been in London only a few months when Thackeray's immense fame began making its impact upon the young man from Dorchester. *Vanity Fair*, published in 1847–8, had obviously not penetrated into the recesses of Higher Bockhampton, and Hardy had to do a lot of reading to catch up. On December 19, 1863, only five days before Thackeray's death, Hardy wrote to his sister Mary: 'About Thackeray: you must read something of his. He is considered to be the greatest novelist of the day. . . . His novels stand . . . high as works of Art or Truth. . . . *Vanity Fair* is considered one of his best'.[10] And the fact that this was not merely a matter of good advice from Big Brother to Little Sister, but represented some of the thinking Hardy had been doing on the subject, is indicated by his pronouncement: 'Looking at novel writing of the highest kind as a perfect and truthful representation of actual life . . . is no doubt the proper view to take'.[10] When Hardy sat down to write *The Poor Man and the Lady*, he had obviously done more than a little thinking about novels.

Hardy's statement that, until 1867, he had taken little interest in prose fiction was coupled with his memory that he had once surprised Blomfield's pupils by expressing 'an indifference to a popular novelist's fame'.[11] The name of this popular novelist is not given, but one wonders whether it was not Charles Reade, whose novel *The Cloister and the Hearth* had appeared in 1861. One wonders also whether Hardy's memory in later years was mixed up with the fact that he and this 'popular' but arrogant and pugnacious novelist had gone together, one day in May 1875, to call on Prime Minister Disraeli. They went as a delegation from the Association to Protect the Rights of Authors, in order to urge the desirability of changes in the Copyright Law. Hardy's later memories were doubtless also complicated by his recalling the day in 1894 when someone discovered that the title of Hardy's new novel, *The Simpletons*, then beginning its run in *Harper's*, had a close resemblance to Charles Reade's *A Simpleton*.

As Hardy proceeded with the writing of *The Poor Man*, he so obviously patterned his satire of the upper classes after Thackeray's that Alexander Macmillan easily recognized the relationship. When, in August 1868, he came to write Hardy about *The Poor Man*, Macmillan observed: 'Nothing could justify such a wholesale blackening of a class but large and intimate knowledge of it. Thackeray makes them not greatly better in many respects, but he gave many redeeming traits . . . ; besides, he . . . wrote in a mocking tone. You seem in grim earnest.' But this comment from the publisher came after Hardy had finished writing the story, and we must now turn our attention back to its composition.

In beginning *The Poor Man*, Hardy, like a good architect, had taken account of the materials he had to work with and the sort of structure he wished to build. His own experience as a 'poor man' and one 'of very humble origin' supplied him with a point of view. He did not plan, however, to tell the story of his own life; he would invent incidents and devise dramatic situations, but would associate these with a young architect who, from a school such as that built by Mrs. Martin at Bockhampton and from a parish church such as that at Stinsford, went up to London in order to make his fortune. Nor would Hardy find it necessary to invent all the incidents, for some occurred to him out of his own experience in London. He remembered that, in awarding him the Royal Institute medal for his essay on the modern use of coloured bricks, the judge had withheld the ten-pound prize that was sometimes given with the medal, because, said the judge, Hardy had 'scarcely gone sufficiently into the subject'. That decision had naturally seemed niggardly to the disappointed young architect, but the young would-be novelist could now make use of the incident. Hardy also remembered having gone with Arthur Blomfield to New Windsor one day, when the memorial stone of a church was laid by the Princess Royal. When Blomfield handed her the trowel, the Princess got her glove soiled with mortar and handed the trowel back to the architect, whispering impatiently, 'Take it! Take it!' That incident, too, could be put to fictional use. As for 'the Lady', Hardy's memories of Mrs. Martin, the mistress of Kingston Maurward House at Stinsford, came to his aid. For the scenes in London, his own observations in the theatre, in Hyde Park, in Covent Garden, and in the art gallery, could all be drawn upon. To add a literary polish to his story Hardy would call on the poets for help—Browning and Shelley and, of course, Shakespeare. Further 'atmosphere' could be obtained by descriptions of architecture and by allusions to Turner and Romney, to Raphael and Rubens and others.

Once this plan had been mapped out, Hardy wrote rapidly and by Christmas the first draft was finished. On January 16, 1868, he began to write out a clean copy and finished this task on June 9. On July 25 he mailed the manuscript to Alexander Macmillan, and in a little more than two weeks received a letter from the publisher, saying that, although he had read the novel 'with much interest and admiration', it seemed to him to have 'fatal drawbacks to its success' and that its descriptions of the upper classes would be sure to strike readers as 'ignorant misrepresentation'. Macmillan added, however, that 'your description of country life among working men is admirable'.

Hardy was of course disappointed. He could not console himself with the thought that this criticism was just one man's opinion, for Macmillan wrote: 'I have shown your MS. to one friend, whose judgment coincides with my own.' We now know that this 'friend' was Macmillan's reader, John Morley, and that he had reported that 'the thing hangs too loosely together', that some of the scenes were wildly extravagant, 'so that they read like some clever lad's dream'. How perceptive Morley was! But he agreed with Macmillan in finding some virtue in the manuscript. 'The opening pictures of the Christmas-eve in the tranter's house are really of good quality: much of the writing is strong and fresh.'

Macmillan mollified his rejection of Hardy's story by giving him a letter of introduction to Frederick Chapman of the publishing firm of Chapman & Hall. On December 8, 1868, Hardy accordingly called on Chapman and left his manuscript with him. A month later, on Chapman's invitation, Hardy again called and was told that the publisher was not prepared to purchase *The Poor Man and the Lady* outright, but that he would be willing to publish it if Hardy would guarantee twenty pounds against possible loss. Hardy was eager enough for publication to agree to this proposal, but two months went by without his hearing anything more about it. Then he received a request from Chapman to come and meet 'the gentleman who read your manuscript' and talk it over with him. This 'gentleman' turned out to be the novelist George Meredith. Hardy went up to London in March 1869, met Meredith, and was told by him that if he proceeded with his desire to have his novel published, he was sure to raise such a storm of censure as would blow him out upon the same kind of hostile sea as Swinburne had had to sail only three years earlier. Meredith's advice was to put *The Poor Man* aside and write another novel—one with a more complicated plot, the sort of thing Wilkie Collins had just done. *The Moonstone* had been published by Tinsley Brothers in 1868.

It occurred to Hardy that the Tinsley firm might not agree with the adverse judgment of Macmillan and Meredith. Hardy himself did not agree with all that had been said to him. Macmillan had written: 'The fault of the book, as it seems to me, is that it lacks the *modesty of nature* of fact. . . . One sees in the papers accounts of gentlemen's daughters running away with their father's grooms, but you are not in that region. . . . Could it happen . . . ?' Obviously, Alexander Macmillan did not know about Lady Susan who had run away with the Irish actor and now lay buried with him in the very 'region' in which Macmillan supposed such things could not happen. Hardy remembered, too, that the Tinsleys (William and Edward) had published Hardy's boyhood favourite, James Grant. It would do no harm to sound out the opinion of a third publisher. Accordingly, on June 8, 1869, Hardy submitted *The Poor Man and the Lady* to the Tinsley Brothers. This firm's reader scrawled a big 'Return' across the face of the letter Hardy had sent with his novel, and for the third time *The Poor Man and the Lady* came back into the hands of its author. This time it stayed there.

When Hardy's *Human Shows* appeared in 1925, it contained a reference to 'the story of *The Poor Man and the Lady*, written in 1868, but never printed and ultimately destroyed'. In view of this fact, the reader may well wonder why so much space has been devoted to it here. 'It is hunting very small deer,' Hardy remarked to Edmund Gosse, when inquiries were being made about Hardy's first attempt at fiction. Gosse, however, did not agree with Hardy, and thought that 'the student of Hardy's mind in its early development' would wish to know all that could be learned about his first faltering attempt to write a novel; and, as we shall shortly see, there is an additional reason for wishing to cast full light on the unpublished *Poor Man*: the rejected manuscript was dipped into by Hardy on at least four subsequent occasions, for use in other works. His ten months' labour on *The Poor Man* was not all wasted.

During the tedious months when the fate of his novel was still undecided, Hardy's old teacher, John Hicks, died. His practice was purchased by a Weymouth architect, G. R. Crickmay, and when the latter found out that Hicks had left unfinished a great many Gothic church commitments on which Hardy had been assisting the Dorchester architect, Crickmay wrote to invite Hardy to help him in carrying out this work. Hardy accepted this invitation, and after the rejection of *The Poor Man* by Tinsley, Hardy migrated to Weymouth and spent the rest of 1869 in Crickmay's employ. He lodged at No. 3, Wooperton Street. By this time Hardy had grown a full beard which made him look much older than he really was. He was now twenty-nine.

Life in Weymouth had its pleasant side. There was a bay on which Hardy liked to go rowing and in which he often went swimming. This bay was the scene sketched by him on the fly-leaf of his French textbook when he was day-dreaming in the evening class at King's College. But most of his leisure time and thought in Weymouth went into meditating about George Meredith's advice to write another novel, one with more plot. Meditation ended in decision. He *would* write another. This time Hardy was able to work more rapidly, not only because of his previous experience in planning and writing *The Poor Man*, but also because he was able to salvage some passages from the rejected work.

Hardy called the new novel *Desperate Remedies*. Discarding Thackeray as his guide and model, Hardy substituted Wilkie Collins, and followed his new model so closely that, as he came later to admit, 'the principles observed in its composition are, no doubt, too exclusively those in which entanglement, surprise, and moral obliquity are depended on for exciting interest'.[12] In describing these entanglements, however, Hardy showed that he had learned to handle the complications of the plot efficiently and clearly. Although he was still, as he said in the 1889 preface to the novel, 'feeling his way to a method', he had learned how to avoid the marks of 'ignorant misrepresentation' which Macmillan had found fault with in *The Poor Man*. He described what lay right in front of his eyes. The Weymouth scenes were written at Weymouth (which Hardy called 'Budmouth'), and the later 'Knapwater' scenes were written at Bockhampton, to which place he returned when he found that life in Weymouth left him too little leisure and quiet for literary activity. For the 'Knapwater' setting, he turned to the manuscript of *The Poor Man* and from it lifted the description of 'the Lady's' Kingston Maurward House, which he now called Knapwater House. In a surprisingly short time he had worked out an elaborate and gruesome murder story, and by the end of February 1870 he had a completed manuscript ready. On March 5 he mailed *Desperate Remedies* to Alexander Macmillan. A month later it was returned to him: another rejection! Later on, Macmillan explained that 'the story was of far too sensational an order for us to think of publishing it'.

Doggedly, Hardy rewrapped the manuscript and sent it to Tinsley Brothers. When the manuscript reached William Tinsley, he was just going out to lunch. He took the sheets with him to the Gaiety Bar and there met an old friend, William Faux. The latter asked about the manuscript Tinsley was carrying. The publisher replied that it was apparently a story by a writer unknown to him and that he had not yet read it. 'Give it to me!' said Faux; 'I'll take it home and read it for you.' Faux read *Desperate Remedies* and advised Tinsley to accept it for publication. Tinsley, however, was a cautious fellow. On May 6 he wrote Hardy that he would be willing to publish his novel if

Hardy would guarantee the costs. Determined now to see the venture through, Hardy agreed to put up seventy-five pounds. During the latter part of 1870 he wrote out a fair copy for the printer; in January 1871 he paid over the money; and on March 25, 1871, *Desperate Remedies* appeared in print—in three anonymous volumes. Hardy had become a published author, even though his name had not yet appeared in print.

' 'pon my soul, Mr. Hardy,' Tinsley exclaimed at a later meeting with the author, ' 'twas a blood-curdling story! You wouldn't have got another man in London to print it! Be hanged if you would!'

A reviewer in the *Spectator* thought that Tinsley too ought to have refused to print such a wild tale. 'This is an absolutely anonymous story,' said the reviewer. 'By all means let the novelist bury the secret of his name in the profoundest depths of his own heart. The law is hardly just which prevents Tinsley Brothers from concealing their participation also.'

There is no denying the fact that *Desperate Remedies* has some wild scenes. In one there are three spectators, unknown to each other and each with a different purpose, who spy in the dark on the guilty Manston. The reader is asked to believe that a murder and a suicide in jail aid in bringing about a happy marriage. The obvious faults of the story ought not, however, to be allowed to conceal the fact that (as Hardy pointed out in a new preface, written in February 1896) 'certain characteristics in my latest story were present in my first'. This is true. Cytherea Graye is the first of Hardy's gallery of fresh, charming, and unstable heroines. The contest between a sensual villain and a devoted, self-sacrificing hero for the possession of the fascinating heroine was a theme which, used in *Desperate Remedies* for the first time, Hardy was to return to again and again.

Nor are the characteristics of *Desperate Remedies* of interest merely because they are the harbingers of better things to come. Two may be mentioned as good in themselves—neither crude nor immature. The rustic characters—the postman, the railway porter, Clerk Crickett—are well done, and their humorous dialogue shows how attentively Hardy had listened to the talk of the Dorset natives and how skilful he was in recording it. Second, his descriptions are fresh and delicate. Cytherea 'glowed amid the dulness like a single bright-red poppy in a field of brown stubble'. The masons, working at a distance, 'appeared little larger than pigeons, and made their tiny movements with a soft, spirit-like silentness'. Nature too is observed with a precise and mature eye. 'The water gurgled down from the old mill-pond to a lower level, under the cloak of rank broad leaves.' 'He halted to listen to the intensely melancholy yet musical wail of the fir-tops, and as the wind passed on, the prompt moan of an adjacent plantation in reply.' As John Morley had said of *The Poor Man*, 'Much of the writing is strong and fresh.'

William Tinsley recognized this fact, and when he happened to meet Hardy on the street in London, one day early in 1872, he asked the young author when he would let him have another novel. Hardy replied that he had already written a short one. 'Let me see it!' said Tinsley. Never again did Hardy have to seek out a publisher or advance any money for the publication of what he had written.

William Tinsley promptly accepted *Under the Greenwood Tree* for publication and paid Hardy thirty pounds for the copyright. Although this sum was only a small fraction of what the novel came eventually to be worth as a piece of literary property, it represented in Hardy's eyes, at this date (1872), evidence that he had taken a step up in the world.

One of the reasons why Hardy had been able to complete the writing of this novel so promptly was that eight of its thirty chapters had been salvaged from the beginning of the rejected *Poor Man*. Just as Knapwater House and its mistress had been lifted from *The Poor Man* into the pages of *Desperate Remedies*, so the tranter and his family, the Stinsford musicians, the woods at Bockhampton, the nightingales on the edge of Egdon Heath, the vicar at Stinsford Church (now called 'Mellstock'), were all transferred into *Under the Greenwood Tree*, the idyllic character of which is suggested by its Shakespearean title. The mistakes of *Desperate Remedies* are avoided. The plot is simplicity itself. The heroine, who (like Cytherea) proves fascinating to two men, conceals from one her promise to the other. That is the only structural device. In *Desperate Remedies* Manston's last words recorded his 'having found man's life to be a wretchedly conceived scheme', but in *Under the Greenwood Tree* all bitterness is left out. It is full of country tunes and birds' notes. Tinsley remarked: 'It is as pure and sweet as new-mown hay.'

The blithe rural atmosphere of the novel is partly explained by Hardy's return to the land of William Barnes and his poems. Once again he was where 'Blackmwore' and 'Trees Be Company' originated. In 1868 Barnes gave Hardy a copy of his *Poems of Rural Life*. Parts of *Under the Greenwood Tree* seem to have been written with one eye upon Barnes's volume. The chapter 'Driving Out of Budmouth' recalls Barnes's 'A Bit o' Sly Coorten' '; the chapter 'A Confession' suggests the poem 'Meaken Up a Miff'; the chapter on 'Yalbury Wood and the Keeper's House' recalls the poem 'The Settle an' the Gret Wood Vire'. Barnes's young lady, 'Fanny', may have suggested the name of Hardy's heroine, Fancy Day. This young lady is vividly portrayed; and, like Cytherea before her and like many more to come after her, she is as unstable as she is fascinating. The most original portraits in *Under the Greenwood Tree* are those of the musicians. The vividness with which they are described has at times led readers to suppose that Hardy was here drawing on his own experiences. The Stinsford ('Mellstock') instrumentalists had, it is true, been organized by Hardy's grandfather, and Hardy's father had, as we have noticed in a previous chapter, played an active and leading part in the music of the parish. But the grandfather had died before Hardy was born, and his father had stopped playing before Hardy was old enough to attend the Stinsford church. In 1904 Hardy wrote: 'So far as I am aware, there are no church string-bands left in Wessex at the present date.' They survive solely in the pages of *Under the Greenwood Tree*.

'Mr. Hardy, I do like your writings,' exclaimed William Tinsley, on the occasion of another chance meeting in the Strand in London. And then Tinsley proceeded to make a proposal that was to have far-reaching effects upon Hardy's future career—upon his methods, plays, characters, fame, and fortune. Tinsley proposed that Hardy write a novel to appear serially in *Tinsleys' Magazine*, and in accepting the proposal Hardy embarked upon a life that committed him for the next twenty-five years to serial production. It also involved him in a new kind of novel; in setting about its composition he made use of recent experiences which have thus far been ignored in our narrative. To them it is therefore necessary to turn before proceeding with a record of the novel-writing.

VI

Excursion into Lyonnesse

WHEN William Tinsley proposed to Hardy that he write a serial for *Tinsleys' Magazine*, the publisher knew exactly what he wanted. In *Under the Greenwood Tree* he had, so he thought, 'got hold of the best little prose idyll I had ever read. . . . But, strange to say, it would not sell. . . . It just lacks the touch of sentiment that lady novel-readers most admire.' If Hardy could give his next novel that 'touch of sentiment', things would go better. Tinsley's request came at a most opportune time, for Hardy had fallen in love. If *A Pair of Blue Eyes* is different from anything that he had as yet written—as it is—the reason lies in the fact that he had taken a trip into Cornwall and had there met the owner of the blue eyes. It was the most important trip he ever took in his whole life—one that left its mark on many a page in books he was yet to write.

The reader will recall that on Hardy's twenty-fifth birthday, when he was still in London, he 'wondered what woman, if any, I should be thinking about in five years' time'. A few months after his return to Bockhampton in midsummer 1867, he thought he knew the answer to his question. He went to Puddletown, only two or three miles from his home, to see the mummers there (like those he afterwards described in *The Return of the Native*), and at Puddletown he met his cousin Tryphena Sparks. She was then sixteen years old. In talking with her, Hardy discovered that she had once attended Mrs. Martin's school at Bockhampton, the same one that he had gone to for one year. Later, Tryphena had gone to a school nearer home, at Athelhampton, the village near Puddletown where John Hicks had

built a new church, one that Hardy had 'written up' for the
Dorset County Chronicle. Hardy found his cousin attractive. He
admired 'her ebon loops of hair' and learned with interest that
she was looking forward to becoming a school teacher. Before
Tryphena's departure in 1869 to Clapham where she enrolled
in the Stockwell Teachers' Training College, she and Hardy
took walks together in the country between his home and hers.
Attempts have recently been made to inflate these meetings into
a romantic affair, with talk of an 'engagement' and the giving of
a ring. This hypothetical 'engagement' rests upon the memory
of Tryphena's octogenarian daughter who was only eleven or
twelve when her mother died but who claimed to remember her
mother's saying 'We used to go for walks together'.

Tryphena eventually qualified as a school mistress, and at the
age of twenty went (in 1871) to Plymouth, there met Charles F.
Gale and in 1877 married him. Tryphena Gale died in 1890.
When the news reached Hardy, he wrote a poem 'Thoughts of
Phena: at News of her Death' (published in *Wessex Poems* in
1898) in which he remarked:

> Not a line of her writing have I,
> Not a thread of her hair.

Those who wish to believe that there had been a formal engagement can find some support in Hardy's reference in this poem to
'my lost prize', and his memory of his attractive cousin may be
responsible for the 'ebon loops of hair' in another poem, 'The
Wind's Prophecy' (not published until 1917), as well as for the
emphasis on the cousin-relationship of Jude Fawley and Sue
Bridehead in *Jude the Obscure*—the novel which was suggested,
so Hardy later explained, 'by the death of a woman' in 1890.

If there was a formal engagement, and if it was broken by
Tryphena at Charles Gale's urging, and if Hardy was pained by
this inconstancy in his cousin and by this losing of his 'prize',
one can be the more inclined to wonder whether any of school-
teacher Phena's personality went into the creation of school-
teacher Fancy Day in *Under the Greenwood Tree* in 1872. C. Day
Lewis sees this heroine 'as the minx she occasionally is', and he
notices that Hardy, far from idealizing her, shows her to be
'capricious, vain, a little snobbish, at the mercy of her feelings,
and—for the heroine of a romance—most unromantic . . . : "I

like Dick, and I love him, but how plain and sorry a man looks in the rain, with no umbrella, and wet through!" But . . . she is not . . . going to confess to Dick how nearly she jilted him . . . "and [she] thought of a secret she would never tell".'¹ Well, if Thomas Hardy was jilted by his capricious and somewhat snobbish cousin, it was a secret he never told; and now, a hundred years later, we shall never know. Any reader of *An Indiscretion in the Life of an Heiress* who wishes to do so may hear romantic echoes of Hardy's walks with Tryphena in some of the scenes between Egbert Mayne and Geraldine Allenville; for example, an episode in Chapter IV: 'Suddenly . . . he seized her hand . . . , kissed it tenderly, and clasped her in his arms. Her soft body yielded like wool under his embrace. As suddenly releasing her, he turned and went. . . . That she had ever seriously loved him he did not hope or dream. . . .' The dates in Tryphena's life, however, and the known facts in Hardy's life at the time of his 1870 trip into Cornwall are all opposed to any easy belief in an engagement to Tryphena Sparks broken by her in 1872.

To return, now, to 1870. The reader will remember that John Hicks had one day gone off to Cornwall to inspect a dilapidated Gothic church at St. Juliot. Hicks died before the planned 'restoration' had been accomplished, and when Crickmay of Weymouth purchased Hicks's practice, he found that there had been no progress whatever on the St. Juliot project. It would have to be begun all over again. Since Crickmay already had more work than he could attend to, he again called on Thomas Hardy for help. Just at this time Hardy was busy with the composition of *Desperate Remedies* and was unwilling to put his writing aside. But when the novel was finally finished, Crickmay happened to repeat his inquiry and this time Hardy accepted. On March 7, 1870, he set out for Cornwall. It was a cold Monday morning and a date he never forgot. 'What rainbow rays embow it!' he exclaimed later.²

Hardy remembered that March day with great vividness. He later wrote:

The weather was exceptionally mild . . . at such a month of the year. . . . Every sound could be heard for miles. There was a great crowing of cocks, bleating of sheep, and cawing of rooks, . . . a robin close at hand, vehicles in the neighbouring roads and lanes. . . . On the morning of departure he rose at half-past three, for . . . it was necessary to start early. . . . The candle-flame had a sad and yellow look. . . . Few things will take away a man's confidence in an impulsive scheme more than being called up by candle-light upon a chilly morning to commence working it out. . . . The raw wind made him shiver till walking warmed him. 'Good heavens, here's an undertaking!' he . . . thought . . . as he went on.³

The circumspect if not apprehensive note of foreboding as he set out is unmistakable.

The trip to St. Juliot took all day and it was dark by the time Hardy reached the rectory of the Reverend Caddell Holder. He found that the rector was sick in bed; his wife (*née* Helen Catherine Gifford) was upstairs attending him; and upon Hardy's arrival he was received by the rector's sister-in-law, Emma Lavinia Gifford. She was now twenty-nine and had come to live with her sister and her brother-in-law.

Hardy learned later that Miss Gifford had been eagerly looking forward to the arrival of the architect who was coming to make plans for the renovation of the old church, and her thoughts on the occasion of his arrival were afterwards put into a poem by him, 'A Man Was Drawing Near to Me'. After the evening meal, Miss Gifford played the piano and sang and thus got herself into Hardy's notebook. Before the week of his stay was over she was in his heart. In his records 'Miss Gifford' soon became 'E.L.G.'

Tuesday, March 8, Hardy spent in drawing and measuring at the church, but on Wednesday he went with Miss Gifford to visit nearby quarries. A poem, 'Green Slates', written fifty years later, recalled this visit. They also went to Boscastle, not far from Tintagel (King Arthur's romantic site), and another poem, 'At Castle Boterel', was later to record this excursion, particularly a hillside incident on the way back from Boscastle:

> It filled but a minute. But was there ever
> A time of such quality, since or before,
> In that hill's story? To one mind, never.

The whole of Thursday, the tenth of March, he spent in Miss Gifford's company. In the morning they went to visit Beeny Cliff on the coast. Emma was an expert horsewoman and she now rode her horse—a mare she called Fanny—with such abandon that Hardy felt sure that 'she must fall, though she never did' (as his poem 'Places' tells us). Beeny Cliff itself made a great impression upon him. Forty-three years later he was still recalling his first visit to that spot on the Cornish coast and wrote one of his most lilting lyrics about it:

> O the opal and the sapphire of that wandering western sea,
> And the woman riding high above with bright hair flapping free—
> The woman whom I loved so, and who loyally loved me.

On their way to the coast Hardy was learning more than Cornish geography. His conversation with Miss Gifford is clearly traceable in the remarks of Egbert and Geraldine in *An Indiscretion in the Life of an Heiress*:

'How long does it take to go to Westcombe?'
'About two hours.'
'Two hours—so long as that? How far is it away?'
'Eight miles.'
'Two hours to drive eight miles—who ever heard of such a thing!'
'I thought you meant walking.'
'Ah, yes; but one hardly means walking without expressly stating it.'
'Well, it seems just the other way to me—that walking is meant unless you say driving.'

And the reader is told that they both were then conscious of the same thought. 'It was that horrid thought of their differing habits and of those contrasting positions which could not be reconciled. Indeed, this perception of their disparity weighed more and more heavily upon him as the days went on.' It was the same awareness of social cleavage that he had felt and described in *The Poor Man and the Lady*. Here it was again, only— this time—a more poignant example in real life. 'Thus they mutually oppressed each other, even while they loved.'

Hardy learned that Emma Gifford's father was a solicitor—a well-educated man who, she said, liked to quote Latin. Her uncle, the Reverend Doctor Edwin Hamilton Gifford, was a canon of Worcester Cathedral; he was destined later to be Arch-deacon of London. Miss Gifford, too, was learning things. She noticed Hardy's Dorset accent but soon became used to it. She noticed that his overcoat was shabby. She discovered that he had written a novel—as yet, it is true, unpublished—and that he had composed poems. She liked his soft voice. She decided that his beard made him look older than he really was, and she eventually learned that he was actually only twenty-nine and less than six months her senior. All in all, the day when they visited Beeny Cliff together was nearly perfect; too perfect, Hardy thought, ever to return. Tennyson's words, 'The tender grace of a day that is dead will never come back to me', occurred to him.

Hardy's return to Dorset was planned for the next day. In order to reach home by night he had to make another early start, but 'E.L.G.' was up to see him off. They had breakfast together 'in the dim of dawn' and spoke of a change in the weather. His poem 'The Frozen Greenhouse' later recorded some of the morning conversation:

> 'There was a frost
>   Last night!' she said,
> 'And the stove was forgot
>   When we went to bed,
> And the greenhouse plants
>   Are frozen dead!'
>
> By the breakfast blaze
>   Blank-faced spoke she,
> Her scared young look
>   Seeming to be
> The very symbol
>   Of tragedy.

Another poem, 'At the Word "Farewell" ' tells us what happened after the discovery that the plants in the greenhouse were frozen. Hardy and Emma Gifford hurried outdoors to look at them:

> She looked like a bird from a cloud
>   On the clammy lawn,
> Moving alone, bare-browed
>   In the dim of dawn.
> The candles alight in the room
>   For my parting meal
> Made all things withoutdoors loom
>   Strange, ghostly, unreal. . . .

Excursion into Lyonnesse

'I am leaving . . . Farewell!' I said,
 As I followed her on
By an alley bare boughs overspread;
 'I soon must be gone!'
Even then the scale might have been turned
 Against love by a feather,
But crimson one cheek of hers burned
 When we came in to-gether.

'That is quite a good poem,' Hardy remarked many, many
years later, perhaps less in honest pride of workmanship than in
pleasurable reminiscence of the crimson cheek that 'burned' on
that frosty morning of March 11, 1870.

By evening of that day he was back at Bockhampton, but the
young man who returned to the parental home was a very
changed person from the diffident man who had 'stepped from
the door' of the house at 4 a.m. on March seventh, and he knew
why. 'He had left his heart in Cornwall.'[4] Later on, he was to
describe his return home in one of the most exuberant poems he
ever wrote. Among the more than nine hundred poems he was
eventually to compose, not one rings with such exultant sounds
of triumph as this one:

When I set out for Lyonnesse
 A hundred miles away
 The rime was on the spray,
And starlight lit my lonesomeness
When I set out for Lyonnesse
 A hundred miles away.

What would bechance at Lyonnesse
 While I should sojourn there
 No prophet durst declare,
Nor did the wisest wizard guess
What would bechance at Lyonnesse
 While I should sojourn there.

When I came back from Lyonnesse
 With magic in my eyes,
 All marked with mute surmise
My radiance rare and fathomless,
When I came back from Lyonnesse
 With magic in my eyes!

It is doubtless not necessary to explain that 'Lyonnesse' as a poetic name for Cornwall was not Hardy's invention but the designation (in Arthurian legend) for the country fabled to have once been contiguous to Cornwall but to have long since sunk beneath the sea. Hardy uses the name as synonymous with Cornwall. He published this poem in 1914, and some time later wrote to a friend: 'I learn from American newspapers that the verses "When I Set out for Lyonnesse" have become quite well known in the United States and much quoted. . . . Not a soul in England . . . has thought anything of them.'

Hardy's words that 'All marked with mute surmise' his rare radiance when he returned from St. Juliot are enough to tell us that his mother was able to 'surmise' what had happened; and when, in August 1870, Hardy had to return to Cornwall to continue with the work of church restoration, he went with such 'magic in his eyes' as made it impossible for his mother to be kept any longer in the dark. For the first time in his life Hardy's prospects seemed to him really bright. Tinsley had agreed to publish *Desperate Remedies*, Hardy had found the young lady whom his 'heart could not but follow',[5] and 'love lured life on'.[6]

His mother, however, sounded a note of caution. After his return from his second excursion into Lyonnesse, she reminded him that rosy prospects do not always result in glowing successes; and, as if to impress this fact upon his mind, he wrote in his notebook (dating the entry 'October 30, 1870'): 'Mother's notion (and also mine)—[is] that a figure stands in our van with arm uplifted, to knock us back from any pleasant prospect we indulge in as probable.' We see from this entry where Hardy's tendency towards fatalistic forebodings came from.

During the August 1870 visit to Cornwall, Hardy went several times with 'E.L.G.' on picnics to Beeny Cliff. On August 19, after they had eaten their lunch, Emma tried to wash their picnic tumbler in a little brook. She

> held the vessel to rinse in the fall
> Where it slipped, and sank, and was past recall.
> . . . There the glass still is.[7]

Three days later, they again returned to Beeny. This time it rained. 'It never looks like summer here,' Miss Gifford remarked ruefully. Years later, Hardy put her words into a poem. In spite

82

of the rain, Hardy sketched two pictures of the scene of the picnic, and (long afterwards) wrote three poems recalling the events of that day: 'Where the Picnic Was', 'The Figure in the Scene', and 'Why Did I Sketch?' While they were there, Emma lost an ear-ring in a crevice between the rocks. That episode was shortly to be made use of in a dramatic way in *A Pair of Blue Eyes*, the novel Hardy was to write for serialization in *Tinsleys' Magazine*.

Now that his thoughts were full of Emma Lavinia Gifford, Hardy set about writing *A Pair of Blue Eyes* with unusual verve and confidence. With only a few notes and a general outline to work with, he began to write. When, towards the end of July, Tinsley asked Hardy whether he could have the first instalment by the middle of August so that he might start the story in the September issue of the magazine, Hardy agreed, even though this meant writing under extreme pressure. He was helped in this hasty performance by making fictional use of his own recent experience in Cornwall. He had already formulated a vague plan for a novel, even before Tinsley had proposed a serial; but now, in line with Tinsley's wishes, Hardy inserted into his plot, a heroine who looked very much like Emma Gifford, who, like her, 'with bright hair flapping free', rode a pony, played the organ at church, lost an ear-ring between the rocks, and visited Beeny Cliff. In order to make sure that the new novel would contain enough of that 'touch of sentiment' to suit Tinsley, Hardy went to the extreme of providing his heroine with four lovers—one who had died, one who was jilted by her, one who succeeded only to resign his prize, and one who married her only to be called upon to provide for her a grave.

The startling surprises, the many coincidences which at times carry credulity to the extreme, and the amazing conjunction of circumstances in the last chapter, may be explained as due partly to Hardy's natural bent towards the sensational, partly to the unconscious influence of Ainsworth and Wilkie Collins, and partly to a justifiable feeling that every instalment in *Tinsleys' Magazine* ought to contain some episode striking enough to make readers notice the narrative and wish for more. The feeling doubtless led to a multiplication of the coincidences in the novel. Mr. Swancourt happens to choose for his secret marriage the very same day that his daughter Elfride had selected for hers.

On her return from London she happens to meet the one person in all Cornwall she wished to avoid. The missing ear-ring happens to turn up at the most embarrassing moment possible. Two of the lovers, Knight and Smith, each attempting to elude the other, happen to take the same train. Some readers are more disturbed by such chance events than are others; and, as we shall shortly see, some readers are not disturbed by this sort of thing at all. As Lord David Cecil has remarked: 'If we are to appreciate Hardy, we must school ourselves to accept his conventions. It is simply no good going to him expecting the eye-deceiving realism of Tolstoy or the psychological subtleties of Proust. We must read him in the spirit [in which] we read . . . *King Lear*, prepared to swallow naive melodramatic plots, full of mystery and coincidences and sensational improbable events, and complete with hero and heroine . . . and comic relief.'[8]

Tinsley apparently had complete confidence in Hardy's industry and ability: he began the publication of *A Pair of Blue Eyes* in the September number of his magazine before Hardy had written out more than a few chapters. Thereafter it became a race with the printer. The novel ran through eleven instalments, from September 1872 to July 1873. In none of them did Hardy's name appear. Tinsley employed an artist, J. A. Pasquier, to draw eleven illustrations for the novel; these were engraved by Edward Evans and one was printed with each instalment.

As the story proceeded, Tinsley's magazine editor, William Croft, began to cast an increasingly critical eye upon Hardy's manuscript as it came in to the publication office. In Chapter XIX he observed that 'a bright star' is called 'he' in one sentence and 'it' in the next sentence. Would not Mr. Hardy prefer to be consistent? Hardy saw no need to be so finicky and the text remained unchanged. When Croft reached the last chapter of the novel, he tried to get Hardy to rewrite it in order to eliminate the tragic conclusion. Hardy refused. 'Such a change would make an inartistic piece of work. . . . It is to be published exactly as I wrote it.'[9] And it was.

At the end of May 1873, after the June number of the magazine had been issued and when there was only the one final instalment yet to come, Tinsley published the novel in book form, in three volumes. And then, for the first time, English readers saw in print the words 'By Thomas Hardy'. The young architect was at last ready to discard his previous anonymity, to give up T-square and ruler, and to devote himself henceforth entirely to writing. He had proved that he could write.

True, in his haste to keep up with the printer, he had allowed some minor points to get by him. On two pages the wife of John Smith, the master-mason, is called Jane; in three other places she is called Maria. In his attempt to keep the printer supplied with copy, Hardy again used the device he had tried twice before: he turned to the rejected manuscript of his first novel and from it lifted as much as he could now use. Mrs. Swancourt's discussions of 'the language of artificiality' and of 'the members of a Fashionable World whose professed zero is far above the highest degree of the humble', and much of the satire on London society in Chapter XIV, are doubtless salvagings from *The Poor Man and the Lady*. Hardy came later-to feel that the pressure under which he had had to write had led him into inartistic prolixity. This he tried to correct in later editions of the novel by making drastic deletions. In the first chapter, for example, he dropped the first nine paragraphs. He omitted six sentences in the second paragraph of what he allowed to remain, and in the fourth paragraph he dropped thirty-six words and omitted an entire sentence. Hardy had never received any training in literary composition but he was learning.

John Morley had criticized *The Poor Man and the Lady* for being 'hung loosely together'. Wilkie Collins had since then taught Hardy how to improve the structural cohesiveness of his work, and this improvement was achieved with far more attention to psychological consistency than Collins had concerned himself with. Hardy showed genuine insight in portraying his characters, especially his heroine, in *A Pair of Blue Eyes*. Elfride's chess game with Knight is described with remarkable understanding of the girl's mind, and the unhappy maiden's thoughts and feelings after capturing and reading Knight's notebook, in which she found observations suggested by her own conduct, are subtly revealed. Accident and coincidence are never allowed to distort the naturalness of characters whom Hardy really knew.

Hardy's indebtedness to Wilkie Collins was candidly acknowledged by him in a preface written for a later edition of *A Pair of Blue Eyes*; and since this preface was afterwards discarded in its entirety, and replaced in 1895 by a wholly new one, it may be of interest to quote part of it here:

> In some of my former novels the object proposed has been to trace the influence of circumstances upon character. In the present story I have reversed the process. The attempt made here is to trace the influence of character on circumstances. The conduct pursued, under a sudden emergency, by a young girl, supplied the foundation on which I have built this book. The same object has been kept in view in the handling of the other characters. . . . Their course of thought and action under the circumstances which surround them is shown to be . . . sometimes right, and sometimes wrong. Right or wrong, their conduct . . . directs the course . . . of the story. . . . In the case of the physiological experiment which occupied a prominent place in the closing scenes of *The Moonstone*, the same principle has guided me. . . .

By the time he came to write this preface, Hardy showed, in speaking of 'the influence of character on circumstances', that he had matured philosophically and was no longer a blind believer in his mother's fatalistic 'notion' about the Figure with arm uplifted to knock one back. We shall have more to say about this development in Hardy's thinking when we come to *The Mayor of Casterbridge*.

One feature of *A Pair of Blue Eyes* will at once strike the reader. Although the action is set in Cornwall, the humour of the Cornish workmen is cast in a familiar Dorset mould. The driver of the dogcart, Martin Cannister, John Smith the master-mason (patterned after one of the workmen employed by Hardy's father), and William Worm are all cousins of the characters familiar to any reader of *Under the Greenwood Tree*. The dialogue is easy and natural, and the humour fresh and piquant. The scene in which the tomb of Lady Luxellian is being prepared is also right out of Dorset, and we know why: it was sketched directly after Lady Susan's vault at Stinsford Church, built by Hardy's grandfather.

One thing in *A Pair of Blue Eyes* appears for the first time in Hardy's writings. The scene in which Knight slips over the edge of the cliff—we easily recognize it now as Beeny Cliff—and is saved from a horrible death by Elfride's resourcefulness and energy is the first indication of Hardy's ability to sustain interest in a tense situation by the sheer power of vivid description. It is not easy to forget the gripping nature of that scene with Knight, when 'Time closed up like a fan before him'. The episode is of interest not only because of the sensational event itself but also because of the psychological results. They are presented by Hardy with all the artlessness of real life.

These many virtues won enthusiastic readers for the novel. The *Saturday Review* declared it to be 'most artistically constructed'. Reginald Brooks, son of the editor of *Punch*, wrote that it was 'worth all the other novels I have read for a long time'. Coventry Patmore, after a first reading of *A Pair of Blue Eyes* in 1875, continued to have his wife read it aloud to him, over and over and over, throughout the next twenty-one years. Each time he felt the same shock of surprise in its pathos and of pleasure in its art. Hardy liked to recall in later years that it was the favourite novel of the Poet Laureate, Alfred Tennyson.

The success of *A Pair of Blue Eyes* in England attracted immediate attention across the ocean. Just as soon as the last instalment had appeared in *Tinsleys' Magazine*, Henry Holt published the novel in New York. Its success in America equalled its popularity at home. The *Southern Magazine*, published in Baltimore, declared that *A Pair of Blue Eyes* 'has much of the vivacity and light, graceful touch that won our admiration in *Under the Greenwood Tree*. . . . There is great power of description, all the more intense because of the simplicity of the language and . . . life-likeness in the statements. . . . We . . . have reason to congratulate ourselves on making the acquaintance of this genial, pleasant, and natural writer.'[10] A Baltimore clergyman wrote: '*A Pair of Blue Eyes* impressed me very favourably. Descriptively it is delightful, morally it is unobjectionable, psychologically it is sound; in plot it is masterly; its literary style is artistic, and its denouement unstrained and surprising to a degree not often achieved by writers of fiction.'

William Dean Howells, editor of the *Atlantic Monthly*, remembered in later years that 'Thomas Hardy I first knew in *A Pair of Blue Eyes*. After I had read this book, I wished to read the books of no other author, and to read his books over and over. I could not get enough of them.' Professor William Lyon Phelps had a similar experience. 'Nearly fifty years ago,' he declared,

'I read my first novel by Thomas Hardy, ... *A Pair of Blue Eyes*. ... Within a year I had read every one of his books.'[11] In Boston, Massachusetts, a reviewer in *The Literary World* called *A Pair of Blue Eyes* 'one of Mr. Hardy's most brilliant novels. ... The unreasoning, irresponsible, impulsive girl of Endelstow Vicarage ... is clearly a favourite with him ... and there is nothing in modern fiction ... [like] those closing chapters. [They] haunt one'.

They have continued to haunt readers now for nearly a hundred years. When, towards the end of his life, Hardy was asked which of his novels was his favourite, he replied '*A Pair of Blue Eyes*', and explained that this was not so much because of its merit as a novel as because of the circumstances that had led to its composition and publication. Without doubt Hardy's excursion into Lyonnesse was the most important journey of his entire life.

VII

'Cornhill' Complications

TEN years before the publication of *A Pair of Blue Eyes*, when Hardy was reading Shakespeare, attending the plays given by Samuel Phelps, and writing Shakespearean sonnets, he had memorized Sonnet CXI. He liked to quote the lines

> O! for my sake do you with Fortune chide,
> The guilty goddess . . .
> That did not better for my life provide.

Fortune tended always to seem a 'guilty goddess' to Hardy, even when his luck proved to be good luck. In 1873, however, his fortune remained consistently good. *A Pair of Blue Eyes* was hardly a month old when Hardy received a letter from Leslie Stephen, editor of the *Cornhill Magazine*, asking him for a novel to be serialized in the magazine of which Thackeray had been editor a decade previously. Before the end of July Hardy had not only accepted Stephen's invitation, but had also, with justifiable pride in the growth of his reputation, had time to let his American publisher know about it. Doubtless to Hardy's surprise, Henry Holt wrote back, on July 27, 1873, to confess that he 'learned your intention of so soon publishing again with regret. Probably no one but Shakespeare has ever been able to accomplish the best class of work . . . with any rapidity.'

Holt didn't know his man, however, for Hardy set about writing his next novel under the same sort of pressure as that under which he had written *A Pair of Blue Eyes*, and within a year he had produced *Far from the Madding Crowd*. It is one of his best. '*Far from the Madding Crowd* is a great novel,' declared

89

James M. Barrie. H. C. Minchin (the biographer of Robert Browning) agreed. 'I have been devoted to this novel from boyhood,' Minchin declared, some years later; 'I have read it over and over again, and it remains my favourite among all the novels, Hardy's or other people's, that I have read.'

Leslie Stephen began publication in the January 1874 issue of the *Cornhill*, before Hardy had finished writing the story. It appeared anonymously for a few months, but the chorus of praise that greeted the beginning soon led to a disclosure of the author's identity. Even the *Spectator*, which had damned *Desperate Remedies*, was enthusiastic about this new novel and (before Hardy's authorship was disclosed) remarked: '*If Far from the Madding Crowd* is not written by George Eliot, then there is a new light among novelists.' There was, indeed, and readers were not slow to discover it. Before the year 1874 was over, *Far from the Madding Crowd* had been published seven times.

Hardy had wisely followed his beaten path. His characters were Dorset rustics, living in or near Puddletown. (He changed the unattractive name of the village to 'Weatherbury'.) His heroine, Bathsheba Everdene, was patterned after a deceased aunt who had lived at Puddletown; Hardy remembered going with his mother to call on 'my Aunt Sharpe' when he was a boy. His hero Gabriel, 'Shepherd Oak', was sketched after 'Maniel' (Immanuel) Riggs, whom Hardy knew as a boy. This shepherd had died only a few months before Hardy began writing his new novel. Sergeant Troy was imagined from Hardy's observation of the soldiers at the Dorchester barracks; and the Harvest Home supper and dance to which 'Squire' Martin had invited these soldiers in 1848, when he wished to provide the girls at Kingston Maurward House with dance partners, was the basis for the harvest supper and dance in Chapter XXXVI of the novel.

When Hardy came to describe the storm that followed the harvest supper, he recalled the fact that in Ainsworth's *Rookwood* there is a chapter entitled 'The Storm'. To save time, Hardy took his copy of the Ainsworth novel from the shelf, opened it to Book II, Chapter I, and proceeded to make free use of Ainsworth's description. He did not copy it word for word, as he had once copied Charles Swain's poem on the back of the door of the grandfather's clock, but he came close to doing so. In both accounts of the storm, the sequence of events is the same: the sultry weather, the confused activity of the animals, the calm, the vivid flash of lightning, the crash of thunder, the black sky, and then the torrent of rain. All this Hardy might, of course, have learned directly from nature; no one will wish to deny him his possession of keenly observant eyes. But nature did not supply Hardy with the long list of identical words—sultry, lurid, metallic look, night, rooks, lightning, flash, peal—which came right out of Ainsworth. The list would have been much longer if Hardy had not skilfully paraphrased Ainsworth, turning 'kine' into 'sheep', 'deer' into 'heifers', 'the grave' into 'a death', 'hazy vapour' into 'hot breeze', 'sighing wind' into 'expiration of air', 'highest branches' into 'summits of lofty objects', and 'pitch dark' into 'black sky'. What resulted was undoubtedly a magnificent chapter—one that has commanded universal admiration. Lionel Johnson was later to remark of it: 'The passage fills me with a strange fear, so magical seems this warning of nature in the night; and with a strange shame, so little should I have understood it.' Hardy was never called upon to identify the man who had taught him how to describe a storm, for he had died before his indebtedness to Ainsworth was noticed. It went undetected for sixty-seven years.[1]

Doubtless one of the reasons for Ainsworth's special appeal for Hardy was the fact that he had a painter's eye for detail. Both writers had the artist's power of visualization. This was one of the aspects of Hardy's art to which Lord David Cecil called attention in 1942 when he delivered the Clark Lectures at Trinity College, Cambridge. 'Before he does anything else,' said Cecil, 'Hardy wants to make you *see*. . . . His creative impulse seems to have instinctively expressed itself in picture. . . . No other English novelist has so great a power of visualization.'

Anyone who has had an opportunity to examine the manuscript of *Far from the Madding Crowd* has perhaps noticed a good illustration of this fact. In the chapter entitled 'Night—Horses Tramping' Jan Coggan and Gabriel Oak are pursuing some supposed horse-thieves. The text describes the marks left in the muddy road by the horses: 'The footprints . . . were full of information' for Coggan. From them he is able to identify 'a stiff gallop', 'a canter', 'a trot', then a walk, and finally a 'lamed' horse—lame in 'the near-foot-afore'. In Hardy's manuscript, however, all these marks are not only described but also illustrated. 'The mystic characters ... of the regular horseshoe shape' were drawn by Hardy, a set of footprints to illustrate each pace graphically. Leslie Stephen, however, did not think that this visual aid to following the text was important enough to reproduce it in the *Cornhill*, and Hardy's sketches were all omitted.[2]

The omission of the footprint drawings in the *Cornhill* does not mean that Leslie Stephen was opposed to pictures. On the contrary, he engaged Helen Paterson to illustrate Hardy's novel. Her twelve drawings (one for each instalment in the *Cornhill*) pleased Hardy greatly, and he later referred to her as the best illustrator he had ever had. Her drawings are not as dramatic as those done by Robert Barnes for *The Mayor of Casterbridge*, or as impressive and poignant as W. Hatherell's illustrations for *Jude the Obscure*; but Miss Paterson had an eye for detail that fully satisfied the Wessex author. Her illustration of the use of Bible and key does, in fact, tell us more about this old method of divination than can be learned from Hardy's text. She obviously knew how the key is tied inside the Bible and is then supported on the wedding-ring fingers of the two women. When the novel was eventually published in book form,[3] each volume reproduced six of the *Cornhill* drawings. When Henry Holt published the novel in a single volume in New York, these illustrations by Helen Paterson were at first omitted, but two years later Holt inserted them.

One other fact learned from an examination of the manuscript of the novel calls for special mention. After the publication of the book by Smith, Elder & Co., the manuscript was put aside in the publisher's office and forgotten. In 1918 it was discovered and then (with Hardy's consent and approval) was put into a Red Cross sale in the last months of World War I. In the course of making arrangements for the sale at auction, the manuscript was subjected to careful scrutiny. It was then discovered that one entire chapter was missing—Chapter XVI in the printed book, 'All Saints' and All Souls' '—in which Fanny Robin fails to get married by the mere chance of going to the wrong church in a strange city. The reader familiar with Hardy's emphasis of the part that chance plays in human lives is likely to regard this chapter as a perfect illustration of his view

of things, or of the working of his mother's notion of the Figure
with the uplifted arm. The discovery made in 1918 was that
Chapter XVI could not really be called 'missing', for the
numbering of chapters and pages showed that it had never
been in the original draft of the novel at all. When Hardy was
asked about this, he admitted that this chapter was an after-
thought: he had sent it in to the publisher only with the proof
sheets.

While praise of the new novel was arising on all sides, Hardy
had two experiences which cast new and unexpected light upon
what a life of authorship might involve. Leslie Stephen wrote
him to say that the story of Fanny Robin would have to be
treated in a gingerly fashion. Some subscribers to the *Cornhill*
were already beginning to write to the editor, voicing their
Grundian objections to certain passages in the story. Hardy was
astounded but accepted Stephen's directions, and accordingly
'Liddy came close to her mistress and whispered into her ear'
the 'wicked story' that readers of the *Cornhill* could guess at but
must not be allowed to read. The second experience was even
more of a surprise to Hardy. A deputation of six 'humanitarians'
from America turned up at Hardy's door one day and said that
they had come to remonstrate against the 'cruel incident' that
occurs after Fanny has been assisted from the Dorchester bridge
to the Workhouse by a stray dog on whom she leans for support.
The deputation objected to the passage in which, upon Fanny's
asking later for her friend the dog, she is told that it had been
stoned away. The 'humanitarians' from America wanted this
scene changed.

The characters in this novel are easily the best portraits so far
painted in words by Hardy. Bathsheba is, of course, a sister of
Cytherea, Fancy Day, and Elfride; but there are differences.
She is more convincingly drawn, more appealingly alive, and
her progress through the novel involves a development of
character, a maturing, that is largely lacking in the preceding
novels. Not all readers approved of Bathsheba, however, and
complaints were heard on both sides of the ocean. 'We cannot
say that we either understand or like Bathsheba,' declared an
anonymous reviewer in New York who turns out to be none
other than Henry James.[4] 'She flirts with Oak in the most heart-
less manner,' complained the *Westminster Review* in London. To

one correspondent Hardy wrote, defending his portrait of his heroine:

I myself, I must confess, have no great liking for the perfect woman of fiction. . . . The majority of women are quite worthy enough in nature to satisfy any reasonable being, but I venture to think that they too frequently do not exhibit that nature truly and simply. . . . I had an idea that Bathsheba, with all her errors, was not devoid of honesty of this kind; it is however a point for readers to decide. I must add that no satire on the sex is intended in any case by the imperfections of my heroines.

In the opinion of many readers, the most entertaining part of the novel was that portraying the company of comedians, the rustic frequenters of Warren's Malthouse. They represent an achievement, says Lascelles Abercrombie, 'which can only be matched in the very greatest literature. In several scenes the elemental comedy of these rustic immortals is without doubt Shakespearean'. With this judgment J. H. Fowler agrees: 'To match the racy humour of Joseph Poorgrass and the rest of the company at the old malthouse, it might indeed be necessary to go back to Bottom and his crew in *A Midsummer Night's Dream* or to the gravediggers in *Hamlet*.' To those who have not made the acquaintance of Henery Fray, Jan Coggan, Joseph Poorgrass (that 'fearfullest man' who said 'sir' to an owl), and Billy Small-bury, it may sound like uncritical exaggeration to compare this group of Hardy's characters with Shakespeare's, but many others have found the unconscious humour and the untutored wisdom of the 'Weatherbury' crew little short of inspired. Critics in Hardy's own day were sometimes inclined to maintain that no such amusing rustics ever lived—'Do labourers really converse like this?' asked *The Academy* (January 2, 1875)—but Hardy vouched for them. There were, he said, half a dozen such humorists on his father's farm, and he once offered to show a visitor where two of them were buried. Henery Fray's real name, he said, was Isaac West, and Joseph Poorgrass was drawn after John Amey.

Perhaps it was because of the fact that Hardy wrote *Far from the Madding Crowd* with the prospect of marriage colouring his thoughts and warming his feelings, that this novel is character-ized by an almost total absence of the bitter thoughts found in his early poems and the gloomy strains and stresses destined to appear in his later work. Here the nightingales sing. True, Hardy had not wholly forgotten his mother's Figure with the uplifted arm: he writes about 'the impersonator of Heaven's persistent irony' on one page, and on another he allows Henery Fray to wail: 'Your lot is your lot, and Scripture is nothing; for if you do good, you don't get rewarded according to your works, but be cheated in some mean way out of your recompense.' But apart from these two sentences, Hardy was here content to postpone judgment of heaven and censure of God.

For nearly a hundred years readers of *Far from the Madding Crowd* have been loud in their praise of the excellence and the variety of its descriptions of nature. Hardy had an eye and an ear for everything. Dry leaves 'simmering and boiling in the breeze', the wailing of trees and murmuring of hedges, the pool that 'glittered like a dead man's eye', the pink flush which arose and overspread the neck and shoulders of a sheep where they were left bare by the clicking shears, a poplar tree that stood out 'like an ink-stroke on burnished tin', the note of the sheep bell, that 'chronic sound that only makes itself noticed by ceasing or altering in some unusual manner from the well-known idle tinkle which signifies to the accustomed ear that all is well in the fold', the 'toad humbly travelling across the path', the 'huge brown garden-slug which had come indoors to-night for reasons of its own'—all are noticed with the eye of a lover and touched into the picture with the hand of an artist. Nor does Hardy stop with mere appeals to eye and ear, but shows an amazing power of passing from the trivial to the cosmic. In the second chapter, describing 'midnight on the shortest day of the year' he begins with 'dry leaves in the ditch', but the reader's attention is shortly directed to 'the twinkling of all the stars' and is told that 'to persons standing alone on a hill during a clear midnight . . . , the roll of the world eastward is almost a palpable movement. . . . The impression of riding along is vivid and abiding.' Hardy then continues:

The poetry of motion is a phrase much in use, and to enjoy the epic form of that gratification it is necessary to stand on a hill at a small hour of the night, and . . . long and quietly watch your stately progress through the stars. After such a nocturnal reconnoitre it is hard to get back to earth, and to believe that the consciousness of such majestic speeding is derived from a tiny human frame.

95

As soon as Hardy had been able to send the final instalment of *Far from the Madding Crowd* to Leslie Stephen, he was glad to turn from literary activity to personal plans. His love affair with Miss Gifford had by now progressed to the point at which they were making definite plans for marriage, but there was one snag: Emma's father did not approve of Hardy. Mr. Gifford is said to have called him a base churl, and it was obvious to Emma that marriage from the Gifford home was out of the question. Her father, John Attersoll Gifford, was at this time residing at Bodmin, Cornwall. When Emma's sister Helen Catherine was wedded to the Reverend Caddell Holder, the marriage took place at Bodmin. Now, however, Hardy and Miss Gifford decided to establish residence in another parish. When the last chapter of the *Cornhill* novel had been sent to the editor, Hardy left Bockhampton, returned to London, and took up residence at No. 4, Celbridge Place, Westbourne Park. Miss Gifford went (to use her own words) 'as country cousin to my brother in London', and her uncle, Dr. E. Hamilton Gifford, Canon of Worcester, agreed to marry them. The date set for the rite was September 17.

Shortly before the wedding date, Hardy received an inquiry from Louis J. Jennings, editor of the *New York Times*, asking whether he could supply that youthful paper with a story. As we have seen, Hardy was quite equal to working under pressure, and five days before the date of his marriage, he mailed the manuscript of a long short-story to the Manhattan paper. 'Destiny and a Blue Cloak' appeared in the *New York Times* on October 4, 1874, with the announcement that it had been 'written expressly for' that paper. Hardy had dashed the story off in a hurry by making fictional use of the young man he had known in Dorchester fifteen years previously—T. W. Hooper Tolbort, one-time student at the school conducted by William Barnes. (This story of 'Destiny and a Blue Cloak' has never been published in England, for reasons which we shall try shortly to surmise.)

On September 17, 1874, Hardy and Miss Gifford appeared at St. Peter's Church on Elgin Avenue, Paddington, and were married. They went off to France and spent a brief honeymoon in Rouen and Paris. It was for both their first experience in a foreign country, but Hardy's years in London made him more at home in a big city than was his young bride from St. Juliot. Visiting the Louvre was, for Hardy, a logical continuation of his National Gallery habit of ten or twelve years previously. For Emma it was a new experience. She kept a little diary, in pencil, and in it recorded her opinion that 'the Louvre is very French'. Upon their return to England, they settled down for the winter of 1874–5 in lodgings at St. David's, Hook Road, Surbiton, south of Kingston. Here they could look across the river Thames to Hampton Court Park.

Shortly after *Far from the Madding Crowd* had ended its serial run in the *Cornhill*—the last instalment appeared in the December 1874 issue—Leslie Stephen asked the author for another novel. Early in the new year, 1875, Hardy was glad to learn from his new publisher, George Smith, that he was preparing to print a second edition of the *Madding Crowd*. Less than four years had passed since Tinsley was able to sell no more than 370 copies of *Desperate Remedies*, and since *Under the Greenwood Tree* 'would not sell'; and of *A Pair of Blue Eyes*, two years previously, only five hundred copies, or less, had been sold. But now—a second edition! Hardy's skies were certainly brightening.

Hardy got promptly to work at Surbiton and submitted the first few chapters of *The Hand of Ethelberta* to Stephen in March. The editor thought well enough of the new novel to start publication in the *Cornhill* in the July 1875 issue, and then began another race between Hardy and the printer; for the novelist did not finish writing the story until six months after it had begun to appear in the magazine. One wonders whether Hardy ever recalled Henry Holt's remarks about hasty work.

At the beginning of the present chapter we quoted the *Spectator*'s conjecture that *Far from the Madding Crowd* was by George Eliot. Strange to say, instead of taking that remark as a compliment, Hardy regarded it as an offensive charge of imitation. 'This discouraged him greatly,' so Mrs. Hardy later stated, 'and he went off at a tangent and wrote *The Hand of Ethelberta* by way of contrast.' It was a great mistake. Mrs. Hardy admitted that she never liked it: 'Too much about servants in it!'

That, however, was not its main defect. Hardy could paint with natural sympathy a portrait of the quiet, dignified butler, Ethelberta's father, but the rest of this story of leisurely Society is a different matter. In spite of Hardy's best efforts to be sprightly, his accounts of dinner parties and his descriptions of lords and ladies at Enckworth Court or at Hotel Beau Séjour are slow and often dull. The simple truth is Hardy was unable to make his people of 'gentility' come alive. He observed them as an outsider and left his readers uncertain as to whether they were expected to admire or despise. Ethelberta herself is an adventuress and her marriage to the dissipated old Lord Mountclere has none of the interest or the vitality that Thackeray once gave to this theme. Lord Mountclere himself was not drawn from real life; Hardy manufactured him by a hasty touching up of the portrait of the sixty-five-year-old Farmer Lovill in 'Destiny and a Blue Cloak', the story he had sent off to the *New York Times* the week before he married Miss Gifford. Certain incidents in the plot of 'Destiny' are similarly repeated in *Ethelberta*. This re-use of material is doubtless the reason, or one of the reasons, why Hardy never collected 'Destiny and a Blue Cloak' and why this story has never been published in England.

No wonder the critical acclaim of *The Hand of Ethelberta* was disappointing! Though Hardy afterwards called it a 'somewhat frivolous narrative', he seems never to have understood what was the matter with it, and consoled himself for the public's lack of enthusiasm by thinking that 'the novel suffered for its quality of unexpectedness—that unforgivable sin in the critic's sight'.[5]

In spite of his disappointment at the critical reception accorded *The Hand of Ethelberta*, Hardy had no reason to complain of the financial returns. The *Cornhill* serialization and the two-volume publication by Smith, Elder & Co. in England were paralleled by serialization in the *New York Times* from June 20, 1875, to April 9, 1876, and by book publication in New York by Henry Holt; and by the time all four of these appearances of *Ethelberta* had been achieved, Hardy and his wife had in hand enough money to permit them to talk of leaving their lodgings and of going to look for a house.

VIII

'Negative Beauty of Tragic Tone'

UPON leaving Surbiton Hardy investigated various other places before he and his wife were able to settle into a house of their own. On June 22, 1875, he visited Wimborne Minster but found nothing available there. While at Wimborne, he noticed a feeble light in the ancient minster; and, tip-toeing in though it was already ten p.m., he found the organist practising by the light of a single candle. Hardy sat down and listened with rapt attention to the organ music. From Wimborne Minster he went on to Bournemouth, and in July brought his wife to lodgings in this 'Mediterranean lounging-place on the English Channel'.[1] His poem 'We Sat at the Window' (not published until 1917) is a record of July 15, 1875, 'when the rain came down' at Bournemouth.

After a brief stay there, the Hardys moved to nearby Swanage, again to lodgings, and there the writing of *The Hand of Ethelberta* was finished. At Swanage, Hardy, like Ethelberta in Chapter XXXI of the novel, 'managed to find a room . . . in the house of one of the boatmen, whose wife attended upon them'. There, too, he managed, at last, to get a poem accepted for publication. His lines 'The Fire at Tranter Sweatley's' appeared in the *Gentleman's Magazine* for November 1875, and in America in *Appleton's Journal*, November 6, 1875. Hardy's poem 'Once at Swanage', though not published until 1925, also refers to this period of sojourning on the English Channel.

In March 1876 the Hardys moved again, this time to Yeovil, and from there, in July 1876, to Sturminster Newton. Here they at last found a house, Riverside Villa, which they were able to

99

occupy all by themselves, and here they spent the next twenty-one months or so—'our happiest time' Hardy later called it.[2] At least three of his poems refer to this Surminster Newton period: 'A Two-Years' Idyll', 'Overlooking the River Stour', and 'The Musical Box'. And here *The Return of the Native* was written. In the opinion of many readers and of some critics, this is Hardy's greatest novel.

Hardy set to work on *The Return of the Native* with the expectation that Leslie Stephen would accept it for serialization in the *Cornhill*. He forgot, however, or recklessly ignored, Stephen's earlier reaction to the stories of Fanny Robin and Ethelberta, for Hardy now planned another rural Dorset story in which an erring heroine named Thomasin was to repeat some of Fanny Robin's experience with Sergeant Troy and was to anticipate some of Tess Durbeyfield's experience with Alec D'Urberville. The new heroine was, like Tess in the later serial, to imagine herself married; she was to be gone from her Dorset home a week, during which she was to have lived with Wildeve as his wife, and then to return home only to discover that she was not married after all. In other words, Thomasin was to be compromised, as was Tess in the serial version of the later novel, by a false marriage ceremony. Hardy, in planning a story like this, seems to have completely forgotten Stephen's earlier warning 'that Troy's seduction of the young woman [Fanny Robin in *Far from the Madding Crowd*] will require to be treated in a gingerly fashion', and to have completely closed his eyes to the significance of Stephen's later comment on *The Hand of Ethelberta*: 'I may be over-particular, but I don't quite like the suggestion of the very close embrace in the London churchyard.'

Stephen *was* over-particular. He obviously lived as much in fear of Mrs. Grundy as did those contemporaries of his whom Frederick Locker-Lampson had in mind when he wrote:

> They eat and drink, and scheme, and plod,—
> They go to church on Sunday;
> And many are afraid of God,
> And more of Mrs. Grundy.

(This quatrain is both pertinent and timely, for in 1878 Locker-Lampson gave Hardy an inscribed copy of his *London Lyrics*.) Thomas Hardy was not afraid of Mrs. Grundy but he learned eventually to know her power. A dozen years later, when he opened his copy of John Hutchins's *History of Dorset* and in Volume III found, at page 671, an account of the wife of Squire Peter Walter of Stalbridge House, Hardy made fictional use of Mrs. Walter in a story he entitled 'Squire Petrick's Lady'; but before the story was accepted for publication in the London *Graphic* (December 1, 1890), the editor, Arthur Locker, insisted on changes. Hardy accordingly had to delete several sentences —112 words on one page and 124 words on another.[3] The manuscript of 'Squire Petrick's Lady' is now in the Library of Congress, where readers can inspect Hardy's irritated marginal comments: 'The above lines were deleted against the author's wish, by compulsion of Mrs. Grundy', and 'deleted solely on account of the tyranny of Mrs. Grundy.'

By the time Hardy had written out enough of *The Return of the Native* to give the editor a good idea of its quality and trend, he sent his manuscript to Leslie Stephen and was startled to have him return it with the statement that he was fearful that the relations between Wildeve and Thomasin 'might develop into something "dangerous" for a family magazine'.[4] He therefore refused to commit himself to an acceptance of the manuscript unless he could see the entire novel. This demand was so contrary to Hardy's previous experience with magazine editors that, instead of finishing the composition and running the risk of having Stephen finally turn the work down after a year's labour had been put into it, Hardy decided to ignore the *Cornhill* and look elsewhere. He finally agreed to publication in *Belgravia*, a monthly magazine published by Chatto & Windus. Hardy's recognition of the fact that *Belgravia* was distinctly inferior to the *Cornhill* is evidenced by his parenthetical reference to 'publication in (of all places) *Belgravia*'.[5]

As it turned out, however, the set-back and delay caused by Leslie Stephen's refusal to accept an only-partly-written novel proved, in the long run, a great advantage. Although Hardy says nothing about it in *The Early Life*, the fact is he subjected his whole plan for the novel to a drastic overhauling. He changed incidents, names, plot, emphases, characterizations, and descriptions, so that when publication was finally begun in the January 1878 issue of *Belgravia*, the story was an immensely improved one. Henry Holt's belief that an author's best work could not be produced rapidly found excellent substantiation in the work Hardy did at Sturminster Newton in the autumn of 1877.

In the course of his quiet meditations at Riverside Villa he came to conceive of his novel as capable of showing a close analogy with classical drama. Its five books could be made, he thought, to correspond to the five acts which his copies of *Sophocles* and *Aeschylus* had made him familiar with. He inserted the names of Plautus and Martial in his manuscript, and though these names were afterwards deleted, he retained, throughout all the subsequent revisions of his text, references to *Oedipus*, to 'the Greeks', and to Aeschylus. As late in his life as 1923, when he described himself as 'old-fashioned enough to think there is a virtue' in the strict preservation of 'the unities',[6] he remembered having attempted to preserve them in *The Return of the Native*. He planned to confine the time of the action to exactly a year and a day. He planned to be even more specific in his emphasis of the unity of time: he would begin the action on November 5, 1842, and would end it on the night of November 6–7, 1843. To enforce his close attention to unity of place, he made himself a map of Egdon Heath, and late in 1878 he thought of letting his readers see this map. He thereupon copied it and sent the sketch to his publisher in London, suggesting that it be used as a frontispiece. 'Unity of place is so seldom preserved in novels that a map of the scene of action is as a rule quite impracticable. But since the present story affords an opportunity of doing so, I am of opinion that it would be a desirable novelty.'[7] Hardy's map of Egdon Heath was accordingly published when Smith, Elder & Co. issued the novel in three volumes in November 1878.

Throughout the novel Hardy had scattered subtle reminders of the Greek drama. The grasshoppers form 'a whispered chorus'; Eustacia plays 'her part in such a drama as this'; and in the 'strange low utterances' which the wind 'breathed into the chimney' Thomasin heard 'the prologue to some tragedy'. In describing his heroine—his 'wayward and erring heroine' Eustacia Vye, as opposed to his 'good heroine' Thomasin (Hardy himself drew this distinction in giving his illustrator, Arthur Hopkins, some suggestions for the depiction of the two girls in the pages of *Belgravia*)—Hardy continued the analogy to

Greek drama. 'Eustacia Vye was the raw material of a divinity. On Olympus she would have done well. . . . She could utter oracles of Delphian ambiguity when she did not choose to be direct.'

Women-readers of the novel have not always approved of the raw, goddess-like qualities, and James M. Barrie once reported having been shown an old library copy of *The Return of the Native* in which he read 'in the handwriting of different ladies: "What a horrid book!" and "Eustacia is a libel on noble womankind", and "Oh, how I *hate* Thomas Hardy!" '. Among saner or less emotionally disturbed readers, Eustacia's heroic, if not divine, stature has been commented upon by every critic who has ever written about *The Return of the Native*. Lord David Cecil, for example, in the Clark Lectures to which attention has been called in a previous chapter, remarks upon the way Eustacia Vye is made 'to assume the impersonal majesty of a representative of all mankind. . . . Eustacia stands for all passionate imprisoned spirits.' She owes this commanding stature, however, to her long evolution during the period when Hardy himself was studying her character. When he began, he regarded her only as 'the local witch' and thought of her merely as an 'unsympathetic agent of romantic heresy'. She was at this stage of the composition called Avice—a name Hardy later discarded, only to resuscitate it fifteen years later in *The Well-Beloved*. But as Eustacia grew under his hand, she lost her witch-like characteristics and became 'lovable after all'. In the *Belgravia* serialization 'she was lovable sometimes'. In the first edition (1878) 'she was not altogether unlovable', and in the Uniform Edition of 1895 'at times she was not altogether unlovable'. Hardy eventually devoted no less than thirty-five years to the study of Eustacia's character, and the results were well worth the time and labour. Leslie Stephen's rejection of the rough manuscript of 1877 doubtless seemed to Hardy another instance of the working of Crass Casualty but it is clear to us that it was really a benefaction of Hardy's guardian angel in disguise.

The writing and rewriting, the amending and revising, of those days of toil at Sturminster Newton often resulted in pages that were so messy as to be almost illegible. Hardy thereupon called upon his wife to make a clean copy, and some of the final 'printer's copy' is in Emma's hand. For the next fifteen years

Mrs. Hardy was to continue in this capacity, and her services as amanuensis have never been given the recognition they deserve.

Thanks to his quiet residence at Sturminster Newton, and thanks to the longer period of time he was able to devote to the composition of *The Return of the Native*, Hardy also had leisure to meditate about the art to which he was now committed. Being a person very much like Mrs. Yeobright in the novel, 'not disinclined to philosophize', Hardy pondered the question: What makes novel-writing worth doing? Or, for that matter, what is the value of any literature, poetry as well as novels? As he thought back over the past ten years and surveyed his own published works, it seemed clear to him that they lacked a theme, a philosophical motif. In June 1877 he wrote in his notebook: 'There is enough poetry in what is left after all the false romance has been abstracted, to make a sweet pattern.' Thus, shortly after he had become thirty-seven years old, he had found the text to guide his work in the future. 'If Nature's defects must be looked in the face and transcribed,' he wrote, 'whence arises the *art* in poetry and novel-writing? I think the art lies in making these defects the basis of a hitherto unperceived beauty, by irradiating them with "the light that never was" on their surface, but is seen to be latent in them by the spiritual eye.' The day he recorded this thought was an important one in the history of Hardy's development, and the quietness of its entry in a notebook should not conceal from us the significance of his arrival at a working formula for the future. Thenceforth 'a hitherto unperceived beauty' is to be his lodestar, a beauty to be sought out by him among the defects of a sorry universe. Fifteen years later, when he came to write the forty-fifth chapter of *Tess of the D'Urbervilles*, he was to rephrase the idea: his purpose was to be 'to reach a new kind of beauty, a negative beauty of tragic tone'. His work henceforth was to be 'tragic'; in the eyes of many readers it was destined to seem 'negative'; but its aim, its art, was 'to reach a new kind of beauty'.

As if to illustrate in *The Return of the Native* the working of this artistic formula, Hardy described a journey taken by Mrs. Yeobright across Egdon Heath:

She came to a spot where independent worlds of ephemerons were passing their time in mad carousal, some in the air, some on the hot ground and vegetation, some in the tepid and stringy water of a nearly dried pool. All the shallower ponds had decreased to a vaporous mud amid which the maggoty shapes of innumerable obscure creatures could be indistinctly seen, heaving and wallowing with enjoyment. Being a woman not disinclined to philosophize she sometimes sat down under her umbrella to rest and to watch their happiness, for a certain hopefulness gave ease to her mind.

That inclination to philosophize on maggots in a mud-puddle is of course Hardy's own.

Other autobiographical elements found in *The Return of the Native* have already been mentioned in several previous chapters. A number of the attitudes or experiences of Clym are reflections of Hardy's own career; and the remarks of Hardy's mother, at the time of his return from London in 1867, are probably the source of some of Mrs. Yeobright's remarks in the novel. Fairway's description of the way Thomasin's father bowed his bass-viol until every window in the church 'rattled as if 'twere a thunderstorm' is a humorous echo of the stories Hardy had heard about the playing of his grandfather. When Wildeve announces (in Chapter I, 9) that he has 'kindred in Wisconsin' and that his uncle is reported (in Chapter IV, 8) to have died in Canada, Hardy was probably recalling that his 'Aunt Sharpe' had gone to Canada and that she had died there. (He is characteristically vague about the place but very specific about the time: his aunt died on August 28, 1859, 'at 4 p.m., at Paris, British North America'! Paris, Ontario, Canada, is about half-way between London, Ontario, and Niagara Falls; but Hardy was always pretty hazy about geographical details when he ventured outside of Wessex.)

Before he had finished writing *The Return of the Native*, Hardy's thoughts were again directed to the other side of the Atlantic by his receipt of a letter of inquiry from J. Henry Harper, the New York publisher. Harper was coming to London and wished to talk with Hardy about the possibility that Harper & Brothers might publish his novels in New York—not only as books but also as serials in one or another of the Harper periodicals. Hardy had heard of the 'almost princely rate of pay' the Harpers were paying to other English authors, and he was therefore glad to accept Mr. Harper's invitation to meet him in London. Hardy came up from Sturminster Newton, called on Harper at his Piccadilly hotel, and the two men then strolled out into Green

Park and sat on a bench while they talked. Harper recalled the attempt his house had made three or four years previously to acquire the American publishing rights in *Far from the Madding Crowd*. This attempt had gone far enough for the Harpers to feel free to announce Hardy's novel in the *Publishers' Weekly* (January 17, 1874) as a 'Forthcoming Publication' of theirs. But then they discovered that James R. Osgood of Boston had already paid the *Cornhill* for serial rights, and Henry Holt insisted on his own book-rights by virtue of a 'gentleman's agreement' with Hardy. The Harpers had thereupon gracefully withdrawn from the field. Now, however, they were ready to enter it again, and this time they proposed to deal directly with the author. Henry Harper's own account tells us something about that Green Park meeting:

Hardy pulled out a roll of paper from his pocket, covered with titles, and asked me to look them over and express my opinion as to which one I thought would be most appropriate for his new serial.

'You can hardly expect a suggestion from me,' I protested, 'when you have always been so happy in your titles. For instance, *Far from the Madding Crowd*, *A Pair of Blue Eyes*, and so on.' I asked him which one of his tentative titles he himself preferred.

'Well,' he reflected, 'I like *The Return of the Native*.'

This title was chosen.[8]

The novel was eventually serialized in *Harper's Magazine*, where it appeared just one month after the *Belgravia* publication; it was issued as a book by Henry Holt in New York just a month after its London publication by Smith, Elder.

Publishers and editors were not always so ready to agree with Hardy as was J. Henry Harper. The editor of *Belgravia*, for example, objected (just as Tinsley's editor had objected in the case of *A Pair of Blue Eyes*) to the tragic ending of *the Native*. In the earlier instance, Hardy had stood his ground. Now, however, he was unwilling to pile trouble with *Belgravia* on top of the *Cornhill* rejection. He therefore agreed to dissipate some of the blackness of his tragic denouement, and accordingly wrote a Sixth Book, with four new chapters, at the end of his story. This of course wrecked his carefully planned analogy to a five-act Greek drama; it ruined his vaunted unity of time; and it cast doubt on his consistency of characterization. He was not at all proud of this yielding to editorial demands, but he did it.

Thirty-four years later, he printed a sop to his own aesthetic conscience, and to Chapter 3 of Book VI he appended a note with these four terse sentences:

The writer may state here that the original conception of the story did not design a marriage between Thomasin and Venn. He was to have retained his isolated and weird character to the last, and to have disappeared mysteriously from the heath, nobody knowing whither—Thomasin remaining a widow. But certain circumstances of serial publication led to a change of intent. Readers can therefore choose between the endings, and those with an austere artistic code can assume the more consistent conclusion to be the true one.[9]

As for 'readers with an austere artistic code', Hardy had good reason to wonder, in 1878, whether any such persons existed. For when the novel was published in November, it was denounced as 'distinctly inferior' to anything he had written. A writer in the London *Athenaeum* took him to task for alleged inaccuracy in the use of the Dorset dialect, whereas a reviewer in the New York *Nation* found fault with him for using dialect at all. 'We are beginning,' said this reviewer, 'to long for a novelist bold enough to permit his people to say good things in English that we can read at sight.' A reviewer in the London *Times* wryly remarked that he had 'found himself taken farther from the madding crowd than ever', and readers in general were attracted to the novel in such small numbers that the publisher cautiously bound only a part of the edition he had printed. Four years later a hundred unbound quires were remaindered. Hardy came to feel that he 'was living in a world where nothing bears out in practice what it promises incipiently'. He must have looked at the words he had placed upon Eustacia's lips in the printed book and have thought how sadly prophetic they were: 'How destiny has been against me! I do not deserve my lot! O the cruelty of putting me into this ill-conceived world! I have been injured and blighted and crushed by things beyond my control! O, how hard it is!'

Curiously enough, the reception given Hardy's novel was more cordial in the United States than that given in the land of Egdon Heath. Dr. Josiah Gilbert Holland, for example, writing in *Scribner's Monthly*, remarked that *The Return of the Native* was not only a book well worth reading, but also one that a reader could profitably return to 'again with pleasure, although the fortunes of the actors are known'. Said Dr. Holland:

Pick it up where you will, there are thoughtful passages, phrases of great cleverness, piquant expressions that no one else uses and that urge one to make a better acquaintance with the writer. . . . Hardy's old liking for rustics who are strangely like Shakespeare's clowns remains. . . . The Shakespearean talk of these dwellers on Egdon Heath is said to be quite true to life. As to the main figure of the book—Eustacia Vye—she is of an excellence that throws other heroines into the shade. . . . In fine, the novel has . . . excellent qualities.[10]

A young graduate of Yale University, Walter Peirce, has more recently put on record his youthful, untutored reaction to the novel:

It was in 1897. I was twenty-two years old and was spending the summer on my father's farm in southern Ohio. One blazing August morning, I found myself out of something to read, and resorted to the back numbers of old magazines in the attic. . . . In *Harper's* for 1878 I came across *The Return of the Native*. . . . All that boiling August day I followed the varying fortunes of Clym and Eustacia and Wildeve and Thomasin and Diggory. . . . By five o'clock I reached the end of the eleventh number, which concluded with the chapter called 'In Spite of Rain and Darkness several walk abroad', the chapter in which the five protagonists were crossing Egdon Heath in the pouring rain of a November night, converging on the weir. And the twelfth and final number of the magazine was missing!

I was fifteen miles from the library at Springfield and motor cars were not yet. The library closed at six. I felt that I could not live until the next day without learning the end of that tragedy, so I mounted my bicycle and got to the library before it closed. I took out the book—what if it hadn't been in!—rode to the edge of the city, threw my bicycle into the ditch when I had passed the last house, and sat down at the roadside and read through to the cataclysm.

Then felt I like some watcher of the skies. *Hamlet* and *King Lear* have left the same impression on me; so have the *Agamemnon* and the *Hippolytus*, but few other works. Hardy, in the prose medium of the novel and with a handful of peasants and yeomen, had achieved an effect equalled only by Shakespeare and the Greeks in high poetic tragedy dealing with kings and princes.[11]

One can only regret that Hardy did not live to read a tribute like this. *The Return of the Native* has long since outlived the chilly reception it received in England in 1878 and has become one of the classics of English literature. But Hardy could not foresee that outcome in 1878. No one told him that his hymn of praise of Egdon Heath was a magnificent piece of writing, and he did not live long enough to hear it called 'in the sweep of its prose a superb poem'. No one remarked on the mastery of design, or on the structural unity of the novel. Readers eager for a romantic love-story did not linger appreciatively over Hardy's eye for nature, and failed to notice his delight in songs and music. They paid little attention to the vividness of his descriptions and ignored the wealth of background detail. Now that the world has had more than eighty-five years in which to read and re-read *The Return of the Native*, it is of course easier to see how rich a storehouse it is of Wessex customs and traditions. The fires that commemorate the Gunpowder Plot, the Village Picnic and dance at East Egdon with the musicians 'sitting in a blue waggon with red wheels scrubbed as bright as new', and, above all, the Christmas play of Saint George as presented by the 'mummers' whom Hardy had known as a boy—all these are part of that historical richness which makes *The Return of the Native* such a delight for all readers who are interested in the past. The picture of humpbacked Father Christmas, swinging his huge club, is one that Hardy obviously enjoyed recalling from his own boyhood:

> Make room, make room, my gallant boys,
> And give us space to rhyme;
> We've come to show Saint George's play
> Upon this Christmas time.

Hardy's service as an antiquarian and historian came in time to be recognized, and in 1889 James M. Barrie contributed to the *Contemporary Review* an article on 'The Historian of Wessex' in which this aspect of Hardy's literary work received warm praise.[12]

Closely allied with these memories of Wessex customs and festivals is the record of superstitions and folklore in which *The Return of the Native* is likewise rich. Johnny Nunsuch's 'crooked sixpence' was prized by him because it would keep witches away. Susan Nunsuch pricked Eustacia in church with a long stocking needle 'so as to draw her blood and put an end to the bewitching of Susan's children'. A wax effigy of Eustacia was stuck full of pins and then held in the fire while it melted slowly away, to the accompaniment of the Lord's Prayer said backwards—all 'to counteract the malign spell' which Eustacia was supposed to be working upon a sick child. Hardy's memory of such stories as these rushed back into consciousness while he was engaged in recounting the experiences of dwellers on the heath, and we can count ourselves fortunate that he had time and leisure enough at Sturminster Newton to weave them into the fabric of his story.[13]

In the course of the more than four-score years during which *The Return of the Native* has been subjected to critical study, no subject has been more frequently debated than Hardy's procedures and techniques as he went about producing a masterpiece. Did he plan his novel as he had planned a church tower or a manor house in his days as an architect? Or did he stagger along, like drunken old 'Sir John' Durbeyfield trying to find his way home to Marnhull? Both views have been defended.

One of the very first of Hardy's critics, Lionel Johnson, expressed the view of those who take the architectonic side in the argument. In *The Art of Thomas Hardy* (1894) Johnson declared: 'The most appreciable mark of Mr. Hardy's power . . . is the tenacity with which his designs hold the memory; it resembles the power of architecture to stamp there its great designs. . . . There is an architectural quality in the designs of Mr. Hardy.' Professor Joseph Warren Beach declared (at the University of Minnesota) that Hardy's plots were 'expressible almost in algebraic formulas',[14] and Arthur McDowall thought that Hardy's habits of work as an architect threatened the spontaneity of his work as a novelist.[15] More recently, Professor Albert J. Guerard has commented on what he calls 'Hardy's gravest weakness, his tendency to shape and plan his novels according to some obvious architectural principle and his failure to conceal the blueprint'.[16]

On the other side in the critical debate is Desmond Hawkins. 'The truth is,' he avers, 'that Hardy's technical progress was like the homing of a drunk—a great deal of tacking, wavering and back-pedalling, but with a final irresistible urge in the right direction.'[17]

The authoritative judge in this debate about blueprints is Dr.

John Paterson of the University of California at Berkeley. Was there a blueprint for the creation of *The Return of the Native?* No, says Paterson, there was not. 'Hardy's procedure ... was ... predominantly experimental and improvisatory. The impulse of the moment, not the diagram, evidently presided over the making of the novel.'[18]

Does this mean that Dr. Paterson agrees with Hawkins that Hardy's procedure resembles 'the homing of a drunk'? No, not at all. Paterson, after a thoroughgoing examination of Hardy's manuscript (now in the library of University College, Dublin) and of the various versions of the novel which appeared in print, from the serialization in 1878 down to the definitive text of 1912, comes to the conclusion that Hardy 'was more self-consciously the artist in fiction than he would himself have cared to admit' (p. 124), and that *The Return of the Native* marks, in its final text, the progress 'of a powerful imagination not [at the start] fully aware of its own nature', but, as time went on, an imagination increasingly 'awake to, and in control of, the possibilities it had itself created' (p. 125). Paterson's careful scrutiny of all six stages in the evolution of this novel constitutes the most detailed study of Hardy's text to be found anywhere, and the only conclusion to which he comes on which there may be said to remain any doubt is the question whether Eustacia Vye committed suicide. For any student of Hardy's fiction, John Paterson's is a most interesting and most informative book.[19] Its publication in 1960 demonstrated the immense distance which critical attitudes towards Hardy had travelled since 1878, when *The Return of the Native* could be branded as 'distinctively inferior'.

Short Stories and Little Ironies

WHILE Hardy was still engaged in writing *The Return of the Native*, he received an inquiry from No. 198, The Strand, where the *Illustrated London News* had its offices. Could Hardy supply a story for inclusion in a children's collection which the *News* was planning to publish shortly before the following Christmas? Remembering how he had succeeded in speedily turning out a short story for the *New York Times* three years ago, Hardy now agreed, in spite of his preoccupation with *the Native*, to write a Christmas story. He had never written anything for children, but he was willing to try. The story need not be long—in fact, it *must* not be long—if it was to be 'relished by boys and girls' as the editor hoped it would be. Hardy accordingly interrupted his work on *the Native* long enough to write 'The Thieves Who Couldn't Help Sneezing'. On Saturday, December 8, 1877, the *Illustrated London News* announced that 'a new claimant, entitled *Father Christmas: Our Little Ones' Budget*' would appear shortly. A week later, the contents of the new publication were announced: Hardy's story was to be given first place—pages 1–3. *Father Christmas* was published immediately thereafter and was almost as immediately forgotten, even by the author. He never mentioned his Christmas story. 'The Thieves' dropped out of sight for sixty-five years and nothing more was heard of it until 1942 when it was republished in America.[1]

Other London editors were likewise attracted by Hardy's growing reputation. Robert W. Buchanan, for example, who had made himself famous (or notorious) half a dozen years previously by attacking Dante Gabriel Rossetti in an article on the Fleshly School of English Poetry in the *Contemporary Review*, had now founded a magazine of his own—a weekly 'Journal of Criticism & Belles Lettres' ambitiously called *Light*. He solicited a contribution from Hardy, and the novelist again interrupted his work on *the Native* long enough to oblige. 'The Impulsive Lady of Croome Castle' was the result.[1] She made her début in *Light* on April 6 and 13, 1878. Fourteen years later, Buchanan dedicated his own novel, *Come Live with Me and Be My Love*, to Hardy. Whether Hardy regarded this dedication as a compliment or not we do not know. Buchanan's novel has been described as a downright plagiarism of *Far from the Madding Crowd* and *The Woodlanders*. As we shall see later, Hardy was to resume relations with Buchanan when he came to writing *The Dynasts*.

Another London editor who was eager for something from Hardy worked in the office of Chatto & Windus, the publishers of *Belgravia*. They also published the *New Quarterly Magazine*. Its editor requested a short story, and once again Hardy dropped his other work long enough to respond to the editorial appeal. As a result, 'An Indiscretion in the Life of an Heiress' appeared in the *New Quarterly* for July 1878, where it ran to more than sixty pages. Hardy achieved a story of this length with such promptness by salvaging about fifteen chapters from his rejected first novel, *The Poor Man and the Lady*.[1] The editor of the *New Quarterly* was pleased enough to ask for more; and in April 1879 'The Distracted Young Preacher' appeared, to be followed in April 1880 by 'Fellow-Townsmen'. Thus, in the months immediately before the publication of *The Return of the Native* and in the period immediately after this novel had begun its run in *Belgravia*, Hardy saw the publication of five short stories. He thus found himself embarked upon a voyage not at all of his own charting, one which was to continue for the next twenty years or more. In all, he produced nearly fifty short stories. Some of them are very good; some, it must be admitted, are very poor. In general, they can be said to show the same characteristics as the novels. They come from the same Wessex environment and deal with the same traditions and superstitions. Obviously, no short story can provide space for the gradual building up of interest in a powerfully drawn character, or for tracing the approach of a gathering storm that finally breaks in a scene of dramatic climax; but, in their own class and judged by their own proper standards, Hardy's short stories are often very well done. A few of them are excellent. 'The Three Strangers' is one of these. In recognition of the fact that the short stories are not as well known as the novels or the poems, they are all listed and annotated (briefly) in the Notes.[1]

Hardy's pleasant two-year idyll at Sturminster Newton finally ended, for he had come to feel that, if he was to pursue an active literary career in the most efficient way, such isolation as that of Sturminster Newton would not do. He ought to reside in or near London. He and Mrs. Hardy accordingly gave up Riverside Villa and moved in March 1878 to Upper Tooting (south-west London) where they established themselves at No. 1, Arundel Terrace, 'The Larches', not far from 'Knapdale', the home of Alexander Macmillan, the publisher.

In June 1878 Hardy's contacts with the literary world were greatly improved by his election to membership in the Savile Club. Edmund Gosse became a member at this same time, and the two thus began a friendship that was to continue until the end of Hardy's life fifty years later.

Once settled into the new house, Hardy was ready to go to work on a new novel. True to his dislike of monotonous repetition, and in line with his hypersensitivity to criticism, he decided to strike out on an entirely new path. When the *Spectator* had thought that *Far from the Madding Crowd* might be by George Eliot, Hardy had foolishly gone off 'at a tangent and wrote *The Hand of Ethelberta* by way of contrast'.[2] Now that a reviewer had declared that *the Native* carried the reader 'farther from the madding crowd than ever', Hardy decided to try yet another tangent. This time he would write a historical novel; and, while he would not desert his own Dorset environment, he *would* depart from the contemporary scene to which he had thus far stuck. He would go back to the days of his grandfather and write a novel about the Napoleonic era.

His thoughts had, in fact, been turning in this direction even before he had left Sturminster Newton. While he was still at Riverside Villa he had written a poem on the siege of Valenciennes and had composed a rollicking song about the time

> When Boney will come pouncing down
> And march his men on London town,

a poem he later inserted into Chapter V of *The Trumpet-Major*. There was nothing surprising about this choice of subject. As a young boy at Bockhampton Hardy had sometimes seen parts of military uniforms and had been told that they were survivals of volunteer-service days, when the Dorset natives had hourly feared invasion by Napoleon. Later, while riding about the country with his father, he saw a heap of bricks and clods on a hilltop and was told that they were the remains of the hut once occupied by a beacon-keeper stationed on the hill in order to light the fire that was to warn the countryside that Napoleon had landed. When he was a young architect at Weymouth Hardy had seen outhouse doors riddled with bullet holes and heard that they had been used as targets in firing-practice in the early days of the century. For years, therefore, Hardy's thoughts had been turned back to that time of tense excitement.

He now found, however, that writing about that time was attended by unexpected difficulty. The new novel must necessarily be based on testimony rather than on observation and experience. Hardy could to some extent trust, or at least make use of, the recollections of old persons whom he had known in childhood, but these recollections did not easily guide him in the construction of a coherent narrative, one event leading logically to another. He became aware, as he said later, 'of the difficulty of ascertaining the true sequence of events'. He accordingly set himself a careful course of reading. He went to the British Museum and there looked up various newspapers, magazines, and other records contemporary with Napoleon, and copied notes, descriptions, dates, etc., into a little notebook.[3] He hunted up the *Army Regulations* for 1801. In early February 1879, in spite of severe winter weather, he went to Dorchester and in the Museum there copied down an 'Address to All Ranks and Descriptions of Englishmen' which he eventually transcribed into Chapter XXIII of the novel. He went on to Weymouth and stayed for several days, making a study of the English Channel. Back in London by mid-February, he began to equip his own library at Upper Tooting with volumes to aid his historical research. He acquired a set of the two massive volumes of C. H. Gifford's *History of the Wars Occasioned by the French Revolution* (London, W. Lewis, 1817), and—even more significantly—he bought a 48-volume set of Sir Walter Scott's Waverley Novels

(Edinburgh, 1877–9). Many years later, Hardy was inclined to look down upon Scott's novels, and declared that 'he preferred Scott the poet to Scott the novelist and never ceased to regret that the author of *Marmion* should later have declined on prose fiction'.[4] In 1878–9, however, Hardy obviously thought otherwise.

When he came to write Chapter XXIII of the new novel, Hardy seemed to run into particular trouble. This is the chapter headed 'Military Preparations'. Hardy began it by opening a copy of his own *Desperate Remedies* and copying thence the first paragraph of Chapter XII, almost word for word. This habit of pilfering from his own works doubtless originated in his having dipped so frequently into the manuscript of his rejected first novel. Now, however, he went further in his 'borrowings'. After copying from *Desperate Remedies*, and after copying the 'Address to All Ranks' which he had found in the Dorset County Museum, he turned next to Gifford's *History of the Wars* and 'borrowed' (without any acknowledgment) about 275 words which he found there. They eventually filled about three pages of the novel. Hardy did this in an attempt to give a vivid account of the drilling of the volunteers at Weymouth; but, without realizing what he had done, he had put his hand into a hornet's nest. The hornets would not emerge to sting him for some months after the publication of *The Trumpet-Major*, but once out of the hive and after him, they never let up their pursuit of the hapless author for the rest of his life. We shall shortly have more to say about this matter.

Hardy's interest in the drilling of the militia had a personal rather than a historical basis: his grandfather, Thomas Hardy the First, had been a volunteer stationed with his company at Weymouth, 'waiting for Bonaparte who never came'.[5] To improve his familiarity with this part of Dorset, Hardy returned to Weymouth in August 1879, this time taking Mrs. Hardy with him. They occupied lodgings there long enough for Hardy to fix 'Overcombe' and 'Oxwell Hall' and 'Gloucester Lodge' (where King George III had had his summer residence from 1798 to 1805) firmly in his mind.

Upon his return to London, Hardy proceeded with the writing of *The Trumpet-Major*, but found it difficult to force historical events into an orderly plot. He found, too, that in

dealing with events in an era before he was born, it was extremely difficult to create a convincing 'atmosphere'. He himself had
never had direct experience with such a national crisis as he was
now trying to depict. At the time of the Crimean War he was
still a schoolboy at Mr. Last's academy, more concerned with
translating Eutropius than with learning about the ineptitudes
of the British Army at Sevastopol. In 1870, at the time of the
Franco-Prussian War, Hardy was occupied with thoughts of
Emma Lavinia Gifford at St. Juliot. Now, as he tried to capture
the excitement of the period from 1800 to 1805, he found—as
his readers also were shortly to find—that his characters refused
to take on the reality of those whose voices he himself had heard
and whose faces he had seen.

Hardy's difficulties were not moderated, either, by talks he
had with Leslie Stephen. Hoping that the editor would be
willing to serialize his novel in the *Cornhill*, Hardy told Stephen
that he was now writing a story about the reign of George III
and about the fears then felt of a Napoleonic invasion. He
proposed to put King George into the novel. Stephen dashed
Hardy's hopes by declaring: 'I think that a historical character
in a novel is almost always a nuisance.' Hardy did not agree
with Stephen, and rather than change his plans for the novel
Hardy again decided to change his magazine. Serialization was
finally arranged for in a monthly called *Good Words*, but this
shift of base served only to introduce a new complication.

Hardy's dealings with the office from which *Good Words* was
published were carried on with the publisher, Isbister, rather
than with the editor, the Reverend Donald Macleod, D.D.,
because of the fact that the editor lived in Glasgow and made
only occasional visits to London. Late in July 1879, Mr. Isbister
invited Hardy to come to the office of *Good Words* on Ludgate
Hill to meet Dr. Macleod. Hardy went. He soon learned that
the shadow of Mrs. Grundy was just as noticeable and just as
domineering in the office of *Good Words* as in the *Cornhill* office.
In Chapter XVI of *The Trumpet-Major* Hardy had described a
lovers' meeting at Dorchester on a Sunday afternoon—a meeting 'not far from All Saints' Church' where Bob Loveday,
brother of the trumpet-major, 'could hear the afternoon service
. . . as distinctly as if he had been one of the congregation'. Dr.
Macleod asked Hardy to change this meeting from Sunday

afternoon to Saturday. Hardy acquiesced. In four or five chapters, Hardy had tried to approximate the language of the soldiers and sailors who appear in the story: 'Good God!' (ch. 18), 'Damn' (ch. 22), 'O Lord!' (ch. 26), and 'By God!' (ch. 31). Dr. Macleod asked Hardy to 'avoid swear-words' and Hardy agreed to do so. After the serialization in *Good Words* was all over, the swearing went back into the text, and Captain Robert Loveday is now allowed to go to meet the girl on Sunday; but even with these attempts at realistic treatment *The Trumpet-Major* cannot be regarded as one of Hardy's great achievements. He finished writing it before the end of 1879, serialization was begun in the January number of *Good Words* and continued throughout 1880, and in October it was published in three volumes by Smith, Elder & Co.[6]

'Napoleon' and 'Waterloo' were obviously names that had close personal and family associations for Hardy, and stories that he had heard from his father interested him. But this novel has never stirred readers deeply and it never will. Hardy simply lacked the sympathy with the spirit of historical romance that enabled three of his contemporaries to create the impressive accounts of Waterloo found in *Vanity Fair*, in *War and Peace*, and in *Les Misérables*.

The plot Hardy planned for his novel is almost as simple as the one he had used in *Under the Greenwood Tree*. The trumpet-major, John Loveday, and his brother Robert both fall in love with pretty Anne Garland. She is graceful and slender and, like so many other Hardy heroines, uncertain of her own mind. Her shuttlecock shiftings from one brother to the other leave the reader bewildered; and when she finally chooses Bob and allows John to go off to lose his life 'upon one of the bloody battle-fields of Spain', there is no feeling of inevitability, of 'rightness', about the conclusion. Festus Derriman is an amusing poltroon, but he probably owes more to Hardy's study of Parolles in *All's Well That Ends Well* than to any observation of such a character in real life.

One of the most amusing scenes is that in which the volunteers drill, dressed in their workaday clothes, but eager to do their duty in repelling the invader.

'As every man was anxious to see how the rest stood, those at the end of the line pressed forward for that purpose, till the line assumed the form of a bow. "Look at ye now! Why, you are all a-crooking in! Dress, dress!" '

The hilarious scene that follows is the one Hardy had lifted out of Gifford's *History of the Wars*. He here did something more than merely paraphrase, as he had done in adapting Ainsworth's 'Storm' for use in *Far from the Madding Crowd*. In *The Trumpet-Major* Gifford's entire description of the drill is reproduced almost word for word in Chapter XXIII of the novel.

Fortunately for Hardy's peace of mind in 1880, there were few if any readers of *The Trumpet-Major* who had also read, or remembered, Gifford's *History*, but in America the situation was different. There, Henry Holt published the novel only a short time after the London publication; but, thanks to the absence of international copyright protection, the novel was pounced upon by piratical publishers with the result that it eventually appeared in more than twenty different American formats.[7] This gave *The Trumpet-Major* a much larger audience in the United States than it had enjoyed in England. One of Hardy's numerous American readers, Charles P. Jacobs of Indianapolis, Indiana, remembered (as he later reported his experience) 'that I had in my library an old book entitled *Georgia Scenes*, which contained, among other things, a humorous sketch of a drill of the rural militia'. This book was by a Methodist minister, the Rev. A. B. Longstreet. Taking it from the shelf, Jacobs copied the drill scene and sent it, together with 'the quotation from *The Trumpet-Major*' to the editor of *The Critic*, and this New York magazine promptly printed 'the deadly parallels' for all the world to see.[8] Hardy might never have seen this demonstration of his plagiarism, but unfortunately it was repeated in London in *The Academy* (February 18, 1882). What reply could Hardy make? He had never seen a copy of Longstreet's *Georgia Scenes* and the American author was totally unknown to him. He decided to say nothing.

It so happened that Hardy was just at this time engaged in correspondence with Thomas Bailey Aldrich, editor of *The Atlantic Monthly*. Aldrich had written to solicit a novel for serialization in the Boston magazine, and Hardy had agreed to supply one. In writing to the New England editor, Hardy found it hard to ignore the charge of plagiarism that had so recently been brought against him, and on March 8, 1882, he wrote to Aldrich thus:

Curiously enough I have never heard of *Scenes in Georgia*—the portions of my drill-scene which accord with the transcript from that book being based on the letter of an eyewitness printed in a *History of the Wars of the French Revolution*, London, 1817. I rather wonder the editors of your [American] reviews, who are usually discriminating enough, did not perceive that to show that a page or two of historical and biographical matter has been embodied in fiction was to show very little. What would the concocters of the parallel columns say if they knew that columns and columns from North's Plutarch are copied almost verbatim into Shakespeare's Roman and Greek plays? —and that, nevertheless, this is not plagiarism—plagiarism in a work of invention being confined to the appropriation of another's inventions.[9]

Here Hardy caught himself in his own trap. For if he had looked into Gifford's *History* more attentively, he would have noticed that Gifford's drill scene is *not* a case of 'historical and biographical matter' but an 'invention'—one which Gifford explicitly stated he had lifted from John Lambert's *Travels through . . . the United States in the Years 1806, 1807 and 1808.*[10] Hardy had doubtless never seen Lambert's book, and Gifford's reference to it went unnoticed. In writing to Aldrich, Hardy invited him to publish some statement absolving the novelist from 'the imputed plagiarism', but Aldrich decided to follow Hardy's example and say nothing. On April 3, 1882, Aldrich wrote to Hardy: 'It seems to me . . . that the charge which has been brought against you by idle letter-writers is not worth consideration. You have proved that it is easier for you to invent than to borrow.'

Other readers, however, were not so easily convinced of Hardy's innocence. The editor of *The Critic* was one of the sceptics. On May 9, 1896, he remarked editorially:

The new edition of *The Trumpet-Major* [published by Osgood, McIlvaine in London in 1896] contains a preface by the author, dated October, 1895, which contains, however, neither explanation of nor reference to the charge of plagiarism made by *The Critic* on 28 January 1882. . . . Thus the matter stands. Mr. Hardy has ignored the charge.

A month later Hardy broke silence, and on July 4, 1896, his reply to the renewed attack was published in *The Critic*:

My publishers have just sent me a cutting from *The Critic* of May 9, which contains a paragraph on a resemblance between the drilling scene in *The Trumpet-Major* and a scene in an American book published in 1840. I know nothing of the latter work. . . . Some of the details of this particular militia drill . . . were suggested by a similar description in Gifford's *History* . . . published in London in 1817—a description which I understood to refer to the English peasantry. This book and the Army Regulations . . . were the only printed matter I used.

With this reply *The Critic* dropped the matter, but other hornets kept on buzzing about the head of the unhappy author, and in 1905, in 1906, in 1910, and even in 1928 (a month after Hardy's death), the charge of plagiarism was repeated.

The most that Hardy was ever brought to admit was his statement in the preface to the 1896 edition of the novel, that on looking more carefully into Gifford he found that he was 'mistaken in supposing the account [of the drill] to be advanced as authentic, or to refer to rural England'. In Volume II (p. 967) Gifford had distinctly described his drill scene as a 'satire upon American discipline', and had stated that this account of how one Captain Clodpole drilled his men would 'give some idea of American tactics'. The sketch was indexed on page 1729 of Gifford under 'American discipline'. Hardy was doubtless careless rather than blind, but he was also disingenuous in his replies to those who had detected his borrowing.

It is not surprising, however, that he was puzzled about the charge; nor is it surprising that many of his readers remained puzzled if not sceptical. For the facts about the amusing drill were extremely complicated and were not all brought to light until as recently as April 1948.[11] The story of this international borrowing is as curious a bibliographical maze as any known to the literary historian. Briefly, it may be stated that the amusing drill scene was the work, the 'invention' (to use Hardy's word), of Oliver Hillhouse Prince. His description of how Captain Clodpole drilled his Georgia militia was published in *The Washington Monitor* on Saturday, June 6, 1807. The *Monitor* was a Georgia newspaper, then edited by Prince's uncle, David P. Hillhouse. Shortly after the newspaper appearance of the sketch, it was reprinted as a pamphlet by Cushing & Appleton in Salem, Massachusetts, and by September 29, 1807, copies of this reprint, entitled *The Ghost of Baron Steuben*, were out.[12] When John Lambert visited Charleston, South Carolina, in January 1808, he picked up a copy of this pamphlet (or another reprinting of Prince's sketch like it) and carried it back to London. There, in 1810, he reprinted it in his *Travels*, the book from which C. H. Gifford lifted it into his *History* in 1817.

In 1835, back in Georgia, the States Rights Sentinel of Augusta published *Georgia Scenes* by A. B. Longstreet. This amusing book attracted so much attention that in 1840 the Harper brothers took it over in New York and issued an illustrated edition; eleven other Harper editions followed, and by the time *The Trumpet-Major* was published in 1880, *Georgia Scenes* had become a widely-known book. One chapter in it was entitled 'The Militia Company Drill'. In a footnote Longstreet credited this chapter to 'the pen of a friend'—i.e., Prince—and stated that it had been 'published about twenty years ago'. That would mean publication in 1815. Thanks to the survival of a copy of the *Monitor* for June 6, 1807, and of at least two copies of the Salem *Ghost* of September 29, 1807, we now know that Longstreet's ascription 'about twenty years ago' was eight years short of the truth.

Thomas Hardy himself of course never learned all these facts; and, if he had, he would doubtless have seen no reason to change the attitude he expressed in 1896 when he apologized to the editor of *The Critic* 'for occupying your space with such a trivial matter as a few sentences in a novel written twenty years ago'. Besides, Hardy felt that he was in good company. Had not Shakespeare copied North's Plutarch 'almost verbatim'?

X

'Troubles in Battalions'

ON June 2, 1880, Hardy was forty years old. In spite of some recent set-backs and disappointments, he had many reasons for feeling encouraged. The future certainly had bright spots. He had just signed a contract with Harper & Brothers for a new novel, not a word of which had as yet been written, but one for which they were willing to pay $6,500—one hundred pounds sterling when he delivered the first instalment, and twelve hundred pounds on the delivery of the completed work. When the New York publishers opened negotiations with Hardy regarding this new serialization, Henry M. Alden (the editor of *Harper's Magazine*) explained that they proposed to start a European edition of the magazine in December 1880 and they would like to have Hardy's manuscript in time for the first number. They proposed to run his story both in London and in New York, and would afterwards publish it as a book in New York, allowing Hardy to make his own arrangements for book publication in London. This was easily the most princely pay Hardy had ever been offered for a product of his pen; he accordingly promptly accepted the Harper offer and began at once to make plans for the new serial-to-be.

In outlining this fresh undertaking he shifted his attention to a part of southern England he had never used before. Six of his seven novels had all dealt with Dorset; one (*A Pair of Blue Eyes*) had described Cornwall. He now decided to make use of Somerset, and selected Dunster and Dunster Castle as his locale, renaming the old Elizabethan structure 'Stancy Castle'. Since he had made a practice of never naming the actual county in any of his novels—Dorset was merely 'South Wessex', Devon was 'Lower Wessex'—he would locate 'Stancy Castle' in 'Outer Wessex' and would transfer the name Somerset to his hero. To facilitate prompt work with the new project, Somerset would be made a young architect, thus once again permitting the author to draw on his own earlier experience. Hardy went promptly to work and before the month of June 1880 was over, he had written seven or eight chapters of *A Laodicean*.

These early chapters reflect Hardy's cheerful spirit at this point in his career. One hesitates to speak of optimism in describing a novel by Thomas Hardy, especially one in which the author regards 'pessimist surmises'—like those of a 'gambler seasoned in ill-luck'—'as a safe background to his most sanguine hopes', but the fact that Hardy did, in June 1880, have sanguine hopes cannot be doubted. What is more, he set down in Chapter V of *A Laodicean* the first evidence to be found in his writings that he had begun seriously to question the accuracy of his mother's idea of the Figure with the uplifted arm as a way of explaining defeat or failure in the world. One may conjecture that Hardy's membership in the Savile Club and his meeting (there and elsewhere) men like George Smith (the publisher), W. H. Pollock, Professor Huxley, Ferdinand de Lesseps, Walter Besant, Matthew Arnold, Browning, Tennyson, Lord Houghton, James Russell Lowell (then American Minister in London), Henry Irving, and others, were beginning to teach him that Chance is not the explanation of all things. Men are, as Cassius claimed, at some time the masters of their fate. In *A Laodicean* Hardy makes Sir William De Stancy remark: 'With a disposition to be happy, it is neither this place nor the other that can render us the reverse. In short, each man's happiness depends upon himself.' This observation marks a distinct advance for Thomas Hardy towards achieving a mature philosophy of life.

When (on May 24, 1880) the Harpers made their agreement with Hardy for *A Laodicean*, they asked him to have 'a large and a small illustration' made for each part—'at our expense, of course'—and eventually George Du Maurier was selected for this work of illustration. Hardy went to Du Maurier's studio and (as the artist afterwards stated) 'gave him points minutely'. As a result, the artist 'felt constrained within these limits' and

produced drawings of so unsatisfactory a nature that Harper's
London agent, R. R. Bowker, finally expressed keen disappointment with them. Whereupon Du Maurier 'owned up that he
was better at working his own will ... than under the limita-
tions of other people's stories'.[1] By July 28 Du Maurier had
finished the illustrations for the first two instalments.

Now that *The Trumpet-Major* was running smoothly towards
the end of its serialization, and now that *A Laodicean* had been
sketchily planned and begun, Hardy decided that the literary
skies were rosy enough to justify a vacation. At the end of July
1880 he and his wife went off to the Continent and spent several
weeks in a leisurely tour of Normandy. Le Havre, Etretat,
Lisieux, and Caen were all destined to reappear a year later in
A Laodicean (Book VI, Chapters 1 and 2). Upon his return to
London, Hardy went on (at Upper Tooting) with the writing of
A Laodicean and well before the dead-line set by Harpers he had
three or four instalments in their hands and the proofs read. In
October he went with Mrs. Hardy to spend a week in Cam-
bridge, and then disaster struck.

While at Cambridge, 'he felt an indescribable physical weari-
ness'. Upon their return to Upper Tooting on Saturday, October 23, he knew he was ill, and on Sunday, when he felt worse,
he summoned a doctor. After observing Hardy's condition for
two or three days, the physician diagnosed it as an internal
haemorrhage. Mrs. Hardy consulted the Macmillans in nearby
'Knapdale'. They sent their own doctor, and he agreed with the
earlier diagnosis. The case was serious. If Hardy was to avoid
a critical operation he would have to lie in bed, with his legs
higher than his head, and remain in that position for an
indefinite period. On no account was he to get out of bed. Thus
'their troubles began',[2] and under these painful conditions *A
Laodicean* was written. For six months Hardy lay immobilized.
Determined not to embarrass the plans of *Harper's Magazine* for
the serial he had agreed to supply, he went doggedly on with its
composition, dictating it to his wife. Day after day, in the intervals of nursing, Mrs. Hardy took down whatever her husband
was able to think up. He fell back on personal reminiscences.
The Rev. Mr. Perkins, the argumentative Scottish minister of
the Baptist Church at Dorchester (with whose Aberdeen-
trained sons Hardy had carried on vehement discussions of

infant baptism during his days of apprenticeship at John Hicks's office) was now recalled to mind to serve as a model for the Rev. Mr. Woodwell, the Baptist minister in the novel who charges Somerset with advocating adult baptism 'in contention and not sincerely'. Hardy recalled—or did Mrs. Hardy remind him?— that in July 1879 they had attended a garden-party given by Mrs. Alexander Macmillan which was interrupted by a thunderstorm which sent all the guests scampering for cover. That could be used as an incident in the novel. Hardy plunged his hero into the technicalities of architecture and filled pages with 'shop-talk'. He made use of his memory of the niggardly treatment he had received at the hands of the Royal Institute of British Architects eighteen years ago, and he once again brought up the old theme of social class-distinctions. When these subjects had been exhausted, he turned to his diaries of travels on the Continent—a trip up the Rhine in 1876 and the visit to Normandy in August 1880—and in this way was able to dictate additional pages to his faithful amanuensis. Unfortunately, none of this was calculated to make a gripping novel, and Hardy was unable to make his characters do more than wander in dull and idle uncertainty through chapter after chapter. When the labouring author decided that it was time to bring the villains into his story, he slipped into a preposterous sensationalism that outdoes anything in *Desperate Remedies*. The scene in the church vestry, in which Dare and Abner Power, each with a revolver in hand, face each other across a table, is pitiful evidence of the author's complete exhaustion.

Even at an earlier point in the story, Hardy had given evidence of the pressure under which he wrote. When he came to describe Sir William De Stancy, he recalled an article entitled 'The Turf' in the *Quarterly Review* for 1833 from which he had once copied a passage by one 'Nimrod' (now identifiable as Charles Apperly). This was a description of 'the late Colonel Mellish' who was, so Apperly said, 'the star of the racecourse of modern times'. Hardy of course knew nothing whatever about racecourses, and was as yet blissfully unaware of the dangers of plagiarizing. He therefore copied somewhat over two hundred of Apperly's words into Chapter V of *A Laodicean*, not knowing that he had once again thrust his hand into a hornet's nest.

The dictating to Mrs. Hardy continued until her husband

was at last, in April 1881, permitted to leave his bed. On May 1 he was finally able to finish *A Laodicean*, 'in pencil'. The novel dragged on in *Harper's* until the end of the year. Late in November it was published in New York by Harper & Brothers, and in December in London by Sampson Low, Marston, Searle & Rivington. Two months later the London publisher remaindered the book to Mudie. No one had to ask why. Hardy knew, and his publishers knew, that this was the poorest novel he had ever written.

Harper & Brothers were not content, however, to let *A Laodicean* merely be forgotten. They wished no reader to labour under the impression that, in printing the novel in *Harper's Magazine*, they indicated critical approval of it. Far from holding it in high esteem, they regarded it as flabby, pale, and trite, and they lost no time in letting their public—and the author!—know this. In the issue of February 1882, the editor of the magazine frankly announced that

Mr. Hardy has pitched his new romance, *A Laodicean*, on a lower and feebler key than usual. Compared with the best of his former novels, its movement is languid, its actors tame and colourless, and its plot and incidents hackneyed. Hitherto one of the most unconventional of modern novelists, in this story he rivals the most conventional. . . . His admirers will . . . look regretfully and vainly through the *Laodicean* for the powerful scenic and dramatic effects and the deep Rembrandt-like tones with which he had made them familiar, or for the intensely realistic delineations of picturesque aspects of common life among the agricultural labourers and peasantry of England, and the vivid descriptions of heath and fen and moorland scenery that have characterized the strongest of his previous performances.

Even before this editorial castigation had reached the public eye, an American reader of *A Laodicean*, Charles T. F. Spoor, had detected the plagiarized passage in Chapter V. Writing to the New York *Nation* on January 9, 1882, he remarked: 'I do not criticize the use made of the scissors . . . by Mr. Hardy, but call attention to it as a specimen of the manner in which the inventive labours of novelists are doubtless often abridged.' The *Nation's* charge of plagiarism (January 19, 1882) was repeated a month later in London, in *The Academy* (February 18). In the face of this double-barrelled attack, Hardy maintained an unbroken silence. Fourteen years later, when *A Laodicean* was about to be reprinted in the Osgood edition of 1896, Hardy quietly revised the plagiarized passage, shortening it, introducing dialect ('zay' for 'say', 'zight' for 'sight'), thus reducing the number of points which had led Charles Spoor to remark in 1882: 'There is, to say the least, a striking similarity apparent.'

While undergoing all these afflictions, Hardy tried to maintain a philosophical attitude. 'This is the chief thing,' he had learned to quote from Marcus Aurelius: 'Be not perturbed.' He also recalled the King's remark in *Hamlet*:

> When sorrows come, they come not single spies
> But in battalions,

and while he lay in bed, Hardy tried to convince himself that 'there is mercy in troubles coming in battalions—they neutralize each other'.[3] He was soon to have a chance to test the truth of this idea, for his troubles were far from over. He came to suspect that Philosophy was just as 'guilty' a guide as he had once thought Fortune to be 'guilty' as a goddess. And in his next novel he was going to write about a young man who 'found that the goddess Philosophy, to whom he had vowed to dedicate his whole life, would not . . . support him through a single hour of despair'.[4]

As soon as Hardy had regained sufficient health to be able to move, he and his wife were quite understandably ready to turn their backs upon the house where their troubles had begun. In June 1881 they moved to Wimborne Minster in Dorset, finding in The Avenue a house called 'Llanherne' conveniently located not very far from the minster where Hardy had once listened to the organist practising late at night. They moved in on June 25 and on that very evening saw in the northern sky the comet about which the newspapers had been talking for some time. The London *Times* of that morning printed (p. 12) a brief note on 'The Comet':

We continue to receive letters from different parts of the country describing the appearance and position of the comet. It was clearly visible last night in London, rather low in the heavens, and almost due north. The nucleus was very large and bright, and the fan tail spread out gracefully. . . . It decidedly outshone the star Capella.

These words are worth quoting because, within a year of

Hardy's arrival at Wimborne Minster, the comet with its graceful fan tail was to reappear in the pages of *Two on a Tower*.

At Wimborne the Hardys soon made friends and found some congenial neighbours. Across the street lived Frank Douglas, brother of Sir George Douglas of Springwood Park in Scotland, whom the Hardys were later to meet and visit. It was to Sir George Douglas that Hardy turned a few years later for the correction of Farfrae's Scottish speech in *The Mayor of Casterbridge*. Another neighbour in Wimborne was Judge Tindal-Atkinson of the County Court. These friendly folk enjoyed communal Shakespeare readings and the Hardys were soon invited to take part in them. Hardy afterwards remembered a young girl, one 'N.P.', who read 'Miranda' in *The Tempest*, and a retired general who read 'Trinculo'. After the general had 'blurted out one of Shakespeare's improprieties ... before he was aware'—('Monster, I do smell all horse-piss, at which my nose is in great indignation')—he told Hardy privately that he was 'in fear and trembling' lest he may do it again'.[5]

Hardy never identified the part or parts that he himself read. This exposure to dramatics in 1881 had, however, interesting personal associations for him. He recalled having appeared twice in pantomimes at Covent Garden in London in December 1865 —once as a 'nondescript' and once 'in a representation of the Oxford and Cambridge boat-race',[6] presumably as one of the crowd of spectators—but even more pointed at this time was his recollection of having recently tried to dramatize *Far from the Madding Crowd*. In or about 1879 he had made a dramatic adaptation of his novel, and when Comyns Carr, a London art-critic, happened to ask him whether he had ever thought of dramatizing any of his work, Hardy sent Carr his play. He had called it *The Mistress of the Farm*. Carr thought that there were some rough spots in it, and Hardy thereupon invited him to try to smooth them out. This Carr did and then, with Hardy's approval, offered the play to Hare and Kendal, managers of the St. James's Theatre. Early in 1880 these managers sent a provisional acceptance of Hardy's play, but later (after Mrs. Kendal had begun to raise objections to her part in it) the acceptance was held up. By November 1880, just when Hardy was put to bed in Upper Tooting, *The Mistress of the Farm* was finally rejected. And now, a year later, while Hardy was enjoying the Shakespeare readings at Wimborne Minster, the St. James's Theatre announced in *The Times* (December 27) that a new play, *The Squire*, by A. W. Pinero, would open the following day. On the 29th the first performance of the new play was reported and commented on. Friends immediately rushed letters off to Hardy in Wimborne, Carr wrote him in great perturbation, and on the first day of the New Year, 1882, Hardy wrote the following letter:

To the Editor of *The Times*:

Sir,

My attention has been drawn to the play entitled *The Squire*, now just produced at the St. James's Theatre, by a somewhat general declaration on the part of the daily Press that the play is an unacknowledged adaptation of my novel *Far from the Madding Crowd*. I should have read this announcement with no strong feelings had my labours in connexion with the subject been limited to writing the novel; but the aspect of the matter is changed by the fact, of which the spectators were ignorant, that the managers of the St. James's Theatre have had in their hands, not only the novel accessible to everybody, but a manuscript play of my own based on the novel. I had long been impressed with the notion that the central idea of the story—a woman ruling a farm and marrying a soldier secretly, while unselfishly beloved through evil and through good report by her shepherd or bailiff—afforded a promising theme for the stage. I accordingly dramatized the story, sent the play to Mr. Comyns Carr, the art critic, who kindly improved it, and offered the play to the theatre above mentioned. I suggested to him that the rank of the personages be raised, particularly that Sergeant Troy should appear as a lieutenant, and that in this case the names should be changed, and he told me that the suggestion was duly presented to the theatre. Moreover, a gipsy who does not exist in the novel, was introduced into our play, and I see that a gipsy figures in *The Squire*. I then learnt that the play was verbally accepted and would soon appear; then that it was rejected. Silence ensued till *The Squire* is proclaimed by many observers as in substance mine. My drama is now rendered useless, for it is obviously not worth while for a manager to risk producing a piece if the whole gist of it is already to be seen by the public at another theatre.

I am, yours faithfully,
Thomas Hardy.

Wimborne, Dorset, Jan. 1.

Pinero replied immediately, stating that he was not acquainted with Hardy's work. The theatre managers wrote to say that Pinero had assured them that his play was original. Comyns Carr replied; others joined the discussion; and for months the argument continued. As late as March 3, 1882, *The Times* stated that 'the controversy over the coincidences between Mr. Pinero's play and Mr. Hardy's novel is not yet at an end'. Hardy himself made no further statement after his New Year's Day letters (he wrote one also to the *Daily News*); but others kept the dispute alive, and echoes of it lasted into the twentieth century. In April 1906 *The Critic* (New York) remarked that 'Mr. Hardy and Mr. J. W. Comyns Carr dramatized *Far from the Madding Crowd*, which had the same plot as Mr. Pinero's *The Squire*, and this fact led to tiresome litigation'. Actually, there was no litigation whatsoever. Not only has no record of any legal action ever been found, but no contemporary reference to the controversy mentions litigation. It was merely a heated newspaper discussion.

Moreover, there is no evidence whatever to support a further statement in *The Critic*, that 'some woman had sold the same plot to Mr. Pinero and to Mr. Hardy without letting either know what she had done'. This report about 'some woman' was repeated years later by Professor Joseph Warren Beach of the University of Minnesota: 'The same woman had sold the plot separately to each of the two authors.'[7] It is now clear that this story is quite false. Hardy had not bought his plot from anyone. After a brilliant piece of detective work, Professor Richard Little Purdy arrived at a solution of the problem: 'Mrs. Kendal was the culprit.' She had not sold Hardy the plot of his novel, but she *had* read the Hardy-Carr play, and she told its plot to Pinero without telling him anything about Hardy's work, either as a novelist or as an adapter of the novel.[8]

Contrary to Hardy's expectations, his play got on to the stage after all. It was produced at Liverpool on February 27, 1882 (*Early Life*, p. 198, says 'during March'), and the disappointed would-be dramatist and his wife went to Liverpool to see it. *The Early Life* also states that 'the play . . . was not . . . to Hardy's liking', and he refers to it as 'a dramatization . . . prepared by Mr. J. Comyns Carr'; but Hardy's letter of January 1, 1882, to *The Times* distinctly refers to 'my drama' and to 'a manuscript play of my own', and the programme of the Royal Globe Theatre in London, where the play opened on April 29, 1882, announced it as 'by Thomas Hardy and Comyns Carr'.[9]

It is easy to understand why, forty years later, Hardy's memory of the whole business was distasteful and why he was inclined to shift responsibility for the dramatization of his novel on to the shoulders of Comyns Carr. His irritated sense of frustration had not worn off by March 8, 1882, when he wrote to Thomas Bailey Aldrich about 'the imputed plagiarism' in *The Trumpet-Major*. 'It is hardly a matter for surprise', he said, 'that, in view of recent events connected with the stage, such a countercharge should have been made.'[10]

Fortunately for Hardy's own peace of mind, he received just at this time from Aldrich (*via* his London agent Stevens) an inquiry as to whether Hardy could and would supply a novel for serialization in the *Atlantic Monthly* in Boston, Massachusetts. Hardy agreed to Aldrich's proposal of a serial to run for eight months only, to begin in the May 1882 *Atlantic*, and promptly got to work writing *Two on a Tower*. He decided to make use of Wimborne Minster as a setting, and to utilize the comet he had seen in June 1881 as the starting-point of a story with an astronomical motif. He would 'set the emotional history of two infinitesimal lives against the stupendous background of the stellar universe'. This poetic idea obviously came from his recent experience during the weary half-year when he lay flat on his back. He had then had plenty of opportunity to 'look out of the window with sad apathy' (like Hannah in Chapter X of *Two on a Tower*) and to meditate on the smallness of his own life in contrast with the bigness of the universe he could see from his bedroom window. At Wimborne, too, his interest in 'the stupendous background of the stellar universe'[11] was increased by the discovery that, in Charborough Park (an estate near Wimborne Minster), there was an old tower which suggested the possibility of its use as an astronomical observatory.

Hardy was reminded of the fact that he had once before seen a comet—in 1858—during his period of study under John Hicks, and had written a poem in ballad stanza about it:

> It bends far over Yell'ham Plain,
> And we, from Yell'ham Height,

Stand and regard its fiery train,
So soon to swim from sight.

When this poem, 'The Comet at Yell'ham', was later published,[12] it was quoted shortly thereafter by a speaker at Oxford;
whereupon Hardy wrote to him (on October 24, 1909): 'I am
honoured by your quoting my little poem about the comet. It
appeared, I think, in 1858 or 1859—a very large one—and I
remember standing and looking at it as described.'

The comet Hardy had seen from Yellowham Hill near Higher
Bockhampton was Encke's Comet, visible in October 1858; and
this date helps us to place the action of *Two on a Tower* in time.
In choosing this decade of the nineteenth century, Hardy sand-
wiched his comet-novel in between *The Return of the Native*, the
action of which was dated 1842–3, and *Far from the Madding
Crowd*, the action of which was dated 1869–73. Hardy was
obviously showing as much care in dispersing his time-
periods over the Victorian Era as he was in dispersing his geographical settings throughout 'Wessex'. For fictional purposes,
however, Hardy transferred to Encke's Comet the characteristics of the comet he had seen on June 25, 1881. We now know
this comet as Tebbutt's, but in 1881 people were like 'the placid
inhabitants of Welland' (Hardy's fictional name for Wimborne
Minster) who, in Chapter X, discuss the new comet: 'Is it
Gambert's? Is it Charles the Fifth's? Or Halley's?' Of course no
one then knew its name, for no one then living had seen it
before. The last time it had been visible was in 547 B.C. When
Hardy wrote (in Chapter XV) that 'the comet . . . was now on
the wane . . . [and] would soon disappear altogether from the
heavens for perhaps thousands of years', he was not far off from
the truth, for astronomers have now been able to inform us that
the period of Tebbutt's Comet is 2428 years. It will not be back
until A.D. 4309.[13]

Other bits of information about the comet determined additional features of the novel. Tebbutt's Comet had been first
observed in Australia, a month before Hardy saw it. It was next
observed at the Cape of Good Hope in Africa, and in Chapter
XV of *Two on a Tower* Hardy's young astronomer wishes to find
'some suitable place for observing . . . ,—say, at the Cape', and
in Chapter XL we are told that he 'made straight for the Cape'.

Knowing that this story of a youthful astronomer from

'Welland' was to appear in a Boston magazine, Hardy decided to send his hero to Boston. He therefore conveniently created the oceanic shipping necessary to permit Swithin to sail, in a single sentence, from Cape Town to Melbourne, back to Cape Town, 'thence ... to America, where he landed at Boston'. There, 'taking no interest in men or cities, this indefatigable scrutineer of the universe went immediately on to Cambridge' (Chapter XL). When Hardy's manuscript reached the office of the *Atlantic Monthly*, this evidence that Hardy knew neither the size nor the site of Cambridge, Massachusetts, was noticed, and the word 'on' was quietly suppressed in the pages of the *Atlantic*, so that the young astronomer could proceed 'immediately to Cambridge'—just across the Charles River from Boston. But when Hardy came to prepare his novel for its London publication in book form, he re-inserted the word 'on'; and then, in later editions of the novel—apparently to make sure that no reader would think that Swithin went from Boston in America to Cambridge in England—Hardy amended his text so that his hero might go 'immediately on to Cambridge, United States'.

Hardy's interest in interstellar space was greater than his interest in the American Cambridge. When Hamlin Garland called on Hardy in Dorchester and happened to mention Harvard University, the visitor was startled to have the novelist ask: 'Is that a girls' school?'[14]

Hardy's preparation of his manuscript was done rapidly, for once again he found himself caught in the awkward position of not having completed the writing of a story until some time after it had begun to appear in print. He dispensed with the usual frills of chapter headings and poetic epigraphs. He wrote at top speed and, as a result, his manuscript became full of suppressions and additions, interlineations, transpositions, afterthoughts and deletions. From time to time as he worked, he called on Mrs. Hardy to make a 'fair copy'; and sometimes, in looking over her transcript, he made fresh revisions of the text. A further complication developed. Knowing that the danger of his manuscript going astray would be greater in the course of an ocean voyage to Boston than he had had to face previously when his manuscripts went no farther than to London, Hardy decided to send *two* manuscripts. On March 8, 1882, he wrote Aldrich: 'Herewith I send Part 2 of the story. A duplicate will follow by the next mail, to guard against accidental loss.'[15] The survival of three parts of this duplicate manuscript, together with five parts of the original manuscript—both now in the Houghton Library, Harvard University—makes it possible to learn that Hardy continued to revise his text in the duplicate manuscript even after he had sent off the original. More than once he made fresh insertions in the duplicate, which thus did not maintain correspondence with the original draft from which the *Atlantic Monthly* text was printed. As a result some of Hardy's after-thoughts never blossomed into print.[16]

Eventually, the eighth and last instalment was finished, and the *Atlantic* serialization ended in December. In late October 1882 *Two on a Tower* was published in London in three volumes by Sampson Low, and by Henry Holt in one volume in New York in December. Hardy's own words (in a Preface written in 1895) tell what happened next:

On the publication of the book people seemed to be less struck with the high aims of the author than with their own opinion, first, that the novel was an 'improper' one in its morals, and, secondly, that it was intended to be a satire on the Established Church of this country. I was made to suffer in consequence from several eminent pens,—such warm epithets as 'hazardous', 'repulsive', 'little short of revolting', 'a studied and gratuitous insult', being flung at the precarious volumes. It is sufficient to draw attention to the fact that the Bishop is every inch a gentleman, and that the parish priest who figures in the narrative is one of its most estimable characters.

In spite of the presence of these 'estimable characters', Hardy's readers refused to be pleased. James Russell Lowell, American Minister in London, began reading the novel but 'did not get on with it'.[17] Aldrich wrote Hardy that 'the concluding chapters . . . were not quite in the line of the *Atlantic*'.[18] Harriet W. Preston denounced *Two on a Tower* as a tale which 'Mr. Hardy's truest admirers must wish most heartily he had left untold'. Its wit (she thought) was 'exceptionally keen' but its intrigue was 'insufferably low', and 'the character of Lady Constantine is, properly speaking, a pathological study'.[19]

No one had anything to say about the tender portrayal of Viviette's unselfish and half-maternal devotion to her young lover, especially during his sickness—a portrayal in which Hardy was obviously recalling Emma's loyal services and attention when he lay sick at Upper Tooting—and of course no one recognized in Swithin's remarks to Viviette evidence that the words were not really those of a zealous young astronomer but those of a sick author gazing in melancholy impotence at the sky. The plain fact is that *Two on a Tower* cannot take a high rank among the Wessex novels simply because it is deficient in the two things that Hardy knew best—rustic Dorset characters and natural phenomena—and his attempts to portray people in polite society were here just what they had been in *The Hand of Ethelberta*, wooden and unconvincing. Amos Fry appears all too infrequently. Mr. Torkingham's amusing efforts in training the choir to sing 'Honwerd, Christen sojers' are reminiscent of Hardy's own observations as a boy at Stinsford Church, but the haste with which he had to compose *Two on a Tower* gave him little opportunity for weaving such incidents and observations into the fabric of his novel.

Haste did not end for Hardy with the writing of *Two on a Tower*. As soon as this story was off his hands, he was called upon to dash off another. On February 25, 1883, he sent the manuscript of a 'hastily written novel' to the editor of the *Graphic* in London, and *The Romantic Adventures of a Milkmaid* appeared in its issue for June 1883. 'It is, if the truth must be told, the most arrant pot-boiler that was ever turned out.'[20] It impressed no one; it disappointed many. A Philadelphia reviewer declared that 'Mr. Hardy's *Adventures of a Milkmaid* will be . . . read . . . with vexation at being so . . . befooled by a clever writer who ought to do better for his admirers'.[21] In Boston, the *Milkmaid* was called 'a weak, inconsequential, unnatural story. . . . If Mr. Hardy's genius is to run itself out in such nonentities as this, he would better lay his pen down and rest . . . on his reputation'.[22] Nothing Hardy wrote seemed to succeed or give satisfaction.

When Hardy remarked of Viviette that 'events mocked her on all sides', he cannot have failed to think of the fact that, ever since his depature from Sturminster Newton in 1878, events had mocked him on all sides. But relief was in sight. When the *Westminster Review* for April 1883 appeared, it contained an anonymous article entitled 'The Novels of Thomas Hardy'. The novelist had no great reason for opening the pages of the *Westminster* with any pleasurable anticipation, for he cannot have forgotten that this was the magazine which, in reviewing *Far from the Madding Crowd*, had characterized its charming heroine as 'hard and mercenary'. Now, however, Hardy not only looked into the *Westminster Review* but was delighted with what he found there.

The article was a full-length critical survey of Hardy's entire literary product—twelve titles in all—treated as literature. Hardy found himself classed with Goethe and George Eliot. The anonymous article was obviously by some one who knew how to write as well as how to appraise and judge. The writer was clearly a person with wide acquaintance with literature. As Hardy read on, his pleasure in having found an appreciative critic increased. The unknown reviewer even singled out for special attention *A Pair of Blue Eyes*—always a favourite with Hardy because of its association with St. Juliot and his own Cornish romance. The article pointed out that

A Pair of Blue Eyes contains the first serious study of Mr. Hardy's favourite hero, who belongs to the class that enters modern literature as 'Wilhelm Meister', and finds its most prominent recent representative in 'Daniel Deronda'.

Hardy was so delighted with this thoroughgoing survey of his novels that, on April 29, 1883, he wrote to his unknown appreciative critic:

My dear Sir:

I have read with great interest your article in the *Westminster* and can inadequately express by letter my sense of your generous treatment of the subject. I consider the essay a remarkable paper in many ways, . . . with . . . charm of style and variety of allusion. . . . The keen appreciativeness which the article discloses sets me thinking. . . . In speaking of men of the Wilhelm Meister and Daniel Deronda class as being my favourite heroes, you are only saying in another way that these men are the modern man—the type to which the great mass of educated modern men of ordinary capacity are assimilating. . . . I hope to read some more of your critical writings in the future and believe I shall discover them without a mark. . . .

Hardy eventually discovered that the article was the work of Havelock Ellis. It was Ellis's very first piece of critical writing. Neither the article nor Ellis's name is mentioned in *The Early Life*; and when, in October 1896, Ellis contributed another article, 'Concerning *Jude the Obscure*', to *The Savoy*, it, too, failed to gain an entry in the index of *The Later Years of Thomas Hardy*. (On four subsequent occasions (in 1930, 1931, 1932, and 1939) Ellis returned to make further comments on Hardy's work, but Hardy had not lived to see them.)

Havelock Ellis had, however, done more than give Hardy momentary pleasure. He had found much to praise but he had also noted that

in Goethe's novel, and in George Eliot's, larger issues are involved than anywhere in Mr. Hardy's. . . . Mr. Hardy . . . is mostly indifferent to these [larger] things; his hero passes through no . . . process of development. . . .

Hardy took mental note of Havelock Ellis's remarks and, when he came to write *The Mayor of Casterbridge* a year later, he not only made a point of having his hero, Michael Henchard, 'develop', but also demonstrated that he himself, the author, was likewise ready, at the age of forty-three, for further progress towards intellectual maturity.

In June 1883 he and Mrs. Hardy left Wimborne Minster.

XI

Portrait of a Man of Character

UPON leaving Wimborne Minster in June 1883, Hardy and his wife spent a few days in London. The novelist dined with Edmund Gosse and shortly afterwards carried Gosse off with him on a house-hunting expedition into Dorset. They looked at houses as far west as Bridport and there had the experience—an unusual one for Hardy—of getting lost. On finding no house to suit him, Hardy finally decided to settle down in Dorchester and, still finding nothing to his taste, he came to the conclusion that there was only one solution to his housing problem: he would have to build. Meanwhile, he rented a house in Shire Hall Lane and to it brought Mrs. Hardy at the end of June. 'To her surprise she found herself in one of the little-used alleys of the town' where one of the neighbouring landmarks was an old arch with a keystone 'mask with a comic leer', the appearance of which was 'so ghastly', especially when seen by the weak glimmer of a street lamp, 'that she could not bear to look at it'. The words here quoted from Chapter XX of *The Mayor of Casterbridge* apply to Elizabeth-Jane, and one would hesitate to transfer them to Emma Lavinia Hardy if one had not learned from Hardy's past practice how ready he was to use for fictional purposes his own and his wife's experience in real life. He himself recognized the unattractive aspects of Shire Hall Lane and admitted that, in the house there, 'the sunshine flaps open and shut like a fan'.[1]

Thus the native returned to Dorchester for a second time. But the man of forty-three who returned was a very different person from the disorganized youth of twenty-seven who had returned from London in 1867. It was not merely a matter of a difference in age, nor the fact that he was now married, nor that he was now the author of nine published novels instead of being merely a disappointed would-be poet. He was now a man with a different outlook upon the world, with a greater maturity of mind, based upon greater experience. He was more serious, with a growth and a broadening of intellectual interests that showed in a number of ways. When *Longman's Magazine* had wanted a contribution while Hardy was enjoying the Shakespeare readings at Wimborne, he had sent the editor the amusing story of 'The Three Strangers'; but when the editor asked for more, Hardy sent him a serious article on 'The Dorsetshire Labourer'[2] in which he not only objected to the labourer's being called 'Hodge' but also anticipated by more than fifteen years the views that were to be expressed by another writer in 'The Man With the Hoe'. Shortly before leaving Wimborne Hardy joined the Society for the Protection of Ancient Buildings and remained a member until his death. After settling in Dorchester, he made at the request of this society several visits of inspection to old buildings in Dorset and wrote out reports on the old tower of the East Lulworth Church and on the White Horse Inn at Maiden Newton. This quickened interest in people and places, quite apart from any thought of their use in his fiction, was, however, only a slight bit of evidence that he had experienced a growth and a strengthening of character. He had not only become more self-reliant but had emerged from his recent troubles with the knowledge that he possessed enough fortitude to meet them. He had been exposed to adversity and had learned to rise above it. Instead of continuing to chide Fortune as

> The guilty goddess . . .
> That did not better for my life provide

Hardy had learned that

> Not from the stars do I my judgment pluck,
> . . . to tell of good or evil luck.[3]

He was getting ready to create a heroic character who could declare: 'My punishment is *not* greater than I can bear.'[4] This does not mean that Hardy had suddenly become your ideal Stoic. He hadn't. But he *was* learning to confront the tragic aspects of life with open eyes and without whimpering. On May 28, 1885, he noted that 'the roar of London . . . is . . . composed of . . . laughter, moans, cries of . . . people . . . playing their parts in the tragedy [of life]. . . . All are caged birds; the only difference lies in the size of the cage. This too is part of the tragedy.'[5]

Nor was the maturing of Hardy's vision confined to sympathetic observation of the outer world. He looked inward as well. The return of the native in 1883 had lasted less than a year when he wrote in his notebook: 'Every error under the sun seems to arise from thinking that you are right yourself because you are yourself, and other people wrong because they are not you.'[6]

Hardy was learning, too, about the wife he had married in 1874. Emma was obviously not wholly pleased at his settling on Dorchester as the place where he would build them a house. She would quite willingly have gone instead to Devon, 'as it is her native country',[7] and as late as March 1885 he remarked: 'Cannot think why we live in benighted Dorset.'[8] Ten years before this, Hardy had quoted Robert Herrick's lines on 'The Poetry of Dress'. One wonders whether he ever quoted, either to himself or to his wife, those lines from the *Hesperides* in which Herrick confessed

> More discontents I never had
> Since I was born than here,
> Where I have been, and still am, sad
> In this dull Devonshire.

By 1883, however, Hardy had learned the truth of the remark that he had already placed upon the lips of Sir William De Stancy: 'With a disposition to be happy, it is neither this place nor the other'—neither Devon nor Dorset—'that can render us the reverse.'

When Hardy remarked that the decision to move to Dorchester in June 1883 was 'a step they often regretted having taken',[9] we may well suspect that the 'regret' in large part reflected Emma's feeling. However, she was not alone. Lord Wynford later told Hardy that he would not live in Dorset for fifty thousand pounds a year!

Unable to find in Dorchester a 'house to suit him',[10] Hardy finally acquired a lot of an acre or two a mile out of town, on the road to Wareham; and there, in the autumn of 1883, he began the construction of the house which was to be his home for the next forty-five years. He remarks in *Early Life* (p. 212) that his chief objection to the site was its 'newness', but when he began to dig the foundations he ran into Roman graves with skeletons! No wonder he was later to observe of Dorchester that it 'announced old Rome in every street, alley, and precinct. It looked Roman, bespoke the art of Rome, concealed dead men of Rome. It was impossible to dig more than a foot or two deep . . . without coming upon some tall soldier . . . of the Empire who had lain there . . . for . . . fifteen hundred years.'[11]

In his desire to preserve at least one link with the past, Hardy decided to name his new home Max Gate. The name has often puzzled people, but its explanation is simple. Only a few yards from the spot where Hardy built his new home there was a little cottage which had long been used as a toll-gate by a man called Mack. In the scene in *The Dynasts* where the beacon is lit on the Ridgeway above Weymouth, one of the characters remarks that the light can be seen at Mack's Gate. Mack had been dead for some time when Hardy began to build, but that point on the Wareham road was still known locally as Mack's Gate, and the little cottage itself lasted until 1964. Hardy felt that he could not call his own house 'Mack's Gate', but he wished to preserve the old Napoleonic association, so he named the new dwelling Max Gate. Construction was begun in October 1883, was continued throughout 1884, and was completed in twenty months. Hardy and his wife moved into Max Gate on June 29, 1885.

According to the evidence of a poem, 'Everything Comes', published long afterwards,[12] Mrs. Hardy found the new abode unattractive:

> 'The house is bleak and cold
> Built so new for me! . . .
> No screening trees abound,
> And the curious eyes around
> Keep on view for me.'

The poem represents her husband as replying:

> 'My love, I am planting trees
> As a screen for you,'

and according to *The Early Life* (p. 226) he planted (with his own hands, if we may believe him) two or three *thousand* small trees. No wonder Max Gate came eventually to be hidden in a miniature forest! A third of a century later, when there was a second Mrs. Thomas Hardy installed at Max Gate, the dwelling had improved little in attractiveness. 'This place', wrote Florence Hardy in 1920, 'is too depressing for words in the winter, when the dead leaves stick on the window-pane and the wind moans and the sky is grey and you can't even see as far as the high road.'[13]

The house admittedly lacked some things. In spite of Hardy's training as an architect, he was satisfied to erect a house without a bathroom and with a water-system that required of the Max Gate gardener, each morning, five hundred strokes of a pump in the kitchen in order to fill the water tanks. Not until after Hardy's death in 1928 was a bathroom installed at Max Gate. But Emma Lavinia Hardy's reaction to her new home was not exclusively a feeling about the house. Even if one got used to its deficiencies, there were other causes of friction: indications, small at first, but gradually increasing both in frequency and in number, that the warm glow of romance begun at St. Juliot in March 1870 had not lasted. 'The brought breeze fainted soon,' Hardy confessed in a poem, 'Fetching Her' (not published until 1922). Just what caused the chill Hardy never knew, or at least professed not to know; but he did admit that he knew exactly when he first became aware of the change in the domestic weather:

> 'Twas just at gnat and cobweb-time, . . .
> That your old gamut changed its chime . . .
> So sank I from my high sublime! . . .
> And never I knew or guessed my crime.

These words are from his poem 'The Rift'.[14] Hardy may have 'guessed' more than he put into the poem. For certainly, by this time, after ten years of marriage, he must have become aware of the fact that Mrs. Hardy was taking increasingly frequent occasion to remind him that she came from a higher social level than he. Her infrequent visits to his parental home at Higher Bockhampton served only to present to her eyes a painful contrast with her own girlhood home at Plymouth.

'My home', she reminisced later, 'was . . . one of exquisite . . . refinement—alas the difference . . . to me!'[15] Moreover, her own conventional and 'orthodox' outlook as the niece of Canon Gifford and the sister-in-law of the Reverend Caddell Holder made Hardy's increasingly outspoken agnosticism distasteful if not repugnant to her. The 'rift' when he sank from his high sublime had already become a noticeable domestic division before they moved into Max Gate; and they had not been in the new house many months when Hardy sat down at the writing table in his new study and wrote: 'He feared anew that they could never be happy together. . . . She was accomplished: he was unrefined. It was the original difficulty, which he was too thoughtful to recklessly ignore, as some men would have done in his place.' (Said of Giles Winterborne, in *The Woodlanders*, Chapter XXXIX.) Hardy was too thoughtful a man to ignore the domestic problem, but his solution was merely to brood upon it. Her solution was different. 'Keeping separate a good deal is a wise plan in crises,' she wrote later. On Hardy's forty-fourth birthday (June 2, 1884) he went alone to call on his parents at Higher Bockhampton and stayed with them until 9 p.m. As he set out for the familiar three-mile walk back into Dorchester, it was 'so silent and still that a footstep on the dead leaves could be heard a quarter of a mile off'.[17] Two months later, Hardy went off with his brother Henry on a vacation trip to the Channel Islands; his visit to Guernsey, Jersey, and Sark was destined to provide Lucetta with a Jersey background where 'they speak French on one side of the street and English on the other'.[18] Emma Hardy's absence from her husband's side began as a rare occasion, an exceptional incident; the time came, however, when he often went without her.

Even when the two were together, all was not serene. They got into the habit of making annual trips up to London, chiefly in the spring and early summer. They were there in June 1883, for example, and again in June 1884; and at garden-parties, such as one given by Mrs. Alexander Macmillan, or at evening parties, such as one given by Mrs. G. Murray Smith (the wife of the publisher), Hardy came to know titled ladies and *grandes dames* who in turn invited him to their own 'crushes'. Lady Carnarvon, Lady Portsmouth, and other hospitable 'noble dames' invited the Hardys; and—doubtless to Emma's surprise—her 'poor man' showed that he enjoyed being lionized by these ladies. He began to notice their dresses. Lady Stracey 'looked remarkably well'. Lady Portsmouth's black brocaded silk gown fitted her well. Lady de Grey was 'handsome, tall, glance-giving, arch, friendly.' Hardy himself made no comparisons, but others who saw Mrs. Hardy at this time have made the comparisons for us. Robert Louis Stevenson's American wife, who saw the Hardys in August 1885, described the Max Gate couple thus: 'Hardy . . . a pale, gentle, frightened little man, that one felt an instinctive tenderness for; with a wife—"ugly" is no word for it! who said, "Whatever shall we do!"'[19]

When Lady Portsmouth invited the Hardys to visit her at her 'seat' in north Devon—Eggesford House, at Wembworthy (a dozen miles north-east of Okehampton)—Hardy was eager to accept the invitation, even though he had not yet finished his work on *The Mayor of Casterbridge*. Mrs. Hardy, one might have expected, would have been glad to revisit her native county, Devon. But when the time came, she could not—or at least did not—go. Hardy went without her. On Friday, March 13, 1885, he went off for a week-end visit with a group of noble dames—Lady Portsmouth, her daughters Lady Dorothea and Lady Camilla, their cousin Lady Winifred Herbert, a married daughter, Lady Rosamond Christie, and others. Mrs. Hardy remained in Dorchester.

All these activities naturally caused a marked lull in Hardy's literary productivity. His writing was only postponed, however, and as soon as the construction of Max Gate was well under way, after designs made by himself, he was ready to go back to work with his pen. In late March or early April, 1884, he began the actual writing of *The Mayor of Casterbridge* and penned the last line of it on April 17, 1885, five weeks after his return from the excursion into Devon.

Hardy worked under unusually favourable conditions. This time he had not committed himself to a magazine dead-line and was able to finish the writing before a word of the story had been put into print. Serialization was not begun until eight months after he had written the last line. Proof-reading, too, proceeded at a leisurely pace. The novel was in type before the end of October, but two more months elapsed before the first instalment was published. Hardy had never before enjoyed so comfortable a schedule.

This propitious pace gave him leeway for careful planning. He had decided to write about Dorchester. This choice of setting was quite natural, for he had always liked to write about his immediate surroundings. When he was living at Bockhampton, he wrote about the Bockhampton environs. When he resided at Weymouth, he wrote about the Weymouth neighbourhood. During his residence at Wimborne Minster, he wrote about that part of Dorset. The only exceptions to this general practice were *The Return of the Native* and *A Laodicean.* 'I always go to a place first,' Hardy once declared, 'before attempting to describe it.' He did not have to go to Dorchester, however, for he had known the town for thirty-five years. In choosing it for use in the new novel, he made it possible to draw upon the wealth of knowledge he had been storing up. No need now to consult histories of Napoleonic wars or to visit astronomical observatories. He had known the brick bridge and its loafers and the stone bridge with its shabby-genteel ever since boyhood. He remembered the iron railing on which as a boy he had climbed up to peer in on the hangman placidly eating his supper the night before a public execution. The grizzled church of St. Peter's, the dark walk along the Froom River, the old Roman Ring, the King's Arms Hotel, and the work-house—all were as well known to him as Egdon Heath.

In planning this new novel Hardy did several things that he had never done before. The more closely one examines *The Mayor of Casterbridge* the more one is impressed with the fresh marks of originality that it shows. With the exception of those stories in which Hardy had made the mistake of trying to deal with polite society, all of his novels had dealt with an agricultural background. The characters had been farmers and shepherds, dairymen and field-workers. He now planned to turn to town life and to deal with merchants, grain-dealers, and other townsmen. In his previous stories, Dorset rustics had been used chiefly to provide comic interludes. He now planned to give the uneducated part of his cast a serious, even though a minor, part in the plot. And as for that plot, he decided to write for the first time a novel that was not, in any important respect, a love story but one in which he would centre the drama in one person. There are three women in the story—Susan, Lucetta, and Elizabeth-Jane—but they are never allowed to assume a major rôle. Even the men are kept under rigid control. Newson hardly appears upon the stage at all, and Farfrae comes on just enough to annoy some envious readers by his unbroken good luck. He also annoys native Scots with his accent (picked up by Hardy in 1881 from a young Edinburgh cab driver; an accent later 'corrected' by Sir George Douglas). But Henchard is a full-length portrait, and Hardy truthfully subtitled the novel 'A Story of a Man of Character'.

In deciding to present 'The Life and Death' of Michael Henchard, Hardy again broke with his former practice. Most of his novels had emphasized the unpredictability of human fate, the inscrutability of the workings of the colossal Prince of the World against whom Eustacia Vye railed. Character after character had echoed Henery Fray's opinion that 'your lot is your lot, and Scripture is nothing'. It is not at all surprising that many readers of the Wessex novels have come to the conclusion that fatalism, defined in one way or another, is Hardy's philosophy of life. These readers have not read *The Mayor of Casterbridge* with the care it merits and rewards. For, during the six months while he lay flat on his back in Upper Tooting, Hardy had had opportunity to plumb the shallowness of Henery Fray's opinion. The novelist had come to realize that a theory which might serve to explain the success or failure of a man working with the soil and the weather would not serve to explain the careers of such men as Hardy had come to know at the Savile Club in London. Edmund Gosse was not Edmund Gosse because of his 'lot'. George Curzon was not George Curzon because of Fate. Novalis, whom Hardy had been reading, summed the point up by writing 'Character is Fate' ,and the novelist now decided to make the life and death of his Man of Character illustrate the truth of Novalis's observation.

The constitution of Henchard's character is worth lingering over for a moment, since he is the most forceful and one of the most original characters that Hardy ever drew. The author conceived of him as a truly heroic man cast in Shakespearean mould. Some critics have, in fact, thought that Hardy's inspiration for Henchard was derived from Shakespeare. Professor Harvey C. Webster, for example, remarks that Henchard's

first folly in selling his wife 'inevitably recalls the first scene of
King Lear', and that Henchard's final defeat and isolation 'inevitably and with even more pathetic force recall Lear's lonely
death. . . . In a sense he is as tragic as Lear . . . ; in another
sense he is still more pathetic, for it is only his Fool, Whittle,
who attends him at his death.'[20] Other critics have sensed
traces of the influence of Aeschylus, or of the Bible, either
directly or by way of Milton's *Samson Agonistes*. Professor De
Sola Pinto, on the other hand—perhaps remembering Hardy's
purchase of *Aristotle* (as translated by Theodore Buckley) with
part of his prize money in 1863—observes that Henchard
'fulfils perfectly Aristotle's definition of the tragic hero: "a man
not eminently good or just, yet whose misfortune is brought
about not by vice, but by some error or frailty"'.[21]

It is not necessary, however, to look as far as to Aristotle and
Aeschylus, to Milton or to Shakespeare, if one is seeking the
immediate source of Hardy's conception of his Man of Character.
Just six months before Hardy began to write about Henchard,
a book appeared in London—the *Autobiography* of Anthony
Trollope—in which we can find all that we need in our search.
Trollope had died on November 3, 1882, and a year later
everyone was reading his *Autobiography*. Hardy had long been
interested in this older novelist. He had bought a copy of
Barchester Towers to send to his sister, for Trollope's 'Barsetshire' was the talk of London when young Hardy arrived there
in 1862. Later, in the seventies, Hardy bought a copy of *The
Eustace Diamonds* and afterwards expressed his admiration for
its construction. 'I like Trollope,' he said to a caller, later on.
'You know, at one time, it was thought he was going to be
recognized as the greatest of the Victorian novelists. Dickens
was said to be too much of a caricaturist; Thackeray too much
of a satirist. Trollope was put forward as the happy mean.'[22]
In the *Autobiography* Trollope had written:

Just before Christmas my brother died, and was buried at Bruges.
In the following February my father died, and was buried alongside
of him. I sometimes look back, meditating for hours together, on his
adverse fate. He was a man of great parts, with immense capacity for
work, physically strong very much beyond the average of men,
addicted to no vices, carried off by no pleasures, affectionate by
nature, most anxious for the welfare of his children, born to fair

fortunes,—who, when he started in the world, may be said to have had everything at his feet. But everything went wrong with him. The touch of his hand seemed to create failure. He embarked in one hopeless enterprise after another, spending on each all the money he could at the time command. But the worst curse to him of all was a temper so irritable that even those whom he loved the best could not endure it. We were all estranged from him, and yet I believe that he would have given his heart's blood for any of us. His life as I knew it was one long tragedy.

This analysis of the character of Trollope's father gives us a catalogue of Michael Henchard's traits. The 'great parts', the 'immense capacity for work', the physical strength, the affectionate nature, the irritable temper, the estrangement from his family, the business folly, the final death in an alien place, all are his. Henchard's life, like that of Trollope's father, was one long tragedy. No one who has previously read Trollope's description of his father can accuse Hardy of overdrawing in his portraiture of the mayor of Casterbridge. And this time there is no ground for talking about plagiarism, since whatever borrowing Hardy may have done was achieved legitimately and executed with utmost skill and originality.

In choosing a time for the action of his novel, Hardy went back to the period when Trollope's father was alive. So specific is the novelist about his dates that it is not only possible, it is quite easy, to reconstruct the calendar he followed in writing *The Mayor of Casterbridge*. Henchard sells his wife on Saturday, September 15, 1827, and on the next day makes his vow to touch no liquor for twenty-one years. The reader who notices that the novel opens with an unspecific reference to 'one evening of late summer before the nineteenth century had reached one-third of its span', may wonder how this vague statement can be translated into 'Saturday, September 15, 1827'. He has only to remain alert, however, ready to take advantage of all the hints the author drops along the way—Candlemas Fair (February 2, 1847), for example, falls on a Tuesday; Henchard's twenty-one-year vow expires on September 16, 1848—to see that Hardy made careful plans to time the action of this novel so that it would follow immediately upon the heels of the action in *The Return of the Native*. The main part of the action in *The Mayor* falls between 1846 and 1849. Working backwards

for twenty-one years from that decade, one arrives at the
eighteen-twenties and is therefore not at all surprised when an
unpublished letter of Hardy's turns up confirming these de-
ductions—a letter that refers to the 'frequent instances [of
wife-selling] here [at Dorchester] between 1820 and 1830, the
supposed time of the sale in *The Mayor of Casterbridge*'. One can
therefore confidently date the arrival of Susan and her eighteen-
year-old daughter in 'Casterbridge' on Friday, September 18,
1846. Just a year later, Henchard's unsavoury past was revealed.
A year after that, his twenty-one-year-old vow expired.

In creating the events which Hardy proposed to fit into this
time-scheme, he showed an amazing resourcefulness as well as a
striking improvement in his handling of the logic of events.
There is a much smaller amount of coincidence in this novel.
One episode is merged so reasonably and naturally into the next
that the gradual decline of Henchard's fortunes seems not only
plausible but inevitable.

The novel is rich in vivid and memorable scenes. Hardy's
invention seems never to flag. The fight in the granary-loft
between Farfrae and Henchard, with one arm of the latter tied
against his side so that his superior strength might be no unfair
advantage to him; Henchard on the brink of Ten Hatches Weir,
planning suicide and horrified to see his own effigy come floating
down the stream as if dead in the water before him; Henchard
on the ramparts of Mai Dun Castle, telescope in hand, spying
on Elizabeth-Jane's meetings with Farfrae; the fatal skimming-
ton-ride of the 'two images on a donkey, back to back, their
elbows tied to one another's; the startling announcement that
'Michael Henchard have busted out drinking after taking nothing for twenty-one years'—these are only a few of the incidents
which are hard to forget. When Robert Barnes came to draw
twenty illustrations for the serialization of this novel in the
Graphic, there was no dearth of dramatic incidents for him to
make use of. In the opinion of some, Barnes's illustrations for
The Mayor of Casterbridge are 'the best of the Hardy serial illustrations', possibly 'because of their close attention to detail and
expression, and their fidelity to the novel'.[23]

Thanks to careful and deliberate planning, *The Mayor of
Casterbridge* appeared simultaneously in the *Graphic* in London
and in *Harper's Weekly* in New York, running from January 2 to

May 15, 1886. After the serialization had ended, the novel was
published as a book—in two volumes in London by Smith,
Elder & Co., and in one volume in New York by Henry Holt.
In both cities, the publishers acted with extreme caution,
though for different reasons. Smith, Elder printed only 758
copies, bound only 650, and sold only 613. This poor showing
ended Smith, Elder's relations with Hardy. They had begun
publishing him in 1874, had dropped him for five years, 1881–5
(the period of *A Laodicean*, *Two on a Tower*, and *The Romantic
Adventures of a Milkmaid*), and had resumed relations with
obvious hesitation. After *The Mayor* had sold less than seven
hundred copies, they were content to let Hardy look elsewhere
in London for a publisher. In New York the situation was
similar but not identical.

Henry Holt's experience with piratical American publishers
led him to issue *The Mayor* not only as a dollar book in his
Leisure Hour series, but also as a thirty-cent paper-back in his
Leisure Moment series. Even this move did not forestall activity
by the pirates. Almost immediately George Munro offered the
novel in New York for twenty cents. His brother Norman L.
Munro and the J. W. Lovell Company soon had two more
twenty-cent editions on the market. M. J. Ivers added another.
Six New York *Mayors* in one year produced no profit for Holt
and of course no royalty for Hardy. Henry Holt decided that he
had had enough. 'By an amicable arrangement' he ceded all his
'rights' in Hardy to Harper & Brothers and received from them
in return their rights in William Edward Norris.

Fortunately for the feelings of the hypersensitive author, there
is more than one kind of success. Commercially unsuccessful
though *The Mayor of Casterbridge* may have been, there can be no
doubt about its great success in the eyes of the critics. Applause
was universal. 'Michael Henchard,' declared William Sharp, 'is
one of Mr. Hardy's most noteworthy creations.' George Gissing
wrote to Hardy to say that in his books he had 'constantly found
refreshment and onward help'. Edmund Gosse wrote to William
Dean Howells in New York that Hardy was without doubt 'our
greatest novelist over here'. Every aspect of the novel came in
for praise. Not only was Henchard acclaimed as one of Hardy's
greatest creations, but almost every other character received a
share of the applause. Elizabeth-Jane has almost as slight a rôle

as has Cordelia in *King Lear*, yet she is depicted with vividness and charm. One critic observed that Hardy had nowhere else ever painted 'a woman with such tenderness, . . . natural delicacy, good sense, and honesty of purpose'. Another declared that she provides a centre of stability in the Casterbridge tragedy not unlike Kent's rôle in *King Lear*. As Professor De Sola Pinto remarks: 'it is fitting that she should speak those last words after the revelation of Henchard's terrible testament, words that express a depth of emotion in simple prose as admirably as any Greek or Elizabethan could have expressed it in verse: "O Donald! . . . What bitterness lies there. . . . But there's no altering—so it must be" '. Professor J. F. A. Pyre later remarked that Elizabeth-Jane is so sympathetically drawn that 'we may easily be tempted' to regard her philosophy of stoic renunciation as Hardy's own.

Even the lesser characters have earned praise. There is not much room for humour in this novel, but Constable Blowbody, Mr. Grower, and Stubberd, who try to find the men responsible for the 'skimmington' ride, provide a moment of entertainment not unlike that provided in another age by Dogberry and Verges. And the Hostess in *Henry the Fifth* may, by her description of Falstaff's death, have taught Hardy how to achieve one of the most poetic passages in *The Mayor*, Mother Cuxsom's touching elegy on Mrs. Henchard: 'Well, poor soul, she is powerless to hinder that or anything now. . . . And all her . . . wishes and ways will all be as nothing!'

Among the delighted readers of *The Mayor of Casterbridge* was Miss Rebekah Owen of New York City. She had become an enthusiastic reader of Hardy's books and had organized among her friends in New York a T.H.B.L. (as she called it): a league of Thomas Hardy Book Lovers, or a Thomas Hardy Book League. In 1892 she and her sister Catharine went to England, settled in Dorchester, and eventually made Hardy's acquaintance. Upon purchasing a copy of *The Mayor of Casterbridge* there, Miss Owen was surprised to discover that the story in her Dorchester copy of the book had a different ending from that with which she had become familiar in America. When she asked Hardy about this, he said that he had changed the ending in revising the serial version for its London appearance in book form, because he had come to believe that it weakened the story to have Henchard go away from Casterbridge twice. Hardy had therefore omitted 'nearly a chapter' dealing with Henchard's return to Elizabeth-Jane's wedding, his purchase of the caged goldfinch, and the slow starvation of the poor bird after his embittered departure from Casterbridge. Miss Owen argued with Hardy, maintaining that he was wrong in thinking that these events weakened the story. She finally convinced him, and he promised that in a new edition of the novel he would restore the goldfinch, the return to the wedding, and the second departure. He carried out his promise in 1895, when *The Mayor of Casterbridge* appeared with a preface. In this edition Hardy called attention to the restoration of the previously omitted passage and stated that it 'was made at the instance of some good judges across the Atlantic, who strongly represented that the home edition suffered from the omission'.[24]

In the course of the nearly four-score years that have passed since the first publication of the novel, *The Mayor of Casterbridge* has attained wide use in schools, colleges, and universities, both in England and America, and tens of thousands of students have thus become acquainted with Hardy's Man of Character. Unfortunately, in presenting Henchard to these students, editorial guidance has sometimes been blind. One textbook edition of the novel assures the unwary student that 'in no other writing is Hardy more clearly a fatalist . . . ; in no other book does he urge more unmistakably his belief that men and women are but helpless puppets in the hands of mischievous fate'. One can only wonder whether this unobservant editor ever read Chapter XVII of the novel. This is the chapter in which we are told that Farfrae's trade increased, *not* because of his good luck. 'Most probably luck had little to do with it. "Character is Fate", said Novalis, and Farfrae's character was just the reverse of Henchard's.' Men *are* sometimes the masters of their fate.

Probably one of the best comments, as well as one of the briefest, ever made on *The Mayor of Casterbridge* was made by Robert Louis Stevenson when the novel was only a few weeks old. 'Henchard is a great fellow,' wrote R. L. S. in 1886, 'and Dorchester is touched in with the hand of a master.'[25] Deservedly, *The Mayor of Casterbridge* has become one of the classics of English literature.

XII

Atmosphere of Cider

THE first novel written by Hardy after he had moved into Max Gate was *The Woodlanders*. The years of its creation, 1886 and 1887, constitute an important period in his career for a variety of reasons. For one thing, he then turned a financial corner. Although Smith, Elder & Co. had sold only a little more than six hundred copies of *The Mayor*, the critical acclaim given this book enabled Macmillan & Co. to dispose of nearly five thousand copies of *The Woodlanders* a year hence. In 1887 Sampson Low issued a new one-volume edition of *The Mayor* and, uniform with it, they published reissues of six other novels by Hardy. This seven-volume 'set' (if the uniform bindings permit us to call it that) constitutes the first collected edition of Hardy's works. The set was not complete, for some of the Wessex novels were missing and it was not designated as a Collected Edition in the books themselves; but the uniform bindings indicated to the public that here was an important author whose 'works' were worth buying, instead of merely getting them from a Rental Library.

Equally important in Hardy's own eyes was his improvement in prestige. Alexander Macmillan had declined to publish *The Poor Man and the Lady*; he had rejected *Desperate Remedies*; he had been so cool over *Under the Greenwood Tree* that Hardy had interpreted his letter as another rejection. After nearly eighteen years of failure in knocking at the Macmillan door, Hardy must have been more than delighted when Mowbray Morris, editor of *Macmillan's Magazine*, suddenly asked Hardy for a serial novel. Morris's inquiry had actually reached Hardy when he was doubly involved—with the erection of Max Gate and the writing of *The Mayor of Casterbridge*—but as soon as those responsibilities had been taken care of, Hardy turned with unusual satisfaction to the writing of *The Woodlanders*. In entering the Macmillan portal at long last, he could (as he once remarked to Robert Louis Stevenson) 'feel several inches taller'. He began work on *The Woodlanders* in November 1885 and finished it in February 1887. The novel was serialized in *Macmillan's Magazine* from May 1886 to April 1887 (twelve monthly parts) and was issued in America in *Harper's Bazar* in forty-eight weekly instalments, May 15, 1886, to April 9, 1887. The shadow of Mrs. Grundy was cast over the London serialization (in Chapter XX, in which Suke Damson and Fitzpiers re-enter Little Hintock at day-break), but, surprisingly enough, this passage remained un-bowdlerized in *Harper's Bazar*.

Hardy set the action of the new novel in the wooded region that lay a dozen or fifteen miles north-west of Dorchester. This was a neighbourhood of which he had made no previous fictional use but one he knew well and was 'very fond of'.[1] He afterwards specified that his woodlanders lived 'in the hamlets of Hermitage, Middlemarch, Lyons Gate, Revels Inn, Holnest, Melbury Bubb, etc.,—all lying more or less under the eminence called High Stoy, just beyond Minterne and Dogbury Gate'. The names 'Little Hintock' and 'Great Hintock' were obviously suggested by Minterne Parva and Minterne Magna, but in referring to 'Little Hintock' in his April 1912 preface to the novel Hardy wrote: 'I may as well confess here . . . that I do not know where that hamlet is.' A statement like this must not be taken too literally. Hardy often took liberties with his settings, stretching or contracting their geography to suit his fictional purposes, and he naturally saw no point in advertising what he had done. But when he wished to, he could find every feature of his terrain—valleys, hills, hamlets, houses, roads, bridges, woods—and could describe them with a fidelity and vividness unparalleled in English literature. One of the places that has often baffled literary-minded tourists is the location of the foliage-hidden mansion of Mrs. Charmond in Chapter VIII of *The Woodlanders*. 'It stood in a hole,' says Hardy, 'but the hole was full of beauty.' But where was that hole? When Donald Maxwell visited Dorset in the course of preparing the illustrations for his book of Hardy landscapes,[2] he could not find Felice Charmond's abode, but Hardy himself finally gave the artist a tip. Maxwell thereupon trekked across country twelve miles and soon located 'this large house' near Blandford, just where Hardy had told him to look. 'Turnworth House is evidently the model, situation and all, for "Hintock House".' The setting for *The Woodlanders* was, as Hardy himself described it, 'one of those sequestered spots outside the gates of the world where ... dramas of a grandeur and unity truly Sophoclean are enacted in the real, by virtue of the concentrated passions and closely-knit interdependence of the lives therein'.[3]

Hardy was equally clear-eyed and specific about the time selected for the action of the novel. The 'new statute' in Chapter XXXVII was a modification of the English divorce law made in 1878. The reference to the 'South Carolina gentleman' (Chapter XLIII) who had left the South after the failure of the Confederate cause (Chapter XXI) helps further to date the action and enables us to discover that Hardy's time-chart was designed to cover two and a half years from Christmas 1876 to March 1879. The action in *The Woodlanders* was thus planned to follow immediately upon the heels of the action in *Far from the Madding Crowd*.

The most important aspect of the corner which Hardy turned in 1886–7 has not yet been mentioned. In *The Woodlanders* he shifted his philosophical point of view. Previous novels of his, up to *The Mayor of Casterbridge*, had expressed with ever-increasing frankness his rebellious feelings about the fundamental conditions of existence in a badly constituted world. From this youthful fist-shaking at the cosmos, Hardy had progressed (as we have seen in the last chapter) to a recognition that man's unhappiness on earth is often due, not to defects in Nature, but to the frailties of human nature. Now, in *The Woodlanders*, he was to turn for the first time to question seriously how far the organization of society itself, how far man-made laws and conventions, are responsible for man's unhappiness. When the passionate gentleman from South Carolina turns up in Little Hintock, he is *not* called the agent of Heaven's persistent irony. When Grace Melbury's marriage proves a failure, Hardy does *not* make her rail at some colossal Prince of the World who ruled her lot; he does *not* allow the philosophizing Fitzpiers to remind her that

Character is Fate. Hardy makes her wonder 'whether God did really join them together' (Chapter XLVII) or whether a law made by Parliament in London was at fault. Or was it her father's foolish social ambition? or her own 'recent off-handedness'?

The interest of this wondering whether God had really joined them together 'does not lie', William R. Rutland observes, 'in whether it is true . . . but in its being there at all. For it . . . strikes a note which is wholly new in Hardy's fiction. . . . His quarrel with human society for its attitude toward sexual relationships . . . is inaugurated in *The Woodlanders*.'[4] A hasty and careless reader of the novel may miss this point, especially if he becomes confused by the fact that Hardy's pen has left traces of *all* his differing ways of looking at the world. Creedle and John South, for example, share Hardy's earlier fatalistic views. Creedle's remark in Chapter XII that 'The words of the faithful be only as wind' might have come out of the pages of *Far from the Madding Crowd*, and Fitzpier's remark in Chapter XXVI on 'how powerless is the human will against predestination' might have been lifted from *The Return of the Native*. But when we hear Melbury's comments on Fitzpiers as a 'forlorn hope' of a husband (Chapter XLVIII), we are again in the atmosphere of *The Mayor* with its reminder that 'Character is Fate'. The first page of Hardy's preface to *The Woodlanders*, however, with its questionings about 'how to afford the greatest happiness to human society', and the references to 'the new law' in Chapter XXXVIII and to 'the laws and ordinances' in Chapter XXXIX and to George Melbury's 'cruel deception' regarding the new law, all point to Hardy's most recently acquired outlook.

The theme of the story is one that Hardy had used before and was to use yet again—the clash between rustic simplicity and urban veneer, between self-sacrificing loyalty and dissatisfied selfishness. George Melbury is eager to make a 'good match' for his daughter; to satisfy him the daughter turns her back on her steadfast rural admirer Giles Winterborne and accepts the attentions of the flashy Dr. Fitzpiers. He is a piece of human flotsam who is as unreconciled to the placid life of the woodlanders as Eustacia Vye was to life on Egdon Heath. The doctor marries Grace, however, just as Eustacia married Clym, and again with tragic results. Giles's happiness founders in the shoals of Melbury's foolish social ambition, and the sophisticated representatives of urban society who come to the woodlands bring nothing but bitterness and death in their train.

The tragedy in *The Woodlanders* is relieved by glowing accounts of the activities of the humble folk who live 'outside the gates of the world'. The cider making, in which Hardy's father was an expert, is described with vividness and affection; and, though the words are applied to Giles Winterborne, we can easily surmise that Hardy saw his own father when he wrote:

He looked and smelt like Autumn's very brother, his face being sunburnt to wheat-colour, his eyes blue as corn-flowers, his sleeves and leggings dyed with fruit-stains, his hands clammy with the sweet juice of apples, his hat sprinkled with pips, and everywhere about him that atmosphere of cider which at its first return each season has such an indescribable fascination for those who have been born and bred among the orchards.

The return not of autumn alone, but of each season, had a fascination for Hardy, and no Wessex novel is richer than *The Woodlanders* in descriptions of the seasons.

Some of the charm of this novel comes from the descriptions of Wessex customs, as in the scene in which the Hintock maids go into the woods on Midsummer Eve 'to attempt some spell or enchantment which would afford them a glimpse of their future partners for life'. Even in scenes of greater dramatic significance—such as that in which Fitzpiers goes riding off to visit Mrs. Charmond, while Grace watches him until both horse and rider become a mere speck—even in such scenes there is quiet picturesqueness. Critics have often found fault with Hardy's prose style: it can be, and often is, gnarled and awkward; but in *The Woodlanders* there are many passages which are stylistically admirable, where the blending of description and drama, of setting and character, is done with simple and effective dignity. The picture of Dr. Fitzpiers on the sleek mare, set in relief against the deep violet of the evening sky, is a striking one, but it is not *merely* a picture:

So the infatuated surgeon went along the gorgeous autumn landscape of White-Hart Vale, surrounded by orchards lustrous with the reds of apple-crops, berries and foliage, the whole intensified by the gilding of the declining sun. The earth this year had been prodigally bountiful, and now was the supreme moment of her bounty. In the poorest spots the hedges were bowed with haws and blackberries; acorns cracked underfoot, and the burst husks of chestnuts lay exposing their auburn contents as if arranged by anxious sellers in a fruit-market. In all this proud show some kernels were unsound as her [Grace's] own situation, and she wondered if there were one world in the universe where the fruit had no worm, and marriage no sorrow.

In Grace Melbury's thought, nature and man are associated as equally subject to the imperfections of the universe. Nature is not the malign cause of human troubles but a fellow-sufferer with man.

Upon the publication of *The Woodlanders*, Hardy had the satisfaction of hearing a chorus of praise that was almost unanimous. The *Saturday Review* announced that this novel contained some of the best writing that Hardy had ever done. The *Athenaeum* declared: 'It should be read by all who can tell masterly work in fiction when they see it.' Robert Louis Stevenson, preparing to leave England for the last time, insisted on carrying away with him the three volumes of *The Woodlanders*. Since he was to sail on Monday, August 22, 1887, he was in London on Sunday the twenty-first ready for the embarkation, but the book shops were all closed. Stevenson appealed to Edmund Gosse for help, and Gosse long remembered how he 'had to scour London that Sunday afternoon' in order to find a copy of 'Mr. Hardy's beautiful romance, *The Woodlanders*. . . . In the evening . . . I . . . returned . . . with the three volumes, borrowed or stolen somewhere.' Later judgments agreed with those of Stevenson and Gosse. '*The Woodlanders* is, to my thinking,' declared Sir Arthur Quiller-Couch, 'Hardy's loveliest if not his strongest book.' Alfred Austin sent Hardy a copy of his *Love's Widowhood* (1889) inscribed 'To the Author of *The Woodlanders*'.

'If I had to name the finest English novel,' Arnold Bennett declared, later still, 'I should undoubtedly choose *The Woodlanders*.' Twentieth-century judgments have echoed those of the Victorian critics. Cyril Aldred called *The Woodlanders* 'the most balanced and satisfying' of the Wessex novels. John A. Steuart remarked: 'Such a book as *The Woodlanders* is enough to make one feel proud of one's generation.'[5] In America the same verdict was rendered. Professor William Lyon Phelps called *The Woodlanders* 'the most beautiful and most noble of Hardy's novels'. Professor Samuel C. Chew described it as 'the most tender of all Hardy's books'. A. Edward Newton regarded it as 'one of the best novels of the last century'. James M. Barrie, after re-reading a number of the Wessex novels, eventually declared: 'I have found that *The Woodlanders* is the most complete, so to speak, of all. I have seldom known any book that makes the reader so much one of the company, that leaves him with the feeling that he was there. It really is an epitome of life with its joys and sorrows, and it is also a very consoling book.' Hardy himself came to share some of these judgments. On April 22, 1912, he wrote to a friend: 'On taking up *The Woodlanders* and reading it after many years, I think I like it *as a story* the best of all. . . . It seems a more quaint and fresh story than *the Native*, and the characters are very distinctly drawn.'[6]

Other critics have followed Hardy's example in comparing one of his books with another. Arthur McDowall declares that *The Return of the Native* 'has no superior among Hardy's tragic novels as a work of art' but he thinks that Michael Henchard is 'the most original as well as the most forcible character Hardy ever drew'. In *The Woodlanders*, however, 'there is no dominating character at the centre . . . and . . . the book is a study of drifting characters'.[7] Few readers are likely to agree that Marty South and Giles Winterborne are 'drifting characters', but Hardy himself once confessed to regarding Grace Melbury in that light. On September 13, 1893, he remarked to Rebekah Owen that 'Grace never interested him much; he was provoked with her all along. If she would have done a really self-abandoned, impassioned thing . . . , he could have made a fine tragic ending to the book, but she was too commonplace and strait-laced and he could not make her.'[8] Grace obviously was no Eustacia Vye.

About Marty South, however, there is only one critical opinion. Every reader comes to recognize that she is the real heroine of the story, not Grace Melbury. Marty South is one of the reasons for the great charm of *The Woodlanders*. The opening scene presents her to us, and the last scene is wholly hers. 'None but a great artist,' Lionel Johnson observed in 1894, 'could have closed his work thus perfectly, with that passionate simplicity of speech, straight from the heart of a noble woman, whose silent and austere suffering . . . had given so grave a beauty to the tragic play.'

Giles Winterborne, like Gabriel Oak, is one of Hardy's long-suffering sons of the soil. He is a milder man than Oak, less ambitious, less confident, less forceful. But he has Oak's sterling character. He is loyal to the core and faithful in that loyalty unto death. He is the only one in all the Wessex novels to give his life for love. Although his dying is not the dramatic death of a Sydney Carton, he earns the supremely simple final eulogy pronounced by Marty South: 'I never can forget 'ee, for you was a good man, and did good things.' Professor Samuel C. Chew, many years later, drew attention to the significance of the admiration which Hardy had so obviously lavished upon a man like Winterborne, a man 'with courage, resourcefulness, patience, endurance, clear-sightedness, tenderness, tolerance, forbearance, and unselfishness', but at the same time a man who (as Chapter XXXIX of the novel tells us) 'was unrefined' in the eyes of polite society. In Chapter XLV the author comments on 'how little acquirements and culture weigh beside sterling personal character'; in reading those words we cannot fail to sense that when Hardy wrote them he had his own domestic situation in mind.

In more recent years critics have been less inclined to show enthusiasm for the beauties of *The Woodlanders* than to express regret over some of its defects. After reading about 'a Wouvermans eccentricity' in Chapter XXVIII, W. J. Dawson comments thus: 'Hardy's constant references to art . . . are so frequent that, without a tolerably competent knowledge of Dutch and Italian pictures many of his allusions will be meaningless to his readers, and in purely rural drama it is irritating . . . to be distracted by such allusions.' In Chapter XVI Dr. Fitzpiers makes Winterborne stand and wait while he quotes—from memory!—an entire Spenserian stanza out of Canto II of Shelley's poem *The Revolt of Islam*. On a number of pages, Hardy the ex-architect takes command and banishes Hardy the novelist. In Chapter XXIII, for example, Grace's visit to Sherton Castle involves us in talk about 'the lower vaulting . . . surmounted by the *crochet* capital', and in Chapter XLVIII Melbury's search for his daughter has to be interrupted long enough for us to learn that the Earl of Wessex Hotel at 'Sherton Abbas'

(Hardy's fictional name for Sherborne) had been 'rebuilt contemporaneously with the construction of the railway'. In Chapter XXVI the references to Heidelberg and Baden-Baden carry us back to Hardy's visit to the Black Forest in 1876—the Rhine tour which he had already made use of in *A Laodicean*. More annoying still, to some readers, are the contrivances of the plot. Sylva Norman, for example, grumbles about how 'the story bumps and creaks by its continued dependence upon accidents with horses, storms, and man-traps'. Cyril Aldred, on the other hand, thinks that the plot is quite plausible and that 'the events unfold naturally'. Professor William T. Brewster agrees that in *The Woodlanders* Hardy tells his story 'without the introduction of chance, caprice, fate, or irony'.

With whatever defects, *The Woodlanders* remains one of Hardy's great works. If, among his greatest, it is the one least frequently read nowadays, this is partly because of the fact that there are four or five even greater among the Wessex novels. The opinion of a Canadian critic (Professor George Herbert Clarke) is a safe one: '*The Woodlanders* is a work in which Hardy's powers as a novelist may be studied to great advantage.'

In any examination of what the years 1886–7 meant to Thomas Hardy one feature is certain to stand out as having, in Hardy's own eyes, extreme importance. The influence of Edmund Gosse is here evident. Gosse—now a friend of ten years' standing—not only wrote poetry; he got it published. In 1885, when his *Firdausi in Exile and Other Poems* appeared, he sent Hardy a copy. In this volume Hardy found a poem entitled 'Two Points of View' which took his fancy. In Chapter XXV of *The Woodlanders* he quoted the third and fourth stanzas of the poem and acknowledged the lines as the work of 'a contemporary poet'. Gosse's reputation as an essayist, critic, and biographer has now, by 1965, so completely effaced his reputation as a poet that readers of *The Woodlanders* have often been puzzled as to the identity of the 'contemporary poet' to whom Hardy referred. They have even wondered whether the novelist was here slyly slipping into the novel a poem of his own. Hardy also inserted lines or words from many another poet besides Edmund Gosse, and the careful reader of *The Woodlanders* will detect at least a dozen: Arnold, Browning, Chatterton, Congreve, Herbert, Homer, Keats, Shakespeare, Shelley, Swin-

burne, Tennyson, and Wordsworth. Gosse was in good company. The result of all this quickened interest in poetry was that
Hardy himself began composing verses once again. For twenty
years, while engaged in the process of earning a living, he had
devoted himself exclusively to prose. This long winter was now
over, and the poetic sap began to flow once again in his veins.
His poem 'The Pine Planters', though not published until 1909
(in *Time's Laughingstocks*), carries a subtitle, 'Marty South's
Reverie', which invites the surmise that it was composed at the
same time as *The Woodlanders*.

Another poem, 'In a Wood', can with even greater confidence
be assigned to the time of *The Woodlanders*, for not only did
Hardy write on his manuscript '*Vide* [see] "The Woodlanders"'
but also added the dates '1887: 1896'—the second date being
that of such revision as he gave to the poem before printing it in
1898 in *Wessex Poems*. (The manuscript of the poem is now in
the library of the Birmingham City Museum.) This important
poem—important for a number of reasons—has had a curious
history. The second Mrs. Hardy thought that it was, like 'The
Pine Planters', a reverie of Marty South, but several lines in the
poem contradict this idea. 'In a Wood' is Hardy's own reverie,
not Marty South's. He is the one who was 'spirit-lame'. Hardy
himself is the one who felt 'city-opprest' and who came to 'this
wood' in search of 'release from men's unrest'. J. Middleton
Murry once referred to this poem as 'the song in *The Woodlanders*',[9] but the poem is *not* 'in' *The Woodlanders*. Murry's error
is understandable, in view of the fact that Hardy's publishers
inadvertently changed his Latin '*Vide*' to read 'From', and the
poem is still designated as 'From *The Woodlanders*' in as recent
an edition of the *Collected Poems* as that of 1952. One of Hardy's
French readers, Georges Lasselin, later pointed out that 'this
poem only summarizes a description in *The Woodlanders*',[10] but
he refrained from trying to identify any specific passage in the
novel. In Chapter XIX Dr. Fitzpiers is allowed to repeat some
of Hardy's own recent experience—a reading of Friedrich
Schleiermacher, for example, and a preferring 'the ideal world
to the real, and the discovery of principles to their application'.
But Fitzpiers never attains to the philosophical conclusion of
the last stanza of 'In a Wood', and there is no one else in the
novel who shares the author's own philosophizing habit and

ability. The poem therefore remains (as stated above) Hardy's own 'reverie':

> Since, then, no grace I find
>   Taught me of trees,
> Turn I back to my kind,
>   Worthy as these.
> There at least smiles abound,
> There discourse trills around,
> There, now and then, are found
>   Life-loyalties.

In view of the fact that some published comments on this poem show a regrettable inability on the part of the commentator to read the lines properly—i.e., as Hardy meant them to be read—it may be well for the reader to notice that Hardy was here using the stanzaic form made famous by Tennyson's 'Charge of the Light Brigade'—eight dactylic dimeter lines, rhyming *abab cccb*. Hardy had recently been re-reading Tennyson; the poet-laureate is quoted or referred to three times in *The Woodlanders*. The use of a dactylic rhythm is admittedly an extremely rare choice by Hardy, but its use in 'In a Wood' is not an unnatural one and no reader of the poem ought to try to distort the rhythm into something else.

In his 'turning back' from trees to mankind, in his finding among men 'now and then . . . life-loyalties', we can notice the further development in Hardy's mind of what was (at the time when Clym Yeobright was being created) no more than a vague desire 'to buckle to and teach men how to breast the misery they are born to'. Life-loyalty to his fellow-men was one of the philosophical 'principles' discovered by Hardy since the date of *the Native*. He had come to see that the writing of novels solely for entertainment or amusement is not enough. He wished to teach men what 'loyalty' means, what social responsibility is, what human relationships imply and involve. On March 4, 1886, Hardy wrote in his notebook: 'The human race [is] to be shown as one great network or tissue which quivers in every part when one point is shaken, like a spider's web if touched.'[11] As a writer in the London *Times Literary Supplement* observed only a few years ago, 'Hardy is not customarily regarded as a social reformer, but is not this idea of the quivering human web the starting-point of the United Nations . . . ?'

The years 1886–7 therefore mark, in addition to all their other features, the development in Hardy's mind of a desire to teach, to 'show' readers what they 'ought' to be shown. The didactic note glimpsed in *The Woodlanders* is destined to become more pronounced in the two great novels yet to be written, but its appearance in 1887 ought not to be missed by the observant student of Hardy's career.

As soon as Hardy had completed his revision of the text of the serial version of the novel for the three-volume edition published by Macmillan & Company, he and his wife went off for a month's tour of Italy—his first visit there. The literary outcome of this excursion was a series of eight 'poems of pilgrimage', as Hardy called them—some sketched on the spot, others composed later, but none of them of any great importance. They testify to the pleasure he took in reading Shelley and Keats, but they also demonstrate that, after twenty years of exclusive addiction to prose-writing, he had not yet attained ease in handling verse.

Upon his return from Italy, Hardy was happy to learn from Frederick Macmillan that *The Woodlanders* had sold so well that the firm was already prepared to reprint the novel—this time in one volume. Hardy again revised the text, making further improvements in style, and was rewarded by a third large printing of the novel before the year 1887 was over.

The House of Macmillan, now that its door had been opened to Hardy, was naturally pleased with the result, and asked Hardy for more. Since no full-length novel was ready, he put five of his short stories together, and *Wessex Tales* was published by Macmillan early in 1888. On Browning's birthday (May 7) Hardy sent him a copy of the new book. He also gave a copy to Mrs. Francis Jeune, one of the London hostesses whose hospitality Hardy had enjoyed. Before a year had passed Macmillan & Company reissued *Wessex Tales* in an edition of twice the number of copies, and in America Harper & Brothers published *Wessex Tales* with a portrait of the author—the first time any reader of Hardy's work had had a chance to see what he looked like. At that date Hardy was wearing a full beard.

A month after sending the birthday gift to Robert Browning, Hardy was forty-eight years old. He was now upon the threshold of his most successful act of literary creation.

XIII

'A Pure Woman
Faithfully Presented'

AS soon as *Wessex Tales* was off his hands, Hardy went with his wife to Paris and spent two weeks there in early June. He had been in Paris thrice before—in September 1874 (on his honeymoon), in 1882 (an October visit of several weeks), and in 1887 (on his way back from Italy). This time he visited the Archives Nationales, probably with no conscious intent of preparing for work on *The Dynasts*, which was still fifteen years off in the future, but with an unconscious instinct for improving his grasp of Napoleonic times.

Upon his return to England, Hardy was greeted with a greatly increased volume of requests from editors and publishers. H. Quilter wanted a story for the *Universal Magazine*, and in August Hardy sent him 'A Tragedy of Two Ambitions' (published in December 1888). Edward Arnold wanted a novel to serialize in *Murray's Magazine*; Mowbray Morris would like something more for *Macmillan's Magazine*; James R. Osgood (London agent for Harper & Brothers) sought Hardy's help in making arrangements for three illustrations for 'The First Countess of Wessex' (to be published in *Harper's Magazine*); and W. F. Tillotson, head of the newspaper-syndicate firm of W. F. Tillotson & Son in Bolton (a Lancashire town, ten miles from Manchester), requested a novel for serialization in their newspapers. From among these offers, Hardy chose the one from Bolton, probably for no more cogent reason than that the Tillotsons offered better terms. Hardy agreed to supply the syndicate with a novel for serialization a year hence.

He began making plans for the new story and in his correspondence with Tillotson referred to it as 'Too Late Beloved'. (The Tillotson firm sometimes called it 'Too Late, Beloved!'[1]) Hardy planned to write about a milkmaid, not about a girl like Margery Tucker, the milkmaid whose 'Romantic Adventures' he had related only five years before, but about a much more carefully conceived heroine who would combine the fire of Eustacia Vye, the charm of Bathsheba Everdene, the emotional nature of Marty South, and the tender resignation of Elizabeth-Jane in *The Mayor*. The new milkmaid would, in short, be a complex creature of heroic stature. Hardy clarified his thoughts as to what 'heroic stature' involved by re-reading Sophocles and by meditating on the essence of tragedy in literary art. He now proposed to write his *Electra*.

In one respect his new heroine would be unlike any of her predecessors: she was planned as a representative of that class which Victorian society liked to refer to as 'fallen women'. As early as 1866, while he was still in London, Hardy had written a poem entitled 'The Ruined Maid', but its somewhat flippant tone prevented—or at least discouraged—its publication until 1902, when it finally achieved print in *Poems of the Past and the Present*. The new heroine, as planned in 1888, was to be sympathetically handled; this would permit Hardy to salvage the idea he had had in mind when he first planned *The Return of the Native*. Thomasin, we remember, was to have been compromised by a spurious marriage. In the revamping of *the Native* which Mrs. Grundy had demanded, this idea had been discarded, but Hardy had never lost sight of his vision of a 'fallen' heroine.

Stories of seduction were, of course, no new thing in nineteenth-century England. Scott's *Heart of Midlothian*, Dickens's *David Copperfield*, George Eliot's *Adam Bede*, and Trollope's *Vicar of Bullhampton* had all dealt with this theme. But in all these stories the unfortunate victim was a weakling; she was set in contrast with the heroine who held the centre of the stage. Scott's Effie, Dickens's little Emily, and George Eliot's Hetty are all overshadowed by their stronger sisters, and Trollope's *Autobiography* explains the reason why. In *The Vicar of Bullhampton*, Trollope had introduced

the character of a girl whom I will call—for want of a truer word that shall not in its truth be offensive—a castaway. I have endeavored to endow her with qualities that may create sympathy. It is not long since the very existence of such a condition of life as was hers, was supposed to be unknown to our sisters and daughters.

Trollope explained that his novel was written chiefly with the object of exciting not only pity but also sympathy for the unfortunate woman, and then he added: 'I could not venture to make this female the heroine of my story.'

That, however, was precisely what Thomas Hardy now proposed to do. He had not forgotten that when *Desperate Remedies* was published, the *Spectator* had ridiculed him for supposing that 'an unmarried lady owning an estate could have an illegitimate child'. He had not forgotten that Leslie Stephen had insisted that the seduction of Fanny Robin in *Far from the Madding Crowd* be handled in a gingerly fashion. Nor had Hardy forgotten that, when *The Woodlanders* was running only two years ago in *Macmillan's Magazine*, Mowbray Morris had asked him 'not to bring the fair Miss Suke to too open shame. . . . Let the human frailty be construed mild.' But various things had been happening to encourage Hardy's hope that, in his next novel, he might be more outspoken. Ibsen's influence was making itself increasingly felt on English thought, and *A Doll's House* (1879) and *Ghosts* (1881) had been receiving a more tolerant hearing. Hardy hoped that his new heroine might win more than toleration. She was to merit sympathy and understanding. He began by calling her Sue Woodrow.

The key to Sue's tragedy was to be her poverty. In the article on 'The Dorsetshire Labourer' which Hardy had written only five years previously, he had told about a family that had come to his notice: 'The father and eldest son were paid eleven shillings a week each, the younger son ten shillings, three nearly grown-up daughters four shillings a week each, and the mother the same.' A grown-up girl—four shillings a week!

One day, when Hardy took a walk with his friend Charles J. Hankinson, they set forth from Max Gate and soon came to a farm which caught Hardy's eye. The disrepair into which the farm buildings had been allowed to fall led Hardy to stop and, while leaning over the rickety gate, he discoursed to Hankinson about the hard life of the farm worker. On another occasion (September 20, 1888) he visited Woolcombe, where some member of the Hardy family had once owned a good deal of property. Now he saw more rickety gates and more dilapidated buildings—and an improverished owner, the father of 'an enormous lot of children'. Not only fences and buildings went to pieces; men deteriorated too, and women. 'So we go down, down, down,' Hardy meditated as he returned to Max Gate. In *The Woodlanders* he had written of 'dangling and etiolated arms of ivy groping in vain for some support, their leaves being dwarfed and sickly for want of sunlight'. The fact that in this respect they 'show them to men akin' was something he had pointed out in his poem 'In a Wood'. Large families were certain to produce weak bodies, sickly characters, dwarfed personalities. The seduction of an impoverished Sue Woodrow would be as natural, as inevitable, as had been the similar fate of Fanny Robin.

Hardy went on with the writing of 'Too Late Beloved' and by midsummer 1889 had the story half done. W. F. Tillotson, of Bolton, had by this time died, but his colleague in the newspaper syndicate, William Brimelow, continued with the arrangements made with Hardy.[2] Since the novel was to be illustrated for the Tillotson serialization, Hardy sent 'a portion of the MS. . . . equal to about one-half, I think' to Bolton on September 9, 1889, so that an artist might begin work on the illustrations. But before the artist had prepared more than three pictures, Brimelow discovered the nature of the story Hardy was writing, and promptly let Hardy know that Mrs. Grundy was just as powerful in Bolton as she had previously shown herself to be in London in the offices of the *Cornhill*, *Good Words*, and *Macmillan's Magazine*.

Tillotson's office at first proposed that Hardy omit certain scenes and rewrite others, but this time Hardy was unwilling to scrap all his plans. He therefore proposed the cancellation of his agreement with the Bolton syndicate, and they agreed. His manuscript was accordingly returned to him before the end of September, and in October Hardy submitted it to Edward Arnold, editor of *Murray's Magazine*. Arnold deliberated a little longer than had the Bolton people, but he eventually reached the same conclusion. Hardy next offered his manuscript to Mowbray Morris, but Morris needed only ten days to decide that *Macmillan's Magazine* could not use a story of seduction. For the third time, therefore, the manuscript of 'Too Late Beloved' came back to Max Gate. The history of *The Poor Man and the Lady* was being re-enacted. It is not surprising that there is no mention of 'Too Late Beloved' in *The Early Life of Thomas Hardy*.

By this time, however, the novelist was determined to see the writing of his story through to the end. Even though three editors had rejected it, Hardy was not ready to give up the Sophoclean tragedy he had formulated in his mind. He did, however, decide to do some revising of his manuscript. He shifted the order of some of the events and changed the name of his heroine. He went through his manuscript and crossed out 'Sue Woodrow' wherever the name occurred and wrote 'Rose Mary Troublefield' in its place. Is it mere coincidence that Charles Lamb's almost forgotten story *Rosamund Gray* has a heroine with a name somewhat similar to Hardy's new choice of name for his heroine, and that Lamb's hero was called Allen Clare? Hardy's hero—if so unheroic a character can be called a hero—is called Angel Clare. Hardy once told Sir Sydney Cockerell that Angel Clare was partly drawn from Charles Moule, the sixth son of the Vicar of Fordington. Perhaps the word 'partly' should be emphasized. For Hardy's 'Clare' found himself unable to submit to the prescribed curriculum at Cambridge University because his reading had undermined his religious faith. Charles Moule, on the contrary, not only went to Cambridge, but eventually became President of Corpus Christi College there. Charles Lamb's Allan Clare, however, had been (so Lamb tells us) 'betrayed into scepticism'. Moreover, Lamb's Clare became a nomad, and Hardy's Clare goes off to Brazil. Lamb's story is a slight and undeveloped piece of work and we have no proof that Hardy ever read it, but the many resemblances in incident and characterization between the two stories are suggestive.

One day, in the period of enforced delay in the process of getting his story written, Hardy happened to be standing at a street corner in Dorchester, not far from the site of the office where he had studied architecture under John Hicks, when a tipsy man staggered past. Hardy heard him muttering 'I've a great family vault over at Bere Regis'. This was the village Hardy had described in *Far from the Madding Crowd*. His curiosity was aroused by the drunkard's assertion. Upon investigation Hardy discovered that, in the old church at Bere Regis, there is not only a large family vault, but also a fine window of stained glass known as the Turberville window. The name Turberville lodged in his mind, and the next time he was in London, he imitated old Simon Stoke in Chapter V of the novel: he conned 'for an hour in the British Museum the pages of works devoted to extinct, half-extinct, obscured, and ruined families', and thus came upon the interesting discovery that, although the name Turberville had died out, there were still a number of very humble families living in Dorset who were descended from the ancient Turbervilles and who now unwittingly hid their honourable surname under various corruptions. One of the commonest of these was Troublefield—so common, in fact, that that was the reason why Hardy had chosen the name for his Mary Rose. He now decided to rename his heroine. Instead of Troublefield he would call her Turberville. In tracing the various ramifications of the name, however, Hardy came upon a Henry John Turberville who had died as recently as 1875. This man turned out to be no genuine Turberville at all, but the brother of Richard D. Blackmore, the author of *Lorna Doone*. Born in 1822, John Blackmore had changed his name to Turberville. This information was suggestive. Hardy had planned to call his villain Smith. Smith now became 'Smith-Turberville'; and readers of the novel will recall the explanation that Smith's father, having made a fortune as a merchant in the north of England, wished to settle afterwards in the south as a gentleman of leisure, and that upon discovering that the Turberville family was practically extinct he simply annexed that name to his own in order not to be too readily identified with his commercial past.

Blackmore the novelist, however, was still alive; and Hardy had no desire to suggest, even indirectly, that he had Henry John Turberville in mind. He therefore again changed his villain's name, first to 'Higgs-D'Urberville', and eventually and finally to 'Stoke-D'Urberville'. Similarly, 'Troublefield' finally shifted into 'Durbeyfield'. Still dissatisfied with his heroine's first name, he gave up 'Rose Mary' and finally chose 'Teresa'. Thus the now-famous milkmaid at last became Tess Durbeyfield. Mrs. Hardy once told Rebekah Owen that Tess had been called 'Rose Mary' so long that it was difficult to think of her as 'Tess'.

Hardy now decided on a new title. 'Too Late Beloved' was

discarded and 'A Daughter of the D'Urbervilles' was chosen. The aged tippler with 'a bias in his gait' who had boasted about his great family vault at Bere Regis became Tess's father. Hardy transferred him from the street-corner in Dorchester to Marnhull, which (according to Hermann Lea) was once reputed to be 'the booziest place in Dorset'. This village is situated in the Vale of Blackmoor, which Hardy had never made use of in any previous fiction. He had, however, long known 'this fertile and sheltered tract of country in which the fields are never brown and the springs never dry', and had written about it on several previous occasions. Ten years before, in an unsigned review of William Barnes's *Poems of Rural Life* (published in the *New Quarterly Magazine* for October 1879) Hardy had used the words just quoted; and after Barnes's death, when Hardy was asked to write an obituary notice for the *Athenaeum* (published on October 16, 1886), he repeated the same description of 'this fertile and sheltered tract of country'. Now he copied his words for the third time into the second chapter of the new novel. In a similar economizing of labour, he copied into Chapters XVIII, LI, and LII, several paragraphs from his 1883 article on 'The Dorsetshire Labourer'.

Another thought occurred to him. Blackmoor, where he planned to have the Durbeyfields live, was a valley of little dairies. Talbothays, where Hardy's father owned a small farm and where he now planned to locate the dairy where Tess was to find employment, was in a valley of great dairies. This contrast in the two places suggested contrasting experiences in the projected life of his heroine, and Hardy saw the possibility of identifying human experience with geographical setting. He therefore assigned Tess's unspoiled childhood to the unsophisticated village of Marnhull; her betrayal by Alec follows a visit to the 'decayed market-town of Chaseborough'; her romantic summer under the eyes of Angel Clare is spent in the lush valley of the Froom where the air is fragrant with the scent of many flowers; at the ancient Wool manor-house her own past catches up with her; and in the sterile fields of Flintcomb-Ash she spends her pitiful months as a deserted wife. When despair overtakes her and she saves her wretched family by selling herself, she moves to the town of 'fashionable promenades', Bournemouth. And finally Stonehenge is chosen for that most beautiful and most pathetic of all the scenes Hardy ever invented—that of Tess falling asleep on one of the Druid stones in that place of ancient sacrifice. This artistic harmonizing of man and nature runs through many of the Wessex novels, but it was never more poetically handled than in *Tess*.

To provide Tess with three dairymaid companions, Hardy drew on his memories of Sunday School days at Stinsford Church. 'As a boy I knew those three dairymaids well,' so the novelist is quoted as having said.³ One milkmaid ('Marian' in the novel) was especially easy to remember. Hardy had been her teacher, and he had never forgotten her amazing ability to quote whole chapters of the Bible by heart. Thoughts of that Sunday School class reminded him, too, of the children singing Thomas Bilby's hymn 'Joyful'. Its words 'Here we suffer grief and pain' were obviously suited in sentiment more to the aged than to the young; but almost from the moment when the hymn was first published in the *Infant School Teachers' Assistant* (1832) it became very popular with children because of the catchy tune to which it was set, and it had extensive use in Sunday Schools during Hardy's boyhood. (It is now Hymn No. 509 in the *Hymnal Companion to the Book of Common Prayer*.) When Tess asks the four little Durbeyfields to sing, their phlegmatic performance in singing 'Joyful' has elicited sarcastic remarks from some critics, but Hardy here knew what he was writing about.

Hardy's memories from boyhood served him also in the development of his plot. When he came to planning the tragic end of his story, he did not have to go back to the story of Clytemnestra in the Greek play he had recently read, for he remembered Martha Brown in Dorchester. She was a kindly soul, wife of an innkeeper, who had often given cakes and apples to schoolboys who passed her door. Hardy as a boy had passed the spot daily on his tramp in from Higher Bockhampton and on his return home at night. He well recalled the shock of hearing one day that Mrs. Brown, in a moment of jealous rage, had killed her errant husband. She was tried and convicted, and was hanged in public. Young Tom Hardy, still a pupil at Mr. Last's academy, was not only present at the execution, but 'stood close to the gallows'.⁴ He never forgot that experience. He remembered, too, how on the evening before the public execution, he had gone down to the hangman's cottage (still standing, a century later, on the bank of the Froom river), had climbed up on the railing and looked in to see the hangman placidly eating his supper. Sixty years later, he referred to this public hanging in one of the very few public speeches he ever made—when he was presented the freedom of the Borough of Dorchester. In 1890, then, while planning *Tess*, Hardy found in the tragic end of Martha Brown complete assurance as to what Teresa Durbeyfield would do under somewhat similar conditions.

Thus the prolonged delay in bringing his novel to completion allowed Hardy abundant leisure for the development of Tess as a fully rounded-out character. The novelist later told Arthur Compton-Rickett that she had been 'built up' from three different persons. In a discussion in which Hardy and Compton-Rickett once took part, Mrs. Hardy remarked that she did not remember the colour of Tess's hair. Compton-Rickett said he thought it was dark. 'Of course it was,' said Hardy decisively, as if speaking about a person in real life, 'dark and very thick'. Hardy recalled having seen a girl once, and only once, riding on a cart on the outskirts of Egdon Heath. She was a handsome girl with 'large innocent eyes'. Hardy told J. Henry Harper that he remembered seeing this typical country lass, sitting on the tailboard of a lumbering farm cart, swinging her legs. Another girl, remembered from early years, suggested 'the stopt-diapason note which her voice acquired when her heart was in her speech, and which will never be forgotten by those who knew her'. 'Something in the phrasing here,' remarks Professor Joseph Warren Beach, 'makes one sure the author is speaking of an actual woman, whose voice he has heard and cannot forget.' Still another feature of the milkmaid can be traced to a dated origin. On July 23, 1889, Hardy was entertained at dinner by Edmund Gosse. The lips and teeth of a lady who talked with the novelist on that occasion reminded him of a poem he had once read and had learned to admire:

> when her lovely laughter shows,
> They look like rosebuds filled with snow.

Hardy could not recall off-hand the authorship of those lines, but he promptly hunted them up and found them in Thomas Campion's poem 'Cherry Ripe'. The author thus prepared himself for writing about Angel Clare's delight in looking at

Tess's mouth: 'He had never before seen a woman's lips and teeth which forced upon his mind with such persistent iteration the old Elizabethan simile of roses filled with snow.'

By one of those 'little ironies' that Hardy liked to write about, he was asked—just at the time of the triple rejection of 'Too Late Beloved'—for a contribution to a series of articles appearing in the *New Review* on 'Candour in English Fiction'. He responded by writing an article (published in the issue for January 1890) in which he lamented 'that the great bulk of English fiction of the present day is characterized by its lack of sincerity' and urged the great desirability of permitting novelists to treat frankly 'the position of man and woman in nature, and the position of belief in the minds of man and woman— things which everybody is thinking but nobody is saying'.

In his attempt to treat frankly and sincerely 'the position of man and woman in nature', and in his desire to contrast with it the position of man and woman as seen through the eyes of conventional Victorian society, Hardy expanded the didactic rôle he had already assumed in *The Woodlanders*, and in *Tess* he 'occasionally foisted incongruous views on some of his characters'.[5] As a rule, however, Hardy kept his tendency to preach under strict artistic control, and one of the guiding principles of his art was to keep his vision focused on his central character. Hardy poured his sympathy out lavishly upon Tess, the most pathetic and pain-enduring of all his heroines, and his passionate note of personal feeling about her is felt all through the book.

As Hardy approached the conclusion of his work, he carefully considered how to avoid a fourth editorial rejection. He decided to make use of the device which had served him twenty years ago, after *The Poor Man and the Lady* had been rejected by three publishers. He had then extracted from its pages, from time to time, a paragraph here and a passage there, and had used them in three subsequently published novels. Then he had eventually salvaged the bulky remnant of the manuscript by giving it a new title, transforming it into a long short-story, and this the editor of the *New Quarterly Magazine* had finally accepted. The dismemberment of *The Poor Man* in the seventies was now paralleled by a similar dismemberment of *Tess* in the nineties. Part of Chapter XIV (in which Tess's baby appears) was extracted and sent to the editor of the *Fortnightly Review*. It was accepted and appeared in the issue for May 1891 under the title 'The Midnight Baptism: A Study in Christianity'. Another fragment dealing with the events that led up to the seduction-scene was now re-entitled 'Saturday Night in Arcady' and was sent to W. E. Henley, then editor of the *National Observer*. In this magazine, Chapter X with its description of 'Chaseborough', the 'decayed market-town', appeared as part of a special literary supplement on November 14, 1891. With the baby and the seduction-scene both removed from the manuscript, Hardy patched up the scars by writing a new paragraph, in which a mock-marriage was made to take the place of the originally planned seduction. This is the story which Tess (while moving in the shadow of Mrs. Grundy) was made to tell her mother:

He made love to me, . . . and he asked me to marry him. . . . I agreed. . . . I drove with him to Melchester, and there . . . went through the form of marriage with him as before a registrar. A few weeks after, I found out that it was not the registrar's house we had gone to, as I had supposed, but the house of a friend of his, who had played the part of the registrar. I then came away from Trantridge instantly, . . . and here I am.

Since this concession to Mrs. Grundy required corresponding changes in the story which Tess told after her marriage to Angel Clare, that passage too had to be rewritten. Hardy crammed the revised confession into a single sentence: 'She entered on her story of the visit with D'Urberville to the supposed Registrar's, her abiding sense of the moral validity of the contract, and her wicked flying in the face of that conviction by wedding again.' The situation at Bournemouth, where Clare found Tess living under the same roof with Alec, obviously called for similar emasculation. When the botched-up job of revision had been finally completed, the manuscript was given a new title. 'A Daughter of the D'Urbervilles' was amended to read *Tess of the D'Urbervilles*, and the now-morally-'safe' story was offered to the editor of the *Graphic* and was accepted.

Even so, Hardy's troubles with Mrs. Grundy were not over. When Arthur Locker, the editor, reached Chapter XXIII, in which Angel Clare carries the dairymaids through the pool of water in the flooded lane, he hastily wrote Hardy to say that it would be better if the girls could be transported through the water in a wheelbarrow. Hardy accordingly rewrote Angel Clare's offer, making him say to the milkmaids: 'I'll wheel you through the pool—all of you—with pleasure, if you'll wait till I get a barrow. . . .'

With such 'improvements' as these, Arthur Locker proceeded to prepare to serialize the novel in the *Graphic*. Sensing that he had a really important work in hand, he arranged for twenty-five illustrations to be made for the story by Professor Hubert Herkomer of the Royal Academy and three of his pupils. The professor and his pupils did not always agree as to what Hardy's heroine looked like, but editor Locker was not as critical of a matter like this as he was about the propriety of Hardy's text. The novel began its serial appearance on July 4, 1891, and ended on December 26.

As soon as the printers returned the manuscript, Hardy began to reassemble his dismembered story. The chapters previously published in the *Fortnightly* and the *National Observer* were reinstated. The ridiculous readings specially written for the *Graphic* were marked in blue ink: 'Alterations in blue refer to serial publication only'; and in two places—the title page and the last page—Hardy made some last-minute changes. On the last page he had originally written: ' "Justice" was done.' In correcting the *Graphic* proofs, he had thought of an addition, and as finally printed in the magazine the last paragraph had begun: ' "Justice" was done, and Time, the Arch-satirist, had had his joke out with Tess.' Now, in preparing the manuscript for the book publication, Hardy thought of an improvement on 'Time, the Arch-satirist'. Those words were accordingly suppressed; and after ' "Justice" was done' Hardy inserted three new lines: 'and the President of the Immortals (in Aeschylean phrase) had ended his sport with Tess. And the D'Urberville Knights and dames slept on in their tombs unknowing.' On the title-page, as the result of a similar last-minute inspiration, Hardy inserted, after the title *Tess of the D'Urbervilles*, the words: 'A Pure Woman faithfully depicted by Thomas Hardy.' And even after this emendation had been written out, he thought of yet another change, and the word 'depicted' was struck out and was replaced by 'presented'.

With these final emendations, the manuscript was sent off to the office of James R. Osgood, McIlvaine & Co. (a new London publishing house with offices at 45 Albemarle Street, just off Piccadilly), where a three-volume edition of the novel was promptly 'put in hand'. This new house was one that Hardy had begun association with when it published *A Group of Noble Dames* on May 30, 1891, about a month after the *Fortnightly* had printed 'The Midnight Baptism'. The head of the firm, James R. Osgood, was an American—the same man who, back in 1873, had paid the *Cornhill* for advance sheets of *Far from the Madding Crowd* with a view to the serialization of the novel in the *Atlantic Monthly*. However, before the arrival of the date for the Boston publication of the novel, Osgood had sold the *Atlantic*, and after another dozen years as a Boston publisher he went bankrupt. For a brief spell he was employed by Harper & Brothers in their New York office and in 1886 was sent by them to London as their English agent. Here Osgood made Hardy's acquaintance and was the go-between for Hardy's arrangements with the New York house. After five years' activity as London agent, Osgood established, in 1891, a firm of his own in London, acting promptly upon the heels of the passage (on December 4, 1890) of the new Copyright Bill by the House of Representatives. Osgood sensed at once that the new law, permitting English authors to enjoy for the first time copyright in America, would place Thomas Hardy in a favoured position. He therefore lost no time in making a proposal of such terms to Hardy as the novelist found it impossible to refuse. The publication of *A Group of Noble Dames* was the first result of their agreement, and plans for the publication of *Tess* followed soon thereafter. On (or about) November 29, 1891, Osgood published *Tess* in three volumes. This was the last time that any of Hardy's novels was published in this multiple-volume form; the reign of the 'three-decker' was over. The binding of *Tess* (smooth tan cloth, with a honeysuckle pattern in gilt) was designed by a young man named Charles Rickett, destined shortly after this to establish the Vale Press and to issue books of his own.

In America *Tess* was published in one volume by Harper & Brothers. They had serialized the story in *Harper's Bazar*, beginning its run on July 18, two weeks after the *Graphic* had begun the London serialization, and ending it on December 26, the same day as the *Graphic's* end. This simultaneous ending was achieved by making the final instalment in the *Bazar* a triple number. Early in January 1892 the Harper edition of *Tess* appeared, in a better binding than any Hardy novel had as yet enjoyed in America. The new Copyright Law which went into effect on July 1, 1891, permitted the Harpers to act without fear of piratical competition, and *Tess* accordingly appeared in a fine copper-coloured cloth binding decorated with a gilt lion *rampant*. This decoration was much more appropriately chosen than Charles Rickett's honeysuckles, for it was based upon Tess's statement in Chapter V: 'We have several proofs that we be D'Urbervilles. . . . We have an old seal marked with a ramping lion on a shield, and a castle over him. And we have a very old silver spoon . . . with the same castle.' In their haste to publish the novel, the Harpers used the text of *Harper's Bazar*, and American readers were thus denied the benefit of Hardy's last-minute changes and textual improvements. The Harper text was revised in 1893, but without bringing it into conformity with the London text. As recently as 1920 the New York edition failed to agree with the London. Hardy himself never saw any proofs of the American edition.

Thus, after more than three years of planning, writing, revising, patching, and persevering, Thomas Hardy at last achieved publication for his tragedy of the ill-fated milkmaid. He little suspected, however, that his dealings with her and with the book about her were far from over. For upon the publication of *Tess of the D'Urbervilles* the author was brought face to face with an explosive situation that made Mrs. Grundy's previous quibblings and simperings seem mild by comparison.

XIV

'High-water Mark of Late-Victorian Fiction'

TESS was on the market in London less than a month before Christmas 1891. It was sold out immediately. A second printing, and then a third, and then a fourth, were printed in as many months. No previous Wessex novel had enjoyed any such brisk sale. Before midsummer 1892, Osgood, McIlvaine & Co. were ready for a fifth printing (they called it a Fifth Edition), and Hardy was asked to write a new preface for it. By one of 'life's little ironies' James R. Osgood did not live to see this new edition. He died on May 20, 1892, and was buried in London—in Kensall Green Cemetery, not far from Thackeray's grave. Hardy went up to London to attend the funeral on the twenty-third, and walked in the procession immediately after Osgood's partner, Clarence W. McIlvaine. 'Very sad,' Hardy reported to his wife in a letter he wrote her that evening from the Athenaeum Club.[1] He had been elected a member of this club in April 1891.

In the new preface to *Tess* which Hardy composed in July 1892, he referred with unconcealed irritation to 'the manipulators of *Tess* . . . of the . . . sort whom most writers . . . would gladly forget: professed literary boxers, . . . sworn Discouragers, . . . who pervert plain meanings, and grow personal. . . .' He was especially bitter about 'a gentleman who turned Christian for half-an-hour the better to express his grief that a disrespectful phrase about the Immortals should have been used' in the novel. It is easy to see from these remarks that the unprecedented sale of his book had brought the author something other than undiluted pleasure. There was sand in his honey. For the more the general public clamoured for copies of the novel, the louder became the outcry against it from reviewers, critics, preachers, self-appointed moralists, agents of Mrs. Grundy and custodians of the Victorian conventions and proprieties. The *Quarterly Review* announced that 'Mr. Hardy has told an extremely disagreeable story in an extremely disagreeable manner.' Andrew Lang (who was the 'gentleman who turned Christian for half-an-hour') was not content to write one denunciation of *Tess*: he returned to the attack with a second, in which he denounced Hardy's novel 'for its forbidding conception, for its apparent unreality, and for its defects of style'. George Moore made fun of Hardy's handling of the seduction scene: 'It is the wildest, the most extravagant occurrence that I ever read. . . . I should call it the worst libel on English maidenhood that has ever been penned.' (This, from the man who in 1894 was to write *Esther Waters*!) Frank Harris laughed at the four girls at the dairy, all four in love with Angel Clare. 'What is more miraculous still,' he scoffed, 'they all confess their love openly to each other. . . . No such four women ever stood together on this . . . earth.' Hardy's old reader and adviser, George Meredith, thought that the novel was 'marred by the sudden hurry to round out the story; and Tess, out of the arms of Alec, into . . . those of the lily-necked Clare . . . is a smudge in vapour'.

Hardy was thin-skinned and these denunciatory splinters easily penetrated and hurt. On January 17, 1892, he wrote a pained letter to his fellow-novelist Walter Besant, asking him whether he thought that Hardy ought to resign from the Savile Club because of the 'fiendish' review of *Tess* 'in yesterday's *Saturday Review*'. What could a novelist say in reply to his critics, especially when they are anonymous? To such a judgment as that of P. T. Forsyth that the first sentence in Hardy's final paragraph was 'the most dreadful sentence in modern English literature', what could an author do other than retort with an angry comment on critics 'who pervert plain meanings'?

Obviously, Hardy's meaning was *not* 'plain' to many of his readers. ' "Justice" was done', he had written, but obviously many readers had failed to see the significance of his sarcastic use of the quotation marks around 'Justice'. As for the 'President of the Immortals', it was equally obvious that readers had failed to grasp the meaning of the words 'in Aeschylean phrase'. The 'professed literary boxers' did not know of Hardy's copy of Aeschylus, bought long ago with his prize-money for architectural design; they did not know that in Theodore Buckley's translation of *Prometheus Bound* Hardy had found the phrase about 'the President of the Immortals', and that in his ironic use of it with reference to Tess he was implying the same sort of *dis*approval that he had implied in his reference to 'Justice'. A pagan dramatist like Aeschylus might have explained Tess's fate as the result of the 'President's' inhuman and ignoble zest for cruel sport. British law would explain her fate, like that of Martha Brown, as the result of long-established legal codes, of prescribed rules of meting out 'justice'. Hardy had expected his readers to understand that the author's own attitude towards Tess's fate was neither of these views. Hardy's was an indictment of an intolerant society that could condemn a woman of Tess's integrity and courage and humility and unselfishness.

While the public outcry against the novel was still going on, Hardy received (in September 1892) a letter from Sir Frederick Pollock, the English jurist (son of Sir William Pollock, remembered as a member of the little society at Cambridge whose debates are celebrated in Tennyson's *In Memoriam*). Pollock wrote to say that he was probably the last person in England to read *Tess* but that he had left it for holiday perusal. And now that he had at last read the novel, it seemed to him the finest, most serious piece of work in modern fiction, approaching in its power the grandeur of Greek tragedy. Pollock doubted, however, 'if any judge or jury would have convicted Tess without a recomemndation to mercy'. Hardy remained unconvinced; he remembered what had happened to Mrs. Martha Brown. Besides (so he remarked to Rebekah Owen in 1893), he had been told by another lawyer who had read *Tess*, a man who had had a great deal to do with reprieves, that it had never occurred to him, while reading the novel, that Tess should *not* be executed. Hardy's own view was that there was no other logical conclusion possible. 'It had to be,' he said sadly, 'it had to be.' In later years he told of having made a special trip to Winchester and of walking moodily up and down outside the gaol where Tess was to be confined, and of asking himself what

other solution there was for the situation as it had developed in
his mind. 'It had to be; there was no other end possible.'

It was not only the execution of Tess that came in for
criticism, nor the seduction, nor the 'extremely disagreeable'
nature of the story: even his last-minute after-thought on the
title-page was debated and denounced. 'A Pure Woman'? What
did Hardy mean by that? *Was* Tess 'pure'? Hardy's own statement (written in his March 1912 preface to the novel) was
that the words 'a pure woman' represented 'the estimate left
in a candid mind of the heroine's character—an estimate that
nobody would be likely to dispute'. 'Alas,' he added, 'it was
disputed more than anything else in the book.' The chorus of
dissent and disagreement was truly amazing. 'It might have
been more tactful to have called her, in Massinger's term "a
very woman" ' (A. St. John Adcock). 'Better if Hardy had
written "A Beautiful Woman" ' (Percy Hutchison). 'To me
that glaring subtitle meant nothing, and I could not see what
it should mean to Mr. Hardy' (Hardy's old admirer Havelock
Ellis). 'Hardy did not call Tess "a pure woman" in order . . .
to placate nice readers of nice novels. He meant the subtitle
as the key to the whole story' (John Macy). 'Why did those
admirably moral prigs forget Tom Hood's immortal line, which
fully explains the novelist's meaning?' (D. F. Hannigan). Does
it? The reference here is to a line in 'The Bridge of Sighs'
(1844), to the last line of this stanza:

> One more Unfortunate
> Weary of breath,
> Rashly importunate,
> Gone to her death! . . .
> Touch her not scornfully;
> Think of her mournfully,
> Gently and humanly,
> Not of the stains of her;
> All that remains of her
> Now is pure womanly.

The debate has continued long after Hardy's death. In 1959
F. B. Pinion wrote: 'The subtitle, *A Pure Woman*, was a gauntlet
deliberately thrown in the face of public opinion. By "pure"
Hardy meant "pure of heart"; Tess is endowed with the highest
Christian virtues listed by Saint Paul.'[2]

183

In the midst of the deafening chorus of disapproval that poured in from pulpit, press, and post office upon Hardy's sensitive ears, there were occasional notes of comfort. Sir George Douglas wrote from Scotland to say that he had fallen in love with Tess. On December 30, 1891, Hardy replied: 'I am so truly glad that Tess the woman has won your affections. I, too, lost my heart to her as I went on with her history.' Hardy's friend Edmund Gosse sent him a consoling letter on the first day of the New Year, 1892:

In *Tess of the D'Urbervilles* you have achieved the biggest success you have made since *The Return of the Native*. Your book is simply magnificent, and wherever I go I hear its praises. If you could have listened to the things that I have heard said about it, by Walter Besant, by Mrs. Humphry Ward, by Henry James, by I know not whom else, you would not,—you could not, care what the *Saturday's* ape-leading and shrivelled spinster said or thought. Your success has been phenomenal. I have not heard a book so earnestly and honestly praised by word of mouth (and that is the praise that tells) for years. You have strengthened your position tremendously, among your own *confrères* and the serious male public. Let them rave!

This was encouraging, but there was something even better in store for the lacerated novelist. When *The Academy* for February 6, 1892, appeared, it carried a review of *Tess* by William Watson. He had not yet become Sir William, but had already made a name for himself as the author of the widely-admired poem 'Wordsworth's Grave'. Watson's review was not a friend's opinion expressed in a private letter; it was a public encomium for all the world to see and hear. In *Tess of the D'Urbervilles*, declared Watson,

we have before us the most mature and . . . most powerful expression of the author's genius. . . . The romance has the power, the intensity, the inevitableness, and above all the warm humanity of the great dramas, ancient and modern. . . . I can well believe what I heard a distinguished author declare, that no man . . . could read this book with sympathy and not thenceforth be of broader mind and more charitable and catholic spirit. . . . Whatever is best in Thomas Hardy's work is to be found in this page from life—humour, pathos, tragedy, marvellous descriptive faculty, and that transforming magic through all, for which there is no other word than the much abused term 'genius'. There are scenes in *Tess* which one cannot but believe will represent the high-water mark of our late-Victorian fiction and there are episodes which must surely touch the hearts and influence the minds of those who come after us almost as profoundly as they do our own.

This splendid tribute ought to have soothed Hardy's anguished feelings, but he was not an author who 'soothed' easily. Instead of remembering the praise in *The Academy* he brooded over the attack in the *Saturday Review*. On April 15, 1892, he wrote in his notebook: 'If this sort of thing continues, no more novel-writing for me. A man must be a fool to deliberately stand up to be shot at.'[3] Even after the passage of three more years, when a new edition of the novel was in preparation—Volume I of a new collected edition of his works—he was still unable, in writing a new preface, dated 'January 1895', to refrain from referring to his own heated words of July 1892 and adding: 'The pages are allowed to stand for what they are worth. . . . Even in the short time which has elapsed since the book was first published, some of the critics . . . have "gone down into silence", as if to remind one of the infinite unimportance of both their say and mine.'

In spite of this disclaimer about 'infinite unimportance', the fact is that just at that moment—January 1895—Hardy was engaged in a project that implied exactly the opposite attitude towards his novel. He proposed to dramatize it. 'He had received many requests for a dramatic version,'[4] and 'almost every actress of note in Europe . . .—among them . . . Mrs. Patrick Campbell, Ellen Terry, Sarah Bernhardt, and Eleanora Duse,'[5] had asked him for an opportunity to appear in the part of Tess, if he would only provide a dramatic version. In addition to the actresses named above by Hardy, Elizabeth Robins and Olga Nethersole also sought to play Tess.

Mrs. Campbell seemed to Hardy the most logical choice. She had appeared in 1893 in *The Second Mrs. Tanqueray*, Pinero's famous success, and Hardy was now sufficiently attracted by the idea of having 'Mrs. Pat' appear as Tess Durbeyfield for him to set about the preparation of a dramatic version for her use. He forgot (or ignored) the frustrations he had suffered in 1882 over his adaptation of *Far from the Madding Crowd*, and now went resolutely about a new attempt at the same sort of thing. In spite of being just then 'overwhelmed with neglected proofs' of the books in the collected sixteen-volume Uniform Edition of his works now being readied by Osgood, McIlvaine & Co., Hardy moved up to London in April 1895 and rented a flat in Westminster, writing (on April 24) to his wife to tell her that 'one advantage of the flat is that Mrs. Patrick Campbell lives in an adjoining block—and if the play goes on that may be convenient. . . .'⁶ By July 1895 he had made sufficient progress to be able to write Mrs. Campbell: 'You *must* be the Tess, now we have got so far. It would be a thousand pities if you were not.' Subsequently Hardy talked with Forbes-Robertson, with a view to his enacting Angel Clare.

But the negotiations dragged on. In December Hardy went to see Mrs. Campbell and Forbes-Robertson in *Romeo and Juliet*, and soon after his return to Max Gate Mrs. Campbell decided to follow him to Dorchester and there attempt to clinch matters. Forbes-Robertson wrote Hardy on January 5, 1896, to tell him that 'Mrs. Patrick Campbell is staying at the King's Arms Hotel . . . and she will be coming over to see you'. She came in characteristic style. She hired a horse at the King's Arms, rode as far as the entrance to Max Gate, and was conveniently thrown from the saddle there. After that impressive first arrival, she called on Hardy a second time and tried to bring him to a decision. The chief trouble was that Forbes-Robertson wished to make changes in the text of the play and this Hardy refused to allow. Upon Mrs. Campbell's return to London, she bought a copy of William Morris's newly published Kelmscott Press edition of Rossetti's *Hand and Soul*, inscribed it to 'Thomas Hardy from Beatrice Stella Campbell in dear remembrance, January, 1896', and sent it to the novelist. But it would take more than a Kelmscott Press gift to pry out of Thomas Hardy permission for someone else to tamper with the text of his play. On January 23 he wrote to Mrs. Campbell: 'I am glad . . . you are safely home and none the worse for Dorset air. We missed your friendly visits much after you had left.' But still there was no decision about the *Tess* play.

Ten days later, Hardy himself was back in London, and there he met another actress, Elizabeth Robins, who, like Mrs. Campbell, was eager to appear as Tess. Miss Robins apparently thought, from something that Hardy said or wrote, that he had promised her the part; and on March 18, 1896, she wrote him to express her surprise on learning that he had 'entered into negotiations with Mrs. Campbell'. Hardy had not only 'entered into negotiations' but had told his wife that he was 'to meet a manager'[7] with a view to arranging the commercial side of the project. In the final outcome, however, nothing was done. Mrs. Campbell was disappointed, Miss Robins was disappointed, and Thomas Hardy was disappointed.

On the other side of the ocean, there was similar interest in the possibility of dramatizing *Tess of the D'Urbervilles*, and the fact that Hardy was thousands of miles away proved an advantage. Hardy sent permission to Harper & Brothers to handle the American negotiations; and, after investigating six or seven possibilities, the publishers turned to Harrison Grey Fiske, an experienced producer, whose wife, Minnie Maddern Fiske, would, they thought, make an acceptable Tess. In England Hardy had insisted that there be no departure from the text of his dramatization, but in America he was not so insistent and told the Harpers to authorize some modification—'a reasonable modification'—of his version if that would help to get the play promptly on to the stage. This permission was passed on to the Fiskes; Mrs. Fiske promptly turned to Lorimer Stoddard, the the thirty-two-year-old son of Richard Henry Stoddard, the poet, and young Stoddard's interpretation of 'a reasonable modification' of Hardy's script was to ignore it altogether. In five and a half days Stoddard turned out a five-act play of his own—really four acts, with two scenes in the last act—and with this play Mrs. Fiske opened at the Fifth Avenue Theatre in New York on Tuesday, March 2, 1897. The play was a great and an instantaneous success. The *New York Journal* called it 'revolutionary'. William Dean Howells wrote it up for *Harper's Weekly*. Edith Wharton reviewed it in the *Commercial Advertiser*. Ella Wheeler Wilcox, Hamlin Garland, Robert Ingersoll, and other well-known Americans, all went to see the play and were ready to agree with the judgment that, in Stoddard's dramatization of Hardy's novel, Tess was presented as 'a character of such strength, of such intensity, so virile with life, so vibrant with emotion, that she is able to hold her audience . . . in rapt attention'.

On the night when the play opened in New York, two members of the audience were those 'good judges across the

Atlantic', Rebekah and Catharine Owen, who had persuaded Hardy to change the ending of *The Mayor of Casterbridge*. Rebekah promptly wrote Hardy an account of Mrs. Fiske's performance, and on March 16, 1897, he acknowledged the report as follows:

Dear Miss Owen:

I received on Sunday your interesting letter and its vivid description of the first night of the play. It was really kind of you to go, and still more kind to put yourself to the trouble of sending me such a full report. . . . I was much entertained, as was my wife also, by your account of how it was done. . . .

Mrs. Fiske seems to be a clever and energetic woman, to whom much credit is due for her persistence in bringing out the play and for the fervour with which she has thrown herself into it. Did you notice whether her intonation was sufficiently near the English to pass on the stage here as that of an English girl without seeming discordant to London ears, in case she should bring the play to England? . . .

Mrs. Fiske never took the play to England. Once again, Hardy put his manuscript away, into a cupboard at Max Gate where it was to lie for more than a quarter of a century, another instance of the correctness of his observation that 'nothing bears out in practice what it promises incipiently'.[8] In 1924 chance events were to lead Hardy to bring forth his script from the cupboard, with developments which we shall postpone describing until a later chapter. A year after Mrs. Fiske's presentation of *Tess* in the New York theatre, Hardy published a poem in which he remarked that

> Time, to make me grieve,
> Part steals, lets part abide:
> And shakes this fragile frame at eve
> With throbbings of noontide.

When these lines were published in *Wessex Poems*, Hardy was fifty-eight years old—in the evening of his life, as he thought; but the 'throbbings of noontide' about *Tess* were still many years off in the future.

Meanwhile, public interest in the novel continued. Because of the death of James R. Osgood in 1892, Hardy's business arrangements with the Osgood firm passed into the hands of Harper & Brothers, with the result that, for four years (1898–

1902), the Harpers acted as the novelist's London publishers as well as his publishers in New York. In 1900 Harpers issued, in London, a sixpenny edition of *Tess*—a salmon-coloured paper-backed edition—the cheapness of which greatly enlarged the audience for Hardy's novel. In 1902, when Hardy's contract with Osgood expired, he transferred all his business to Macmillan & Company, where, as far as London publication is concerned, it still lies. As a result, Macmillan began publishing *Tess* in 1902. Six printings of this edition, in addition to four printings of a 'Pocket Edition' on thin paper, followed prior to 1912; and in this last-named year Hardy again revised the text before the publication of *Tess* in the definitive Wessex Edition of 1912. *Tess* also appeared in the *de luxe* Mellstock Edition of 1919, in a Limited Autograph Edition (with forty-one wood-engravings by Vivien Gribble) in 1926, in a two-shilling edition in 1928, in Macmillan's Cottage Library series in 1937, and in their current editions in various formats. About ten years ago, *Tess* finally made its way into the list of novels 'accepted' for academic examinations in England, and a Scholar's Library edition was published in 1959 with an excellent introduction and notes by F. B. Pinion of Sheffield University. *Tess of the D'Urbervilles* had come a long way since Mowbray Morris said 'No' to Hardy's offer of this story.

In America there has been a similar multiplicity and variety of *Tess* editions, not only by Harper & Brothers, but also (since under the American copyright law *Tess* fell into the public domain at an earlier date than in England) by other publishers as well. In 1923 there was a so-called 'Photoplay Edition' partially illustrated by scenes from an American 'movie'. One of the pictures shows Blanche Sweet as a very un-Dorset-like Tess at Stonehenge, surrounded by a posse of seven men, all obviously American in garb and posture. In 1935 the Harpers published an annotated edition which was greeted by Professor Joseph Warren Beach with the announcement that 'Hardy may now be studied line-by-line like Chaucer and Shakespeare';[9] in 1951 Random House published a Modern Library edition with an introduction and glossary by Carl J. Weber; and in 1960 Dodd, Mead & Co. published a 'Great Illustrated Classics' edition which marks the admission of *Tess* into the category of classic and gives it the accolade of 'great'.

Nor has the fame of the Dorset milkmaid reached only those who read English. Even before the close of the nineteenth century *Tess* began to appear in translations into various European languages, and by the time of Hardy's death the translating had spread to Asia. In this way the fame of the novel helped to extend Hardy's reputation and influence throughout the world.[10]

In addition to her appearance in the book and on the stage, Tess Durbeyfield has had the distinction of being put into an Italian opera. The music was composed by Frederic D'Erlanger; the Italian words were written by Luigi Illica; the first performance of the opera was given at Naples, April 10, 1906; and on July 14, 1909, Hardy and his wife saw and heard the first London performance. The opera has been published with an English prose translation by Claude Aveling (London, Ricordi, 1909).

About two years before his death, Hardy was invited by *John O' London's Weekly* to comment on the change that had come about in the world's attitude towards *Tess* in the course of the thirty-five years of its history. In the issue of the *Weekly* for October 24, 1925, Hardy wrote:

It has been remarked that the experiences of the heroine could not have led to such an issue nowadays. Well: I for one am sceptical on this point, and think it just as likely to have happened last week as fifty years back, in which view I am supported by many men with large knowledge of the world.

In 1941, on the fiftieth anniversary of the novel, the library of Columbia University mounted a Jubilee Exhibition of *Tess of the D'Urbervilles* in which fifty editions were displayed, and the library of Colby College (Waterville, Maine) published a Catalogue entitled *The Jubilee of 'Tess'* with thirty-five illustrations. Hardy himself had not lived to see either of these tributes to his great novel, but there can be little doubt that, if he had lived, he would have taken great pleasure in the Jubilee occasion. Henry Van Dyke, of Princeton, once recalled an incident in a London club. 'A luncheon was given for me,' he wrote, 'to meet Thomas Hardy. . . . Alone with him at last, I asked: "Which of your books is your favourite?" Thinking a moment, he answered simply and frankly, "*Tess of the D'Urbervilles*". "That is because you love her the best of all your characters, isn't it?" "Yes," he said gravely, "I love her best of all." '

'I am sure,' concluded Van Dyke in reporting this incident,[11] 'that Hardy put into *Tess* his most intense personal feeling and that the book marks the height of his tragic power.' Professor Robert Shafer agrees: '*Tess* is, by general consent, one of the few great English novels.'[12]

'Anyhow,' said Hardy himself, 'I have put in it the best of me.'

XV

An Interlude

IN the course of concentrating upon *Tess of the D'Urbervilles* we have necessarily omitted a number of incidents in Hardy's literary career to which we must now return.

Shortly before *Tess* began making its serial appearance, Hardy found himself put into a poem by another English author under conditions which require detailed explanation. In the *Collected Verse* of Rudyard Kipling there is a poem entitled 'The Rhyme of the Three Captains'. It is dated 1890, and according to an explanatory note prefixed to the poem it 'appears to refer to one of the exploits of the notorious Paul Jones, an American pirate. It is founded on fact.' But when Kipling wrote that note about 'the notorious Paul Jones' he had his tongue in his cheek: the reference in the poem is really elsewhere and Thomas Hardy is one of 'the Three Captains'. Readers of Kipling have often been puzzled by this poem, and Hardy himself never made any reference to it or to the incidents that led up to its composition; but their explanation is not difficult.

During the summer of 1890, while Hardy was at work upon the dismemberment of *Tess of the D'Urbervilles*, Harper & Brothers issued Kipling's *The Courting of Dinah Shadd and Other Stories* as No. 680 in their paper-backed 'Franklin Square Library'. This 'book' was made up largely of stories already issued and paid for by Harpers, but it was put on the American market without Kipling's knowledge. When the news reached him in the form of a royalty check from the publishers, he was furious. He blew off steam by sending an angry statement to the London *Athenaeum* for October 4, denouncing the New York

firm and declaring: 'When an author is unknown to fame, they
... content themselves with insulting him; when he is celebrated, they insult and rob him.'

Within ten days Kipling's blast arrived in New York. On the
fourteenth Harper & Brothers mailed 'A Reply' to the *Athenaeum*
(published in the issue for November 1), in which they defended
their action, explaining the commercial situation that confronted the American publisher of any English author in the
absence of copyright protection. Kipling, however, was not to
be appeased. He thought the Harpers were incorrect in their
statements, and 'A Counter Reply' from him appeared in the
Athenaeum for November 8. There the matter might have ended,
but Hardy was not a man to remain silent when injustice had
been done. He was as ready to speak out in behalf of a foreign
publisher as of a Dorset milkmaid. Ever since his meeting with
Henry Harper in Green Park he had been on friendly terms
with the New York publisher and their business relations had
always gone smoothly. Two other English authors, Walter
Besant and William Black, men with whom Hardy often dined
at the Savile Club, had likewise had satisfactory business
experience with Harper & Brothers. When, therefore, the
charge of unethical conduct by the Harpers was repeated with
all the force of Kipling's invective, the three authors united in
sending to the *Athenaeum* a letter of remonstrance, dated November 17, 1890. It appeared in the issue for the 22nd:

It seems a clear duty to us, who have experienced honourable treatment from this firm, to enter a protest against the sweeping condem-
nation passed upon them. We wish to record the fact that in the
course of many years' friendly business relations with Messrs. Harper
and Brothers we have always found them as just and liberal in their
dealings as any English house.

This letter made Kipling more furious than ever. Hot words
boiled from his pen, and before they had cooled off 'The Rhyme
of the Three Captains' had been sent to the *Athenaeum*, where it
appeared on December 6. The poem was an angry allegory,
beginning

At the close of a winter day,
Their anchors down, by London town, the Three Great Captains
lay;

And one was Admiral of the North from Solway Firth to Skye,
And one was Lord of the Wessex coast and all the lands thereby,
And one was Master of the Thames from Limehouse to Blackwall,
And he was Chaplain of the Fleet—the stoutest of them all.

No reader of the present book will have to be told who 'was Lord of the Wessex coast and all the lands thereby'. By 1890 everybody knew that Thomas Hardy was Lord of Wessex.

Kipling's poem continued in vigorous verse to tell the story of the 'Yankee brig' that had stolen his wares and of the infuriating interference of his three fellows who had announced to the world that the Harper 'price is fair'. Kipling wished to wash his hands of all such friends. So he called to his 'crew':

We'll out to the seas again—
Then fore-sheet home as she lifts to the foam—we stand on the outward tack.
We are paid in the coin of the white man's trade—the bezant is hard, ay, and black.

'The bezant is hard, ay, and black!' Besant, Hardy, and Black made no further response, and Hardy went on with the job of dismembering the manuscript of *Tess of the D'Urbervilles*.

In the intervals of this work Hardy found time to compose several poems, at least four of which are worthy of identification here:

1. 'Tess's Lament', expressing the milkmaid's feelings at Flint-comb-Ash. The poem indicates Hardy's interest in stanzaic experimentation, but it falls far short of attaining the emotional power of Tess's letters in prose.
2. 'In a Ewe-leaze near Weatherbury', a poem which shows Hardy's improvement in metrical fluency. It is possibly closely related to the one that follows next in this list.
3. 'Thoughts of Phena': this poem was suggested by the death of Hardy's cousin, Tryphena Sparks, to whom we gave some passing attention in Chapter V.
4. 'Lines Spoken by Miss Ada Rehan': this was an Epilogue recited by the actress at the Lyceum Theatre on July 23, 1890, at a performance on behalf of Mrs. Francis Jeune's Holiday Fund for City Children. 'Mary Jeune' (as Hardy had come to call her) was one of the London hostesses whose hospitality he enjoyed, and when she asked him to compose a poem for Ada Rehan to recite, Hardy could not refuse. He wrote the lines at the Savile Club at midnight on July 22. Two days later he

wrote to his wife (she had remained at Max Gate): 'Miss
Rehan read my verses. I was not there myself. The *Daily News*
says they are spirited; the *Globe* that they are poor stuff.'[1]

In addition to composing these verses, none of which were
published at this time, Hardy was able to market a number of
short stories—those that we have already given attention to in
Chapter IX. Of the stories listed in the first Note to that chapter, no fewer than seventeen (numbered 21–37) were published
in the course of the period (1889–92) when *Tess of the D'Urbervilles* was Hardy's chief literary concern.

One of the results of the bitter and abusive attacks made upon
him after the publication of *Tess* was his determination that his
next appearance in print should not offend anyone. He recalled
a tale he had sketched more than twenty years before, when he
was 'virtually a young man, and interested in the Platonic Idea'.
It now occurred to him that he might dig up this early sketch,
modify and develop it; and, 'bygone, wildly romantic fancy'
though it was, it might, he thought 'please Mrs. Grundy and her
Young Person, and her respected husband, by its absolutely
"harmless" quality'. This was the explanation Hardy made to
his friend Gosse to account for the immense contrast between
the Platonic story of 1892 and the novels which preceded and
followed it—*Tess* on one side and *Jude the Obscure* on the other—
for *The Pursuit of the Well-Beloved* is like neither.
    The origin of this story in Hardy's mind goes back to his early
days of reading Shelley in London, since his approach to 'the
Platonic Idea' was by way of Shelley. Of all the poems which
Hardy remembered, none was more frequently in his consciousness than 'Epipsychidion'. He had quoted it in 'An Indiscretion
in the Life of an Heiress'. He quoted it again in *The Mayor of
Casterbridge*, and again also in *The Woodlanders*. Within a few
years he was going to quote it yet again in *Jude the Obscure*. Two
lines from this poem suggested the 'romantic fancy' which
Hardy now decided to develop:

> In many mortal forms I rashly sought
> The shadow of that idol of my thought.

In *The Woodlanders* Hardy had made Fitzpiers talk about 'joy
accompanied by an idea which we project against any suitable

object'. In *The Pursuit of the Well-Beloved* Hardy now conceived of a sculptor, one Jocelyn Pierston, who was to feel 'joy accompanied by an idea'. The sculptor's name, Jocelyn, reminds us of the fact that there was a Jocelyn in William Harrison Ainsworth's *The Star Chamber* (1854) and of the fact that Ainsworth was Hardy's favourite author in boyhood.

Jocelyn Pierston was to pursue his Platonic Ideal in the form of Avice Caro. Hardy named his heroine 'Avice' after the seventeenth-century daughter of the Talbots—the family who had, in the days of Henry VIII, owned a small farm near the site of Max Gate known as Talbot-hays. This farm was now the property of Hardy's father, and from its name Hardy had already drawn the name of the dairy, Talbothays, where Tess met Angel Clare. Now, in *The Pursuit of the Well-Beloved*, he planned to make further use of these old family associations.

Pierston, then, as a young man of twenty, was scheduled to pursue Avice Caro, and there is nothing surprising in that pursuit. But when, twenty years later, Pierston as a man of forty pursues the Ideal in the form of Avice's daughter, and when, later still, Pierston as a man of sixty pursues the Ideal in the form of Avice's granddaughter, the plot tends to become ludicrous. Hardy meant it to be 'fanciful', but 'farcical' is what most readers of the story have found it to be.

Hardy did not linger long over *The Pursuit of the Well-Beloved*. As soon as his manuscript was finished he sent it to the *Illustrated London News* which had taken two of his stories in the past. The editor arranged for Walter Paget to make two illustrations for each of the twelve weeks during which the novel was to be serialized, and the *Pursuit* was finally run in the *News* from October 1 to December 17, 1892. It thus followed *Tess of the D'Urbervilles* by exactly one year.

But what a difference between the two! Hardy's labours with *Tess* had obviously exhausted his creative powers. There is a monotony and an inventive sterility about *The Pursuit* which make it impossible to call it anything other than a failure. The characters remain stone cold. Even apart from the fantastic plot of the story, it remains quite unconvincing. Hardy himself was not enthusiastic about it and, becoming involved (as we have seen) with plans for the dramatization of *Tess of the D'Urbervilles* and with other matters yet to be described, he allowed four years to go by before taking steps to prepare *The Pursuit* for publication as a book. It was finally published in March 1897 as the seventeenth volume in Osgood, McIlvaine's Uniform Edition of Hardy's Works.

The author was then subjected to the painful experience of having the book called something worse than a failure. He was 'grieved by a ferocious review',[2] and by the fact that 'certain critics affected to find unmentionable moral atrocities in its pages'.[3] Hardy thought that these critics were 'blinded by malignity'; he charged them with 'mendacious malice';[4] but nothing—not even subsequent praise of the book by Marcel Proust[5] and by D. H. Lawrence[6]—has been able to redeem it. *The Well-Beloved* (the title was shortened when the story was published as a book in 1897) has never been reprinted except as a part of Hardy's Collected Works. We need not linger over it here.

In the spring following the serialization of *The Pursuit of the Well-Beloved*, Hardy and his wife followed their annual custom of spending 'the season' in London. For ten days, however, in the latter part of May they left London in order to pay a visit to Ireland. On the eighteenth they went by train to Llandudno in Wales, and crossed to Dublin on the nineteenth. This Irish expedition was not the result of Hardy's having developed an interest in Ireland, but of his having been invited to be the guest in Dublin of the Lord-Lieutenant, the second Baron Houghton, and of the Baron's sister, Florence Milnes Henniker. She was the wife of a young army officer, Major Arthur H. Henniker, but while he was away from England on active duty with the British army, she served her brother as hostess at the Viceregal Lodge in Dublin. Mrs. Henniker, now thirty-eight years old, had literary ambitions. She had turned novelist just at the time when *Tess of the D'Urbervilles* was appearing, and had published *Sir George* in 1891, *Bid Me Good-bye* in 1892, and *Foiled* in 1893. The Hardys remained as her and her brother's guests in Dublin for ten days, arriving back in London on Monday, May 29, 1893.

Shortly after Hardy's return to Max Gate, Mrs. Henniker also returned to England and took up residence at Southsea, a section of Portsmouth. Letters began to fly back and forth between Max Gate and Southsea. In June Hardy gave Mrs.

Henniker a copy of *Tess*; in July, a copy of *A Laodicean*; in September, a copy of *Desperate Remedies*. In October, they began to collaborate in writing a gruesome story called 'The Spectre of the Real'.[7] Prior to the appearance of this story Mrs. Henniker had published a book of short stories entitled *Outlines*. It was dedicated 'To my friend Thomas Hardy'. She gave him a copy of the book in February 1894. Later in this year, Hardy helped her to get at least one of her stories into the pages of the *English Illustrated Magazine*.

All of this activity with Mrs. Henniker naturally clouded the domestic skies at Max Gate. 'Mrs. Hardy's growing eccentricities were [already] painfully manifest'[8] during the May 1893 visit to Dublin, and the events that followed her return to Max Gate increased the rift between the novelist and his wife.

At the end of the week that marked Hardy's return from Dublin to London, his one-act play *The Three Wayfarers* was performed at Terry's Theatre in London. The date was Saturday, June 3, 1893, the day after Hardy's fifty-third birthday. *The Three Wayfarers* was Hardy's own dramatization of his short story 'The Three Strangers' which James M. Barrie had suggested. Hardy and his wife saw the performance, taking 'Mary Jeune' with them. (Mrs. Jeune had now become Lady Jeune.) 'The little piece was well received,'[9] and on June 16 Hardy wrote to the chief actor, Charles Charrington: 'Your performance of the hangman was extraordinarily powerful and took everybody by surprise.'

The play was again performed in 1911 at Dorchester, and also in London and in Weymouth. On June 21, 1926, it was performed at Keble College, Oxford. In later years Hardy tended to scoff at it—in writing to Sydney Cockerell on November 9, 1911, he called it 'a mere trifle I did for a freak twenty years ago and should be horrified to write now'—but he really had no need to look down upon the amusing skit. Barrie's judgment about it was quite sound, and *The Three Wayfarers* has merits not found in *The Well-Beloved*.[10]

XVI

Sad Music of Humanity

ABOUT ten days after he had seen the performance of *The Three Wayfarers* Hardy did something that he had long promised himself to do: he visited Oxford. As far back as the early eighteen-sixties, when he had been a young assistant architect in London, he had written his sister Mary: 'Oxford must be a jolly place. I shall try to get down there some time or other.' Mary Hardy had been to Oxford several times, but for one reason or another her brother's desire to visit the University city had apparently never been satisfied.[1] Now, however, he had a special reason for wishing to see Oxford; he had decided that his next novel would deal with the keen desire of a poor boy for an Oxford education and with the tragic frustration of that desire. Chance or accident was to play almost no part in the new novel. Jude's frustration was to be brought about not by Crass Casualty—Hardy had by now outgrown any desire to emphasize that view of things—but by the callously indifferent and irresponsible action of Victorian society. In this theme Hardy felt that 'there is something the world ought to be shown, and I am the one to show it to them'.[2]

On or about Monday, the nineteenth of June, 1893, he accordingly went to Oxford and took a room in a small hotel near Carfax, 'a spot' (as he explains in Chapter II, 6, of the novel) 'called The Fourways [Quatre voies] in the middle of the city'. He remained in Oxford all through the 'Commemoration' period, watched the boat races, strolled about the college quadrangles, familiarized himself with the main thoroughfares—Broad Street, 'the High', 'the Corn' (Cornmarket Street)—noted 'the cross in the pavement which marked the spot of the

Martyrdoms' of Cranmer, Latimer, and Ridley, looked up at the Bodleian, 'the looming roof of the great library into which he hardly . . . had time to enter', and allowed his gaze to travel over 'the varied spires, halls, gables, streets, chapels, gardens, quadrangles, which composed the *ensemble* of this unrivalled panorama.'[3] When 'a bell began clanging' from under 'the ogee dome' of one of the colleges, he counted 'till a hundred-and-one strokes had sounded. He must have made a mistake, he thought: it was meant for a hundred.'[4] The college with the ogee dome had been founded by Cardinal Wolsey, and Hardy recalled that it was called 'Cardinal College' in Ainsworth's novel *Windsor Castle*. Hardy felt that, in the novel now taking shape in his mind, he could use the same name as that used by Ainsworth; and, the better to describe 'Cardinal College', he went and 'stood in a corner' of 'the great green quadrangle' and watched 'the figures walking along under the College walls'.[5]

Hardy remained in Oxford long enough to become aware of the fact that the University with its many colleges was only one side of the place. 'He began to see that the town life was a book of humanity infinitely more palpitating . . . than the gown life' and that the 'struggling men and women before him were the reality', whereas 'the floating population of students and teachers' were not Oxford 'in a local sense at all'.[6]

During these days of familiarizing himself with the University city, Hardy passed unnoticed in the crowds assembled for the boat races and for 'Commem', and, like Jude Fawley, 'knowing not a human being' there, he 'began to be impressed with the isolation of his own personality'.[7] When the time came for him to begin to write the new novel, it was inevitable that many aspects of the author's own personality and experience were transferred to his fictional characters. He had of course done this in all his novels, but in *Jude the Obscure* this subjective identification of himself with his characters became more pronounced than ever.

In making a statement like this the biographer is well aware of the fact that it contradicts an assertion made by Hardy himself. In *The Later Years* Mrs. Hardy is quoted as having written a letter at Hardy's request and obviously at his dictation: 'To your inquiry if *Jude the Obscure* is autobiographical, I have to answer that there is not a scrap of personal detail in it, it having

the least to do with his own life of all his books.'[8] This assertion
is so obviously untrue that one wonders why Hardy made it. In
the next chapter we shall try to arrive at an answer to the question 'Why?', but in the meantime the reader is entitled to know
just what grounds exist for regarding many things in *Jude the
Obscure* as autobiographical in spite of the author's explicit
statement to the contrary.

Hardy was born two miles from Stinsford ('Mellstock') and
Jude Fawley 'comes from Mellstock, down in South Wessex'.[9]
'Hardy was a born bookworm,'[10] and in *Jude* 'the boy is crazy
for books, that he is'. Once upon a time Hardy was stopped in
Dorchester by a boy who drove a baker's cart; the boy wanted
to borrow Hardy's Latin grammar. In the novel Jude asks 'for
some grammars, if you recollect', and is described as having
'driven old Drusilla Fawley's bread-cart'. When young Tom
Hardy became old enough to take his studies seriously, he
taught himself Homer by using Clarke's edition of the *Iliad*, just
as Jude Fawley 'dabbled in Clarke's *Homer*'. In February 1860,
while he was still studying architecture under John Hicks,
Hardy acquired a copy of Griesbach's edition of the New Testament in Greek (it was sold on May 26, 1938, in Lot 22 at the
sale of Hardy's library). He studied the book diligently in order
to fit himself for carrying on arguments about infant baptism
with the Perkins boys, the sons of the Baptist minister at
Dorchester. In *Jude the Obscure* young Fawley obtains 'by post
from a second-hand bookseller' a copy of the 'New Testament
in the Greek, . . . Griesbach's text', in which he was later described
as 'earnestly reading'. In 1863 Hardy bought a copy of Buckley's
translation of *Aeschylus*, from which he lifted the 'Aeschylean
phrase' which so annoyed some readers of *Tess of the D'Urbervilles*. In *Jude* (Chapter VI, 2) Fawley quoted from that same
book, citing (from the *Agamemnon*): 'Things are as they are, and
will be brought to their destined issue.'

On June 20, 1873, Hardy went to Cambridge and spent a
night at Queens' College as the guest of his friend Horace M.
Moule, just as Jude Fawley calls on Phillotson at Oxford. Jude
thinks of 'entering the Church' and 'keeping the necessary terms
at a Theological College' exactly as Hardy, in August 1865, had
thought of 'keeping terms'[11] at Cambridge with a view to fitting
himself for 'a curacy in a country village'—a career 'towards

which he had long had a leaning'. By this time Hardy had grown a dark beard, and in *Jude* (Chapter III, 3) Fawley wears a dark beard. Jude shares Hardy's view that Salisbury Cathedral is 'the most graceful architectural pile in England', and (in Chapter II, 3) 'the great waves of pedal music' which 'tumbled round the choir' of Oxford Cathedral affected Jude precisely as the organ music had affected Thomas Hardy on June 22, 1875, when he listened to it in Wimborne Minster. In *Jude* (Chapter IV, 5) Fawley quotes Hardy's favourite poem by Browning, 'The Statue and the Bust', and (in Chapter II, 6) shows himself to be familiar with Hardy's favourite *Book of Job*.

In view of this multiplicity of proved and reliable echoes, we are probably justified in surmising that in the novel we hear further echoes out of Hardy's own past. In Chapter III, 6, Jude remarks to Sue: 'We are cousins, and it is bad for cousins to marry', and (in II, 6) Jude is told: 'Don't you be a fool about her! . . . If your cousin is civil to you, take her civility for what it is worth, but anything more than a relation's good wishes it is stark madness for 'ee to give her'. One wonders whether Hardy was here recalling remarks made to him in 1868 when he was 'walking out' with his cousin Tryphena Sparks. In *Jude* (Chapter III, 8), after Sue had announced her intention to marry Phillotson, Fawley 'projected his mind into the future' and imagined his cousin Sue 'with children . . . around her'. However, 'the consolation of regarding them as a continuation of her identity was denied to him . . . by the wilfulness of Nature in not allowing issue from one parent alone'. Was this Thomas Hardy's own thought when, in 1877, his cousin Tryphena married Charles Gale? Their daughter, also called Tryphena, was born in 1878. After Hardy's cousin had died in 1890, he went to call on her daughter. In Chapter III, 8, Jude Fawley remarks: 'If at the . . . death of my lost love I could go and see her child—hers solely—there would be comfort in it.'

Nor is autobiography confined to Jude Fawley. Richard Phillotson shares Hardy's knowledge of Bernardin de St. Pierre and his familiarity with Shelley's poetry. Sue Bridehead is endowed with Hardy's knowledge of John Stuart Mill's *On Liberty* and she shares his familiarity with Swinburne's poems. She knows Hardy's favourite poem by Shelley, 'Epipsychidion', and she anticipates *The Dynasts* by at least ten years in expressing

Hardy's view that 'the First Cause worked automatically like a somnambulist and not reflectively like a sage'. In one of the most moving chapters of the novel (VI, 2), Sue, in a moment of uncontrollable grief, exclaims: 'There is something external to us which says "You shan't!" First it said "You shan't learn!" Then it said, "You shan't labour!" Now it says "You shan't love!" ' Sue had obviously been made to adopt the 'notion' of Mrs. Thomas Hardy, Senior, about the Figure with arm uplifted, ready 'to knock us back from any pleasant prospect'.

Hardy made similar use of the experience of other members of his family. His sisters, Mary and Katherine ('Kate'), had gone to a Teachers' Training School at Salisbury; he had once visited them there. In 1891 he visited the Training College for Schoolmistresses at Whitelands, and was reminded by that visit of the painful restrictions to which his sisters had been subjected during their period of training. Out of these memories came his description of that 'species of nunnery known as the Training School at Melchester' to which Sue Bridehead goes.

Hardy also drew on other family associations. His father had died in 1892—just a year before the novelist went to explore Oxford. This bereavement was the first time death had visited Hardy's immediate family since he was a boy. His grandmother Hardy had died when he was seventeen. She is the 'One We Knew' in the 1907 poem of that title. Hardy recalled his grandmother's stories of the first dozen years of her life, when, as a little girl named Mary Head, she had endured such hardships at Great Fawley in Berkshire, near Oxford, that she had never been willing to return to that spot after she had once left it. Hardy himself went to take a look at Great Fawley in October 1892 when the story of Jude was taking shape in his imagination. He decided to call his ambitious boy Fawley, and to rename the place where Mary Head had spent her girlhood 'Marygreen'.

With characters and incidents thus taking shape in his mind, Hardy decided to repeat, in general outline, the plot of *Tess of the D'Urbervilles*. For *Jude the Obscure* is *Tess* turned round about. The same sort of triangle is presented, with the sexes reversed. In place of the two men, Alec and Clare, involved in relations with Tess, Hardy created two women, Arabella and Sue, involved in relations with Jude. Both novels present the same contrast between selfish sensuality and fastidious aloofness. As we have noted in a previous chapter, Hardy's memory of a girl he had once seen riding in a farm cart suggested the physical appearance of his milkmaid; so now, his memory of the Dorchester boy who drove the baker's cart gave him a starting-point for his conception of young Jude Fawley. Corresponding to the death of the horse at the beginning of *Tess*, the killing of the pig serves to set things in motion in *Jude*. Fawley's failure to mention to Sue his marriage to Arabella corresponds to Tess's similar failure to speak of her past to Angel Clare. Jude's eventual 'confession' to Sue 'that he had married a wife . . . and that his wife was living still' parallels Tess's eventual confession to Clare. Just as the run-down property near Marnhull suggested an environment in which to place the shiftless Durbeyfields, so Mary Head's painful memories of Great Fawley suggested a suitable spot at which to begin the career of the intellectually eager but impecunious boy. And since Great Fawley was near Oxford—near enough (at least in Hardy's romantic imagination) for the spires of Oxford to be visible in the sunlight—Oxford rather than Cambridge was the logical place for the main action of the novel. Hardy decided to call the city 'Christminster'.

Hardy was well informed about the history of Oxford, particularly its Victorian history. He knew about the meeting of the British Association for the Advancement of Science at Oxford in 1860, when Bishop Wilberforce had been confronted and soundly defeated by T. H. Huxley. (Hardy had since met Huxley in London.) He knew that in 1863 Benjamin Jowett of Balliol College (called 'Biblioll' in *Jude*) had been prosecuted for heresy in the Vice-Chancellor's Court, and that a year later there was a debate in the Oxford University 'Congregation' in which Jowett was charged 'with holding and affirming doctrines subversive to the Church's faith'. Hardy was thus quite prepared, when Jude Fawley proposes to 'go and sit in the Cathedral', to make Sue Bridehead reply: 'I'd rather sit in the railway station. That's the centre of the town life now. The Cathedral has had its day.'

Once his theme and atmosphere, his characters and setting, his plot and tragic denouement, were all fixed in his mind, Hardy returned to Max Gate and began to write. As he warmed to the task, his heart became painfully involved. He was as

much distressed over the frustration of Jude Fawley's high hopes
as he had been over the sad fate of Tess Durbeyfield. For in Jude
Fawley, Hardy conceived of another character of genuine
worth—a man who was obscure and weak, it is true, but a man
of high ideals, true humility, steadfast courage, and affectionate
loyalty. Tess Durbeyfield had been endowed with some of these
same qualities, but there is one important distinction between
hero and heroine. In the end Tess had been crushed into a shell
of her real self, so much so that Angel Clare hardly recognized
her when he found her at Bournemouth. But nothing was to
stamp out the manhood in Jude's character. Scourged, disgraced, starved, deserted, ridiculed, tricked, despised, even
when he has been plied by Arabella with 'plenty of good liquor',
he refused to bow his head. 'Don't say anything against my
honour!' cried Jude hotly, standing up when he had hardly
strength enough in his legs to stand with. 'Listen to me, Arabella. You think you are the stronger; and so you are, in a
physical sense, now. You could push me over like a ninepin. But
I am not so weak in another way as you think. I made up my
mind. . . .'

Hardy, too, had made up his mind. He was going to write his
King Lear. There would be no room now for amusing rustics; no
idyllic descriptions of apple orchards or poetic accounts of the
seasons; no dallying with sensational feats of sword play or
dramatic scenes of sleep-walking or of cliff-hanging; no sorting
out of ill-mated couples to make a 'happy' ending; no soothing
sop of faith in a life hereafter in which the wrongs of this world
would be righted; no pretence, in short, that the worthy receive
any other reward than that which Shakespeare's Cordelia
shared with Goneril and Regan. And if some reader of the Wessex novel should, like Shakespeare's Kent, ask: 'Is *this* the
promised end?', Hardy was prepared to answer: 'Somebody
might have come along that way who would have asked him his
trouble, and might have cheered him. But nobody did come,
because nobody does.'

In writing lugubrious lines like these, Hardy was of course
hoping to move his readers not only to sympathize with Jude's
unhappy lot but also to stir them into wishing to *do* something
about it. He had not forgotten having written in *The Return of
the Native* his keen sense of the need for 'somebody to . . . teach

the world how to breast the misery they are born to'. Other novelists have influenced events; why not Thomas Hardy? 'O, I have ta'en too little care of this': he could echo King Lear's words. Unfortunately, Hardy's zeal for reform ran away with him. He was eager not only to reform Oxford and the Church, not only to modernize Education and banish the empty ritualism of a formal and stagnant religion, but also to humanize Parliamentary legislation about divorce and to liberalize social attitudes towards 'emancipated' women like Sue Bridehead. In an ambitious programme of such scope, Hardy was of course doomed to failure. A man of more practical experience would never have attempted so much.

Not that novels are impotent as vehicles of reform. On the contrary, they can be quite effective. E. M. Forster's *A Passage to India* thirty years later was to give a brilliant demonstration of how a novel can change the climate of thought. British colonialism was not only changed, but changed so completely and so promptly, as to leave little doubt about Forster's novel deserving its reputation as the most successful propagandist novel of the twentieth century. If Hardy failed, as he did, it was not because the novel, as an art-form, is unfitted to bring about social reform; it was because Hardy's aim was too sweeping, his skill too defective, and—it must be admitted—his artistic control too frenzied.

As Hardy went on with his tragic theme, he began to realize that, as a novel intended for serialization in a magazine, it was not going to prove satisfactory to any editor. His recent experience with *Tess* had taught him that English editors were still far from being willing to take what he had to offer; and the editor of *Harper's Magazine*, who had offered to take Hardy's new novel, had made it clear that attitudes and timidities in New York were not unlike those that confronted Hardy in London. The New York editor had written to explain to Hardy that *Harper's* was a 'family periodical' and that it could not publish a serial along the lines of *Tess*. Hardy had replied that the novel he was now working on 'would not bring a blush to a schoolgirl's cheek' (the phrase is J. Henry Harper's), but after the story got under way, Hardy found that 'the characters had taken things into their own hands' and the result was not at all what the author had expected. He therefore wrote in April 1894 to ask *Harper's* to release him from his agreement with the magazine. The New York publishing house was not eager to give up the idea of having a famous author appear in its periodical and therefore advised delay. Let Hardy go on with the writing of his story and when it was all finished, he and the publishers could again discuss the matter.

Hardy completed his manuscript, and in October 1894 he and J. Henry Harper had another meeting in London. The result was just what Hardy had foreseen. His story was much too outspoken for Harper acceptance, but (under New York urging) he finally agreed to do for *Jude* just what he had done three or four years previously for *Tess*. He would rewrite certain passages, he would delete others, and would patch up the scars left by this mutilation. Back to Max Gate Hardy went. Jude's illegitimate children were transformed into adopted orphans, and in a few weeks Hardy had a 'safe' manuscript in the hands of the publishers.

The first instalment appeared in the December 1894 issue of *Harper's New Monthly Magazine*. The story was there entitled *The Simpletons*. This title immediately aroused comment because of its resemblance to Charles Reade's *A Simpleton*. When, therefore, the second instalment appeared in the January 1895 issue of the magazine, the title of the novel was changed to *Hearts Insurgent*, and under this title it ended its run in the November 1895 number. W. Hatherell had been employed to make twelve illustrations for the novel, and Hardy was especially pleased with the results achieved by this artist. On November 10, 1895, he wrote to Hatherell: 'Allow me to express my sincere admiration for the illustration of "Jude at the Milestone". The picture is a tragedy in itself, and I do not remember ever before having an artist who grasped a situation so thoroughly.' Hardy later put these illustrations up on the wall of his study. They are now in the Hardy Room of the Dorset County Museum in Dorchester.

As soon as the magazine had finished with his manuscript, Hardy set about correcting its mutilated condition for Osgood, McIlvaine's printers.[12] He had marked it: 'Alterations and deletions in blue and green are for serial publication only.' In August 1895 he prepared a preface, in which he tried to disarm criticism by reminding readers that the story was 'addressed by a man to men and women of full age'. The title was now changed to *Jude the Obscure,* and under this title the book was published in November in both London and New York. The London edition (out on November 1) contained a frontispiece etching by Macbeth-Raeburn; the New York edition (published by Harper & Brothers two weeks after the London edition) reproduced the twelve illustrations prepared by Hatherell for the magazine.

Immediately bedlam broke loose. Reviewers and critics were violent in their denunciations. The clergy and the genteel world tore their passions to tatters. In the January 1896 *Blackwood's Magazine,* Mrs. M. O. W. Oliphant 'screamed' (the word is Hardy's own) that the novelist was trying to establish a wicked 'anti-marriage league'. The Reverend W. W. How, Bishop of Wakefield, threw Hardy's book into the fire—at least he publicly announced that he had done so—and sent a scandalized remonstrance to London with the result that *Jude the Obscure* was promptly withdrawn from Smith's Circulating Library. A lecturer in Liverpool, discussing Hardy's novels at some length, told his audience that 'this author has a curious mania for exploiting sewers; filth and defilement he faces with the calm, unshrinking countenance of a Local Board labourer'.

The noise of alarm was just as loud in America. The *Bookman* called *Jude* 'a novel of lubricity', and *The Critic* announced that Professor Harry Thurston Peck had branded it as 'one of the most objectionable books he had ever read'. In the *New York World* for December 8, 1895, Jeannette L. Gilder hysterically announced:

Thomas Hardy has scandalized the critics and shocked his friends. What has gone wrong with the hand that wrote *Far from the Madding Crowd?* I am shocked, appalled by this story. *Jude the Obscure* . . . is almost the worst book I have ever read. . . . No wonder that *Harper's Magazine* could not print it all. The only wonder is, that it could print any of it. . . . I do not believe that there is a newspaper in England or America that would print this story . . . as it stands in the book. Aside from its immorality, there is its coarseness which is beyond belief. . . . Mr. Hardy's mind seems to be grovelling all through this story. He goes out of his way to write of nastiness. . . . When I finished the story I opened the window and let in the fresh air.

In the uproar two or three quieter and saner voices could hardly be heard. Swinburne wrote to Hardy to say: 'The tragedy is equally beautiful and terrible in its pathos.' In a new magazine called *Cosmopolis*, Hardy's friend Gosse wrote: '*Jude the Obscure* is an irresistible book'; but, he explained, somewhat apologetically, that Hardy had here 'aimed higher than he ever aimed before, and it is not to be maintained that he has been equally successful in every part of his design'.

Few critics and reviewers in the eighteen-nineties were able to grasp Hardy's idealistic vision of the possibilities of human life. That vision had beckoned Hardy just as the gleaming 'city of light', Oxford, had beckoned Jude in his youth. It was a vision of a society in which laws and conventions would more nearly coincide with individual human needs. 'Is there anything better on earth than that we should love one another?' At least one of Hardy's more recent critics has acquired the insight to see and the courage to declare that 'the love of Jude and Sue, with all its error and its agony, most nearly approaches the ideal love, and this is the one love that we are allowed to see persisting into years of married life'. Hardy's mind was genuinely philosophical; he brooded over what he saw. He had listened so intently to what Wordsworth called 'the still sad music of humanity' that he had become attuned to its tragic chords. The tragedy in *Jude the Obscure* is not that the President of the Immortals had ended his sport with Jude; it is not that of a divine Miltonic lawgiver handing out punishment for wrongdoing; it is not a seasonal catastrophe that can be repaired in sunnier days. It is, simply and finally, without possibility of repair, tragedy—stark, blank, and unrelieved.

Jude the Obscure, more than any other of the Wessex novels, is full of fancies and dreams. There is more talk and less incident. Sue is one day made to exclaim: 'You are Joseph the dreamer of dreams, dear Jude. And sometimes you are Saint Stephen, who, while they were stoning him, could see Heaven opened.' Hardy, too, was a dreamer of dreams. Unfortunately, his readers in the eighteen-nineties were unable to see his vision. Years later, the novelist remarked that it had always been his misfortune to pre-suppose a too-intelligent reading public. In a preface which he wrote for the 1912 reissue of *Jude the Obscure* he remarked:

In my own eyes the sad feature of the attack was that the greater part of the story—that which presented the shattered ideals of the two chief characters, and had been more especially, and indeed almost exclusively, the part of interest to myself—was practically ignored by the adverse press of two countries; the while that some twenty or thirty pages of sorry detail deemed necessary to complete the narrative, and show the antitheses in Jude's life, were almost the sole portions read and regarded.

In presenting the shattered ideals of his characters Hardy had hoped to be able to influence the world's way of thinking and doing. In this he failed. 'The only effect of it on human conduct that I could discover,' he grimly remarked years later, was 'its effect on myself—the experience completely curing me of further interest in novel-writing.' He never wrote another.

Now that seventy years have passed, *Jude the Obscure* can be read with a quieter pulse, even though the critics still disagree. H. C. Duffin calls *Jude* 'the greatest of Hardy's novels' and finds in it 'a vastness, an inexhaustibility, that . . . carry us out into the illimitable spaces of thought. . . . I cannot see how *Jude the Obscure* should ever die for any man or any age.'[13] W. R. Rutland, on the other hand, sees in *Jude* only 'Hardy's deliberate determination to create a nasty taste'. He finds the description of the pig-sticking 'physically sickening', and thinks that Hardy 'deliberately did all he could to horrify and outrage his readers'.[14] In the long run Swinburne's judgment is likely to prove the best. *Jude the Obscure* is a great tragedy, 'beautiful and terrible in its pathos'. It is Hardy's most sustained effort, his bitterest piece of fiction, the one in which he was most seriously in earnest. In it he tried, as he declared in 1895, 'to deal unaffectedly with the fret and fever, derision and disaster, that may press in the wake of the strongest passion known to humanity: to tell, without a mincing of words, a deadly war waged between flesh and spirit; and to point the tragedy of unfulfilled aims'. It is an unpleasant and at times a painful work. So is *King Lear*. But any reader of mature mind may take it up with the assurance 'that certain cathartic, Aristotelian qualities may be found therein'. At any rate, that was Hardy's hope in writing the novel.

XVII

Deep Division

THE 'poor lady' (as Hardy called her in the 1912 preface to *Jude*) who 'screamed' in *Blackwood's Magazine* that there was an unholy anti-marriage league afoot was not the only one whose attention was caught by the fact that, in *Jude the Obscure*, Hardy seemed to dwell with uncommon and unnecessary repetition upon the theme of marriage and mismating. Professor Bruce McCullough, of New York University, eventually made the same observation and decided that there was 'some evidence of a failure of temper' on the part of the author. No careful reader of the novel can fail to notice the vehemence with which the subject of mating is discussed. 'A marriage ceremony . . . is only a sordid contract, based on material convenience' (Chapter IV, 2). 'Fewer women like marriage than you suppose; . . . they enter into it for . . . the social advantages it gains them' (V, 1). 'Wifedom has not yet squashed up and digested you in its vast maw' (III, 9). 'I think I should begin to be afraid of you, Jude, the moment you had contracted to cherish me under a Government stamp, and I was licensed to be loved on the premises' (V, 1). 'Arabella . . . has made me feel more than ever how hopelessly vulgar an institution legal marriage is' (V, 3). Hardy once pointed out to a friend in private that all these remarks occur in dialogue—it is Jude or Sue talking, not Hardy himself—and that these five quotations are only five, in a book of five hundred pages; but we who have noticed the many autobiographical features in the novel will not be easily convinced by Hardy's disclaimer. Nor are we likely to be over-impressed by the arguments of those who stress the fact that the subject of marriage and divorce was on everyone's lips in England in 1890, at the time when the notorious Parnell Case filled the newspapers.

Hardy's private correspondence points to a nearer source of his interest in this subject—nearer both in time and in space—for at Lady Jeune's dinner-table in London Hardy often heard discussions of the problems presented by the British divorce laws. Sir Francis Jeune (later created Lord St. Helier) held the post of Judge-Advocate-General and had many a story to tell—some amusing, some tragic—about his Divorce Court experience. Hardy later set down two of these stories in *Later Years* (p. 110). He was particularly impressed with the difficulties of separating ill-mated couples, with the problems involved when there are children, and with the rigidity of the legal code. Hardy remembered one conversation he had listened to shortly after his visit to Oxford—one in which the Duchess of Manchester, Lady Londonderry, and Lady Jeune had discussed the divorce law; and he remembered a similar occasion, again at the home of Lady Jeune, when the Duchess of Abercorn was present and took part in the discussion. Hardy afterwards sent her a copy of *Jude the Obscure*, knowing (he said) that she would 'understand and sympathize with the shadowy personages it concerns'.

In spite of all these circumstances, the fact remains that there is in *Jude* a vehemence and a bitterness of tone in the remarks on marriage which inevitably invite surmises that their explanation involves something other than dinner-table conversations, something that touched Thomas Hardy more closely than Parliamentary laws. Lord David Cecil has remarked that 'there is a noticeable similarity between Sue's story and that of Rebecca West. Both are "emancipated" women. . . .'[1] Professor Richard Little Purdy does more than note a similarity: he speaks of cause and effect. He has stated[2] that Sue Bridehead was in part drawn from Mrs. Florence Henniker, whom Hardy had visited in Dublin in May 1893 and with whom he collaborated in writing a short story during the months when *Jude the Obscure* was being written. One can here find a possible explanation of Hardy's reluctance to have anyone think that *Jude the Obscure* was in any way autobiographical.

We can, however, come even closer than that to an understanding of the strained conditions at Max Gate, and fortunately we do not have to rely upon guesses or gossip. Independent and corroborating evidence is available to make it quite clear that Hardy's sensitiveness on the subject of *Jude the Obscure* was related to his wife's attitude towards this novel. For twenty years Emma Hardy had worked with him as he composed his novels. She had often been called upon to make 'fair copies' of his manuscripts, and in one case—*A Laodicean*—she had had to write out much of the novel at his dictation. Except for the first two anonymous stories, *Desperate Remedies* and *Under the Greenwood Tree*, Mrs. Hardy had had her hand upon, if not actually *in*, all his manuscripts. Her physician (Dr. Fred B. Fisher) later remarked: 'She gave me the impression she revised them pretty freely.' This was probably only the doctor's impression, and most certainly an erroneous one, but he was not the only person to be given such an impression. A French visitor to Max Gate, M. Henri Davray, came away with the belief that Mrs. Hardy was quite willing to have him think that it was her hand that put the finishing touches to her husband's rough drafts. Davray noticed that Hardy maintained an attitude of simple dignity and remained silent when Mrs. Hardy spoke of collaborating with her husband; the French caller thought him timid and resigned to a situation he could not change. T. P. O'Connor in London also reported having heard Mrs. Emma Hardy make claims of having done part of the writing: ' "I have it all here", pointing to her ample bosom.' Of one thing there can be no doubt: many pages of the surviving manuscripts of the Wessex novels are in her handwriting.

In 1894, however, this long-established custom changed. When Mrs. Hardy came to read what her husband had written in *Jude the Obscure*, she threw the pages away from her in disgust, so she told Dr. Fisher, and vowed that 'she'd never have anything more to do with any book he wrote'. Those scandalous remarks about holy matrimony, those shocking lines about being 'licensed to be loved on the premises', those coarse comments. . .! They ought never to be put into a book. Quite apart from any possibility that she recognized Florence Henniker in the portrait of Sue Bridehead—and this is perhaps more than a possibility—Emma Hardy was convinced that *Jude the Obscure* was not fit to be printed. If her husband's judgment had become so befouled and if his taste had sunk so low, something ought to be done to stop him before he disgraced both himself and her.

Mrs. Hardy accordingly made a special trip up to London and applied to Dr. Richard Garnett at the British Museum for help in persuading her husband that he ought to burn his vicious manuscript. Dr. Garnett, even though he enjoyed a reputation (at least in Mrs. Hardy's eyes) as Dean of Letters, assured her that he had no powers as Court Censor; and, in the final outcome, Mrs. Hardy had to return, defeated, to Max Gate. Unfortunately, Garnett reported the incident to his own family circle; and, upon hearing the story, the young Garnetts were either appalled or amused, depending upon their age and their own individual leanings. But, between horrified gasps and sophisticated snickers, the news got around in the British Museum that Dr. Garnett had been appealed to by the novelist's wife for aid in getting a perfectly awful book suppressed, but that the shocker was apparently going to appear in print after all. This of course only helped to advertise the book. Within three months of its publication *Jude the Obscure* was in its twentieth thousand. Hardy reported (truthfully enough) that his experience with *Jude* had 'completely cured him of further interest in novel-writing'—'No more novel-writing for me!'— but he said nothing about the ironical fact that *Jude* put more money into his purse than any book he had written. Not only did *Jude* sell briskly, but every copy sold helped to stir interest in the dozen novels that had preceded it.

Mrs. Hardy's refusal to 'have anything more to do with any book he wrote' was, of course, not a first step, but the culmination of a series of events that led up to the estrangement now felt at Max Gate. She thought back over the ten years she had spent in Max Gate, 'the house . . . built so new for me',[3] and meditated on the shadows cast upon its happiness by an increasingly long parade of women: society leaders like Lady Jeune, actresses like Mrs. Campbell, novelists like Mrs. Henniker, admirers like Rebekah Owen, portrait-painters like Winifred Hope Thomson, to say nothing of the duchesses, marchionesses, countesses, and other 'noble dames' whose tea-tables and dinner-parties and theatre-halls Hardy was taking increasing delight in gracing. Here we have no need to rely upon conjecture or surmise. T. P. O'Connor has reported how Emma Hardy one day blurted out to him that her husband was really 'very vain and very selfish. And these women that he meets in London society only increase these things. They are the poison; I am the antidote.'

Hardy himself eventually came to comment on Emma's inability to refrain from using 'words inept'[4] like these. The habit grew upon her, and testimony about it comes from many sources. Sir Desmond MacCarthy (editor of the *New Quarterly* and later co-editor of *Life and Letters*) remembered Mrs. Hardy's saying to him sharply at tea one day: 'If you listen to what *I* am saying, you will find it as well worth hearing as Mr. Hardy's remarks.' Rebecca West once heard her say: 'Try to remember, Thomas Hardy, that you married a lady!'

Unfortunately, what Hardy did remember was that he had married

> an ageing shape
> Where beauty used to be;
> That her fond phantom lingers there
> Is only known to me.[5]

In contrast with Emma's ageing shape, Lady Jeune 'looked handsome', Mrs. T— was 'the most beautiful woman present', Lady Yarborough was 'very pretty', the Duchess of Manchester was a 'laughing-eyed woman', Lady P— was 'the most beautiful woman there', Miss —— was a 'handsome girl', Mrs. R. C. and Mrs. A. G. were 'a pair of beauties' and the latter 'was the more seductive'. Emma Hardy obviously had some reason for thinking 'They are the poison; I am the antidote.' And Hardy not only set down these notes about feminine charm and seductive beauty in his notebooks but eventually, thirty years later, took steps to see that they all attained publication in his autobiography.

The contrast between Mrs. Hardy's 'shape where beauty used to be' and the 'pair of beauties' between whom Hardy once sat at a London dinner-table made a striking impression upon Mrs. Gertrude Atherton (author of *The Doomswoman*, 1892) when she came from California to pay a visit to London. William Sharp and his wife gave an afternoon reception for Mrs. Atherton, to which Hardy came, alone, and impressed the California visitor by his 'almost excessive refinement of feature and air of gentle detachment'. Later, at the home of the Duchess of Sutherland, Mrs. Atherton saw Hardy again. 'In his wake was an excessively plain, dowdy, high-stomached woman with her hair drawn back in a tight little knot.' It was Mrs. Hardy. Gertrude Atherton thought that 'no doubt Hardy went out [into society] so constantly to be rid of her'. Mrs. Atherton had no way of knowing that Mrs. Hardy often stayed away, or remained at home at Max Gate, of her own desire and choice: it was her means of keeping aloof from a situation that was, as she thought, spoiling her 'very vain and very selfish' husband.

Hardy's own thoughts at this time of stress and strain can be gauged by anyone who will read his three poems entitled 'In Tenebris'. Though not published until 1902 in *Poems of the Past and the Present*, they are all three dated '1895–96'. In the first he speaks of 'my bereavement pain' and consoles himself with the thought that 'love can not make smart . . . his heart who no heart hath'. In the second he thinks of himself as 'one born out of due time, who has no calling here'. In the third, he has 'learnt that the world is a welter of futile doing', and that 'sweets to the mouth, in the belly are bitter and tart'. In a poem called 'The Division' Hardy spoke of 'that thwart thing betwixt us twain which nothing cleaves or clears',[6] but it will by now be clear to the reader that there was more than one 'thwart thing' between the two persons who dwelt together at Max Gate.

Emma's social snobbery and her exaggerated ideas about her own literary powers, his eye for feminine beauty and his blindness to the jealousy he was arousing in 'the woman whom I loved so, and who loyally loved me',[7] their inability to see eye to eye in matters of religious faith—all these causes of friction might have been surmounted without bringing the couple to what Hardy called 'our deep division and our dark undying pain',[8] if there had been present in the marriage one other item—perfect sexual compatibility. About a matter like this it is obviously impossible to speak with any assurance. Neither of them, naturally enough, ever made any comment on this aspect of their marriage; and one must be cautious about jumping to rash conclusions based on Hardy's frequent references to Diana (as 'the goddess whom Bathsheba instinctively adored' in *Far from the Madding Crowd*) or to Artemis (the goddess who represented a larger part of Grace Melbury's constitution in *The Woodlanders* 'than [did] Aphrodite') or to women like Sue Bridehead ('a phantasmal, bodiless creature . . . who had so little animal passion'). It is quite possible that none of this has any autobiographical significance whatever. On the other hand, there is a note written down by Hardy on August 13, 1877, when he and Mrs. Hardy were living at Sturminster Newton. At that date they had been married nearly three years. In his notebook Hardy wrote: 'We hear that Jane, our late servant, is soon to have a baby. Yet never a sign of one is there for us.' Obviously, Hardy would never have written a note like this if there had been no reason for thinking that there *might* have been a baby. Nor is it likely that he would have published this record fifty years later— as he did—unless he had felt that his failure to acquire a child of his own seemed to him Emma's fault rather than his own. No one knows, of course, and conjecture is dangerous. In any case, the possibility exists that physical incompatibility contributed to the 'deep division and dark undying pain' at Max Gate.

The pain was, of course, not felt only by Hardy. Mrs. Hardy suffered too. Here, again, we are not guessing or gossiping, for the evidence of her distress has survived in her own handwriting. On August 20, 1899, she wrote to Mrs. Kenneth Grahame, who (at the age of forty) married the man who was shortly to become world-famous as the author of *The Wind in the Willows*. Mrs. Grahame wondered how a woman might best insure success in her marriage to a man who was a public figure and a man of letters; she applied to Mrs. Thomas Hardy as one who would know. Mrs. Hardy replied, identifying herself as 'one who has just come to the [end of her] twenty-fifth year of matrimony':

I can scarcely think that love proper, and enduring, is in the nature of men. . . . There is ever a desire to give but little in return for our devotion and affection. . . . Keeping separate a good deal is a wise plan in crises . . . and expecting little, neither gratitude, nor attentions, love, nor *justice*, nor anything you may set your heart on. . . . Love . . . is usually a failure— . . . some one comes by and upsets your pail of milk in the end. . . . Years of devotion count for nothing

. . . hundreds of wives go through a phase of disillusion—it is really a pity to have any ideals in the first place.[9]

It is unlikely that Hardy ever saw this unhappy letter, or knew its contents, but he did not need to. He was already well aware of the fact that all genial warmth had disappeared from his life at Max Gate. As the nineteenth century straggled towards its drab end in December 1900, he sat in his study composing the lines of a poem, eventually to be called 'The Darkling Thrush':

> The ancient pulse of germ and birth
> Was shrunken hard and dry,
> And every spirit upon earth
> Seemed fervourless as I.

XVIII

The End of Prose

'NO more novel-writing for me!' Hardy had exclaimed when the barbed arrows were flying in his direction. And after *Jude* he never wrote another. This does not mean, however, that his concern with his novels ended. On the contrary, he now proceeded to give them, in some ways, more careful attention than he had ever before found it possible to give. Now that the creative effort was over, he embarked upon two decades of polishing his work.

On April 24, 1895, Hardy wrote his wife from the Athenaeum Club in London: 'I am overwhelmed with neglected proofs which I want to get at.'[1] Osgood, McIlvaine & Co. had begun issuing the seventeen-volume Uniform Edition of his works, one volume each month, and in addition to carrying this heavy load of proof-reading Hardy was writing a new preface for each volume. In January (1895) he had written the preface for *Tess*; in February, one for *The Mayor*; in March, for *A Pair of Blue Eyes*; and in April, for *Far from the Madding Crowd*. After a May 'season' in London, he went on with the work. A preface was written in June for *The Return of the Native*; in July, for *Two on a Tower*; in August, for *Jude the Obscure*; in September, for *The Woodlanders*; in October, for *The Trumpet-Major*; and in December, for *The Hand of Ethelberta*.

His task was not merely a matter of composing a preface each month; it involved also a careful combing of the entire text of each novel. In some cases hardly a page of the book escaped revision. Syntax was strengthened, metaphors were added, dialect was revised, awkwardness was removed, and various

219

infelicities were deleted. Miss Rebekah Owen won her point with regard to the ending of *The Mayor of Casterbridge* and the caged goldfinch went back into the text of that novel. The same exhausting pace was kept up in 1896. In January there was a new preface to *A Laodicean*, in February to *Desperate Remedies*, in April to *Wessex Tales*, in June to both *A Group of Noble Dames* and *Life's Little Ironies*, and in August to *Under the Greenwood Tree*. Hardy spent a well-earned vacation in Belgium in the autumn, and wrote the last of the new prefaces—that for *The Well-Beloved*—in January 1897.

After Macmillan & Co. took over the business of publishing Hardy in 1902, they continued to issue the seventeen-volume edition for which James R. Osgood had made the arrangements with Hardy; but shortly after the novelist's seventieth birthday in 1910, his publishers proposed a definitive edition of his works; whereupon the whole business of textual revision, new preface-writing, and proof-reading had to be repeated. In October 1911 Hardy accordingly wrote a General Preface for the new set of books—it was to be called the 'Wessex Edition'[2]—in which Osgood's seventeen volumes were to reappear but in a somewhat different order; and eventually seven more volumes were added to it: an eighteenth volume of prose in 1913 (*A Changed Man and Other Tales*), in which Hardy collected a dozen previously published short stories (see Chapter IX); five volumes of verse, 1912–26; and a posthumous volume of poetry in 1931. In preparation for this Wessex Edition, Hardy wrote a new prefatory note for *Tess* in March 1912; in April, new prefaces for *Jude the Obscure* and *The Return of the Native*; in May, for *The Mayor of Casterbridge* and *Wessex Tales*; in August, for *Desperate Remedies*; and (somewhat later) a brief note added to the preface of *Wessex Tales*.

In all this later handling of the novels, Hardy's work was by no means confined to writing prefaces and reading proofs. A careful comparison of the text of the definitive edition with earlier versions of the novels shows that Hardy put a vast amount of thought and care into his revisions. His deprecatory remarks about his novels, especially those uttered in moments of extreme depression, are apt to mislead the reader and blind him to the fact that Hardy toiled through the novels, line by line, word by word, with extreme patience. He was tireless in the attempt not only to correct faulty punctuation and grammar —Lionel Johnson once sadly observed that Hardy, like Fanny Burney, was 'an inveterate patron of the split infinitive'—but also to strengthen diction, beautify rhythm, clarify thought, and enrich the suggestive power of his lines. Learned allusions were added, quotations were checked and specified, geography was made more specific and accurate, and the handling of dialect was greatly improved. In *Tess of the D'Urbervilles*, for example, Hardy devoted himself with great care to making the dialect serve more effectively in characterization. Mrs. Durbeyfield was assigned an increased number of dialectal words, while Tess was restricted in her use of the Dorset dialect. In *The Woodlanders* Hardy was noticeably eager to eliminate stilted speeches and to render the dialogue more natural. Some of the novels emerged from this grooming with a text quite renovated. Of the 508 pages in the current Harper edition of *Tess of the D'Urbervilles*, there are only 160 which carry no trace of revision.

This late polishing of Hardy's style accounts for some of the differences between twentieth-century praise of his prose and the sneers of some of his Victorian critics. Ninety years ago *The Athenaeum* could remark: 'Though his style is often admirable, Hardy gives us monstrous periphrases . . . till we almost despair of him.'[3] As J. H. Fowler has more recently observed:

Hardy's style has the great merits and the real defects of a self-taught style. . . . It is in some ways a learned style, possibly a too learned style, full of allusions to scientific facts and theories, to art and to literature. . . . It betrays the lack of that academic training which perhaps produces its greatest triumph in the finished art of Thackeray.[4]

If Hardy had been a student under Adam Smith at Edinburgh, he would have been assigned Jonathan Swift as a model for the improvement of his style; but instead of reading Swift, he read William Harrison Ainsworth. As a result of his 'lack of academic training', Hardy was, after fifty years' experience in writing English prose, still capable of perpetrating an autobiographical sentence like this:

In the same month he arranged with Messrs. Smith and Elder for the three-volume publication of *The Trumpet-Major*, which had been coming out in a periodical, and on the 27th started with Mrs. Hardy for Boulogne, Amiens—'the misfortune of the Cathedral is that it does not look half so lofty as it really is'—and several towns in Normandy, including Etretat, where they put up at the Hotel Blanquet, and stayed some time, bathing every day—a recreation which cost Hardy dear, for being fond of swimming he was apt to stay too long in the water.[5]

An additional reason for the unevenness of Hardy's style was his curious belief that prose 'comes along' like the wind, naturally; not like organ music, controlled and ordered. When Hamlin Garland called on Hardy in the mid-nineteen-twenties, Hardy told him that Professor Joseph Warren Beach of the University of Minnesota had recently called at Max Gate and had left a copy of his book *The Technique of Thomas Hardy* (Chicago, 1922). 'Upon reading it,' said Hardy, 'I found he had made no reference to my technique as a poet. There isn't any technique about prose, is there? It just comes along of itself.'

In his General Preface of 1911 Hardy selected one topic as worthy of special mention. 'The geographical limits of the stage here trodden were not,' he declared, 'forced upon the writer by circumstances; he forced them upon himself from judgment. I considered that there was quite enough human nature in Wessex for one man's literary purpose.'

Curiously enough, however, in spite of this 'judgment', Hardy liked to let his imagination range far abroad, and whenever he did so, he allowed errors and incongruities to creep into his stories—errors which remained uncorrected through all the years of revising and amending. In *A Pair of Blue Eyes* Stephen Smith goes off to Bombay. In *Far from the Madding Crowd* Troy works his passage to the United States, where Hardy would have us believe he made 'a precarious living in various towns as Professor of Gymnastics'. In *The Return of the Native* Wildeve announces that he has 'kindred in Wisconsin'. In *Two on a Tower* the young astronomer lands at Boston, but taking no interest in cities he goes, as we have already noticed, 'immediately on to Cambridge'. In *The Mayor of Casterbridge*, Newson went to Canada, where he was washed overboard, but 'got ashore at Newfoundland'. Most incongruous of all is 'that South Carolina gentleman of very passionate nature' who turns up in the moonlit pages of *The Woodlanders*.

The most grotesque distortion of foreign lands in all the Wessex novels is found in five chapters of *Tess of the D'Urbervilles* in which Brazil figures. The reason for this intrusion of Brazil is of some biographical interest. During the three years immediately preceding the publication of *Tess*, hundreds of thousands of agricultural labourers had emigrated from Europe to Brazil. In August 1890, as Hardy and his brother Henry were setting out from Southampton to cross the English Channel on their way to France, they passed a huge Brazilian ship. The little Channel steamer was, so Hardy thought, 'almost overwhelmed by the enormous bulk' of the South American vessel. He was reminded of the notices published in *The Times* throughout the preceding year, warning emigrants about the epidemics, fevers, fraudulent agents, heat, rain, and other hardships likely to be encountered in Brazil. Hardy also recalled from earlier days that there had been previous emigration to the 'empire' of Brazil. In 1868–9 there had been a large exodus of Algerian French to a spot near Curitiba, and about 1880 two thousand Russians from the Volga had also settled in the neighbourhood of Curitiba. Both these colonizing attempts had resulted in failure. The outcome of all these recollections, mixing vaguely in Hardy's memory, was the fantastic land to which he makes Angel Clare emigrate. Hardy never bothered to learn that Curitiba, delightfully situated on a high and healthful plateau, is two thousand miles south of the rainy, clay lands of the Amazonian plain. To represent Clare, on mule back near Curitiba, as riding on Amazonian clay and under Amazonian heat and rain is as curious a mixture of climates as it would have been to describe Michael Henchard as staggering down a Dorchester street under the heat and over the sands of the Sahara. When Hardy forsakes his own native region, the result is almost always unconvincing.

In Wessex, however, he is just what Kipling called him— 'Lord'. There he reigns supreme. His knowledge is not only extensive, it is intimate and accurate in detail, and it is amazingly varied. Many critics have commented on the skilful artistry shown by Hardy in dealing with the geographical and topographical variety found in the small compass of Dorset. When Donald Maxwell was engaged in making his 'artist's anthology of the landscape of the Wessex novels',[6] Hardy advised him to concentrate his attention on ten of the novels. Hardy explained the omission of four of his fourteen full-length novels by stating that in these four he had not had 'much chance of getting a complete atmosphere for each'. Hardy therefore thought that *Desperate Remedies, The Hand of Ethelberta, A Laodicean,* and *A Pair of Blue Eyes* might well be ignored by Maxwell. The artist took Hardy's advice and soon discovered that, in the other ten novels, the settings differ essentially, the two most nearly alike being *Under the Greenwood Tree* and *The Woodlanders.* Each of the ten has a different geographical atmosphere, as it were, a different literary climate.

Moreover, these same ten novels show that Hardy was equally alert to making use of the possibilities of historical atmosphere. He kept his periods of time just as distinct as his geographical regions. In one of the earliest magazine articles on Hardy, James M. Barrie called him 'the historian of Wessex'. The fact that Hardy covered almost the entire nineteenth century in his accounts is made clear when we take the ten novels he recommended to Maxwell's attention and arrange them in the order of the historical periods to which they refer. The action of the stories is dated as follows:

The Trumpet-Major	1800–1808
Under the Greenwood Tree	1835–1836
The Return of the Native	1842–1843
The Mayor of Casterbridge	1846–1849
The Well-Beloved	1852–1892
Jude the Obscure	1855–1874
Two on a Tower	1858–1863
Far from the Madding Crowd	1869–1873
The Woodlanders	1876–1879
Tess of the D'Urbervilles	1884–1889

By common consent Hardy's readers have reduced this list of ten to six by dropping into the second rank four of the above titles: *The Well-Beloved, Two on a Tower, The Trumpet-Major,* and (regretfully) *Under the Greenwood Tree.* Many who share Tinsley's feeling that the *Greenwood Tree* is 'the best little prose idyll ever' will still agree that its slightness must prevent its being classed among the greatest of the Wessex novels.

The remaining six are those on which Hardy's fame as a

novelist must depend. Critics have disagreed, and doubtless will continue to disagree, about the order in which the great half-dozen are to be ranked. *The Woodlanders*, for instance, the novel least frequently referred to and, of the six, the one least widely known, is by some regarded as the best. Hardy himself, we remember, liked it 'as a story' best of all. Among his readers, however, there is a fairly general consensus of opinion that *Tess of the D'Urbervilles* ranks first. When Osgood, McIlvaine & Co. began issuing the Uniform Edition of 1895–6, they put *Tess* first. When Macmillan & Co. began publishing the 'Wessex Edition' of 1912, they put *Tess* first. When the first edition of the present biography was published in 1940, *Tess* was listed (page 184) in first place among those novels on which Hardy would have to 'risk his chance of survival'. When John Dewey was asked, in his days as Professor-Emeritus of Philosophy at Columbia University, to select, among books published in the last half-century, the twenty-five which he regarded as the most influential, he named *Tess of the D'Urbervilles* first among English novels and put it in sixth place on his list of twenty-five books. Today (1965) *Tess* still maintains her leadership among the Wessex novels.

The position of the others fluctuates, going up and down somewhat like the position of the boats on the river at Oxford in the races of Eights Week. In the last chapter of *Jude the Obscure*, Arabella joins the crowd 'going down to the river to see the boat-bumping. Collegians of all sorts ... watched keenly for "our" boat.' At the end of the week of racing and bumping, the results are published in a final chart which shows that some college Eights have gone up, some have gone down, and some have maintained their position on the river unchanged. If Hardy's six major novels were charted in somewhat similar fashion, the result of seven decades of 'bumping' might be recorded like the figure on the following page.

Novels are, of course, not racing shells, and critical appraisals are often of no greater value or permanence than are statistics of 'popularity'. We can, however, at least notice that all these Wessex novels are 'doing well' a hundred years after Hardy's first appearance in print in London. We can also observe that five of the six books here listed are tragedies. Hardy himself wanted readers to call them 'tragic' rather than 'pessimistic'. In the General Preface of 1911, written for publication in Volume I of the 'Wessex Edition', he wrote his reply to those critics who had condemned his books as 'pessimistic':

'Differing natures,' he pointed out, 'find their tongue in the presence of differing spectacles. Some natures become vocal at tragedy, some are made vocal by comedy, and it seems to me that to whichever of these aspects of life a writer's instinct for expression the more readily responds, to that he should allow it to respond.' Hardy had made of the English novel, as no other English novelist has done, a completely satisfactory medium for high tragedy. That is one reason why he has been called 'the Shakespeare of the English novel'.

Osgood, McIlvaine in 1895	Macmillan in 1912	*Hardy of Wessex* in 1940	Reappraisal in 1965
1. *Tess*	*Tess*	*Tess*	*Tess*
2. *Crowd*	*Crowd*	*Native*	*Mayor*
3. *Mayor*	*Jude*	*Mayor*	*Native*
4. *Native*	*Native*	*Crowd*	*Crowd*
5. *Woodlanders*	*Mayor*	*Jude*	*Woodlanders*
6. *Jude*	*Woodlanders*	*Woodlanders*	*Jude*

XIX

The First Book of Poems

AMONG the books which Hardy owned was a flimsy copy of *Tennyson*—a handy volume of selections from the verse of the poet laureate—which he liked to carry with him when travelling. Its light weight made the book attractive, but its contents too had attractions for Hardy. He had quoted 'In Memoriam' in *A Pair of Blue Eyes* and again in *Tess*, and he was to quote Tennyson in the 'Apology' prefixed to *Late Lyrics* in 1922. Tennyson's 'Break, break, break' is quoted in *A Pair of Blue Eyes* and 'Princess Ida' is quoted in *The Mayor of Casterbridge*. Hardy went to Tennyson's funeral in 1892 and on October 2 wrote to his wife—Emma had remained at Max Gate—that at the funeral he had 'had a very good place' in Westminster Abbey and had 'looked into the grave' on his way out.[1]

At the time of Tennyson's funeral, his poem 'The Lotos-Eaters' was almost sixty years old. Published in 1833, it had long been known to everyone of Hardy's generation; and, although Hardy did not quote it in any of the Wessex novels, there can be no doubt that he could easily have quoted it. The lines of the Choric Song of the long-buffeted companions of Ulysses were once too familiar to need quoting in a book like the present, but in these un-Tennysonian days it may be well to place the lines before the reader before we proceed to comment on them:

> Let us swear an oath, and keep it with an equal mind,
> In the hollow Lotos-land to live and lie reclined
> On the hills like Gods together, careless of mankind.
> For they lie beside their nectar, and the bolts are hurl'd
> Far below them in the valleys, and the clouds are lightly curl'd

Round their golden houses, girdled with the gleaming world:
Where they smile in secret, looking over wasted lands,
Blight and famine, plague and earthquake, roaring deeps and fiery
    sands,
Clanging fights, and flaming towns, and sinking ships, and praying
    hands.
But they smile, they find a music centred in a doleful song
Steaming up, a lamentation and an ancient tale of wrong,
Like a tale of little meaning tho' the words are strong;
Chanted from an ill-used race of men that cleave the soil,
Storing yearly little dues of wheat, and wine and oil;
Till they perish. . . .

It does not require a very vivid imagination to conjecture
Hardy's thoughts when he brooded upon these lines, with their
bitter picture of the Gods smiling at the praying hands of the
'ill-used race of men'. What a contrast there was between the
way the public had received these lines by Tennyson and the
way that same public had reacted to Hardy's Aeschylean
phrase about the President of the Immortals who had ended his
sport with Tess. The contrast convinced Hardy that unconventional ideas could be more safely expressed in poetry than in
prose fiction. The more he thought about this, the more certain
he became that, if he were ever again moved by a desire to com-
municate with the public, he would do so in verse.

On October 17, 1896, he recorded his conviction that, to cry
out in a passionate poem that the Supreme Mover must be
either limited in power (i.e., *not* Omnipotent), or unknowing
(i.e., *not* Omniscient), or cruel (i.e., *not* Beneficent), would cause
the reader to do no more than shake his head at such an un-
orthodox utterance, whereas to put precisely the same idea into
argumentative prose would make readers sneer, or foam at the
mouth, and would set them all 'jumping upon me, a harmless
agnostic'. Within less than four months of having recorded this
observation in his notebook, Hardy had decided to publish a
book of poems. What he had been unable to achieve in 1862–7
he would now, thirty years later, set about doing.

Fortunately, all economic pressure had been lightened at Max
Gate by the immense boost which notoriety had given to the
sale of all his books. Hardy was no longer dependent upon the
marketing of new works to keep the wolf from the door. He

could now do as he liked. If he had been a man of indolent habits, he could easily have withdrawn for the rest of his life into the seclusion of Max Gate and never have written another word. Had he been asked why he chose a more energetic course, he might well have used Hamlet's words in reply:

> Sir, in my heart there was a kind of fighting
> That would not let me sleep.

Pent up within Thomas Hardy's artistic soul there was still something crying for expression, something that none of the fourteen novels had satisfied. Poetry had been his chief literary interest before he wrote a word of fiction, and throughout the thirty years since his early days in London he had never lost this interest. During the quarter-century devoted to novel-writing, he had kept this interest alive chiefly by quoting lines of poetry in his novels; but, as we have noted in Chapter XII, he began, shortly after he had settled into Max Gate, to renew his efforts at original metrical composition. Some of these efforts have been mentioned on previous pages. In 1893 Hardy wrote 'He Wonders about Himself', 'The Young Glass-stainer', 'Rake-hell Muses', and 'A Thunderstorm in Town'. In 1894 he composed 'The Slow Nature'. In 1895–6 (as we have seen in a previous chapter), he relieved his anguished feelings by writing three poems entitled 'In Tenebris'. In 1897 he composed 'The Dead Quire' and 'In Gibbon's Old Garden'.

Thus, by the time *The Well-Beloved* was off his hands, Hardy had a considerable number of poems in manuscript, and the desire to publish them, or at least some of them, ripened. As he went about turning over the sheets of these poems in his Max Gate study, another idea came to mind. Some of the poems dealt with long-familiar sights: why not sketch them and use the sketches to illustrate the poems? This thought served to revive for Hardy a habit that carried his mind back to a period in his past now more than thirty years gone—when he had sketched the Weymouth coastal landscape on the fly-leaf of his French textbook, or landscapes in Cornwall near Beeny Cliff. Now, in 1897, he began to carry a sketching-book with him when he went on solitary walks away from Max Gate; and when good weather permitted, he stopped and sketched many an old familiar scene: the Stinsford Church, the Roman Ring at Dorchester, the High

West Street near the site of his 1883 residence, and the West Walk that figures in *The Mayor of Casterbridge*.

Nor was Hardy now confined to an area to which he could go on foot. Like so many of his contemporaries, he was caught up in the craze for bicycling, and found that with a bicycle he could travel much farther afield. On February 3, 1896, he wrote from London to tell his wife: 'I have seen the loveliest "Byke" for myself—would suit me admirably—"the Rover Cob". It is £20! I can't tell if I ought to have it.'[2] This use of a bicycle enabled him to sketch the landscape seen from the Ridgeway on the road to Weymouth; and as soon as he had become expert enough as a cyclist (at the age of fifty-seven), he was able to visit even more distant places. Salisbury Cathedral was sketched on one page of his drawing-book—not the familiar outside view of the Cathedral but an unusual inside sketch showing the congregation seated in the nave—and a view of the two towers of Exeter Cathedral was sketched on another page. All these views testify to the pleasure Hardy was finding in this revival of his sketching habits of long ago. It was, as he told his friend Edward Clodd, 'a novel amusement'. By the time he had selected two-score and more poems to put into the projected volume, he had nearly as many illustrations to go with them.

When Harper & Brothers took over the business of Osgood, McIlvaine & Co. in 1897, Hardy laid his proposal of a book of poems before them. Knowing that this new venture would be attended by some risk, he offered to assume financial responsibility for the publication; but the Harper firm was willing to trust the commercial value of Hardy's name and therefore accepted the full risk. They showed, however, that they knew that the risk was a real one by printing only five hundred copies. Hardy wrote a brief preface for the book in September 1898, and *Wessex Poems* was published in December. An American edition was issued in New York a month later. Thus at the age of fifty-eight Hardy embarked upon a second career—one which was to end only with his death thirty years later.

The reader who knows only the seventy pages that make up the section of Hardy's *Collected Poems* in which *Wessex Poems* is now reprinted can have but a poor idea of what the 1898 volume was like. It contained only fifty-one poems, but these were printed with such wasteful spacing—twelve pages wholly blank;

ten sonnets so broken up as to require twenty pages—that the book was made to bulk up to 210 pages. It contained thirty-one illustrations. (The title-page states: 'with 30 illustrations', but, counting the frontispiece, there are thirty-one. In preparing his manuscript for the printer, Hardy redrew his illustrations with pen and ink.) Of the fifty-one poems, only four had been previously published: one in the *Gentleman's Magazine* in 1875, two in *The Trumpet-Major* in 1880, and one in 'The Three Strangers' in 1883.

If Hardy had taken Robert Browning's advice as given in the last line of 'Respectability'—'Put forward your best foot!'—he would never have begun *Wessex Poems* as he did. For Hardy put forward his worst foot. He opened his book with a poem of Sapphics—six stanzas in one of the most awkward of metres as far as the English language is concerned. Its use by Horace and Catullus was, of course, known to Hardy, and he may have been familiar with the fact that the Sapphic stanza was also used in Gregorian hymns. But the probability is that he was chiefly influenced by Swinburne. Hardy had recently been in correspondence with Swinburne about *Jude the Obscure*. He knew that Swinburne had written Sapphics. After the publication of *Wessex Poems*, he sent Swinburne a copy. But it was an unfortunate influence.

No one opening Hardy's new book and reading those Sapphics could fail to get the impression that an ex-novelist was now, at the age of fifty-eight, trying to teach himself new tricks. The public had no way of knowing that Hardy's metrical experimentations dated back over more than thirty years. To reviewers and critics, *Wessex Poems* seemed awkward and inexperienced, and Hardy was unprepared for the unanimity with which his new venture was condemned. Instead of examining the reasons for the failure of his poems to appeal to readers, he was characteristically ready to lay the blame on the reader rather than on the poem, just as he blamed the reviewer who 'had tried to scan the author's sapphics as heroics'.[3]

Unfortunately, the choice of Swinburnian Sapphics was not the only source of trouble. Hardy's early—and continued—admiration for Shakespeare led him not only to compose ten sonnets of Shakespearean pattern, but also to use an archaic vocabulary made up of such Elizabethan words as 'eyne',

The First Book of Poems

'cicatrize', 'moils', 'maledict', and 'misprize'. The influence of William Barnes is easily seen in Hardy's use of such dialectal words as 'lewth', 'tardle', 'lynchet', 'shrammed', 'garth', and 'snocks'. Similarly, Browning's influence may be suspected when we come to such words as 'subtrude', 'ostent', and 'miscompose'. In a previous chapter we have noticed Hardy's addiction to words in 'un—': 'unware', 'unknows', and the like. Some of these annoying habits of speech were already familiar to readers of the novels. In *Tess*, for example, there had been horrible Latinizations like 'dolorifuge' and 'heliolatries'. Angel Clare had talked to Tess about a 'grotesque prestidigitation', and the Valley of the Great Dairies heard strange talk about 'ecstasise', 'photosphere', and 'concatenation'. But in a short poem this sort of vocabulary can seem even more incongruous, and few readers were found ready to agree with Hardy's claim (expressed in the preface to *Wessex Poems*) that he had had 'good grounds' for his use of 'an ancient and legitimate word' because there was 'no equivalent in received English'. In time, Hardy's most successful poems, published later, were to offer convincing proof that 'received English' was quite equal to all poetic demands.

Hardy's inability to understand his own difficulties is made clear by his reaction to the adverse criticism his poems drew forth. He wanted his readers to know that he was really quite an old hand at writing poetry!

If any proof were wanted that Hardy was not . . . the apprentice at verse that he was supposed to be, it could be found in an examination of his studies over many years. Among his papers were quantities of notes on rhythm and metre: with outlines and experiments in innumerable original measures, some of which he adopted from time to time. These verse skeletons were mostly blank, and only designated by the usual marks for long and short syllables, accentuations, etc.[4]

One may be quite prepared to agree with Hardy's definition of poetry—'emotion put into measure'—and to subscribe to his statement that 'the emotion must come by nature, but the measure can be acquired by art',[5] but this does not mean that one must agree with his idea that that art can be acquired by writing down 'verse skeletons . . . designated by . . . marks for long and short syllables'.

Fortunately, Hardy did not always limit himself to the use of verse skeletons, and several of the most successful of the *Wessex Poems* demonstrate the source of his most reliable metrical inspiration. In a previous chapter we have had occasion to comment on 'In a Wood'—the poem written in the stanzaic form of 'The Charge of the Light Brigade'—and to note the fact that here was a ready-made poetic form into which Hardy could pour his thoughts and emotions. The best of all the ready-made forms available to Hardy were those of the church music he had been familiar with from boyhood. The hymns and doxologies set up musical patterns in his ears, and (whether consciously or unconsciously) he often responded successfully to them. The last of the *Wessex Poems* runs thus:

> I look into my glass,
> And view my wasting skin,
> And say, 'Would God it came to pass
> My heart had shrunk as thin!'

> For then, I, undistrest
> By hearts grown cold to me,
> Could lonely wait my endless rest
> With equanimity.

Here we have no vocabulary trouble and no rhythmical problem. Hardy's painful awareness of the strained situation at Max Gate where a 'heart [had] grown cold to him' here found poignant expression; but what enabled him to achieve that expression artistically was not any experimenting with a verse skeleton but his choice of the 'short-metre doxology' stanza. He had known this form for fifty years. His copy of *Hymns Ancient and Modern* contained numerous examples of this stanza (Hymns 30, 37, 48, 69, 70, and 380 may be instanced for the curious), and readers unfamiliar with Hardy's hymnal can easily identify the form by recalling 'The breaking waves dashed high' (in Felicia Hemans' poem, 'The Landing of the Pilgrim Fathers') or Charles Wesley's familiar hymn, 'A charge to keep I have'.

Another example of the effective influence of hymn music on Hardy is seen in 'The Impercipient'. The illustration which accompanied this poem in the 1898 edition of *Wessex Poems* shows that the 'bright believing band' of the first stanza was attending a church service in Salisbury Cathedral. Hardy in this poem made use of the 'common-metre doxology'—the familiar ballad stanza of 'Sir Patrick Spens' and of 'The Wreck of the Hesperus'.

As a young man Hardy had thought of entering the Church. This purpose had never been carried out, but the Church had entered him. Its tunes and responses, its hymns and litanies, its chants and refrains, had all sung themselves into his memory; and when emotions welled up in his heart and cried for expression, he was often able to forget his verse skeletons with their marks for longs and shorts, and wisely followed the familiar hymn forms.

Despite the lack of enthusiasm shown by those who read *Wessex Poems*, Hardy persevered along his newly chosen path, and by 1901 he had a second volume, one of ninety-nine poems, ready to offer the public. *Poems of the Past and the Present* appeared in November 1901 and received a more favourable reception than had its predecessor. There were nearly twice the number of poems, with much greater variety among them, and with a marked improvement in quality. 'The Levelled Churchyard' (recalling what Hardy had seen in the graveyard at Wimborne Minster) again made use of the common-metre ballad stanza; and 'To Life' again used the 'short-metre doxology' form, and used it successfully:

> But canst thou not array
> Thyself in rare disguise
> And feign like truth, for one mad day,
> That Earth is Paradise?

The best evidence to be found in the *Poems of the Past and the Present* that Hardy had improved in poetical skill may be seen in 'The Darkling Thrush'. This is one of the best poems Hardy ever wrote. Even his most dubious readers were ready to call it excellent. It has been suggested that Hardy got the idea for his poem from W. H. Hudson's 'Nature in Downland' (1900), in which a thrush 'in rough or gloomy weather . . . singing his best' brought to Hudson's mind the thought that 'such sounds' indicated a 'contentment and bliss' beyond our own. Shelley's 'Skylark' may also have contributed to Hardy's idea. But in the expression of wistful tenderness, in the perfect fusion of subject, mood, and technique, Hardy never did anything better than this. A fellow-poet, Alfred Noyes, has written a perceptive comment:

Hardy's poem, 'The Darkling Thrush', is a lyric of rugged strength, that peculiar strength which comes from understatement and the sense of something in reserve; a lyric of such pathos and beauty as can be compared with the best that has ever been done in our great lyrical language; and that is to say one of the finest lyrics in the world. From the first line to the restrained and intense rapture of the close, the poem bears upon it the stamp of a truth and sincerity beyond praise.

Another of the titles in *Poems of the Past and the Present* is 'God-Forgotten'. This and other verses associated with it—'By the Earth's Corpse', 'The Sick Battle-God', 'The Mother Mourns', 'The Bedridden Peasant to an Unknowing God'—deal with a subject that was never very far from Hardy's mind—the fact that Earth is not Paradise. The surprising thing is that Hardy was able to deal with this theme in such a variety of ways and to do so without ceasing to be poetic. This achievement was the subject of remarks made by Professor John Crowe Ransom of Kenyon College when he spoke to the Ohio English Association on April 6, 1951:

[Of] the Major Poets of our period . . . none . . . will outweigh or outlast . . . Thomas Hardy. . . . About the turn of our century . . . he began . . . with a theme topical in England forty years before but now somewhat stale for his intellectual society: the hideous contrast between the indifferent universe, as science had taught the moderns to conceive it, and the gentler order of the affections and decencies of the human spirit. . . . There will always be young people who have to make their painful adaptation to the brute universe, and . . . this body of poetry [by Hardy] will be perennially of use; it is the best record, the classic, of his experience. . . . Technically, his recording is most interesting. . . . He writes his poetry according to the book. When he is full of his subject, he goes about putting it to its metrical expression. Hardy's poetic language could not have been formed otherwise . . . but at the bottom of his sixty-year-old mind is so rich and pure a deposit of sensitive experience that the metrical beauty has no trouble finding the words. They are true homely words. . . . In the eight hundred pages . . . there is rarely an unrewarding page or poem. There are plenty of fine ones to register that this is a Major Poet.[6]

This 'major poet' was now ready, at the age of sixty-two, for the most ambitious undertaking of his life. He had always preferred the large aim of an unskilled artist to the trivial aim of an accomplished one. As he himself put it, he was 'more interested in the high ideas of a feeble executant than in the high execution of a feeble thinker'. Here, of course, he was once again echoing Robert Browning:

> That low man seeks a little thing to do,
>   Sees it and does it:
> This high man, with a great thing to pursue,
>   Dies ere he knows it.
> That low man goes on adding one to one,
>   His hundred's soon hit:
> This high man, aiming at a million,
>   Misses a unit.

Thomas Hardy was a 'high man'. He might miss by a unit; he might die ere he attained his 'great thing'; but he had a high goal to pursue, and in *The Dynasts* he pursued it.

XX

'The Dynasts'

THE title page of *The Dynasts* calls it 'An Epic-Drama of the War
with Napoleon, in Three Parts, Nineteen Acts, & One Hundred
& Thirty Scenes'. By emphasizing in this way the sheer bulk of
his epic-drama Hardy was letting the reader know at once that
this was no mere by-product of the author's earlier concern
with Napoleon Bonaparte. In 1880 *The Trumpet-Major* had
dealt with the fears of invasion remembered in Dorset two
generations later, and two years after the publication of the
novel, when Harpers advertised Hardy's 'Tradition of Eighteen
Hundred and Four' they called it 'Napoleon's Invasion'. Now,
however, in *The Dynasts*, Hardy proposed to range far beyond
the limits of a short story or of a novel. By calling his work an
epic he announced his determination to try to rival Homer. By
calling it a drama he demonstrated his readiness to be compared
to Shakespeare. But even these implications fail to mark the full
extent of Hardy's design. His was an incredibly ambitious plan,
and a careful analysis of the project leaves one amazed that such
an undertaking could have been attempted by a frail man over
sixty years of age.

In writing about F. Scott Fitzgerald and his wife Zelda,
James Thurber once remarked that 'there were four or five
Zeldas and at least eight Scotts, so that their living room was
forever tense with the presence of a dozen disparate personalities'.[1] In writing *The Dynasts* Thomas Hardy demonstrated that
he too was the possessor of a dozen disparate personalities. He
was, in fact, himself well aware of this multiple diversity in his
make-up and called attention to it in a poem entitled 'So

237

Various'. He there described a jury of twelve men: 1. a brisk-eyed man, quite young; 2. a stiff old man of cold manner; 3. a staunch, robust man; 4. a fickle man; 5. a dunce; 6. a learned seer; 7. a man of sadness; 8. 'a man so glad, you never could conceive him sad'; 9. an unadventurous, slow man; 10. a man of enterprise, shrewd and swift; 11. a poor old fellow who forgot anything said to him; and 12. a vindictive man who forgot nothing.[2] And then, in a concluding stanza, Hardy added:

> All these specimens of men . . .
>   Curious to say
> Were *one* man. Yea,
>   *I* was all they.

This piece of self-analysis was quite true, and the preceding chapters of this book have shown Hardy acting as musician, architect, playwright, artist, editor, antiquary, poet, philosopher, and novelist. It is no exaggeration to say that he carried a dozen personalities around inside him, and when he sat down to write *The Dynasts* he put the entire dozen to work. The reader will find the bulky epic-drama easier to understand if, before looking at its hundred and thirty scenes, he pauses long enough to identify the dozen rôles that Hardy played in its composition.

1. The first is that of historian: Hardy planned to do what Edward Gibbon had done. 'The smoothly shaven historian'[3] had written about the decline and fall of the Roman empire; Hardy would write about the decline and fall of the Napoleonic empire. Gibbon liked to recall how, as he sat in Rome on the fifteenth day of October in 1764, 'musing amidst the ruins of the Capitol', the idea of writing 'the decline and fall of the city first started to his mind'. Similarly, Hardy liked to recall that 'on a belated day about six years back'—i.e., in 1897—'the following drama was outlined'.[4] He too had sat 'musing' and had been struck by the fact that 'slight regard' had been paid 'to English influence and action throughout the struggle' against Bonaparte 'by those Continental writers who had dealt imaginatively with Napoleon's career' and that there was therefore 'room for a new handling of the theme'. Hardy noted the fact that London was the only capital in Europe that the French soldiers had not entered. This was not Hardy's first interest in Gibbon. The

historian was mentioned in the 1895 preface to *The Woodlanders*. Sue Bridehead reads him in *Jude the Obscure*, and Jude himself remembers that Gibbon 'used to look friendly in the old days'. He looked friendly to Thomas Hardy now. Gibbon's systematic acquisition of a reliable library was imitated by Hardy's painstaking acquisition of a Napoleonic library. Before he had finished he owned an extensive collection, most of which is now preserved in the Hardy Room of the Dorset County Museum in Dorchester.

Hardy's historical research was done with extreme care. When, in 1904, a London reviewer of Part I of *The Dynasts* criticized Hardy for making Pitt, in a speech in the House of Commons, give utterance to Schopenhauerian ideas of the Immanent Will, Hardy was quick to point out that Schopenhauer had nothing whatever to do with Pitt's final speech; that he (Hardy) had used Pitt's actual words, uttered in Parliament before Schopenhauer was ever heard of.

When Hardy was unable to buy books with which to stock his own library, he turned to the British Museum and there went conscientiously about the task of informing himself. A little later, he acquired, unsought, an assistant who helped him in this historical research. Sometime in 1904, Mrs. Florence Henniker came to Max Gate to call, bringing with her a young friend, Miss Florence Emily Dugdale. Miss Dugdale was then twenty-five years old. She had literary ambitions and eventually became known as the author of half a dozen or more children's books, such as *The Adventures of Mr. Prickleback* and *The Book of Baby Birds*. When the conversation at Max Gate made it clear to Miss Dugdale that Hardy's work on *The Dynasts* involved a lot of investigation in the British Museum, she offered to be of assistance to him, if he ever needed some detail looked up. It was not long before Hardy called on Florence Dugdale for help, and as he went on with Parts II and III of *The Dynasts*, she made various trips to the British Museum reading room for him. In later years Miss Dugdale was sometimes referred to as Hardy's secretary, but she herself denied that she had ever been his hired or paid assistant. She worked for him for the sheer pleasure of helping a famous author.

2. Hardy's second rôle was Homeric. He planned a work of epic proportions. He was not going to sing the wrath of Achilles,

but he would attempt to present a character who had all of the pride and the arrogance of an Achilles or—a better analogy—of a Miltonic fallen angel. Both the *Iliad* and *Paradise Lost* are mentioned in the preface to *The Dynasts*, but the epic characteristics drawn from Milton's poem are doubtless more numerous and more prominent than are those traceable to Homer. The forescene of Part I contains a description of Europe, lying like 'a prone and emaciated figure, . . . the peninsular plateau of Spain forming a head . . . and . . . lowlands . . . from the north of France across Russia like a grey-green garment'—a vista which reminds one of Satan's first view of Eden. When Milton's builders of the tower of Babel are frustrated, the dwellers in Heaven are described as

> looking down to see the hubbub strange
> And hear the din;

and in Hardy's fore-scene 'the point of view sinks downwards through space and draws near to . . . where the peoples . . . are seen writhing, crawling, heaving, and vibrating' in a fashion not unlike Milton's 'hubbub strange'. Milton's skilful reduction of Satan as a figure of heroic proportions at the beginning of the epic, to the despicable wretch who is eventually hissed by his own followers, was skilfully imitated by Hardy's portrayal of Bonaparte's gradual deterioration, both physical and spiritual. Napoleon looks well at first, but soon we read that he is growing fat. In Spain his unhealthy face is mentioned. In Part II his 'stoutening figure' is accompanied by unchivalrous conduct. In Part III his puffed calves and continual cough are merely the physical counterparts of a psychological brutality which shows itself again and again. Napoleon's final spiritual collapse is symbolized by his seeing infidelity in everyone around him, even in those who have served him most faithfully.

3. Hardy's third rôle is that of dramatist. In this capacity he worked under a double inspiration: that of Shakespeare and of Robert Buchanan. Shakespeare's hand may be seen everywhere. His *Richard II*, *Henry IV*, *Part I* and *Part II*, and *Henry V*—a twenty-act historical drama with eighty scenes—corresponds in volume to Hardy's nineteen acts with one hundred and thirty scenes. Hardy had quoted from all four of these Shakespearean plays in five of his novels. Shakespeare's skilful building up of the

character of the wayward Prince Hal until he becomes the 'ideal' English hero, King Henry the Fifth, the conqueror of England's foes, taught Hardy not a little about how to build Wellington up into a commanding dramatic figure, qualified to stand as the impressive emblem of England's implacable resistance to Napoleon.

Many other Shakespearean features will be obvious to any careful reader of *The Dynasts*: the lively dialogue, the pathetic passages, the use of songs, the tense climaxes, the sharp contrasts in characterization, the use of the Shakespearean soliloquy for the purpose of psychological penetration into the heart of a dramatic situation—all these features in the easily-recognized Shakespearean tradition need no emphasis here. Josephine's last words in *The Dynasts* and the Queen's words in *Richard II* would call for similar emotional powers in an actress. Hardy's plans for these aspects of his great drama enabled him to make use of what he had learned from and about Shakespeare in London theatres.

As for Robert Buchanan, Hardy's indebtedness was (and is) less obvious, and it was certainly more carefully concealed. Not until 1952 was it disclosed that Hardy's 'A Drama of Kings', as he had at first proposed calling his work, owed many of its features to Buchanan's *The Drama of Kings* (1871).[5] Buchanan had published his work just about the time when he drew universal attention to himself by attacking Dante Gabriel Rossetti in the notorious Fleshly School article in the *Contemporary Review*. Seven years later, when Buchanan had become editor of *Light*, he solicited a contribution from Hardy and (as we have noticed in Chapter IX) obtained and published 'The Impulsive Lady of Croome Castle'. In 1892 Buchanan published a novel of his own, *Come Live with Me and Be My Love*, and dedicated it to Thomas Hardy. Dr. John A. Cassidy has characterized this novel as 'a downright plagiarism of *The Woodlanders* and *Far from the Madding Crowd*'.[6] In borrowing from Buchanan's *The Drama of Kings* Hardy was merely following Buchanan's own example. (He was of course also following the precedent set by his own previous borrowings from Ainsworth, Prince, Apperly, Burke, and others.)

Buchanan treats the downfall of Napoleon in a 'Choric Interlude' in which (as Professor Fairchild has pointed out)

'Buchanan's Chorus . . . expresses . . . the sorrows and hopes of Hardy's Pities'. Buchanan's 'Celestial Spectators' and his Deserter pave the way for Hardy's 'supernatural spectators' and his deserters. Fairchild points out many other parallels, including such verbal echoes as 'strange Intelligences' (Hardy's 'Phantasmal Intelligences'), 'ancient Shadow' (Hardy's 'Ancient Spirit'), and the like.

4. In the preface to *The Dynasts*, Hardy made a point of stating that his drama was 'intended for mental performance and not for the stage'. This permitted him to include lines and passages which might otherwise not have been admissible, and these passages in turn help to explain Hardy's quoting Wordsworth and Coleridge in his preface. Hardy's fourth rôle is, in short, that of a poet. Acting in this rôle, he wrote some descriptive lyrics of great beauty—one, for example, that Wordsworth himself might have been proud of, written as it is in the rhythm of one of Wordsworth's poems:

> The eyelids of eve fall together at last,
> And the forms so foreign to field and tree
> Lie down as though native, and slumber fast.

In the Semichorus of the Years, on the next-to-the-last page of *The Dynasts*, Hardy writes of the All-mover who 'Ever urges on and measures out the chordless chime of Things'. In writing these words, Hardy's thoughts travelled back forty-five years to the day when, in London, he bought a copy of the lyric poet Horace to whom he had been introduced by Horace Moule. In his early study of *Horace*, Hardy came to a passage in the *Epistles* (I, 12) in which the poet asked: 'quid velit et possit rerum concordia discors?' C. Smart, the English translator, had rendered this passage thus: 'What is the intention and power of the jarring harmony of things?' Young Hardy was struck both by the thought and by the language of this passage and wrote a marginal note on 'the jarring harmony of things'. Forty-five years later, he took down his copy of *Horace* from the shelf and paraphrased the Latin poet's 'concordia discors' as the 'chordless chime of Things'.

5. As Hardy embarked upon the fifth rôle in his repertoire, he recalled Robert Browning's abilities as a satirist, especially in amusing passages. Browning did not always write in verse—for

example, the six students in *Pippa Passes* talk in prose; when the three Policemen converse, they too talk in prose. Hardy wisely decided that some of his satirical scenes would be better in prose. Hence, in the scene near Astorga in Spain, when five deserters hide in a cellar, Hardy writes in a vigorous prose that has often been singled out for critical praise. Browning's Person of Quality who scratched his head to see if the hair had turned wool is no more amusing than Hardy's two sentinels, Jem and John Whiting, the Dorset rustics on guard on Egdon Heath, ready to give the alarm in case Napoleon should effect a landing. The reader cannot fail to recognize that these sentries are cousins of Shallow and Silence, the Shakespearean pair who are mentioned in *The Mayor of Casterbridge*.

6. When Hardy wrote his preface to *The Dynasts*, he mentioned 'the Greek Chorus' and 'classical precedent' and 'the triumphs of the Hellenic theatre'—three references which are enough to identify for us the sixth rôle he was prepared to play. While he had come to feel that the Greeks had 'used up' their theology and that he could no longer make use of the 'celestial machinery' that had served Aeschylus and Sophocles, he was none the less ready to play the part of Classical Tragedian at least to the extent of making use of their 'contrasted Choruses'.

7. In his handling of these Choruses Hardy assumed the rôle of a formal philosopher. Perhaps 'formulistic' would be a better word than 'formal', for in his preface Hardy warns his readers that his remarks are 'advanced with little eye to a systematized philosophy'. In his appearance in this rôle Hardy was influenced by his philosophy-teacher Goethe. Hardy did not read German —at least not well enough to read *Faust* in the original—but he knew about the German poet and his work from Carlyle's essay on Goethe in *Critical and Miscellaneous Essays* (1839); and when, in *The Mayor of Casterbridge*, Hardy had described Faust as 'a vehement gloomy being who had quitted the ways of vulgar men without light to guide him on a better way', the novelist was merely paraphrasing what Carlyle had said. Shortly after the publication of *The Mayor*, Hardy bought a copy of Goethe and read him in the course of the year 1887. At the end of *Faust* he found the semi-dramatic, contrasted, philosophical reflections which seemed to him an improvement upon the Greek Chorus as well as an advance over the Shakespearean soliloquy.

Goethe's philosophical reflections thus provided the suggestion for the whole supernatural framework of *The Dynasts*, one of its striking features.[7] The spectacle of the Napoleonic wars is seen through this *Faust*-inspired framework; in deciding to play the philosopher in this way Hardy was well aware of the fact that he was making 'an independent plunge' and turning his back upon literary conventions in English, but he hoped that he would be credited with 'embodying the real, if only temporary, thought of the age'.[8]

In introducing this supernatural element into his work, Hardy did not stick too closely to Goethe's literary device, nor did he present his supernatural spirits as they had been presented in Robert Buchanan's work, where they constitute a single-minded body. Instead, Hardy created a dramatically contrasted quartet, in the make-up of which we can recognize further echoes of Shakespeare. Hardy thus assumed four supernatural rôles, identified by him as the Spirit Ironic, the Spirit Sinister, the Spirit of the Years, and the Spirit of the Pities. The reader who hears these names for the first time is not likely to get much out of them; but with a little effort, and with a little help from Shakespeare, we can discriminate among these vague creatures and clarify their function in the epic-drama. No mere generalization about the supernatural spirits will do; a separate identification of each of the four is needed.

8. The Spirit Ironic is a jester, a witty, disillusioned 'realist', as if some Mercutio of supernatural dimensions were able to cast his cynicisms out over the Cosmos. When there is a reference to 'this terrestrial tragedy', the Spirit Ironic jokingly interrupts with a 'Nay, comedy!'

9. The Spirit Sinister is a malicious Iago of cosmic proportions. Like the President of the Immortals, he enjoys cruel sport. Like Mephistopheles in *Faust*, he takes delight not only in seeing evil in the world but also in causing it. 'Good,' he exclaims, as Napoleon's designs get under way. 'That is good, and spells blood.'

10. The Spirit of the Years is a hardened old Stoic; or, if 'hardened' is too harsh a term, a resigned philosopher; a Horatio who has learned to take fortune's buffets and rewards with equal thanks; a Marcus Aurelius who has resolved to 'be not perturbed'. The Spirit of the Years has long ago learned that

The Moving Finger writes, and having writ,
Moves on; nor all your piety nor wit
  Shall lure it back to cancel half a line
  Nor all your tears wash out a word of it.

This stoical resignation was a lesson that Hardy would have
liked to learn—he thought that his father had learned it—but he
himself had too much of the Spirit of the Pities in his make-up
for it to be possible for him to enact Horatio in real life.

11. The Spirit of the Pities comes nearest to speaking the
language of Hardy's own heart. In a letter of March 22, 1904,
the author explained: 'The Pities are, of course, merely Humanity, with all its weaknesses.' But by 'weaknesses' he meant kindness, pity, solicitude, mercy, tenderness, sympathy. By 'humanity' he meant humane feelings. It is the Spirit of the Pities that is
most poignantly moved by human suffering. 'O the intolerable
antilogy,' it exclaims, 'of making figments feel!' This is the
Spirit who is puzzled as to the reason for all the suffering in the
world. 'More ills?' it asks. 'Why any?'

It is the Spirit of the Pities who, four pages from the end of
the drama, is allowed to echo the Christian Bible. Paraphrasing
the Magnificat in the first chapter of *Luke*, the Spirit sings
sublimely:

To Thee whose eye all Nature owns,
Who hurlest Dynasts from their thrones,

We sing, . . . yea, Great and Good, . . . we hail,
Who shak'st the strong, who shield'st the frail,

Who hadst not shaped such souls as we
If tendermercy lacked in Thee!

In arguing thus from the presence of pity in mankind to a
belief in the existence of tendermercy in the all-Great-and-
Good, Hardy made use of an idea familiar to him from Brown-
ing's *Saul*—the idea that the love felt by young David for King
Saul is evidence of the similar but Infinitely Superior Love that
God must feel for Saul.

These four Spirits, then, contemplate the human spectacle
and talk the sorry Napoleonic situation over as if they were all
retired emeritus professors of philosophy! (Professor Barker
Fairley's idea.) In the course of their discussions they have a
lot to say about 'It', for Hardy had rejected the idea of a

personal, loving God in favour of the blind, deaf, dumb, 'view-less, voiceless Turner of the Wheel' who, in the first line of *The Dynasts*, is called 'the Immanent Will' and is often thereafter referred to merely as 'It'. Where did Hardy get 'It'?

12. When *The Dynasts* was published (Part I in 1904, Part II in 1906, Part III in 1908), Hardy's friends began writing to him about 'It', pointing out that a neuter It could not logically be conceived of as possessing volition. 'The Will', therefore, is (they thought) a contradiction in terms. To Edward Clodd, Hardy wrote on March 22, 1904: 'What you say about the Will is true enough, if you take the word in its ordinary sense. But in . . . a secondary sense . . . that of effort exercised in an . . . unconscious manner', Hardy thought the word permissible. To Edward Wright he wrote (on June 2, 1907): 'I quite agree with you . . . that the word Will does not perfectly fit the idea to be conveyed—[that of] a vague . . . urging . . . force'; but he again defended his use of the word and claimed that his theory about the Will 'settled the question of Free-will [hyphenated] vs. Necessity'. He accordingly had made the Spirit of the Pities declare:

> We hold that Thy unscanted scope
> Affords a food for final Hope.

In answering Edward Wright, Hardy claimed that this idea was original with him. 'That the Unconscious Will of the Universe is growing aware of Itself, I believe I may claim as my own idea solely.'

In saying this, Hardy ignored, or forgot, the book he had bought for five shillings back in 1889 or 1890—a copy of Mrs. Karl Hillebrand's translation of Schopenhauer's doctoral dissertation at Göttingen, *On the Four-fold Root of the Principle of Sufficient Reason* (London, Bell, 1889; the first publication of this work in English). Hardy's use of the term 'the Immanent Will' in *The Dynasts* had, of course, made many a reader think that Schopenhauer was its source, but Hardy was always inclined to be evasive on that point. When Helen Garwood earned a Ph.D. degree at the University of Pennsylvania with a dissertation on *Thomas Hardy, an Illustration of the Philosophy of Schopenhauer* (1911) and sent Hardy a copy of it, he replied, somewhat cryptically: 'My pages show harmony of view with Darwin, Huxley, Spencer, Hume, Mill, and others, all of whom I used to read more than Schopenhauer.'

Hardy's copy of *The Four-fold Root* has, however, survived and can now tell us more about what he read than he himself was willing to tell. He not only read but marked the passages that had special interest for him. It was not an easy book to read. Some pages are in Latin, some of the passages marked by Hardy are in Greek, and there are numerous quotations in French and in German. But Hardy stayed with the philosopher clear through to page 375 with its scornful defence of the author's pessimistic view of things and its reference to 'the monstrous, nameless evil—the awful heartrending misery in the world'. In short, Hardy not only read Schopenhauer but studied him diligently and long—not *The World as Will and Idea* as so many people have supposed, but *The Four-fold Root of the Principle of Sufficient Reason*. Hardy's marginal explanation of the meaning of 'Reason' is: '[Reason] for the existence of things.'

Here, then, in Schopenhauer we find the source of Hardy's twelfth rôle—that of a hopeful theologian. An inspection of *The Four-fold Root* thows light on a number of pages in *The Dynasts*. In a passage marked by Hardy (p. 236) Schopenhauer declares: 'The fundamental truth of my doctrine, which places that doctrine in opposition with all others that have ever existed, is the complete separation between the will and the intellect. . . . I am the first who has asserted that a *will* must be attributed to all that is lifeless. . . . With me, the will is not . . . an accident of cognition and therefore of life; but life itself is manifestation of will.' Page 238 of the Schopenhauer book emphasizes the need 'to distinguish Will from Free-will' (hyphenated) and 'to understand that the former can subsist without . . . a brain . . . implying deliberation and choice'. Again, on page 309, the philosopher teaches Hardy how to talk about consciousness being 'itself a manifestation of will'.

Hardy thus came to glimpse a different aspect of 'It'—one that 'affords a food for final Hope'. This enabled him to end *The Dynasts* on an optimistic note. For man, like the Pities, could look forward to eventual 'deliverance . . . from the darts that were', and could trust that the day will eventually come when

Consciousness the Will informing
It will fashion all things fair.

Thus a note of optimistic Hope was distilled by the imagination of a poet from the doctoral dissertation of a pessimist.

This prolonged analysis of the dozen personalities that contributed to the composition of *The Dynasts* will have served, if it does nothing else, to emphasize the magnitude of what Hardy attempted. He proposed to take elements gleaned from Aeschylus, Browning, Robert Buchanan, Gibbon, Goethe, Homer, Horace, *Job*, Marcus Aurelius, Milton, *Saint Luke*, Schopenhauer, Shakespeare, Sophocles, and Wordsworth—he would stir all these ingredients up vigorously in the mixing-bowl of his own imagination, and then bake them in an epic mould or form of his own designing. No one could call this a modest plan. Few persons would have prophesied for it anything other than failure.

When Part I was published early in January 1904, Henry W. Boynton promptly called it 'a failure in the colossal style'.[10] Many readers seemed to agree, and Hardy was so discouraged that he was not sure whether he would go on with the work. Shortly after his sixty-fifth birthday, he went to call on his old mentor and critic George Meredith. On July 2, 1905, Meredith wrote to a friend:

Hardy was here some days back ... and ... questioned me as to *The Dynasts*. I spoke . . . in favour of his continuing it, now that it had a commencement. It was useless to say, as I think, that he would have made it more effective in prose, where he is more at home than in verse, though here and there he produces good stuff.

As to the 'good stuff', not everyone agreed with Meredith. One critic announced that 'lyrical charm is completely absent'; another, that 'there is not a line of poetry in *The Dynasts*'; a third remarked that some of the lines seemed to have strayed in out of Gilbert & Sullivan:

> Should the corvette return
> With the anxious Scotch colonel,
> Escape would be frustrate,
> Retention eternal.

Instead of singling out for praise such vivid, dramatic scenes as that of the insane George III receiving the news that 'he' had won a battle, or of the French soldiers found frozen to death by the fireside in Russia, or of the Empress Josephine being told of the intended divorce, or of the contemptible Regent's frenzied perplexity as to how to 'get over this infernal woman', or the colloquy between Lord Uxbridge, hit by a cannon ball, and Wellington:

'I have lost my leg, by God!'
'By God, and have you! I felt the wind o' the shot!'

instead of praising scenes like these, the reviewers took delight in ridiculing Hardy's vocabulary—'walm', 'fugle', 'incarn', 'pulsion'—and in laughing at the artificiality of some of the dialogue on the battlefield. When an officer gallops up to Wellington at Waterloo to report that two-thirds of the 95th Brigade have been killed, Hardy makes him say:

> We bow to the necessity of saying
> That our brigade is lessened to one-third,
> Your Grace.

Hardy himself was not blind to some of these defects, but he had not been able to discipline himself by delaying publication until the blemishes could all be removed from the poem. He was therefore all the more grateful when an appreciative reader occasionally turned up. One such commentator on *The Dynasts* was Sir Henry Newbolt. After his article had appeared in the *Quarterly Review*, Hardy wrote to him:

You approach the book from the right side, which so few critics have done. Instead of saying to themselves, 'Here is a performance hugely defective: is there anything in it notwithstanding the huge defects?' they have mostly contented themselves with picking out bad lines, which any child could do, there being myriads of them, as I knew too well before they said so.

Hardy sent a copy of the book to George Meredith, whose letter of acknowledgment supplies a brief but sound appraisal of the entire work:

The book was welcome all the more as being a sign that this big work was off your mind. How it may have been received I cannot say, but any book on so large a scale has to suffer the fate of Panorama, and must be visited again and again for a just impression of it to be taken. I saw that somewhere in your neighbourhood it was represented in action. That is the way to bring it more rapidly home to the mind. But the speaker of Josephine's last words would have to be a choice one.

Meredith correctly recognized that the scale of Hardy's epic-drama is so great that the human eye cannot, in a single glance, take it all in. No single reading of *The Dynasts* will serve to reveal all its varied riches.

In time, however, and with more deliberate reading, critics came to be increasingly impressed not only with the magnitude of Hardy's attempt, but also with the degree of success he had had in carrying out his intention. An anonymous American reviewer, for example, wrote as follows:

Four years ago we gave a dazed and tentative notice to the first part of Mr. Hardy's huge closet drama. . . . On the appearance of the second part, . . . we began to suspect that we had not done justice to the first part. Now, with the publication of the third and last part, that suspicion has become a certainty. We have read the final volume with the complete absorption of every faculty, and going back from it to read again the first and second parts, . . . we have become aware of a work marked . . . by a colossal unity and a staggering significance—a fitting and in a way a triumphant climax to that long series of novels in which Mr. Hardy has embodied both his poignant knowledge of the world of men and his grim, undeluded philosophy. . . .

In the 'After Scene' . . . , Mr. Hardy has prepared . . . the final utterance of that virile philosophy. . . . Most readers . . . would have expected the debate to end . . . in the temper of an ironic agnosticism. But the true lover of Hardy, who has pondered the eternally optimistic implications of human sympathy, . . . will not be surprised to find that the very last lines of the whole vast panorama . . . are given, not to the Spirit Ironic, but to . . . the Pities. . . .

It would be easy . . . to point out technical flaws . . . , but . . . infelicities of detail . . . should no more disturb us than swallow nests . . . on the façade of the 'awful past'. The answer to technical criticism of *The Dynasts* is: There it is; a complete and powerfully moving whole.[12]

When, in the dark days of World War I, Granville-Barker made a stage abridgement of *The Dynasts* and produced it at the Kingsway Theatre in London (November 25, 1914; 72 performances), Rebecca West went to see it and afterwards testified to the fact that it 'emerges as one of the greatest plays that have been on the English stage'. She admitted that it was not *wholly* successful—'mixed magic and clumsiness'—for there undoubtedly are 'places as rough and bare as the wall of a barn'; but in spite of this fact she maintained that 'never before was so large a vision of the lot of man'.[13]

This view of Hardy's work has, in time, come to be much more widely held; and, though carping critics have not all vanished, they are now in the minority. It is now generally recognized that 'through *The Dynasts* a noble voice speaks. The poem is, indeed, one of the glorious achievements of English literature.'[14]

Even in Hardy's own lifetime, some of those who continued to regard the poem as a failure came to see it as a notable achievement, worth more than some successes. Hardy himself had observed that 'the failure may be greater than the success. To have strength to roll a stone weighing a hundredweight to the top of the mount is a success, and to have the strength to roll a stone of ten hundredweight only half-way up that mount is a failure. But the latter is two or three times as strong a deed.' *The Dynasts* did not reach the top of the mount. At the age of sixty-eight Hardy was unequal to all that his colossal attempt would have required for success. But the world gradually came to a belated recognition that here was a heroic work that merited applause. This acclaim was appropriately signalized on July 19, 1910, when the King invested Hardy with the Order of Merit.

XXI

'Magic Lights'

WHILE focusing attention upon *The Dynasts* we have purposely
passed without comment a number of incidents in Hardy's life
to which we must now return. On April 3, 1904, his mother died
at the age of ninety-one. Hardy sent obituary notices to *The
Times* and to the *Dorset County Chronicle*, and offered the *Graphic*
a portrait of his mother, 'as I have written more for the *Graphic*
than for any other illustrated paper'.[1] Shortly after this loss, he
wrote a poem of five stanzas, 'After the Last Breath',[2] about his
mother, and also a sonnet, 'A Church Romance', in which he
described how his mother had first seen his father in Stinsford
Church.[3]

A year after his mother's death, Hardy received the most
notable public distinction that had as yet come his way. Aberdeen University awarded him the honorary degree of Doctor of
Laws, and in the first week of April 1905 he went to Scotland to
receive this public honour.

By the time Part II of *The Dynasts* was in print, Hardy had
also obtained further evidence of his growth in fame and prestige: he was solicited by a French portrait-painter, Jacques-
Emile Blanche, for an opportunity to sketch the poet's portrait.
This was not the first time that Hardy had been asked to pose
for a portrait. In 1895-6 he had sat to Miss Winifred Hope
Thomson[4] (sister-in-law of Kenneth Grahame), and in 1897 he
had sat for Mr. (later Sir) William Rothenstein, who was subsequently to become Principal of the Royal College of Art.
Monsieur Blanche's application, however, served as a pleasant
indication that Hardy's reputation was no longer confined to

England and America but had crossed the Channel. A French translation of *Tess* had appeared in Paris in 1901, the work of Madeleine Rolland; and a year before this, Mlle Y. Blaze de Bury had published a book, *Les Romanciers anglais contemporains*, which one can only hope Hardy did not see, for it is full of fantastically erroneous statements about him. The cavalier treatment of Hardy by French writers is well illustrated by the fact that 507 pages of *The Return of the Native* are reduced to 284 pages in the French translation by Madame Eve Margueritte, *Le Retour au Pays Natal.*

Hardy agreed to sit for Monsieur Blanche, with results that were not wholly satisfactory.[5] The artist accordingly thought he would like to try again, and in the spring of 1907 Hardy again sat for Blanche—this time with better results: the portrait was hung in the Paris Salon of 1909. While Blanche was engaged in this second, more carefully studied work, Mrs. Hardy turned up in London and, upon meeting the French portrait-painter, remarked: 'Don't make him look miserable!' Blanche's portrait may not make Hardy look miserable, but it certainly makes him look worn and tired. Blanche had obviously noticed Hardy's white hands with fingers a little swollen, his pale bald head and wrinkled skin, his face so deeply lined that it looked like the back of a leaf, his eyes deep-set, and his cheeks thin.

On June 2, 1907, Hardy was sixty-seven years old. Shortly after his birthday, he and his wife were invited to a Royal Garden Party at Windsor Castle; and since Monsieur and Madame Blanche were also invited, the four went together. They entrained at Paddington station, and upon arrival at Windsor discovered that they were only a very small part of the large number of people arriving for the Court festivity. The crowd was so great that there were not nearly enough conveyances to carry everybody from the station up the steep hill to the Castle. Mrs. Hardy, wearing a long green veil, promptly took a place in one of the royal carriages and invited Madame Blanche to come and sit beside her. The latter declined, urging Hardy to take the seat and save himself the weary climb up the hill in the July-like heat. He was so obviously frail that other guests who were headed for Windsor Castle followed Mme Blanche's example in urging Hardy to ride. Mrs. Hardy, however, settled the matter in emphatic words which Blanche never forgot. He later reported the incident: 'Mr. Hardy ride? Why, that walk up the hill in the sun will do him a lot of good!'

So up the stony hill to Windsor Castle Thomas Hardy and his portrait-painter trudged on foot, following the open carriage with its driver in King Edward's scarlet livery and its Devonshire lady in a green veil, seated under a bright silk parasol. Two years later Hardy published a poem entitled 'The End of the Episode', in which he gave himself some advice:

> Ache deep; but make no moans:
> Smile out; but stilly suffer;
> The paths of love are rougher
> Than thoroughfares of stone.

Just how rough his path had by now become, no one but he really knew. But for many years now there had been no possibility of concealing the fact that it *was* rough. When Charles J. Hankinson took Madame Sarah Grand (author of *The Heavenly Twins*) to call on Hardy at Max Gate, the conversation eventually drifted into the subject of general philosophical views of life. Hardy expressed his abhorrence of pious pretensions which have no counterpart in conduct—the sort of view he had already defined in *Tess* and *Jude*—and Madame Grand was amused to observe the vehemence of the little man. But Mrs. Hardy was shocked. After the guests had left she wrote Hankinson a note, saying that she hoped he would not take any of Mr. Hardy's remarks seriously, that of course he didn't really mean them, that he was really a very religious man who read the Bible quite regularly, and read the New Testament *in Greek*! Hankinson later reported having received similar notes from Max Gate 'on several other occasions'.

When the Hardys went to London, the domestic discord moved thither with them. After listening to Mrs. Hardy, T. P. O'Connor came to the conclusion that 'her whole bitter purpose was to belittle, irritate, and discourage her husband'. The time had obviously passed when she felt able to take pride in Hardy's literary work or bask in the sunlight of his reputation as a man of letters. When he was invested with the Order of Merit, she was not present. If Hardy had been a man like Browning's 'faultless painter', Andrea del Sarto, he might have observed that a common greyness silvered everything, now that his wife was no longer

at the point of your first pride in me;
That's gone, you know.

As for pride, when Hamlin Garland came from America to
'Casterbridge' and visited Hardy's birthplace at Higher Bockhampton, the tenant repeated to him the local gossip that Mrs.
Hardy was much prouder of being the niece of an archdeacon
in the Church than of being the wife of Thomas Hardy. Once
upon a time she had signed her name in a copy of *The Woodlanders*, in the manuscript of which she had written out more
than a hundred of its 498 leaves; but there is nothing to tell us
whether, in her copying, she ever saw any significance in
Hardy's remark in Chapter XLV about 'how little acquirements and culture weigh beside sterling personal character'.

If Hardy had been thick-skinned, his 'dark undying pain'[6]
would have been much less grievous; but unfortunately he was
thin-skinned, and he brooded over injuries to his pride and self-
esteem. In a poem, 'The Wound', he wrote of

> that wound of mine
> Of which none knew,
> For I'd given no sign
> That it pierced me through.[7]

In *Late Lyrics* Hardy published a poem about Max Gate
entitled 'The Strange House'. One of the strangest aspects of its
strangeness is the fact that, as he sat in his study penning poems
about the 'deep division' and his 'dark undying pain', his wife
sat under the same roof also composing verses. She had begun
doing this shortly after the publication of his *Wessex Poems*. Even
before he had composed his poem about 'The Darkling Thrush'
she had written a poem of her own about a thrush:

> There's a song of a bird in a tree,—
> A song that is fresh, gay, and free,
> The voice of a last summer's thrush,
> Shaking out his trills—hush! hush!

Mrs. Hardy sent these verses to the *Sphere*, edited by Clement K.
Shorter. The embarrassed editor deliberated but finally printed
the poem, called 'Spring Song', in his issue for April 14, 1900,
with this masterful comment: 'We all know that Mr. Thomas
Hardy began his literary career by writing poems. It is interesting to know that his wife has also written poems. Mrs. Hardy

sends me the following verses, which I am happy, as one of the most enthusiastic admirers of her husband's books, to print in the *Sphere*.'

A year later, Mrs. Hardy sent off another poem, this time to the editor of *The Academy*. In the issue for April 27, 1901, the editor printed the poem with the remark: 'This week Mrs. Thomas Hardy tells us in the following interesting lines how rose trees are planted in Wessex.' A visitor to Max Gate later recalled Hardy's reference to these poetic effusions of his wife and the 'rather wry smile' with which he alluded to them. Ford Madox Ford called one day at Max Gate but found Hardy out. Whereupon he had to listen to Mrs. Hardy, 'in her Junonian blondeness', read her own 'innocuous poems', some of which were about her pet cats.

Four years after the Royal Garden Party at Windsor, the *Fortnightly Review* published (in April 1911) twelve short poems by Hardy entitled 'Satires of Circumstance'. These are the bitterest, most cynical comments he ever made on marriage and mismating. Hardy once ridiculed people who are such 'geese' as to 'believe that everything written in the first person has been done personally'. We need not make that mistake. We recognize that the dozen 'Satires of Circumstance' do not hold the mirror up to actual occurrences at Max Gate. But the spirit in which these poems were written is obviously hard and bitter, and when Edmund Gosse came to review them (after they had been collected in a volume[8]) he remarked: 'The wells of human hope have been poisoned for him by some condition of which we know nothing.' Gosse of course knew much more than he was ready to admit in a published review.

Hardy himself later tried to pass these poems off as 'humorous productions . . . issued with a light heart',[9] but such a claim is nonsense. The 'satires' were not humorous, and they were *not* 'issued with a light heart'. The truth of the matter is indicated in a letter which Hardy wrote to Gosse in 1914: 'The little group of satires cost me much sadness. . . . The scales had not fallen from my eyes when I wrote them, and when I reprinted them they had.' That is to say, sometime between April 1911, when the *Fortnightly* printed the mordant satires, and November 1914, when Hardy's volume of poetry was published, the scales fell from his eyes. To translate Hardy's metaphor into a simple statement of fact: Mrs. Hardy had died of heart-failure on November 27, 1912, three days after her seventy-second birthday.

Immediately, the Max Gate atmosphere was cleared. Some grief at the loss of a wife with whom he had lived for thirty-eight years might have been taken for granted, but it might have been even more safely assumed that his grief would be moderated by the relief he was certain to feel as soon as the irritations and the barbs of recent years had finally ceased. But no one could have guessed what happened next. Once the source of the poet's unhappiness at Max Gate was removed by the hand of death, he reacted by pouring forth some of the tenderest poetry he had ever written. Bitterness was forgotten. Love poem after love poem surged up from the depth of his being. Before Mrs. Hardy had been a month gone, he had written a number of poems, one of which, 'The Voice', exhibits, from its poignant first line to the intense and heart-broken pathos of its close, a perfect fusion of subject, mood, and technique. To quote Alfred Noyes once again: the poem 'bears upon it the stamp of a truth and sincerity beyond praise'. It begins:

> Woman much missed, how you call to me, call to me,
>   Saying that now you are not as you were
> When you had changed from the one who was all to me,
>   But as at first, when our day was fair.

Before a year had gone by, Hardy had produced a body of lyrical verse which, for many readers, has had much greater appeal than anything else he ever wrote.

In November 1913 Hardy went to Cambridge to be invested in the Honorary Fellowship to which he had been appointed at Magdalene College. He told the President of the College, A. C. Benson, that he had been writing some poems about his wife but didn't know whether he ought to publish them. They were, Hardy explained, 'very intimate, of course', and he knew that there were people who still held the Victorian view that an author sought not to invite the public into his private life. Robert Browning's words on this subject were well known:

> Sonnet-sing you about myself?
> Do I live in a house you would like to see? . . .
>   Unlock my heart with a sonnet key?

'Magic Lights'

No: thanking the public, I must decline.
A peep through my window, if folk prefer;
But, please you, no foot over threshold of mine!

But Thomas Hardy was not Robert Browning. 'The verses came,' Hardy said to A. C. Benson; 'it was quite natural. One looked back through the years and saw some pictures; a loss like that makes one's old brain vocal.'

Hardy finally decided to publish, and when *Satires, Lyrics, and Reveries* appeared in 1914, it contained a section called 'Poems of 1912–13'. As a subtitle to this group of poems, Hardy added three words which he remembered, characteristically enough, from his studies of more than sixty years in the past. When he was a schoolboy under Isaac Last, his mother had given him a copy of Dryden's translation of Virgil's *Aeneid*, and later he learned to read Virgil in the original. In this way he became acquainted with Dido and her pathetic love story. Her phrase about recognizing 'the traces of an old fire'—*veteris vestigia flammae*—had remained in Hardy's retentive memory and now that he was preparing to publish his own 'vestiges' he decided to append Virgil's words to the title 'Poems of 1912–13'.

The world has been unanimous in applauding the poet's decision to publish. Edmund Blunden has called these poems 'the most unconventional and impressive elegies in English'.[10] Henry C. Duffin wrote: 'These poems are almost unique. . . . Of all preceding love-poetry in English none has the peculiar quality of intimacy that characterises these poems. . . . With such insistent beauty is the chord of poignant memory and haunting loss played on' that Hardy here gives us 'an intenser and more lyric *In Memoriam*'.[11] Arthur McDowall observed that 'no modern poems of the kind are more wistfully tender than these; they have a selfless pathos which transcends regret'.[12] Professor Samuel C. Chew called these poems 'both touching and extraordinary, quite unlike any other elegies in the language'.[13] In them, declared J. E. Barton, 'the thrill of grief is raised to monumental beauty'.[14] When Professor C. Day Lewis addressed the Congress of the West Country Writers' Association at their meeting in Weymouth in June 1954, he remarked: 'Hardy's qualities of patience, moral courage and integrity are manifest in his poems. After his first wife's death, when he was seventy-two, he released some of the finest love poetry—the best in our language. No other English poet was so tender.' And Douglas Brown has, still more recently, pointed to these verses as 'Hardy's supreme achievement in poetry; among these elegies are his finest single poems'.[15]

Of all the poems in the *Veteris Vestigia Flammae* group, none has been more generally admired than one in which Hardy sends his thoughts back to his Cornish romance of 1870—a poem called 'Beeny Cliff':

> O the opal and the sapphire of that wandering western sea,
> And the woman riding high above with bright hair flapping free—
> The woman whom I loved so, and who loyally loved me.

In the 1914 volume there were thirty-two poems addressed to or inspired by Emma Lavinia Gifford; and when, three years later, Hardy published *Moments of Vision* (1917), he added thirty-three more poems about his wife. In *Late Lyrics and Earlier* (1922) there were twenty-five more poems about or to the first Mrs. Hardy, and in *Human Shows* (1925) sixteen more. In all, nearly six-score poems deal with Emma. One hundred and sixteen of these poems were finally assembled on the fiftieth anniversary of the 'Beeny Cliff' poem and published as a unit with a long introduction on 'Hardy's Cornish Romance'.[16]

One of the poems in *Late Lyrics* is entitled 'The Marble Tablet'. It refers to the memorial stone which Hardy erected in the St. Juliot Church in Cornwall where Emma Gifford had once played the organ. The inscription on this stone reads:

To the dear Memory of Emma Lavinia Hardy, born Gifford, the wife of Thomas Hardy, author, and sister-in-law of the Rev. C. Holder, formerly incumbent of this parish: before her marriage she lived at the Rectory 1868–1873, conducted the church music, and laid the first stone of the re-built aisle and tower; she died at Dorchester 1912, and is buried at Stinsford, Dorset. Erected by her husband 1913.

Hardy's poem refers to this 'cold white' record of bygone days. No marble, however, could recapture her 'voice like the purl of a brook', and Hardy never forgot the day when he first heard that voice and saw that pair of blue eyes. On March 7, 1924, when he was nearly eighty-four years old, he made an entry in his notebook: 'E. first met 54 years ago.' In his poem 'Looking at a Picture on an Anniversary' he recalled that on

'Magic Lights'

this day of the year
(What rainbow-rays embow it!)
We met, strangers confessed,
But parted—blest.

On her gravestone in the Stinsford churchyard he placed these
words: THIS FOR REMEMBRANCE. And in one of the poems in
Human Shows (1925)—the last volume which he lived to see in
print—he remembered with gratitude what 'E' had done for
him:

She opened the door of the West to me,
    With its loud sea-lashings,
    And cliff-side clashings
Of waters rife with revelry.

She opened the door of Romance to me,
    The door from a cell
    I had known too well,
Too long, till then, and was fain to flee.

She opened the door of a Love to me,
    That passed the wry
    World-welters by
As far as the arching blue the lea.

She opens the door of the Past to me,
    Its magic lights,
    Its heavenly heights,
When forward little is to see!

In referring to the 'magic lights' which Hardy saw when he
looked through the door of the Past, he demonstrated that, like
Shakespeare's banished duke in *As You Like It*, he had learned
to find 'good in everything'— even in adversity and in domestic
discord; and if Shakespeare's Amiens had been permitted to
leave the Forest of Arden long enough to look in at Max Gate,
he might well have remarked to the poet dwelling there:

Happy is your Grace
That can translate the stubbornness of fortune
Into so quiet and so sweet a style.

Hardy knew his Shakespeare well enough to have replied: 'I
would not change it.' In spite of all the pain and sorrow that
thirty-eight years of domesticity with Emma had brought him,
she had also brought him love and inspiration and was now
opening to him the door of the Past with its 'magic lights'.

260

XXII

'Let Me Enjoy the Earth No Less'

ON that day in 1904 when Mrs. Florence Henniker brought a young friend to call at Max Gate, she introduced the young lady to Hardy as a distant relative of his. Florence Dugdale had been told by her father that the Dugdales were an old Dorset family remotely related to the Hardys, and any reader of the minor short-story, 'Alicia's Diary', may remember that an 'old feeble Mr. Dugdale' appears in it. In 1904, however, Hardy promptly made it clear to Miss Dugdale that he had little desire to talk about family matters; instead, he asked her if she had ever read Crabbe. No, she had not; but she had read something better: she had read all the Wessex novels, and she knew the short stories too. 'On the Western Circuit' was her favourite.

How had Miss Dugdale come to be such a diligent reader of Thomas Hardy? She had one day stumbled upon *Half Hours with Living Writers*. In this book, there was a selection from *A Pair of Blue Eyes*—the sensational chapter in which Knight falls over the cliff and is saved by Elfride. That was Florence Dugdale's introduction to the work of Thomas Hardy. In the light of his own fondness for his Cornish novel, that provided Miss Dugdale with a good opening gambit.

Florence Emily Dugdale was one of the five daughters of Edward Dugdale, headmaster of a church school at Enfield, just north of London. Her mother was Emma Taylor Dugdale. Born on January 12, 1879, Florence had hoped to follow her father's profession, but ill health interfered with this plan. She therefore turned to writing and, in time, earned a modest reputation as the author of children's books. Among these were *Cousin Christine*, *In Lucy's Garden*, *Old Time Tales*, and *Tim's Sister*.

Miss Dugdale's residence at Enfield made it possible for her to go to the British Museum without too much trouble, and (as we have noted in the chapter on *The Dynasts*) she offered her services and was eventually helpful in finding for him material which made its way into Part III of the epic-drama. Hardy showed his gratitude for this service by giving Miss Dugdale autographed copies of his books. In June 1907 he inscribed a copy of *Wessex Poems* 'To Miss Florence Dugdale, with the Author's kind regards'.

When Hardy's work on *The Dynasts* had come to an end, his personal interest in his young assistant replaced his gratitude to her, and the wording of the inscriptions in gift-copies changed. In July 1907 Florence Dugdale received a copy of *The Rubáiyát of Omar Khayyám* inscribed simply 'F.E.D. from T.H.' In 1908 Hardy gave her a copy of his edition of the *Poems* of William Barnes, inscribed to 'Miss F. E. Dugdale, with the Editor's kind regards'. In 1909 he gave her a copy of *The Mayor*; later still, a copy of *Tess* inscribed 'To Florence Emily Dugdale, with best wishes from Thomas Hardy'. In 1910, when she was at work on a story called 'Blue Jimmy, the Horse-Stealer', Hardy wrote out a number of lines for her to insert in her text; and one may perhaps surmise his aid in obtaining publication for this story in the *Cornhill Magazine* in February 1911.

Florence Dugdale's abilities were not confined to literary matters. After the death of Mrs. Emma Hardy, the Max Gate household was thrown into temporary confusion. The aging poet found himself with no one except distracted servants to protect him from the ever-increasing crowd of celebrity-seekers who forced their way into the Max Gate grounds. The reports of their intrusions are almost incredible. One day, so Hardy later informed his friend Newman Flower, the maid brought him a visiting-card on which he found written 'Herbert Spencer'. Hardy's first thought was: 'It's odd that Spencer should be in this neighbourhood,' but not wishing to be rude, he told the maid to show the caller into the drawing-room. When Hardy went down to meet the man, he found that it wasn't Herbert Spencer at all, but a total stranger who had used this ruse to

get a sight of the Great Man. When these strange intruders
failed to get a glimpse of the author, they walked about his
grounds, tore branches from his bushes, rooted up his flowers
to carry away as souvenirs, and did all they could to render
Max Gate an impossible place for poetic labours. In despair
Hardy turned to Florence Dugdale for help. Before Christmas
1912 she came to Max Gate and there soon brought order and
system into the household arrangements. She learned that
Hardy liked quiet, and she saw to it that he got it. Before the
year 1913 was half over, she not only had a firm hand on the
helm of the domestic ship, but had also proved herself able to
deal with the marauders who came to the front door. 'Florence
is my chucker-out', Hardy once remarked to St. John Ervine.
In a poem called 'After the Visit'[1] he recalled Florence's
ability to transform his home, with its secluded garden, into
a place of quiet retreat where her feet,

> That were light on the green as a thistledown ball,
> [Hastened with] . . . mute ministrations to one and to all
> Beyond a man's saying sweet.

When Rebekah Owen visited Dorchester in November 1913, in
order to witness a dramatization of *The Woodlanders*,[2] she called
at Max Gate and was surprised to discover that the household
was functioning smoothly and happily under the efficient
administration of Miss Dugdale. A few days later Miss Owen
drove out to Moreton, in the *Tess* country, to call on Miss
Teresa Charlotte Fetherstonhaugh-Frampton to whom Hardy
had introduced Miss Owen in 1892. Rebekah reported what
she had observed at Max Gate, and Miss Fetherstonhaugh
later commented: 'I am so glad you found all going so happily
and harmoniously there. I shall like to think of dear Mr. Hardy
as happy and comfortable and in good hands.'[3] Rebekah Owen
sensed that it would not be long before Max Gate saw a second
Mrs. Hardy and her guess proved correct.

On February 10, 1914, Hardy and his brother Henry went
to Enfield, Miss Dugdale's parental parish, and there Florence
and her sister Margaret joined them at the altar. Hardy and
Miss Dugdale were married—he at the age of 73; she, at 35.
Hardy was well aware of what this second marriage did for
him. In a poem called 'I Sometimes Think',[4] he paid his

grateful tribute to Florence. With tender solicitude she had
come to care for him

> And, spiriting into my house, to, fro,
> Like wind on the stair,
> Cares still, heeds all, and will, even though
> I may despair.

In 1917, when *Moments of Vision* was published, Hardy grate-
fully inscribed 'The First Copy / Of the First Edition / To the
First of Women / Florence Hardy'.

'When I married,' Florence wrote Rebekah Owen on September 22, 1916, 'I remember how it was impressed upon me
that I must "keep off" people'—i.e., keep people off. And she
did. Hardy responded to the changed conditions with such
obvious improvement in mood that every visitor to Max Gate
noticed the change. When Miss Fetherstonhaugh went to call,
she observed that Hardy 'looked most cheerful and unworried.
I have seldom seen him with such a happy expression.'[5] The
daughter of Curator Henry J. Moule (Mrs. Edward Leslie)
wrote in the same vein. Hardy, she said, had written her
husband 'as if he were very happy'. On January 1, 1918, Mrs.
Sheridan of Frampton Court called at Max Gate and told
Florence, while Hardy was out of the room, how successful she
had been in making his life happy. 'She said the title of his
book, *A Changed Man*, applied to him, for she remembered his
careworn look and knew what his life used to be.'[6]

This improvement in the atmosphere at Max Gate left its
trace in his writing. Back in 1909, in one of the most successful
of the lyrics in *Time's Laughingstocks*, Hardy had exultantly
declared:

> Let me enjoy the earth no less
>   Because the all-enacting Might
> That fashioned forth its loveliness
>   Had other aims than my delight. . . .
>
> From manuscripts of moving song
>   Inspired by scenes and dreams unknown,
> I'll pour out raptures that belong
>   To others, as they were my own.

It was easier, however, to *talk* about pouring out raptures than
to feel or express such emotions; and Hardy's experience in the

three or four years that followed the writing of that poem had not been of a nature to invite ecstatic moods or to inspire rapturous thoughts. By the end of 1916, however, three years after his second marriage, Hardy was aware of a distinct change in his attitude. He admitted in one of the autobiographical poems of *Moments of Vision* that he 'had never cared greatly' for Life and confessed that 'in earliest years' he had not showed 'much zest for its dance'. Now, however, Life has 'uncloaked a star', one which now beams so brightly upon him that he is able to forget 'the rough highway' of the past.

> And so, . . .
> I pace hill and dale
> Regarding the sky,
> Regarding the vision on high,
> And thus re-illumed have no humour for letting
> My pilgrimage fail.

In this spirit of rededication, he produced, in *Moments of Vision*, a larger body of poems (160) than in any previous (or in any later) volume and achieved a quality not found in the others, except for a rare exception like 'The Darkling Thrush'. There is general agreement with the critical judgment of John Middleton Murry that *Moments of Vision* is 'the volume which contains Hardy's finest lyrical poetry'.[7]

One of its poems, 'The Oxen', has been so universally admired that many a reader, merely on seeing the title here, will feel inclined to pause long enough to quote from memory Hardy's wistful description:

> Christmas Eve, and twelve of the clock,
> 'Now they are all on their knees,'
> An elder said as we sat in a flock
> By the embers in hearthside ease.

It had never occurred to Tom Hardy as a boy to doubt that 'the meek mild creatures' all knelt in adoration on Christmas Eve. In these later years he was of course well aware that 'so fair a fancy few would weave', and we who read the poem fifty years later still must remind ourselves that the poem was published in the London *Times* on Christmas Eve in 1915, the second Christmas of World War I. But despite the horrors of war, despite the blasting of the 'fair fancy', despite the disillusionments of old age (Hardy was now seventy-five), he still felt that

> If some one said on Christmas Eve,
>   'Come; see the oxen kneel,
> In the lonely barton by yonder coomb
>   Our childhood used to know,'
> I should go with him in the gloom,
>   Hoping it might be so.

Another poem in the *Moments of Vision* volume is one entitled 'To Shakespeare After Three Hundred Years'. This poem was written early in 1916 for the tercentenary of Shakespeare's death in April of that year; the impressive growth in Hardy's reputation as a poet was signalized by the fact that his verses were given first place in the 1916 *Book of Homage to Shakespeare*. (See manuscript as reproduced on pages 267–268.)

Later in this same year Hardy brought out a small volume called *Selected Poems*, in Macmillan's Golden Treasury Series, the contents of which were his own choosing. Four years later, Hardy once again recorded his interest in the English poets— this time in John Keats. He wrote two poems: 'At a House in Hampstead', written on or for the centenary of Keats's 'Ode to a Nightingale', and 'At Lulworth Cove a Century Back', re- calling Keats's landing on the Dorset coast on his voyage to Italy in 1820, at which time, so Hardy believed, Keats 'com- posed the sonnet, "Bright star, would I were steadfast as thou art".' These two poems, one composed in July 1920 and the other in September 1920, are not only interesting as tributes to John Keats but also as excellent poems in themselves. Both were published in *Late Lyrics* in 1922.

It is worth remarking here, in passing, that these poems to or about Shakespeare and Keats were not Hardy's first metrical testimonials to earlier English poets. After Swinburne's death in April 1909 Hardy had written 'A Singer Asleep',[8] and after Meredith's death only a little more than a month after Swin- burne's, Hardy wrote an eighteen-line poem 'George Meredith'.[9]

One of the reasons for the improvement in the quality of Hardy's verse was the fact that he was learning to take more time to revise, and was enjoying the relaxed conditions necessary for such work. His autobiographical lines on 'A Poet' provide a good illustration of the care he put into this sort of polishing.

To Shakespeare

After Three hundred years.

Bright-baffling
~~Braenzorm~~ Soul, least capturable of themes,
Thou, who display'dst a life of commonplace,
Leaving no intimate word or personal trace
Of high design outside the artistry
    Of thy penned dreams
Still shalt remain at heart unread eternally.

———

Through human orbits thy discourse to-day,
Despite thy formal pilgrimage, throbs on
In harmonies that ~~drowns~~ cow Oblivion,
And, like the wind, with all-uncared effect
    Maintain a sway
Not fore-desired, in tracks unchosen & unchecked.

———

And yet, at thy last breath, with mindless note
The borough clocks ~~in sameness~~ tongued the hour,
The Avon ~~edverdpasd Herzowhed~~ tower,
    just as always glasses the

———

Thy age was published on thy passing-bell
    But in due note
With other ~~neowisrthatupera~~ dwellers' deaths accorded a like knell.

———

And at the strokes some townsman (met, maybe,
And thereon queried by some squire's good dame
Driving in shopward) may have given thy name,
With, "Yes, a worthy man & well-to-do;
    Though, as for me,
I knew him but by just a neighbour's nod, 'tis true.

"I' faith, few knew him much here, save by word,
He having elsewhere led his busier life;
Though to be sure he left with us his wife."
—" Ah, one of the tradesmen's sons, I now recall....
Witty, I've heard....
We did not know him.... Well, good-day. Death comes to all."

So, like a strange bright bird we sometimes find
To mingle with the barn-door brood awhile,
Then vanish from their homely domicile —
Into man's poesy, we wot not whence
Flew thy strange mind.
Lodged there a radiant guest, & sped for ever thence.
February 14. 1916.

In that poem he asked his readers to come to his graveside some
evening, when they had heard that he had 'doffed this wrinkled
gear'; he asked them, on reaching his grave, to pause there
and say:

> 'Whatever the message his to tell,
> Two thoughtful women loved him well.'
>
> Stand and say that amid the dim:
> It will be praise enough for him.

Dissatisfied with the wording of these couplets, Hardy revised
and reworked the lines, so that they now read:

> 'Whatever his message—glad or grim—
> Two bright-souled women clave to him;'
>
> Stand and say that while day decays;
> It will be word enough of praise.

In the final outcome, 'word of praise' was multiplied far beyond the limits of two short lines. Early in 1919 Siegfried
Sassoon conceived the idea of preparing a 'Poets' Tribute' to be

presented to Hardy on his seventy-ninth birthday. Sassoon explains:

Some such token of homage was certain to be forthcoming in the following year, but my eagerness could not wait for his eightieth birthday. . . . Having disclosed the plan to Mr. Gosse, who welcomed it warmly, I set to work . . . with him, Walter de la Mare, and Sir Henry Newbolt as the presiding committee. About forty representative writers of all generations were asked to contribute an autograph poem. . . . Robert Bridges undertook to write a short foreword. . . . The Poets' Tribute was a labour of Love. . . . When I journeyed to Max Gate, bearing the Poets' Tribute which I had been privileged to place in his hands, I found him in excellent spirits. After he had taken it from me and was sitting at a table quietly turning the leaves, I felt that this was as good a moment as any I had known.[10]

Hardy had a similar feeling. 'The mark of recognition so appealed to him that he determined to answer every one of the contributors by letter. . . . It was almost his first awakening to the consciousness that an opinion had silently grown up, as it were in the night, that he was no mean power in the contemporary world of poetry.'[11]

Before another year had passed, he had two further demonstrations that his position as a poet was secure. On October 10, 1919, his *Collected Poems* was published, bringing together for the first time some five hundred and more of his poems. And three or four months later, Oxford University decided to forget all about the uncomplimentary portrayal of the University in *Jude the Obscure* and awarded Hardy the honorary degree of Doctor of Letters. On June 2, 1920, he was eighty years old; he had without doubt become the Grand Old Man of English literature.

XXIII

'Throbbings of Noontide'

IN the chapter on *The Dynasts* we have noticed how Hardy's interest in Bonaparte resulted in his collecting a Napoleonic library. At 'The Knapp' in nearby Bradpole, near Bridport (fifteen miles from Dorchester), lived Alexander Meyrick Broadley (1847–1916) with interests and habits that often paralleled Hardy's. Broadley, too, assembled a Napoleonic library, and by the time of the publication of *The Dynasts* this library had become large enough to justify cataloguing it. In 1905, under the title *Collectanea Napoleonica*, a catalogue of the Broadley collection was published in London by W. V. Daniell. This gained more than a local reputation for Mr. Broadley and he was invited to lecture on the subject of 'Napoleon's Threatened Invasion of England'—the theme of Hardy's novel *The Trumpet-Major*. A committee was formed in Dorchester to arrange for a public lecture there, and Broadley's appearance was eventually scheduled for February 8, 1908. Meanwhile, the publication of *The Dynasts* had proceeded and Broadley was asked by the editor of *The Tatler* in London to review Hardy's epic-drama. The review appeared in *The Tatler* for February 26, 1908.

Serving on the committee to arrange for the Dorchester lecture was Hardy's Dorchester acquaintance, Alfred Herbert ('Bertie') Evans, who operated a pharmacy near the King's Arms Hotel. Evans was a man of many interests and skills, including music and dramatics, and it now occurred to him that it might add to the attractiveness of the lecture by A. M. Broadley if the programme could include a 'dramatic interlude' based on some of the pages of *The Trumpet-Major*. Evans laid this proposal before Hardy; the novelist gave his approval; and Evans thereupon made a dramatic adaptation of the supper scene in the miller's house in the fourth and fifth chapters of the novel. When February 8, 1908, arrived, the 'dramatic interlude' proved the hit of the evening. Evans thereupon decided to dramatize the entire novel, and by the following autumn he had his play ready. *The Trumpet-Major* was given in Dorchester on November 18, 1908, and was a great success. This was the beginning of what developed into annual performances by 'the Hardy players', as the Dorchester Debating and Dramatic Society came eventually to be called.

On the evening of November 18 Hardy was unable to attend, but Mrs. Hardy was present in the audience. So was Maurice, the seven-year-old son of A. H. Evans. Maurice Evans was later to become internationally known as a Shakespearean actor; his father's dramatization of Hardy's *Trumpet-Major* was the first play he ever saw. A violent storm interrupted the performance, with the result that it was quite late when the play ended—much too late for a seven-year-old boy. Young Maurice was therefore sent home in the company of Mrs. Hardy, and fifty years later the distinguished actor could still recall how Mrs. Hardy held on to him with one hand while with the other she tried to keep the wind from tearing off the voluminous cape she was wearing.

Maurice Evans was not the only one who remembered Mrs. Hardy's cape. People in Dorchester had long ago learned that Emma's clothes were something to look at. She often wore a long velvet dress—'pavement-sweepers' such skirts were then called—and the sight of her coasting down High East Street on her bicycle became a familiar one to Dorchester people. Mrs. Hardy's bicycle was not a modern one with a coasterbrake, but was equipped with a foot-rest on the front fork, so that when she wished to 'free-wheel' down hill, she had only to place her feet on the foot-rest and leave the pedals to spin round and round.

Following up his success with *The Trumpet-Major*, A. H. Evans turned his attention in 1909 to *Far from the Madding Crowd*, and Hardy was magnanimous enough to say, after witnessing a rehearsal, that Evans's was a 'neater adaptation' of the novel than Comyns Carr's (i.e., Hardy's own) dramatization of 1881–2. The Dorchester players produced *Far from the Madding Crowd* on November 17 and 18, 1909, and once again young Maurice Evans was present. In order to regale the cast after the performance, 'Bertie' Evans had bought two kegs of cider. They were tapped prematurely, however, with the result that the local lad who was expected to play the part of Cainy Ball (from Chapter XXXIII of the novel) was in no state to appear before an audience. Young Maurice Evans was thereupon hastily summoned to make an impromptu début upon the stage; fortunately Cainy Ball's rôle consisted chiefly of coughing. A week later the Hardy Players repeated their performance in London under the auspices of the Society of Dorset Men in London.

In 1910 Evans's choice of a Wessex novel for dramatization was *Under the Greenwood Tree*. Hardy himself selected the words and music for the Christmas carols used in the play. Evans called his adaptation *The Mellstock Quire*. It was given in Dorchester on November 16 and 17, 1910, and was repeated in London on December 1.

When the time came for planning a 1911 programme, the secretary of the Dramatic Society, Mr. H. A. Martin, raised with Hardy the question as to what they might best attempt next. In March Hardy suggested his own little play *The Three Wayfarers*, which (he pointed out) 'is quite ready to be put on the stage as it stands'. Hardy of course knew that it would not fill an entire evening's programme, but Mr. Martin's committee (so Hardy thought) might 'ask Mr. Evans to do what he was thinking of at one time, . . . make a little play . . . out of *The Distracted Preacher* (one of my *Wessex Tales*)'.[1] Hardy's 'double-feature' suggestion was adopted and carried out; the two little plays were presented in Dorchester on November 15 and 16, 1911, and were repeated in London on November 27.

In 1912 Evans contented himself with revising the text of his 1908 dramatization of *The Trumpet-Major*, and this revised version was presented in Dorchester on November 27 and 28, 1912, and in London on December 5. On the evening of the first Dorchester performance, it was announced from the stage that Mrs. Thomas Hardy had died that morning.

The Dorchester Debating and Dramatic Society had thus,

by the beginning of 1913, had five years of modest success in staging adaptations of Hardy's novels; but in 1913 'modest success' was changed into something much more impressive, and the reason for the change is not hard to find: the Hardy Players acquired a new actress. A. H. Evans dramatized *The Woodlanders*, and for this play the company needed someone to play the rôle of Marty South. They soon found the actress they were seeking.

Gertrude Bugler was the seventeen-year-old daughter of a Dorchester baker and confectioner, and in the opinion of everyone who saw her she made an ideal Marty. She had had no dramatic training of any kind, but her simple sincerity, her beauty, and her native Dorset dialect, combined to fit her perfectly for Marty South's part. Hardy came to one of the rehearsals, and Gertrude Bugler was then introduced to him. She asked him for advice as to how she should speak her touching final eulogy of Winterborne, but Hardy would say no more than that she should speak the lines just as she felt them. 'So, I did!'[2] *The Woodlanders* was given at Dorchester on November 19 and 20, 1913, and (as we have noted in a previous chapter) Miss Rebekah Owen come down from the Lake District, where she now lived, to attend the performance. The play was repeated in London on December 8, 1913, and was also given in Weymouth on January 22, 1914. The fame of the Hardy Players was obviously spreading.

The outbreak of World War I caused an interruption of four years (1914–17 incl.) in the performances by the Dorchester actors,[3] but when the war was finally over, the demand for a revival of an annual Hardy Play become too insistent to be denied. Mr. T. H. Tilley of Dorchester finally took Mr. Evans's place as adapter—the latter having left Dorchester by this date—and Tilley began with *The Return of the Native*.

Gertrude Bugler, now twenty-four years old, was invited to play Eustacia Vye. When Hardy saw her, he remarked: 'She is exactly the physical type I had in mind when I imagined Eustacia Vye—tall and dark.' He made this remark to Vere Collins on December 27, 1920, with the added information that 'the *Daily Mail* man came down here [from London] and fell in love with her'. So did Thomas Hardy. He came often enough to the rehearsals to feel on easy terms with the actors, and in talking with Miss Bugler told her things that have apparently left no record elsewhere than in her memory of the great novelist. Hardy told her that there had never been a real Eustacia Vye—she was wholly imaginary—but that, when Hardy was young, a boy had drowned in Shadwater Weir and young Tom was on hand when the lad's body was taken from the water. The wet clothes of the drowned person made Hardy think for a moment that it was a girl, and this incident was recalled by him when, later, at Sturminster Newton, he was writing the tragic conclusion of *The Return of the Native*.

Hardy's relaxed and easy relations with the players provided Gertrude Bugler with another unusual experience. Few persons ever heard Hardy laugh. But Miss Bugler did, and she remembered the sound of his voice forty years later. 'I can still hear him laugh, as he laughed when I told him of what happened during a performance of *The Return of the Native*. During the proposal scene with Clym Yeobright, I had to say: "Ah, but you don't know what you have got in me." Before I could go on, a man's voice in the audience said "Hear! Hear!" '[4]

The Return of the Native was given with great success at Dorchester on November 17 and 18, 1920. Pictures of scenes of the play were printed in the London *Graphic* (November 27), and on January 27, 1921, the play was repeated in the Guildhall School of Music Theatre in London. Everyone sang the praises of Gertrude Bugler.

In 1921, for one reason or another, the Hardy Players departed from their usual custom, and instead of a November performance they tried a March presentation; and instead of a new dramatization, they gave (on March 30 and 31) scenes from two of the novels: 'An Old-time Rustic Wedding' from *Under the Greenwood Tree*, and 'Bathsheba Everdene and her Lovers', four scenes from *Far from the Madding Crowd*. In 1922 the company reverted to their previous schedule, and on November 15, 16, and 17, they gave *A Desperate Remedy*, an adaptation by T. H. Tilley of Hardy's first published novel. This play was repeated in London on November 21, 1922.

All of this dramatic activity revived anew Hardy's earlier interest in theatrical adaptations, but it now had a wholly unforeseen and unexpected result. Hardy was eighty-two years old

—quite entitled to sit 'by the embers in hearthside ease,'[5]—
but to everyone's amazement he wrote a new play, *The Famous
Tragedy of the Queen of Cornwall*.[6] Hardy took great pleasure in
this play. He asked the manager to insert in the programme a
reproduction of a water-colour drawing of Tintagel which
Emma Lavinia Gifford had made during her residence at St.
Juliot; and for the book published by Macmillan in November
1923 Hardy drew a frontispiece entitled 'Imaginary View of
Tintagel Castle at the Time of the Tragedy' in which he made
further use of Emma's water-colour. In the course of the year
during which the London, Bournemouth, and Glastonbury
performances (cited in Note 6) took place, Hardy had a forty-
two-page pamphlet made of the play and took obvious delight
in privately distributing it. *The Queen of Cornwall* is the only one
of his works for which he wrote a dedication. It is dedicated 'In
affectionate remembrance of those with whom I formerly spent
many hours at the scene of the tradition'.

When the secretary of the Dorchester Debating and Dramatic
Society consulted Hardy on the subject of 'What next?', the
novelist-poet recalled his dramatizing activities of twenty-eight
years before, when he had adapted *Tess of the D'Urbervilles* with
Mrs. 'Pat' Campbell in mind. The old manuscript, never used,
had been lying in a cupboard at Max Gate for more than a
quarter of a century. It was now brought forth and offered to the
Hardy Players if they wanted to use it. H. A. Martin at once
assured Hardy that they did want it, but the question immediately arose: who could play Tess? Hardy queried: 'Could
you get Miss Bugler to do it?'

But Miss Bugler was no longer Miss Bugler: she had married
her cousin, Ernest Bugler, and was now not only Mrs. Bugler
but also the mother of a baby daughter, born in March 1924.
Moreover, she no longer lived in Dorchester but in Beaminster,
nearly twenty miles away, and transportation between the two
towns was none too good in those days. The possibility of getting
Gertrude Bugler to play 'Tess' did not look very promising.
However, T. H. Tilley made a special trip over to Beaminster;
he talked with Mrs. Bugler; and she agreed to see whether
arrangements could be made which would permit her to attend
rehearsals in Dorchester. She admittedly 'loved acting' and
felt proud of the fact that Thomas Hardy had thought of her

as a possible 'Tess'. In the final outcome, the arrangements were made and rehearsals began.

Hardy's interest in Gertrude Bugler as a seventeen-year-old Marty South and in her as a twenty-four-year-old Eustacia Vye was mild indeed when compared with the fascinated interest he now took in seeing—at long last—his own dramatization of *Tess of the D'Urbervilles* come to life. Mrs. Bugler was now twenty-eight, more beautiful than ever, and—with more dramatic experience behind her—much more capable of meeting the demands of the tragic rôle now offered her. Hardy was delighted with her response to these demands. He not only attended many of the rehearsals at the Corn Exchange in Dorchester but also invited the company to come to Max Gate for further rehearsing; he also proposed that they all make a trip out to Wool to visit the old Elizabethan manor-house which had been used for Tess's honeymoon and for the famous confession-scene. On the ride to Wool, Hardy sat beside Mrs. Bugler. She remembered him on this ride as 'a happy, smiling and almost excited little man'. The novelist himself has apparently left no recorded comment on Mrs. Bugler's acting, but Sydney Cockerell, who came down from Cambridge, has been more helpful: his notes about 'the attractive and talented young actress' tell us that Gertrude Bugler played Tess 'with reserve, pathos, and charm'.

Hardy was more than delighted. In the last stanza of his *Wessex Poems* he had confessed that

> Time shakes this fragile frame at eve
> With throbbings of noontide,

but now, at the age of eighty-four, the throbbings were of such a violent sort as to distress Mrs. Florence Hardy. Sydney Cockerell noted that she was 'greatly disturbed . . . about his infatuation for the local "Tess" ' and that, according to Florence 'all the company of players were talking about it', and that it was 'the subject of much gossip in Dorchester'.

Gertrude Bugler herself was blissfully unaware of what was going on. She was happily married, with a baby daughter and a devoted husband. To her, Thomas Hardy was an old man, nearly eighty-five. The nearest she came to an awareness of Hardy's feelings was when, one day at Max Gate while the two of them were alone in the drawing-room, he asked her a

number of questions about her baby daughter. Mrs. Bugler
later recalled how he had then 'looked a little sadly and wistfully beyond the object on which his eyes happened to be resting,
and, instinctively, I knew it was one of "life's little ironies"
that he had no child of his own'.[7] Usually, upon her departure
from Max Gate at the end of a rehearsal, Hardy said good-bye
to her in the 'porch' of the residence; but one evening he walked
with her all the way out to the highway, where a motor-car
was waiting to carry her back to Beaminster. Half-way to the
road he suddenly stopped and said: 'If anyone ever asks you
if you knew Thomas Hardy, say "Yes, he was my friend".'

The *Tess* play was given in Dorchester on four nights,
Wednesday through Saturday, November 26–29, 1924, and was
repeated in Weymouth on December 11. After one of the Dorchester performances, Mr. H. A. Martin (who had played the
part of Boldwood in *Far from the Madding Crowd* and the part
of Giles Winterborne in *The Woodlanders*) came back stage to
ask Mrs. Bugler to come with him to meet Mr. Frederick
Harrison, the manager of the famous Haymarket Theatre in
London. Harrison surprised her by asking at once how she
would like to play 'Tess' at the Haymarket. Would she! On
January 8, 1925, after his return to London, Harrison wrote
Mrs. Bugler to say 'how much I should like you to play "Tess"
... here'. Gertrude Bugler hurried over to Max Gate to consult
Hardy's opinion on this subject and was pleased to receive his
approval of the idea.

Sydney Cockerell happened to be visiting at Max Gate just
at this time, and from him we learn how very disturbing this
prospect appeared to Mrs. Florence Hardy. Her husband's
'infatuation' cast a cloud over Max Gate. Cockerell urged Mrs.
Hardy to regard the whole business 'as a comedy', but she
found it hard to do this. Hardy had 'spoken roughly' to her, she
said, and had ignored her birthday (she was forty-six on
January 12, 1925). Cockerell pointed out that Mrs. Bugler
lived as far away as Beaminster and that Hardy neither met
her nor corresponded with her apart from the performances of
Tess, but Mrs. Hardy's distress remained unallayed.

Mrs. Bugler returned to Beaminster and there walked with
her head in the clouds, pushing her daughter's 'pram' up and
down the steep hills of the town and dreaming all the time about

the stage of the Haymarket. One day Mrs. Hardy turned up at Beaminster. 'She was agitated and said her husband did not know she had come to see me'—so Mrs. Bugler later reported in a talk she gave on April 7, 1959, at the Corn Exchange in Dorchester—'she said Mr. Hardy was very excited about the play going to London; he was in a nervous state. She feared he would want to go up to town to see it, and, at his age, it would not be good for him. . . . She asked me not to go to London. . . . So, in the end, I wrote . . . to Frederick Harrison . . . [that] I had decided not to play "Tess" after all.'

On February 7, 1925, Hardy wrote: 'Dear Mrs. Bugler: I have just heard from Mr. Harrison of your decision not to go to London. . . . No doubt you have come to a wise conclusion, though . . . I do not believe that any London actress will represent Tess so nearly as I imagined her as you did.'

Florence Hardy's expedition to Beaminster had proved more successful than had Emma Hardy's expedition to London in 1895 when she tried to block the publication of *Jude the Obscure*. Gertrude Bugler did finally appear as 'Tess' in London but not until after Hardy's death. Florence's action prevented his ever seeing Mrs. Bugler on a London stage.

As a result of Mrs. Hardy's appeal to the actress at Beaminster, it came about that, when Hardy's play of *Tess* did finally open at the Barnes Theatre in London on September 7, 1925, another actress played the part of Tess; Gwen Ffrangçon-Davies enacted the tragic rôle; but with Gertrude Bugler absent from the cast, Hardy had apparently lost his interest in the play. He did not go up to London to see it. His friend Henry Arthur Jones went and afterwards wrote Hardy about the performance, but by this time Hardy had turned his thoughts to other matters.

Whether he ever learned how Florence had frustrated Gertude Bugler's hopes of appearing at the Haymarket is uncertain. Probably not. But of one thing we can feel sure: Hardy's forgetting Florence's birthday in 1925 was not the last time that she, too, experienced frustration. In 1927 Hardy hired a car in Dorchester and took his wife for a ride to Yeovil, where he and Emma had lived for three or four months back in 1876. The ride was through the country of *The Woodlanders*, which Hardy always enjoyed seeing. When the car arrived at Yeovil,

Mrs. Hardy wished to stop for tea at Maynard's Café, but Hardy ordered the chauffeur to drive on. They finally stopped at Evershot (the 'Evershead' of Chapter XLIV in *Tess of the D'Urbervilles*, where Tess 'made a halt' and 'breakfasted a second time') and there the Hardys had tea at the unpretentious Strangway Arms. It was obvious to the driver, however, that Mrs. Hardy was not pleased, 'as she had set her heart on having tea at the café in Yeovil'.

It is of course possible that the driver of the car placed a wrong interpretation upon Mrs. Hardy's facial appearance, for everyone who knew her commented, sooner or later, on the habitual gloom of her countenance. One of Sydney Cockerell's correspondents (Mrs. Edmund J. Webb) once wrote him: 'Mrs. Hardy was the most melancholy person I have ever seen. I think she smiled once, but the smile only expressed sadness.' Siegfried Sassoon later remarked: 'Florence Hardy was a person who enjoyed being gloomy.'

With the question of the production of *Tess* off his mind, Hardy turned to the business of preparing another volume of verse for the press. On July 29, 1925, he sent a manuscript containing 152 poems to Macmillan, and late in November *Human Shows, Far Phantasies, Songs*, and *Trifles* was published. The entire edition of five thousand copies was sold out immediately, and two further printings followed before the end of the year. Hardy had no reason to doubt that he had 'arrived' as a poet. Almost as soon as this book of poems was off his hands—the last one he was to see in print—he began work on another; and by the end of 1927 he had made good progress in assembling 105 more poems, planning to have them ready for publication on his eighty-eighth birthday. He failed of attaining this goal by about five months.

The 257 poems in these two final collections (*Human Shows* in 1925 and *Winter Words* posthumously in 1928) brought the sum total of his poetic output to 918 poems. Their dispersal among his eight volumes can be conveniently summarized as shown in the table on the next page.

Hardy never rearranged these poems and never attempted any such classification of them as that by which William Wordsworth annoyed so many editors in later years. Readers are therefore left to their own devices in considering the more than

nine hundred poems left by Hardy. The poems fall into eight
general categories, two of which can be very quickly dismissed.
Hardy wrote a number of war poems, one series during the
Boer War and another during the first World War. As patriotic
expressions of national feeling they are of mild interest, but as
poetry they are quite unimportant. Closely allied to these war
poems is a group of songs, not more than five per cent of his
total output, in which he made an ineffectual attempt to write
a lyric to rank with Ben Jonson's 'Drink to me only with
thine eyes'. Hardy was simply not lyrical in this way.

Title	Publication Date	Number of Poems
Wessex Poems	1898	51
Poems of the Past and the Present	1901	99
Time's Laughingstocks	1909	94
Satires . . . , Lyrics and Reveries	1914	106
Moments of Vision	1917	160
Late Lyrics and Earlier	1922	151
Human Shows, Far Phantasies	1925	152
Winter Words	1928	105
		———
	Total	918

The most distinctive group of his poems, those that Hardy
alone could have written, is one that for want of a better designation may be called 'philosophical'. 'Hap' is one of the earliest
in this class of poems, and 'The Absolute Explains' is one of the
latest. They were written fifty-six years apart. The persistence
of this kind of poem throughout volume after volume has in
some quarters resulted in a misconception as to the bulk if not
the importance of this sort of thing in Hardy's poetic work.
Actually only about seven per cent of the poems are philosophical. 'Nature's Questioning', 'God's Education', and 'By the
Earth's Corpse' are good representatives of this class.

Almost equal in number are the poems which Hardy wrote
on special occasions—on the anniversaries of poets, on the
deaths of friends or relatives, on the occasion of visits to historic
spots, or crises and catastrophes such as the sinking of the
'Titanic' in 1912. Many of these memorial poems are more
successful than such 'occasional' verses usually are, and we

have already given some attention to the poems on Shakespeare, Keats, and Swinburne.

One of the great surprises in generalizing about Hardy's poetry is the discovery that only a relatively small number are devoted to Nature. Of his 918 poems, less than one hundred remind us that 'he was a man who used to notice such things', The comparatively small number is concealed by the fact that in this category are found some of Hardy's very best poems. 'The Darkling Thrush', 'The Oxen', 'In a Wood', 'Afterwards', and 'The Blinded Bird', are all of such unquestioned superiority that they lead to the false inference that much of Hardy's metrical composition was inspired by Nature. This is not so. In fact, all the five classifications thus far mentioned, taken together, do not account for more than one-third of his poems. The other two-thirds are of three sorts: personal poems (autobiographical reminiscences and records), poems of love or of sorrow, and narratives of one kind or another.

Fully a quarter of the poems fall into the class here loosely designated as narrative. Some are in dramatic form; some are dialogues; but all tell a story. 'The Curate's Kindness' is a good representative of this class, and 'Panthera' is another striking member of the narrative group.

No matter what the category, no matter what the subject or the nature of the poem, the reader must be prepared to come upon words that belong to science or philosophy, to rhetoric or logic, rather than to poetry. Just as in *The Dynasts* one reads that Marshal Ney's ignominious death was 'but technically deserved', so in the poems one may come upon a 'culminating sight' or may read of something that is 'warranted up to date'. In one poem day dawns with such a chill 'as to render further cheerfulness intolerable now'. This does not mean, of course, that Hardy was never able to achieve a lovely line. In landscape painting he could write: 'The yachts ride mute at anchor, and the fulling moon is fair.' In portrait-painting he could sketch a girl

> With cheeks whose airy flush outbid
> Fresh fruit in bloom.

In the poetry of action he could picture 'a ghost-girl-rider' who still rides gaily, 'draws rein and sings to the swing of the tide'. In a philosophizing mood he could remark that 'The vows of man and maid are frail as filmy gossamere.' The attentive reader will, in short, find among the 918 poems abundant evidence to convince himself that 'this is a Major Poet'.

During one of the rehearsals of *Tess* at Max Gate, Gertrude Bugler noticed how Hardy sat listening, with 'his hand resting idly on the head of "Wessie", his wire-haired terrier'. On December 27, 1926, 'Wessie' died; and, according to a letter which Florence Hardy wrote to Rebekah Owen on January 26, 1928, Hardy 'never quite got over the loss' of his pet. *Winter Words* contains a poem 'Dead "Wessex" the Dog to the Household' which memorializes Hardy's affection for the dog.

Earlier still, he had written a poem, 'Last Words to a Dumb Friend',[8] in which he recalled 'Snow-dove', a cat, 'purrer of the spotless hue':

> Strange it is this speechless thing,
> Subject to our mastering,
> Subject for his life and food
> To our gift, and time, and mood, . . .
> Should—by crossing at a breath
> Into safe and shielded death,
> By the merely taking hence
> Of his insignificance—
> Loom as largened to the sense,
> Shape as part, above man's will,
> Of the Imperturbable.

This poem reminds us that, no matter from what angle we approach Hardy's mind, we come sooner or later upon this brooding, philosophizing habit of thought, whether about 'the Imperturbable' or about the Inscrutability of Life.

XXIV

'Afterwards'

HARDY's eighty-first birthday 'was remembered by the newspapers' and was made especially memorable for him by his receipt of 'an address . . . signed by 106 younger writers'.[1] The address (probably the work of St. John Ervine who had originated the idea of presenting it to Hardy) is particularly eloquent as a demonstration of the 'grateful homage' now paid by a younger generation of Englishmen and as a graceful and noble definition of the position Hardy had come to hold in their eyes. It read, in part:

We, who are your younger comrades in the craft of letters, wish on this your eighty-first birthday to do honour to ourselves by praising your work, and to thank you for the example of high endeavour and achievement which you have set before us. In your novels and poems you have given us a tragic vision of life which is informed by your knowledge of character and relieved by the charity of your humour and sweetened by your sympathy with human suffering and endurance. We have learned from you that the proud heart can subdue the hardest fate, even in submitting to it. . . . In all that you have written you have shown the spirit of man, nourished by tradition and sustained by pride, persisting through defeat. You have inspired us both by your work and by the manner in which it was done. The craftsman in you calls for our admiration as surely as the artist. . . . From your first book to your last, you have written in the 'high style' . . . and you have crowned a great prose with a noble poetry. We thank you . . . for all that you have written . . . but most of all, perhaps, for *The Dynasts*. We beg that you will accept . . . our grateful homage.[2]

283

It was natural that fellow-writers, 'comrades in the craft of letters', should express admiration for Hardy's work and for 'the manner in which it was done', but in the eyes of other people as well, men and women not primarily interested in craftsmanship, Hardy had come to symbolize an admirable stoicism which lifted him, as a man, above his position as a novelist and as a poet. They had learned, not only from his books but also from his life, 'that the proud heart can subdue the hardest fate, even in submitting to it'.

There have been readers who, in the light of what has just been said here, have wondered why Hardy was not honoured as other English writers had been, and have since been, honoured: Sir Walter Scott, Sir James Barrie, Sir Walter Besant, Sir Edmund Gosse, Sir John Squire, even Sir Hugh Walpole. Why not Sir Thomas Hardy?

The answer to this question is that Hardy *was* offered a knighthood but his self-effacing shyness led him to decline it. According to Hardy's near-neighbour, Albert Bankes of Wolfeton House, he had 'three times refused'[3] this honour. Hardy himself characteristically says nothing about all this in *The Later Years*. When Barrie was made a baronet, Hardy promptly wrote him (on June 3, 1913) 'to express my pleasure at what I see in the papers to-day; for though you did not require the ornament it is the best thing we can do in our English clumsy way'.[4]

Hardy silently retained in his correspondence files the letter in which the Court offer of 'the ornament' was made to him, but for our knowledge of what Albert Bankes said we are indebted to Rebekah Owen. In her indefatigable pursuit of annotations for all of Hardy's writings, she came to his statement in 'The Lady Penelope'[5] that as you go out of Dorchester by the low-lying road which eventually conducts to the town of Yeovil, 'you see on the right hand an ivied manor-house, flanked by battlemented towers, and more than usually distinguished by the size of its many mullioned windows'. This dwelling was known as Wolfeton House, and in time Miss Owen and her sister were invited within its portals by Mr. and Mrs. Bankes and there heard from Albert Bankes himself the report that 'Hardy had three times refused a knighthood'.

Rebekah Owen is also the source of our information about Lascelles Abercrombie. He produced one of the earliest twentieth-century critical studies of Hardy[6]—a book which eventually attracted enough attention to obtain for its author the distinction of being invited to contribute the article on Hardy to the fourteenth edition of the *Encyclopaedia Britannica*. Miss Owen's note, written in 1912, reads: 'Mr. Hardy said Mr. Abercrombie came to see him one day, "a young man on a bicycle", and as he did not know him, he feared he was "a little short with him". The preface [of Abercrombie's book] leads one to think Mr Hardy had admitted him to friendship and confidence.'[7] This admission to 'friendship and confidence', if not made prior to 1912, was at least achieved by the time the 'young man on a bicycle' had become Professor of English Literature at the University of Leeds; and when Abercrombie wrote his article on Hardy for the *Britannica*, he was able, on the basis of the confidence Hardy had reposed in him, to make one disclosure which, up to that time, had been a carefully guarded secret. So quietly did Abercrombie make his revelation that its significance escaped many a reader: 'In 1928 appeared his *Memoirs*, written in the third person.'[8] This reference was to the book we now know as *The Early Life of Thomas Hardy*.

In the course of preparing his autobiography, as we can now call it, Hardy found an opportunity to allow the public to share in a knowledge of some matters which had, up till then, remained hidden (like the offer of knighthood) in his correspondence files. Late in 1920, for example, Alfred Noyes was quoted in the London *Morning Post* as having said in a public lecture that Hardy's philosophy of life involved a belief that 'the Power behind the Universe was an imbecile jester'. The announcement annoyed Hardy, and on December 13, 1920, he wrote Noyes: 'As I hold no such "philosophy", . . . I should be glad if you would inform me whereabouts I have seriously asserted such to be my opinion.' Pages 216–218 of *The Later Years* are devoted to the correspondence that followed, and any reader interested in reading Hardy's own comments on his philosophy of life should look these pages up. Two summarizing sentences can be quoted here:

My sober opinion . . . of the Cause of Things . . . is . . . that the said Cause is neither moral nor immoral, but *un*moral. . . . This view . . . I am quite unable to see as 'leading logically to the conclusion that the Power behind the universe is malign'.[9]

The preparation of his autobiography also gave Hardy an opportunity to pay off some old scores. He ticked off Henry James and Robert Louis Stevenson as 'the Polonius and the Osric of novelists'.[10] Both men were now safely dead, and if the reader is puzzled by this exhibition of animus in a man who was usually as mild-mannered as was Thomas Hardy, the explanation may be found in the *Letters of Henry James*, published in 1920. Up to this time, Hardy's feelings about James had been, if not cordial, at least not hostile. He and James had known each other for nearly forty years. As fellow-clubmen in London, they often saw each other. They sat near each other at a service in Westminster Abbey, they both attended the same fashionable society wedding, and at the annual dinner of the Rabelais Club in 1886 they sat amiably side by side. In 1898 Hardy told William Rothenstein that 'certainly nobody' could do a brief comment on George Gissing 'so well' as Henry James could do it. In January 1916, when James was admitted to the Order of Merit, Hardy wrote in his capacity as President of the Incorporated Society of Authors to express to James his 'sincere felicitations on your appointment to the Order of Merit ... and ... to hope that your health, which by recent reports has been seriously endangered, is now restored'.

In the autobiography, however, Hardy spoke of James as 'a writer who has no grain of poetry, or humour, or spontaneity in his productions', and recorded his memory of James's 'ponderously warm manner of saying nothing in infinite sentences'. What had happened may be easily surmised. When the *Letters of Henry James* was published, Hardy learned what he and Stevenson had been saying about Hardy behind his back. The Osric and Polonius of English novelists had discussed *Tess of the D'Urbervilles* back in 1892 and '93 and now their opinions were published for all the world to read.

On March 19, 1892, James had written to Stevenson: 'The good little Thomas Hardy has scored a great success with *Tess of the D'Urbervilles*, which is chock-full of faults and falsity.' Stevenson, who had once upon a time declared 'I would give my hand to be able to write like Hardy', now echoed James's derogatory remarks; and on February 17, 1893, James wrote again: 'I grant [what] you [say about] Hardy with all my heart. ... I am meek and ashamed where the public clatter is deafening—so I bowed my head and let *Tess of the D'Urbervilles* pass. But oh yes, dear Louis, she is vile. The pretense of "sexuality" is only equalled by the absence of it, and the abomination of the language by the author's reputation for style.'

The abomination of the language! Hardy was not the man to let words like those be forgotten or overlooked. Years before this, Andrew Lang had written Hardy's friend Edward Clodd: 'I am sorry Hardy takes criticism so much to heart. My word, we should cultivate a little stoicism.' But Hardy was thin-skinned and remained so to the end of his life. In the course of preparing his autobiography, he now wrote an account of his attending, in December 1879, the inaugural dinner of the Rabelais Club—a group of writers brought together by Walter Besant 'as a declaration for virility in literature'. Hardy's comment in *The Early Life* reads: 'Hardy was pressed to join as being the most virile writer . . . then in London; while, it may be added, Henry James . . . was rejected for the lack of that quality, though he was afterwards invited as a guest.'[11] But when Henry James sat beside Hardy at the annual dinner of the Club in 1886, he was not there 'as a guest' but as a regular member. What is more, he was a charter-member. When Robert Browning was solicited on June 23, 1879, to join the Club, he was told that Hardy and Henry James were both 'already inscribed' as 'original members'. Later on, when the Club published its *Recreations*—three volumes of them, 1880–88—Henry James was named in each volume as a member, and in the first volume his name was distinguished by an asterisk to mark him as a charter-member of the Club.

Hardy had a set of these *Recreations* in his own library,[12] and he thus had every opportunity for knowing that Henry James had not been kept out of the Club for lack of virility. If this strikes the reader as a sorry exhibition of petty retaliation, he will be the more inclined to join Andrew Lang in exclaiming: 'My word, we should cultivate a little stoicism!'

If Hardy's relations with James had, by 1920, become a little soured, there were others with whom he maintained cordiality to the end. His old friend Gosse, now Sir Edmund, delighted his heart one day by writing: 'Dearest and most admired of friends: Thank you for the unbroken record of nearly 45 years of precious intercourse. May we both live to celebrate our jubilee of Friendship.' They came very near to achieving that goal. In June 1927 Gosse visited Hardy at Max Gate. The two sat in the garden, Gosse holding one of Hardy's cats on his lap, while they talked of many things. Upon his return to London, Gosse wrote to a common friend to report on Hardy at eighty-seven:

He is a wonder, if you like! . . . Very tiny and fragile, but full of spirit and a gaiety not quite consistent in the most pessimistic of poets. He and I collogued merrily of past generations, like two antediluvian animals sporting in the primeval slime.

Gosse was nine years Hardy's junior, but he survived Hardy by only a few months.

In October 1927, four months after Gosse's visit, a Roman pavement was discovered in Fordington—the section of Dorchester where Hardy as a boy had attended the church of the Reverend Henry Moule—and despite Mrs. Hardy's protests (for a cold north wind was blowing) Hardy insisted on going to the site of the excavations and examining the Roman remains. In September 1908 he had similarly gone to the Roman amphitheatre—'the Ring' of *The Mayor of Casterbridge*—where (as he wrote his first wife) he got drenched, 'with sticky chalk-mud half way up to our knees'.[13] This time he was equally eager to see what was going on. The pavement discovered in Fordington was removed to the Dorset County Museum on November 9, 1927, but Hardy's exposure during the inclement weather was probably too much for a man of his age. Early in December he complained of inability to work, and after Christmas he found the stairs at Max Gate too fatiguing for his failing strength, and he thereafter remained upstairs.

During the evening of January 10, 1928, Hardy asked Florence to read Browning's 'Rabbi Ben Ezra' to him. He wished none of the 192 lines skipped. Here are six of them:

> As it was better, youth
> Should strive, through acts uncouth,
> Toward making, than repose on aught found made:
> So, better, age, exempt
> From strife, should *know*, than tempt
> Further. Thou waitedst age: wait death nor be afraid!

Nor was Hardy afraid. On the evening of January 11, only a

few hours before he breathed his last, he asked Florence to re-peat to him 'that stanza in the *Rubáiyát* that begins "Oh Thou, who man . . .".' Hardy had given Florence Dugdale a copy of Omar Khayyám's poem in July 1907, but she apparently had never memorized it as had he. Fortunately, his own copy of the *Rubáiyát* was on his bedside table. She soon found the stanza he wanted and read it to him:

> Oh Thou, who Man of baser Earth didst make,
> And ev'n with Paradise devise the Snake;
>   For all the Sin wherewith the Face of man
> Is blacken'd—man's forgiveness give—and take!

And in wanting to hear that final defiant 'and take!' Hardy signalized the entire integrity of the philosphical side of his life. There was to be no canting dishonesty, even on his deathbed.

In a letter George Eliot had once written, she described the exultation she had felt on being 'liberated from the wretched giant's bed of dogma' on which her mind had been 'racked and stretched ever since it began to think'; and then she spoke of the dismay of discovering 'after a year or two of reflection' that one might need 'the crutches of superstition' to help one to hobble about in one's 'miserable weakness'. Gosse had found Hardy 'very tiny and fragile' but he needed no 'crutches of superstition' on which to hobble about. Hardy's reflecting was not a matter of 'a year or two', for he had lived his whole life in intellectual honesty.

As soon as the news of Hardy's death reached London, the suggestion was immediately made that his ashes be buried in Poets' Corner, Westminster Abbey. The proposal was at once accepted, for there was general recognition of the fact that no other place would serve. 'The death of Thomas Hardy', wrote Virginia Woolf, 'leaves English fiction without a leader.' In the words of John Macy, 'On the day of Hardy's death, the world knew, that is, everybody but the Nobel Prize Committee knew, that the greatest man of letters in the world had gone and that there was no one quite clearly second to step into his place.'

Three simultaneous church services were held on Monday afternoon, January 16. In Dorchester, there was a memorial service at St. Peter's Church, attended by the Mayor and other officials of the town. At Stinsford Church, in the presence of Hardy's brother Henry and of a rural population, there was a simple service under the great yew-tree in the corner of the churchyard. Emma Lavinia Gifford, who had 'opened the door of romance' to Hardy in 1870, now opened a door for him once again: for his heart, which had been removed from his body before it was sent up to London for cremation, was now buried in the grave of his first wife.

The Abbey service was, of course, the most impressive of the three. Among the pall bearers were Barrie, Galsworthy, Gosse, A. E. Housman, Kipling and Shaw. The hour of the funeral was 2 p.m., but thousands of people turned out, in spite of the cold January rain that fell, and a queue began forming as early as ten o'clock in the morning. It eventually stretched from the door of the Abbey, past St. Margaret's Church, and on towards the Gothic tower of the Houses of Parliament. Newspaper reporters who were on hand noticed that in this huge crowd of Hardy's admirers there was none of the levity or idle curiosity of ordinary sightseers. These people obviously knew Hardy's books and liked to talk about them. English was far from being the only language heard in the conversations that helped to fill the four-hour wait before the doors of the Abbey were thrown open. Frenchmen and Germans, Dutchmen and Swedes, Italians and Poles, mingled in the crowd. Turbaned Hindus stood with solemn patience, and American reporters pretended to be able to recognize accents from Boston, Alabama, and Kansas. The whole assembly waiting in the rain belonged to that undistinguished mass of average humanity in which Hardy had taken delight, from which he had himself sprung, and about which he had written. His funeral was attended by a concourse of grateful readers. So numerous were they that, when the doors were finally opened, they could not all get into the Abbey.

The newspaper reporters who overheard the conversations of the waiting men and women noted the fact that there were many varying views of Hardy expressed. One man was grateful for the characters of Tess and Jude. Another rated the description of Egdon Heath as the most glorious passage of English prose produced by the nineteenth century. A third preferred

Hardy's poetry, 'because it was more personal'. Another re-called that Hardy had a keen eye for nature, and that he had written about birds on a wintry day, about sheep in storms, about horses labouring up Ludgate Hill towards St. Paul's, and about the agony of poor animals shot by callous hunters.

If those who braved the cold rain on that January morning did not put a further thought and a subtler feeling into words, that thought and feeling were doubtless present in the funeral crowd none the less, for they appeared in printed reports of the funeral later on. In the eyes of many who came to the Abbey Thomas Hardy had come to symbolize an intense personal loyalty. In the darkness and gloom of post-war depression, the flame of human loyalty shone the more brightly. Against the challenge of despair first brought by nineteenth-century science and later intensified by the chaos of a world war, Hardy had steadfastly vindicated the soul of man. He had spoken for all Englishmen when he had placed on Wellington's lips those words in *The Dynasts*:

> Despite their fierce advantage here, I swear
> By every god that war can call upon
> To hold our present place at any cost.

England had learned to take courage from a man who, like Wellington, was determined 'to hold out unto the last'. Hardy, too, had possessed this same moral quality. Even when he wrote about nature, he had never for long averted his eyes from men. From the trees of 'In a Wood' he had turned back to his kind where he found 'life-loyalties'. In all his novels he had lavished his affection upon men and women of courage, resourcefulness, patience, endurance, tolerance, sympathy, unselfishness, and love. As Henry W. Nevinson remarked: 'No Englishman since Wordsworth has heard the still sad music of humanity with so fine an ear, and none has regarded the men and women of our country with a compassion so profound and yet so stern, as they pass with tears and laughter between the graves and the stars.'

As Virginia Woolf remarked, Hardy's writings had freed men from the cramp and pettiness imposed by life. Our imaginations have been stretched and heightened. . . . It is no mere transcript of life at a certain time and place that Hardy has given us. It is a vision of the world and of man's lot, as they revealed themselves to a powerful imagination, a profound and poetic genius, a gentle and humane soul.[14]

Hardy's ashes were deposited in Poets' Corner next to the grave of Charles Dickens and within a few feet of the grave of Alfred Tennyson.

And after the funeral was over, what was to ensue? Tennyson had once cynically commented on the likelihood that

> when modern things are thrust
> By death below the coffin lid,
> Our liberal sons will spurn our dust
> And wonder what it was we did.

Hardy, too, had had his moments of wondering about the future, and even of making cynical comments on the human scene. In 'Christmas 1924' he had written:

> 'Peace upon earth!' was said. We sing it,
> And pay a million priests to bring it.
> After two thousand years of mass
> We've got as far as poison-gas.

But in better moments his wondering about the future took a kindlier form. In his poem 'Afterwards'[15] he had written:

> When the Present has latched its postern behind my tremulous stay,
> And the May month flaps its glad green leaves like wings,
> Delicate-filmed as new-spun silk, will the neighbours say
> 'He was a man who used to notice such things'?

Yes, the neighbours did say just that—they have, in fact, been saying that for nearly a hundred years; for, as far back as 1871, Hardy had demonstrated that 'he was a man who used to notice such things'. In *Desperate Remedies* he had commented on the 'pink dawns and white sunsets' of April; 'with the third week, the cuckoo had appeared; with the fourth, the nightingale'. He had noticed the way his heroine 'glowed amid the dulness like a single bright-red poppy in a field of brown stubble'. But it is by now clear that Thomas Hardy's 'afterwards' is not going to be confined to a mere matter of remembering that he was a man who used to notice natural phenomena. The signs that he is to have a much more significant future have multiplied everywhere since the date of his death nearly forty years ago, and some of these signs may be briefly noted.

Mrs. Florence Hardy survived her husband by only nine years—long enough to see into print the two volumes of his autobiography. Before her death on October 17, 1937, she arranged for the reconstruction of Hardy's study in the Dorset County Museum, and (although she herself did not live to see this Hardy Memorial Room) it was opened to the public by the poet laureate, John Masefield, on May 10, 1939. Since that time, it has attracted a never-ending procession of visitors, scholars, tourists, admirers, and students. The birthplace at Higher Bockhampton has similarly become a shrine attracting great numbers of visitors.

At the time of the centenary of Hardy's birth, the second World War prevented any suitable notice of the occasion in England; but *Music and Letters* managed to publish a series of articles on 'Hardy and Music' by Eva M. Grew and others.[16] In America, the one-hundredth anniversary was observed by a notable exhibition of Hardy's works (including manuscripts and letters) at the Grolier Club in New York City, and by similar exhibitions in the libraries of Columbia University and of Wells College. In Baton Rouge, Louisiana, a special Hardy Centenary issue of *The Southern Review* was published, with excellent critical articles by Donald Davidson and others.[17] The first edition of the present biography was also published at that time.

In Hardy's native land, when Lord David Cecil of New College, Oxford, was invited to deliver the Clark Lectures at Trinity College, Cambridge, in 1942, he chose Thomas Hardy as his subject because, he said, this choice offered an opportunity to study Hardy's 'special nobility . . . —a union of unexpected elements—the sternness of his integrity and the tenderness of his heart'. Since the date of Lord Cecil's lectures, Hardy's books have come to be more and more widely studied in schools, colleges, and universities. Hundreds of theses and dissertations have been written on the Wessex novels and poems, and the scholarly examination of Hardy's manuscripts has thrown a great deal of light upon the workings of his mind.

The combination of moral qualities mentioned by Lord Cecil

has appealed to thinking men and women far beyond the boundaries of English-speaking lands. In Heidelberg University a special Hardy Room has been set up devoted to the interests of its English Seminar, and in the pages of *Archiv* learned reports on Hardy studies all over the world are given respectful attention. In Japan, an active Thomas Hardy Society has been formed, enrolling hundreds of enthusiastic members who attend annual meetings at which papers on the Wessex writings are discussed with insight and appreciation. In a previous chapter, we have had occasion to list the translation of *Tess of the D'Urbervilles* into Japanese. That translation has been widely read in Japan. Ten years ago, when a Tokyo newspaper sponsored a post-war essay-contest on the subject 'Hopes of a Twenty-year-old', second prize was won by a girl named Michiko Shoda who had read *Tess* in Japanese. Her prize-winning essay made use of Tess's familiar analogy of the blighted apple: Michiko Shoda called it 'worm-eaten'. Thomas Hardy received further emphatic attention in Japan when, three years later, this winner of the second prize became engaged to Crown Prince Akihito and eventually married him.

Kipling, one of the honorary pall bearers at the Westminster Abbey funeral, once called Hardy 'Lord of the Wessex Coast', and by the end of Queen Victoria's reign everyone in England was ready to acknowledge this lordship. In the twentieth century the spread of Hardy's reputation and influence throughout the world has been phenomenal: his works can now be read in more than a score of foreign languages.[18] Hardy's audience today is world-wide, for men and women everywhere have learned to turn to him for solace and inspiration.

A hundred years ago Hardy used some of his London prize-money to purchase a copy of Lucretius' *On the Nature of Things* (London, Bohn, 1851), translated into English verse by John Mason Good. On page 348 Hardy marked a six-line passage that had special appeal for him:

> For, far from mortals and their vain concerns,
> In peace perpetual dwell th' immortal gods;
> Each self-dependent, and from human wants
> Estranged for ever. There no pain pervades,
> Nor dangers threaten; every passion sleeps,
> Vice no revenge, and virtue draws no boon.

'Afterwards'

Hardy's own life had demonstrated his success in rising to a moral plane superior to that of the 'immortal gods' described by Lucretius. For Hardy did *not* dwell far from mortals; he was *not* estranged from human wants; he was *not* indifferent to vice and virtue. His 'comrades in the craft of letters' who addressed him on his eighty-first birthday praised him for his 'vision of life' and for his 'knowledge of character'; they acknowledged the charity of his humour and testified to the healing benefit of his 'sympathy with human suffering and endurance'. 'We have learned from you,' they wrote, 'that the proud heart can subdue the hardest fate.' Today, men and women all over the world have learned that same lesson from Hardy. He has taught them how the spirit of man can persist through defeat, and he continues today to inspire readers to strive towards noble conduct in an imperfect world.

Notes and References

I. BIRTH AND BOYHOOD AT BOCKHAMPTON (*pages 1–17*)

1 *The Early Life of Thomas Hardy* (hereafter abbreviated *Early Life*), p. 8.
2 *Early Life*, p. 28.
3 See William Archer's 'Real Conversation' with Thomas Hardy, in *The Critic*, New York, April 1901, p. 309.
4 *Jude the Obscure*, Chapter VI.
5 *Under the Greenwood Tree*, Chapter I.
6 *The Mayor of Casterbridge*, Chapter XXXII.
7 The lines were printed in the issue of the *Times Literary Supplement* for August 23, 1947, under the title 'Hardy's Earliest Verses'.
8 *Early Life*, p. 43.

II. IN SEARCH OF A PROFESSION (*pages 18–29*)

1 *Early Life*, p. 35.
2 *Early Life*, p. 43.
3 *Early Life*, p. 10.
4 *Early Life*, p. 15.
5 *Early Life*, p. 26.
6 *Tess of the D'Urbervilles*, Chapter XIV.
7 *Early Life*, p. 38.
8 *The Later Years of Thomas Hardy* (hereafter abbreviated *Later Years*), p. 196.
9 *Jude the Obscure*, Chapter I, p. 7.
10 Published in the *Detroit Post*, March 15, 1885.
11 The article was reprinted in book-form by the Colby College Library, Waterville, Maine, in August 1942.
12 *Early Life*, p. 43.
13 In *Early Life* (p. 43) there is a mention of these accounts, 'prepared,' said Hardy, 'for the grateful reporter of the *Dorset [County] Chronicle*'. Thanks to the assiduity of Professor Richard Little Purdy in running these accounts to earth (see his *Thomas Hardy: a Bibliographical Study*, 1954, p. 291), we now know that Hardy wrote one in 1856, another in 1857, two more in 1859, one in 1860, one in 1861, and two in 1862—eight in all.
14 *The Return of the Native*, III, I.

Notes and References

III. LONDON TRIED (pages 30–44)

[1] *Scribner's Magazine*, May 1893.
[2] W. R. Rutland, *Thomas Hardy*, Oxford, 1938, p. 25.
[3] *A Pair of Blue Eyes*, Chapter XXVI.
[4] *Time's Laughingstocks*, 1909.
[5] The reader interested in details about this trail can find them in an article on the 'Twin-Voice of Shakespeare' in the *Shakespeare Association Bulletin*, April and July 1934. After reading this article the second Mrs. Hardy wrote to its author: 'I consider this article one of the best that has been written about my late husband. I don't think even you would realize how truly you have written. Only a few hours before his death Mr. Hardy spoke of Shakespeare.'

[6] The thirty-four are:

Giotto (1276–1337)	Rubens (1577–1640)	Hobbema (1638–1709)
Angelico (1387–1455)	Van Alsloot (15??–1626)	Kneller (1648–1723)
Gozzoli (1420–1497)	Sallaert (1590–1648)	Greuze (1725–1805)
Crivelli (1430–1493)	Poussin (1594–1665)	Romney (1734–1802)
Perugino (1446–1523)	Van Dyke (1599–1641)	Nollekens (1737–1823)
Holbein (1460–1524)	Velasquez (1599–1660)	Flaxman (1755–1826)
Dürer (1471–1528)	Rembrandt (1607–1669)	Turner (1775–1851)
Raphael (1483–1520)	Douw (1613–1675)	Wiertz (1806–1865)
Sebastiano (1485–1547)	Terburg (1617–1681)	Danby (1816–1875)
Del Sarto (1486–1531)	Lely (1618–1680)	Van Beers (1845–??)
Correggio (1494–1534)	Murillo (1618–1687)	
Guido Reni (1575–1642)	Ruysdael (1628–1682)	

[7] *Jude the Obscure*, II, 1.
[8] *Early Life*, p. 65.
[9] *Desperate Remedies*, Chapter III.

IV. LONDON FOUND WANTING (pages 45–58)

[1] Lines from 'A Singer Asleep', published in 1914 after Swinburne's death in 1909.
[2] *Early Life*, p. 22.
[3] Published in *Poems of the Past and the Present*, 1902.
[4] In his 'Apology' in *Late Lyrics*, 1922.
[5] *Early Life*, p. 64.
[6] *Early Life*, p. 70.
[7] *Early Life*, p. 64.
[8] In 1866 he called this poem 'Chance', but later changed the title to 'Hap', the title by which it is now known.
[9] *Jude the Obscure*, Chapter IV.
[10] *Early Life*, p. 63.
[11] *Early Life*, p. 70.
[12] R. W. King, 'The Lyrical Poems of Thomas Hardy', *London Mercury*, December 1926.
[13] *The Return of the Native*, Book Third, Chapter I.
[14] *Under the Greenwood Tree*, Chapter I.

V. 'THE POOR MAN' AND THE CRITICS (pages 59–74)

[1] *The Return of the Native*, Chapter 20.
[2] *The Return of the Native*, Chapter 21.

Notes and References

[3] *Early Life*, p. 75.
[4] *Under the Greenwood Tree*, Part III, Chapter 3.
[5] *Early Life*, p. 74.
[6] *Early Life*, p. 84.
[7] W. L. Phelps, *Autobiography*, New York, 1939, p. 391.
[8] *Early Life*, p. 79.
[9] *The Atlantic Monthly*, December 1939, p. 811.
[10] *Early Life*, p. 53.
[11] *Early Life*, p. 75.
[12] In a preface to *Desperate Remedies*, written in January 1889.

VI. EXCURSION INTO LYONNESSE (*pages 75–88*)

[1] C. Day Lewis, 'Introduction' to *Under the Greenwood Tree*, Glasgow, 1958.
[2] 'Looking at a Picture on an Anniversary', in *Moments of Vision*, 1917.
[3] *An Indiscretion in the Life of an Heiress*, published eight years after Hardy's early-morning start for Cornwall on March 7, 1870.
[4] *Early Life*, p. 100.
[5] From Hardy's poem, 'The Discovery'.
[6] From Hardy's poem, 'Lines: To a Movement in Mozart'.
[7] 'Under the Waterfall', 1914.
[8] David Cecil, *Hardy the Novelist*, London, Constable, 1943, p. 42.
[9] See Edmund Downey (who for five years, 1879–84, was employed in Tinsley's office at 18 Catherine Street in London and there heard Croft's story from his own lips), *Twenty Years Ago*, London, Hurst, 1905, p. 245. See also the report of Clarence Darrow, the American lawyer who called on Hardy, in the *Saturday Review of Literature*, New York, May 26, 1945, p. 19.
[10] *Southern Magazine*, September 1873, p. 365.

VII. 'CORNHILL' COMPLICATIONS (*pages 89–98*)

[1] See 'Ainsworth and Thomas Hardy' by Carl J. Weber, in *The Review of English Studies*, April 1941, pp. 193–200.
[2] Some of the sketches were reproduced in the catalogue of the Grolier Club Centenary Exhibition of the Works of Thomas Hardy, compiled by Carroll A. Wilson: Waterville, Maine, 1940, facing p. 15.
[3] London: Smith, Elder and Co., 1874, 2 vols.
[4] In *The Nation*, New York, December 24, 1874.
[5] The Preface to *The Hand of Ethelberta*, written in December 1895.

VIII. 'NEGATIVE BEAUTY OF TRAGIC TONE' (*pages 99–111*)

[1] *Tess of the D'Urbervilles*, Chapter LV.
[2] *Early Life*, p. 156.
[3] The reader interested to see how harmless these deleted passages are, from a twentieth-century point of view, can find them printed in *The Colophon*, New York, 'Summer' [September] 1938, p. 403, in 'Thomas Hardy in America' by Carl J. Weber.
[4] F. W. Maitland, *Life and Letters of Leslie Stephen*, London, 1906, p. 276.
[5] *Early Life*, p. 154.
[6] *Later Years*, p. 235.
[7] *Early Life*, p. 160.

Notes and References

[8] J. Henry Harper, *I Remember*, New York, 1934, p. 166.

[9] See 'Hardy's Grim Note in *The Return of the Native*' by Carl J. Weber, *Papers of The Bibliographical Society of America*, New York, March 1942, pp. 37–45.

[10] *Scribner's Monthly*, April 1879, p. 910.

[11] Quoted from *Hardy in America* by Carl J. Weber, Waterville, Maine, Colby College Press, 1946, p. 137.

[12] See also Donald Davidson, 'The Traditional Basis of Thomas Hardy's Fiction', *The Southern Review* (VI: 162–178), Baton Rouge, Louisiana, June 2, 1940.

[13] This wealth of folklore has been thoroughly examined in another book which Hardy did not live to see: Ruth A. Firor, *Folkways in Thomas Hardy* (Philadelphia: University of Pennsylvania Press, 1931). See also Professor J. O. Bailey's 'Hardy's "Mephistophelian" Visitants' in *PMLA* (1946, pp. 1146–1184), in which Diggory Venn as the embodiment of such a 'visitant' is given expert consideration.

[14] J. W. Beach, *The Technique of Thomas Hardy*, Chicago, 1922, p. 94.

[15] Arthur McDowall, *Thomas Hardy, A Critical Study*, London, 1931, p. 70.

[16] A. J. Guerard, *Thomas Hardy, The Novels and Stories*, Cambridge, Massachusetts, Harvard University Press, 1949, p. 12.

[17] D. Hawkins, *Thomas Hardy*, London, 1950, p. 34.

[18] J. Paterson, *The Making of 'The Return of the Native'*, Berkeley, University of California Press, 1960, p. 127.

[19] Paterson's conclusions have recently received impressive substantiation at Heidelberg University, where Dr. Dieter Riesner has been carrying on some painstaking researches into Hardy's methods as a literary artist and craftsman. See Riesner's 'Kunstprosa in der Werkstatt: Hardys *The Mayor of Casterbridge* 1884–1912' in a *Festschrift für Walter Hübner* (Berlin, Erich Schmidt Verlag, 1964), pp. 267–326.

IX. SHORT STORIES AND LITTLE IRONIES (*pages 112–122*)

[1] Hardy's forty-seven stories are here listed in the chronological order of publication, which may be assumed to approximate the order of their composition:

(1) 'Destiny and a Blue Cloak': published in the *New York Times*, October 4, 1874, and never reprinted by Hardy, possibly because he had used incidents and characterization from this story in *The Hand of Ethelberta*. This story was republished by the Colby College Library in Waterville, Maine, in February 1940, in *Revenge Is Sweet*, edited by Carl J. Weber.

(2) 'The Thieves Who Couldn't Help Sneezing': published in *Father Christmas*, London, 1877. Never collected by Hardy. There is no copy of *Father Christmas* in the British Museum, and no copy in the Fitzwilliam Museum at Cambridge where Sir Sydney Cockerell actively collected Hardy items in the twentieth century. The Bodleian Library at Oxford has the only copy of *Father Christmas* known to the present biographer. The story was republished in an edition of one hundred numbered copies by the Colby College Library, December 1942, with a foreword on 'Hardy's First Christmas Story' by Carl J. Weber. The first sentence in this story, with its mention of 'oak-trees now past their prime', serves to remind us that Hardy marked the words 'centenary oaks' when he came upon them in the French textbook he used at King's College, London.

(3) 'The Impulsive Lady of Croome Castle': published in *Light*, London, April 6 and 13, 1878. Apparently, no copy of this short-lived weekly has reached an American library; there are copies in the British Museum and in the Bodleian Library at Oxford. See 'A Masquerade of Noble Dames' by Carl J. Weber, *PMLA*, LVIII (June 1943), 558–63.

(4) 'An Indiscretion in the Life of an Heiress': published in the *New Quarterly Magazine*, London, July 1878. Serialized in *Harper's Weekly*, New York, June 29 to July 27, 1878 (five instalments). This is the longest of the 'short' stories for the reason that Hardy here salvaged about fifteen chapters from his rejected first novel, *The Poor Man and the Lady*. He hastily rewrote what was left of the original story after the previous borrowings for use in *Desperate Remedies*, *Under the Greenwood Tree*, and *A Pair of Blue Eyes*. He changed the names of the characters, substituted the third person for the first person of the original novel, and covered up the scars left by the successive extractions. Hardy was not proud of the result. He never reprinted 'An Indiscretion', never referred to it. After the serialization in *Harper's Weekly*, Henry Holt proposed to make 'a little volume' out of the story but he never did. Hardy perhaps dissuaded him. After the novelist's death, the second Mrs. Hardy had the story privately printed (one hundred copies) in October 1934. It was published as a book, with an introduction on 'Hardy's "Lost" Novel' by Carl J. Weber, by the Johns Hopkins Press, Baltimore, in 1935, in an edition planned and executed before knowledge of Mrs. Hardy's privately printed edition became available.

(5) 'The Distracted Young Preacher': published in the *New Quarterly Magazine*, April 1879; serialized in *Harper's Weekly* in April and May 1879; collected by Hardy in *Wessex Tales* (1888). In August 1893 Hardy told some American visitors that 'he knew one of the smugglers' who figure in this story, but he refrained from adding that these smugglers had often made stops at the house of the author's father in Higher Bockhampton. In reprinting the story in *Wessex Tales* Hardy dropped the word 'Young' from the title.

(6) 'Fellow-Townsmen': published in the *New Quarterly Magazine*, April 1880; serialized in *Harper's Weekly* in April and May 1880; collected in *Wessex Tales* (1888).

(7) 'What the Shepherd Saw': published in the *Illustrated London News*, December 5, 1881; collected in *A Changed Man and Other Tales* (1913).

(8) 'Benighted Travellers': published in the *Bolton Weekly Journal*, December 18, 1881, and in *Harper's Weekly*, December 10 and 17, 1881; collected in *A Group of Noble Dames* in 1891, at which time Hardy changed 'Lucetta' to 'Laura', 'Portpool' to 'Toneborough', 'seven' to 'half-dozen', and 'hotels' to 'taverns'. He also re-entitled the story 'The Honourable Laura'—the tenth of the Noble Dames.

(9) 'A Legend of the Year Eighteen Hundred and Four': published in *Harper's Christmas*, November 25, 1882. This story about Napoleon's threatened invasion of England is a by-product of Hardy's work on *The Trumpet-Major*. He collected it in *Life's Little Ironies* (1894), at which time he changed the title from 'A Legend' to 'A Tradition . . .' In 1912 the story was transferred from *Life's Little Ironies* to *Wessex Tales*.

(10) 'The Three Strangers'; published in *Longman's Magazine*, March 1883; collected in *Wessex Tales* (1888), where it was deservedly assigned first place. It is one of Hardy's best. One day in 1896, when Hardy told Rebekah Owen that he thought 'The Son's Veto' was his best short story, she replied that she did not agree with him, that she placed 'The Three Strangers' far above it—'and above all his and other people's short stories' (see *Hardy and the Lady from Madison Square* by Carl J. Weber, Waterville, Maine, 1952, p. 114). 'Mr. Hardy seemed surprised,' Miss Owen recorded. She was certainly right about 'The Three Strangers'. It deals with the sort of freak coincidence that Hardy delighted in. A hangman, his intended victim, and the victim's brother, all happen, plausibly enough, to meet on a rainy night at Shepherd Fennel's cottage. The suppressed terror of the escaped but unrecognized thief,

drying himself in the chimney-corner while the hangman expresses his delight in the prospect of professional employment on the morrow, and the embarrassed terror of the thief's brother, who stumbles upon the scene and then darts out into the rain again, are excellently contrasted. The brother's impulsive flight leads to an amusing climax which, in spite of the sensational nature of the preceding events, has been so naturally prepared for that the whole acquires the semblance of truth rather than of fiction. James M. Barrie saw the stage possibilities of this story and suggested that Hardy dramatize it. 'The Three Wayfarers' (1893) was the result; the play, produced at Terry's Theatre, London, June 3, 1893, was published in New York, with an introduction and notes by Carl J. Weber, by Scholars' Facsimiles and Reprints in 1944.

(11) 'The Romantic Adventures of a Milkmaid': this story, which Hardy called 'a short hastily-written novel', was first published in the London *Graphic* in June 1883, after which it was, Hardy said, 'not deemed worth reprinting'. In America, however, after being serialized in *Harper's Weekly* (seven instalments) from June 23 to August 4, 1883, the story was snapped up by piratical publishers and issued at least ten times. Hardy waited thirty years and then quietly collected this worthless trifle in the last volume of his collected stories, *A Changed Man and Other Tales* (1913). He sold the manuscript of the story to J. Pierpont Morgan.

(12) 'Our Exploits at West Poley': this story of over twenty thousand words was advertised in Boston in the *Youth's Companion* (November 22, 1883) but in the final event was not published there. It eventually appeared in *The Household* (Boston) in six instalments from November 1892 to April 1893, by which time Hardy had apparently forgotten all about this story. The mysterious history of this nine-year silence was reported by Richard Little Purdy in *Thomas Hardy: A Bibliographical Study* (1954), pp. 301–3. After a brilliant piece of detective work by Professor Purdy, this boys' story was discovered by him and was republished in 1952 by the Oxford University Press with an introduction by Professor Purdy. 'Our Exploits' deals with adventures in a cave in the Mendip Hills. In writing to the Boston editor about this story Hardy declared: 'The important features of plot and incident have received my best attention.'

(13) 'Emmeline, or Passion vs. Principle': first published in *The Independent* (New York), February 7, 1884. 'Emmeline' is Lady Emmeline of Stroome Castle; but not until 1943 was she detected as being no other than the impulsive Lady Saxelbye of Croome Castle in disguise. See Story No. 3 above and the *PMLA* article there mentioned.

(14) 'Interlopers at the Knap': published in the *English Illustrated Magazine*, May 1884; collected in *Wessex Tales* (1888). The story describes a traveller who, on a dark night, came to a fork in the road and had to climb the sign-post and strike a match in order to try to learn which way to go. Hardy once told an American visitor: 'It was my father who rode along . . . and was obliged to climb the guide post . . . , finding nothing on the fingers of the post.'

(15) 'Ancient Earthworks, and What Two Enthusiastic Scientists Found Therein': published in Detroit, Michigan, in the *Detroit Post*, March 15, 1885; reprinted in the *English Illustrated Magazine*, December 1893, at which time the title was changed to 'Ancient Earthworks at Casterbridge'. The story was finally collected in *A Changed Man* (1913) under the title 'A Tryst at an Ancient Earthwork'.

(16) 'A Mere Interlude': published in the *Bolton Weekly Journal*, October 17, 1885; collected in *A Changed Man* (1913).

(17) 'Alicia's Diary': published in the *Manchester Weekly Times*, October 15 and 22, 1887; collected in *A Changed Man* (1913).

Notes and References

(18) 'The Withered Arm': published in *Blackwood's Magazine*, January 1888; collected in *Wessex Tales* (1888). Hardy had a high opinion of this gruesome tale, the events of which were all, so he stated, drawn from real life—except that the details were 'in some respects more gruesome than in the story as he told it'. The real name of the hangman was Davies; he was an old friend of the Hardy family. In this story the reader is carried back into the company of Susan Nunsuch in *The Return of the Native*, with her hallucinations and superstitions. Coincidence plays a large part in the action, but Hardy's subtle analysis of the normal human motives and feelings of the deformed bride and her alienated husband makes the story seem natural enough and leads the unsuspecting reader up to a powerful climax.

(19) 'The Waiting Supper': published in *Murray's Magazine*, January and February 1888; collected in *A Changed Man* (1913). The first half of this story is reminiscent of *The Poor Man and the Lady* and is marred by the same sort of stilted dialogue and artificial situation that are found in Hardy's earliest work. But after the story has got well under way, it develops into a very characteristic piece of Hardyan irony. For seventeen years Mrs. Bellston and Nicholas Long dutifully await the return of an absent husband who all that time lies drowned under a waterfall on the estate. The story is told without comment other than to quote, with wry ironic significance, Robert Browning's advice in 'The Statue and the Bust': 'Better wait.'

(20) 'A Tragedy of Two Ambitions': published in *The Universal Review*, December 1888; collected in *Life's Little Ironies* (1894). This story deals with two aspiring sons of a drunken father. With motives of the highest sort they attempt to provide a suitable marriage for their sister, and in a moment of hesitation they allow the disreputable father to drown. That act weighs so heavily upon their consciences that their ambitions turn to ashes, and only too late do they come to realize that true greatness of character would have required them 'to have endured the cross'. This is not a pleasant story, but it is a striking one, and one that gains force from the simplicity and directness with which it is told.

(21) 'The First Countess of Wessex': published in *Harper's New Monthly Magazine*, December 1889. The 'Countess' was Elizabeth Horner, wife of the first Earl of Ilchester, whose story Hardy had found in Volume II of Hutchins's *History of Dorset*. Hardy collected the tale in *A Group of Noble Dames* (1891).

(22) 'The Lady Penelope': published in *Longman's Magazine*, January 1890. Hardy found the story of his heroine, Lady Penelope Darcy, in Volume III of Hutchins's *History of Dorset*. He collected this story in *A Group of Noble Dames* (1891).

(23) 'The Melancholy Hussar': published in the *Bristol Times and Mirror*, January 4 and 11, 1890; reprinted in *Three Notable Stories* (London, Blackett, 1890), and collected in *Life's Little Ironies* (1894). In 1912 Hardy transferred this story to *Wessex Tales*.

(24) 'Barbara of the House of Grebe': published as the first of the Noble Dames in *The Graphic* (London), December 1, 1890. Hardy made Barbara his Dame Number Two when the story was collected in *A Group of Noble Dames* (1891). The heroine was Barbara Webb, wife of the fifth Earl of Shaftesbury, whose story is told in Volume III of Hutchins's *History of Dorset*.

(25) 'The Marchioness of Stonehenge': published in *The Graphic*, December 1, 1890; collected in *A Group of Noble Dames* (1891).

(26) 'Lady Mottisfont': published in *The Graphic*, December 1, 1890; collected in *A Group of Noble Dames* (1891).

(27) 'The Lady Icenway': a companion-piece with 'Lady Mottisfont', just listed.

Notes and References

(28) 'Squire Petrick's Lady': a companion-story to the two preceding. This is the story Hardy was forced to bowdlerize; his marginal comments on the deletions forced upon him by 'the tyranny of Mrs. Grundy' have been quoted in the preceding chapter. This story was collected in *A Group of Noble Dames* (1891).

(29) 'Anna, Lady Bixby': in real life this lady was Anne, Lady Digby of Sherborne Castle, whose story is told in Volume IV of Hutchins's *History of Dorset*. Published originally in *The Graphic*, December 1, 1890, the story was collected in *A Group of Noble Dames* (1891).

(30) 'The Intruder': published in the *Dorset County Chronicle*, Dorchester, December 25, 1890, as 'A Legend of the Chronicle Office'; republished on October 4, 1938, by the Fairfield Publishing Co., Fairfield, Maine. After the appearance of this American edition, the story was found to be a rewriting (with some slight expansion) of 'The Waiting Supper', Short Story No. 19 above. Mrs. Wake, Bellston, Christine, and Nicholas Long of 'The Waiting Supper' were all renamed; they here appear as Mrs. Waye, Belland, Cecilia, and Nathaniel Arden. In 1913, when Hardy was preparing to collect 'The Waiting Supper' in *A Changed Man and Other Tales*, he revised the text, eliminating a number of the marks of similarity between 'The Intruder' and the story that had appeared in *Murray's Magazine*. 'The Intruder' was reprinted in the *Dorset County Chronicle* on December 23, 1937.

(31) 'The Doctor's Legend': published in *The Independent* (New York), March 26, 1891; never printed or published in England; never collected by Hardy. Professor R. L. Purdy thinks that this may be a rejected portion of 'the Old Surgeon's story' in *A Group of Noble Dames*, the story of Barbara, daughter of Sir John Grebe (see Purdy, *Thomas Hardy*, 1954, p. 299). The story was again published in *Revenge Is Sweet* (1940) by the Colby College Library, Waterville, Maine.

(32) 'Wessex Folk': published in *Harper's Magazine*, March to June 1891; collected in *Life's Little Ironies* (1894), in which book the title was changed to 'A Few Crusted Characters'. Some readers of Hardy have professed to see resemblances between his 'crusted characters' and some of Robert Browning's 'men and women'.

(33) 'For Conscience' Sake': published in the *Fortnightly Review* (London), March 1891; collected in *Life's Little Ironies* (1894).

(34) 'The Duchess of Hamptonshire': published in *A Group of Noble Dames*, May 30, 1891, in which volume the Duchess is the ninth of the Dames. Half a century after the publication of this story, it was discovered that Batton Castle, the setting of this story, is the same as Croome Castle (in Short Story No. 3) and the same as Stroome Castle (in Story No. 13), and that these three stories are essentially the same. The revisions, suppressions, additions, and changes by which the versions of 1878, 1884, and 1891 were made to appear different were described in 'A Masquerade of Noble Dames' by Carl J. Weber, *PMLA*, June 1943, pp. 558–63.

(35) 'To Please His Wife': published in *Black and White* (London), June 27, 1891; collected in *Life's Little Ironies* (1894).

(36) 'On the Western Circuit': published in the *English Illustrated Magazine*, December 1891, and in *Harper's Weekly*, November 28, 1891; collected in *Life's Little Ironies* (1894). This story is generally regarded as one of Hardy's best. Florence Emily Dugdale rated it even higher: she thought it the very best of all Hardy's stories. It deals with a young lawyer who 'played the disturbing part in two quiet feminine lives', those of Mrs. Harnham and her maid Anna. The instability of character which has been noticed in the heroines of many of

Notes and References

Hardy's novels is here again observed. Charles Raye (the lawyer) falls in love with the writer of letters he receives; but, because of Mrs. Harnham's deception in allowing him to think that Anna wrote the letters, he marries the maid and learns the truth only when it is too late. It is another 'irony' in which honourable purposes and sincere intentions are followed by blighted hopes and an unhappy future of 'dreary resignation'.

(37) 'The Son's Veto': published in the *Illustrated London News*, December 1, 1891; collected in *Life's Little Ironies* (1894). On November 23, 1896, Hardy told Rebekah Owen that he thought this story was his best, and 'seemed surprised' when she said frankly that she could not agree with him. (See *Hardy and the Lady from Madison Square*, p. 114.)

(38) 'The Fiddler of the Reels': published in *Scribner's Magazine* (New York), May 1893; collected in *Life's Little Ironies* (1894).

(39) 'Master John Horseleigh, Knight': published in the *Illustrated London News*, June 12, 1893, and in *McClure's Magazine* (New York), July 1893; collected in *A Changed Man* (1913).

(40) 'The Spectre of the Real': written in collaboration with Florence E. H. Henniker: published in *To-Day* (London), March 17, 1894; collected in *In Scarlet and Grey* (1896).

(41) 'An Imaginative Woman': published in the *Pall Mall Magazine*, April 1894. In 1896 Hardy collected this story in a new edition (the third) of *Wessex Tales*, giving it first place, but in 1912 he transferred it to *Life's Little Ironies*, which was (he said) 'more nearly its place, turning as it does upon a trick of Nature'.

(42) 'A Committee Man of "The Terror"': published in the *Illustrated London News*, November 22, 1896; collected in *A Changed Man and Other Tales* (1913).

(43) 'The Duke's Reappearance': published in *The Saturday Review* (London), December 14, 1896; collected in *A Changed Man* (1913).

(44) 'The Grave by the Handpost': published in *St. James's Budget*, November 30, 1897; collected in *A Changed Man* (1913).

(45) 'A Changed Man': published in *The Sphere* (London), April 21, 1900; collected in *A Changed Man* (1913).

(46) 'Enter a Dragoon': published in *Harper's Magazine*, December 1900; collected in *A Changed Man* (1913).

(47) 'Old Mrs. Chundle': published in the *Ladies Home Journal* (Philadelphia), February 1929, a year after Hardy's death. Published by arrangement with the second Mrs. Hardy, the story was subsequently reprinted as a separate book (New York, Crosby Gaige, 1929).

2 Mrs. Emma Hardy, quoted in *Hardy and the Lady from Madison Square*, p. 68.
3 The notebook is now in the Dorset County Museum in Dorchester.
4 *Early Life*, p. 64.
5 *Early Life*, p. 14.
6 In America Hardy tried to get *The Trumpet-Major* into the *Atlantic Monthly* in Boston, but failed. Then, after several unsuccessful attempts in New York, he placed it (with the help of Henry Holt) with *Demorest's Monthly Magazine*.
7 For details about these pirated editions see Carl J. Weber, *Hardy in America*, Waterville, Colby College Press, 1946, pp. 273–88.
8 *The Critic*, January 28, 1882.
9 Weber, *Hardy in America*, 1946, p. 67.
10 Lambert's book proved very popular in London: first edition by Phillips, 1810; second edition by Cradock and Joy, 1813; third edition by Baldwin, 1816.

11 See 'A Connecticut Yankee in King Alfred's Country' by Carl J. Weber, in *The Colophon* (New York), n.s. I (June 1936), 525–35, and 'A Ghost from a Barber Shop' by Carl J. Weber, in *The New Colophon* (New York), I (April 1948), 185–9.

X. 'TROUBLES IN BATTALIONS' *(pages 123–138)*

1 E. McC. Fleming, *R. R. Bowker*, Norman, Oklahoma, 1952, p. 156.
2 *Early Life*, p. 163.
3 *Early Life*, p. 189.
4 *Two on a Tower*, Chapter IX.
5 *Early Life*, p. 197.
6 *Early Life*, p. 72.
7 J. W. Beach, *The Technique of Thomas Hardy*, Chicago, 1922, p. 6.
8 See R. L. Purdy, *Thomas Hardy: A Bibliographical Study*, 1954, p. 29.
9 The programme is reproduced on page 448 of *The Colophon*, n.s. II, New York, July 1937.
10 See page 692 in 'Thomas Hardy and his New England Editors' by Carl J. Weber, in *The New England Quarterly*, XV (December 1942), 681–99.
11 Preface to *Two on a Tower*, July 1895.
12 In *Poems of the Past and the Present*, 1902.
13 See 'Hardy's Comet' by Carl J. Weber, in *English Language Notes*, Boulder, Colorado, I (March 1964), 215–18.
14 Hamlin Garland, *Afternoon Neighbors*, New York, Macmillan, 1934, pp. 91–92.
15 See 'Thomas Hardy and his New England Editors' by Carl J. Weber, *New England Quarterly*, XV (December 1942), 686.
16 Their loss is unfortunate, for Hardy's first thoughts were not always his best. He sometimes made a third or fourth attempt at a word or a phrase, and in such persistent efforts at subtler refinements of meaning he was often more successful at the end than at the beginning. In this search for the right word, he finally preferred 'partner' to 'match', 'a movement' to 'certain sounds', and 'excommunicatory' to 'excommunicating'. He decided that 'I'll go on reading' was clearer than 'I'll read', and that 'vehement firmness' was better than a mere 'vehemence'. But not one of these readings in the duplicate manuscript got into the *Atlantic*. See 'The Manuscript of Hardy's *Two on a Tower*' by Carl J. Weber, in the *Papers of the Bibliographical Society of America*, XL (March 1946), 1–21.
17 See 'Lowell's Dead Rat in the Wall' by Carl J. Weber, *New England Quarterly*, IX (September and December, 1936), 468–72 and 686–8.
18 Weber, *Hardy in America*, Waterville, 1946, p. 75.
19 *Century Magazine*, XLVI (July 1893), 356.
20 Joseph Warren Beach, *The Technique of Thomas Hardy*, Chicago, 1922, p. 125.
21 *Lippincott's Magazine*, September 1883, p. 336.
22 *The Literary World*, Boston, July 28, 1883, p. 245.

XI. PORTRAIT OF A MAN OF CHARACTER *(pages 139–153)*

1 *Early Life*, p. 220.
2 Published in *Longman's Magazine*, July 1883.
3 Shakespeare, *Sonnet XIV*.
4 *The Mayor of Casterbridge*, Chapter XLIII.
5 *Early Life*, p. 224.

6 *Early Life*, p. 215.
7 *Early Life*, p. 222.
8 *Early Life*, p. 222.
9 *Early Life*, p. 210.
10 *Early Life*, p. 212.
11 *The Mayor of Casterbridge*, Chapter XI.
12 Published in *Moments of Vision*, 1917.
13 *Hardy's Love Poems*, edited by Carl J. Weber, London, Macmillan, 1963, p. 94.
14 Published in *Late Lyrics and Earlier*, 1922.
15 *Love Poems* (see note 13 above), p. 22.
16 *Love Poems* (see note 13 above), p. 52.
17 *Early Life*, p. 216.
18 *The Mayor of Casterbridge*, Chapter XXII.
19 *Dearest Emmie*, Hardy's Letters to his First Wife, edited by Carl J. Weber, London, Macmillan, 1963, p. 5.
20 Harvey C. Webster, 'Introduction' to *The Mayor of Casterbridge*, New York, Rinehart, 1948, p. ix.
21 De Sola Pinto, 'Introduction' to *The Life and Death of the Mayor of Casterbridge*, London, Macmillan, 1934, p. xvi.
22 Vere H. Collins, *Talks with Thomas Hardy at Max Gate*, New York, Doubleday, Doran, 1928, p. 16.
23 Carroll A. Wilson, *Catalogue of the Grolier Club Centenary Exhibition of the Works of Thomas Hardy*, Waterville, Maine, 1940, p. 26.
24 See Weber, *Hardy and the Lady from Madison Square*, p. 110.
25 *Early Life*, p. 235.

XII. 'ATMOSPHERE OF CIDER' *(pages 154–165)*

1 *Later Years*, p. 152.
2 Donald Maxwell, *The Landscape of Thomas Hardy*, London, Cassell, 1928.
3 *The Woodlanders*, Chapter I.
4 W. R. Rutland, *Thomas Hardy: A Study*, Oxford, Blackwell, 1938.
5 John A. Steuart, 'The Neglect of Hardy's Novels', *Sunday Times*, London, January 22, 1928.
6 *Later Years*, p. 151.
7 Arthur McDowall, *Thomas Hardy: A Critical Study*, London, Faber, 1931, pp. 68, 72, 75, 77.
8 Weber, *Hardy and the Lady from Madison Square*, p. 89.
9 Murry's review of Hardy's poetry in the *New York Times*, July 29, 1923: III, 5, 5.
10 Felix W. Crosse, *The Human Pair in the Work of Thomas Hardy*, London, Toulmin, 1930, p. 67. *The Human Pair* is a translation by Crosse of *Le Couple Humain dans l'Oeuvre de Thomas Hardy*, Paris, 1928, by 'Pierre D'Exideuil'—the nom-de-plume of Georges Lasselin.
11 *Early Life*, p. 232.

XIII. 'A PURE WOMAN FAITHFULLY PRESENTED' *(pages 166–179)*

1 See Richard Little Purdy, *Thomas Hardy*, 1954, pp. 72–73.
2 Purdy, op. cit., pp. 72–73.
3 *The Critic*, New York, April 16, 1892.
4 *Early Life*, p. 37.
5 F. B. Pinion, 'Introduction' to *Tess*, London, Macmillan, 1959, p. ix.

Notes and References

XIV. 'HIGH-WATER MARK OF LATE-VICTORIAN FICTION' (pages 180–191

[1] See *Dearest Emmie*, ed. Weber, London, Macmillan, 1963, pp. 19–20.
[2] *Tess of the D'Urbervilles*, ed. F. B. Pinion, London, Macmillan, 1959, p. 519.
[3] *Later Years*, p. 7.
[4] *Later Years*, p. 32.
[5] *Later Years*, p. 33.
[6] *Dearest Emmie* (see note 1 above), p. 32.
[7] *Dearest Emmie*, p. 38.
[8] *Early Life*, p. 201.
[9] *Modern Language Notes*, Baltimore, LI (April 1936), 262.
[10] The following list of a score of translations of *Tess* into foreign languages shows the time and the extent of the dispersal of the novel throughout the world:
Russian (Moscow, 1893), translated by V. S.
Polish (Lwow, 1893).
Swedish (Stockholm, 1900), translated by Vera Branting.
Danish (Copenhagen, 1905).
Spanish (Madrid, 1924), translated by M. Ortega y Gasset.
French (Paris, 1924), translated by Madeleine Rolland.
Danish (Copenhagen, 1924), a different translation from that of 1905.
Bohemian (Prague, 1927), translated by J. J. David.
Japanese (Tokyo, 1928), translated by Shinsaburo Miyajima.
Polish (Warsaw, 1929), translated by Janiny Sujkowskiej.
Russian (Moscow, 1930), translated by A. V. Krivtzova.
Italian (Rome, 1930), translated by Gian Dauli.
Swedish (Stockholm, 1931), translated by Kerstin Wenström.
German (Leipzig, 1934), translated by Paul Baudisch.
Dutch (Amsterdam, 1934 or earlier).
Lettish (Riga, 1935), translated by Zenta Maurina.
Chinese (Shanghai, 1936), translated by Chang Ku-Jo.
Icelandic (Reykjavik, 1942), translated by Snaebjorn Jonsson.
Norwegian (Oslo, 1948), translated by Margrethe Kjaer.
Polish (Warsaw, 1954), translated by Roza C. Heymanova.
[11] See 'Noteworthy Modern Novels', pp. 283–305 in *The Man Behind the Book: Essays in Understanding* by Henry Van Dyke, New York, Scribners, 1929.
[12] See Robert Shafer, 'Thomas Hardy', pp. 235–81 in *Christianity and Naturalism*, New Haven, Yale University Press, 1926.

XV. AN INTERLUDE (pages 192–198)

[1] *Dearest Emmie*, Hardy's Letters to his First Wife, London, Macmillan, 1963, p. 6.
[2] *Later Years*, p. 61.
[3] *Later Years*, p. 59.
[4] *Later Years*, p. 60.
[5] Proust, 'Extrait de La Prisonnière', *Revue Nouvelle*, Paris, February 1928, p. 55; English translation in the *Colby Mercury*, VI (May 1938), 181.
[6] D. H. Lawrence, in *John O' London's Weekly*, March 12 and 19, 1932.
[7] Published in *To-Day*, November 17, 1894.
[8] R. L. Purdy, *Thomas Hardy*, 1954, p. 344.
[9] *Later Years*, p. 20.
[10] *The Three Wayfarers* was published in March 1944, with an introduction and notes by Carl J. Weber, by Scholars' Facsimiles and Reprints, New York.

Notes and References

XVI. SAD MUSIC OF HUMANITY (pages 199–210)

[1] Clive Holland suggests, in *Thomas Hardy, O.M.*, London, Herbert Jenkins, 1933, p. 54, that Hardy had been at Oxford in 1864, but the evidence he cites is unconvincing.
[2] *Early Life*, p. 272.
[3] *Jude the Obscure*, Part II, Chapter 6.
[4] *Jude the Obscure*, II, 1.
[5] *Jude the Obscure*, II, 3.
[6] *Jude the Obscure*, II, 6.
[7] *Jude the Obscure*, II, 1.
[8] *Later Years*, p. 196.
[9] *Jude the Obscure*, I, 2.
[10] *Early Life*, p. 35.
[11] *Early Life*, p. 66.
[12] For detailed information about the text of *Jude the Obscure* from manuscript to the definitive edition in 1912, see Robert C. Slack's doctoral dissertation at the University of Pittsburgh: *A Variorum Edition of 'Jude the Obscure'*. An abstract of the dissertation was published in the *University of Pittsburgh Bulletin*, L (1954), 8–11. See also Robert C. Slack, 'The Text of "Jude the Obscure",' *Nineteenth-Century Fiction*, XI (1957), 261–75.
[13] H. C. Duffin, *Thomas Hardy*, University of Manchester Press, first edition, 1916, p. 203; second edition, 1921, p. 188.
[14] W. R. Rutland, *Thomas Hardy*, Oxford, Blackwell, 1938, p. 249.

XVII. 'DEEP DIVISION' (pages 211–218)

[1] David Cecil, *Hardy the Novelist*, Indianapolis, Bobbs-Merrill, 1946, p. 189.
[2] Richard Little Purdy, *Thomas Hardy: A Bibliographical Study*, Oxford University Press, 1954, p. 345.
[3] 'Everything Comes', published in *Moments of Vision*, 1917.
[4] 'You Were the Sort that Men Forget', a poem published in *Moments of Vision*, 1917, p. 16.
[5] 'Memory and I', published in *Poems of the Past and the Present*, 1902, p. 256.
[6] 'The Division' was published in *Time's Laughingstocks*, 1909, p. 55. On December 5, 1949, Siegfried Sassoon wrote to Sir Sydney Cockerell: 'The Division . . . obviously refers to Emma.'
[7] From 'Beeny Cliff', in *Satires of Circumstance*, 1914, p. 119.
[8] From the last line of 'Had You Wept', published in *Satires of Circumstance*, 1914, p. 167.
[9] *Hardy's Love Poems*, edited by Carl J. Weber, London, Macmillan, 1963, p. 52.

XVIII. THE END OF PROSE (pages 219–226)

[1] *Dearest Emmie*, London, Macmillan, 1963, p. 31.
[2] This London 'Wessex Edition' should be carefully distinguished from the fifteen-volume 'Wessex Edition' published by Harper and Brothers in New York in 1900 and from their twenty-volume 'Wessex Edition' (in a different format) published in 1905. Neither of these American editions contains Hardy's definitive text, and he saw proofs of none of these American books. See Weber, *Hardy in America*, pp. 98–102.
[3] *The Athenaeum*, December 5, 1874, p. 747.

Notes and References

[4] J. H. Fowler, *The Novels of Thomas Hardy*, English Association Pamphlet No. 71, Oxford University Press, 1928.

[5] *Early Life*, p. 181.

[6] Donald Maxwell, *The Landscape of Thomas Hardy*, London, Cassell, 1928.

XIX. THE FIRST BOOKS OF PROSE (*pages 227–236*)

[1] *Dearest Emmie*, London, Macmillan, 1963, p. 21.

[2] *Dearest Emmie*, p. 37.

[3] *Later Years*, p. 79.

[4] *Later Years*, p. 79.

[5] *Later Years*, p. 78.

[6] *Kenyon Review*, XIII (August 1951), 445–54.

XX. 'THE DYNASTS' (*pages 237–251*)

[1] *The Reporter*, 'a fortnightly of facts and ideas', April 17, 1951.

[2] 'So Various' was published posthumously in the *Daily Telegraph*, London, March 22, 1928.

[3] *Jude the Obscure*, Part II, Chapter 1.

[4] The Preface to *The Dynasts*.

[5] See *Early Life*, p. 290. Hardy's indebtedness to Buchanan is the discovery of Professor Hoxie N. Fairchild, of Hunter College. See his 'The Immediate Source of *The Dynasts*', *PMLA*, LXVII (March 1952), 43–64.

[6] *PMLA*, LXVII (March 1952), 43.

[7] Barker Fairley, 'Notes on the Form of *The Dynasts*', *PMLA*, XXXIV (September 1919), 401–415.

[8] *Later Years*, p. 104.

[9] See Carl J. Weber, 'Hardy's Copy of Schopenhauer', *Colby Library Quarterly*, IV (November 1957), 217–24.

[10] *Atlantic Monthly*, XCIII (May 1904), 713.

[11] *Quarterly Review*, London, January 1909.

[12] *The Nation*, New York, LXXXVI (April 16, 1908), 353–4. I regret that I have been unable to identify this perceptive anonymous reviewer.

[13] *The New Republic*, New York, I (December 26, 1914), 25–26.

[14] Harold Orel, *Thomas Hardy's Epic-Drama: A Study of 'The Dynasts'*, Lawrence, Kansas, University of Kansas Press, 1963, p. viii.

XXI. 'MAGIC LIGHTS' (*pages 252–260*)

[1] Letter of April 10, 1904, to Heath Joyce of the London *Graphic*.

[2] Published in *Time's Laughingstocks*, 1909.

[3] This sonnet was printed in the *Saturday Review*, September 8, 1906, p. 293.

[4] Miss Thomson's portrait of Hardy is reproduced facing page 62 in *Letters of Thomas Hardy*, edited by Carl J. Weber, Waterville, Colby College Press, 1954.

[5] Blanche's sketch of Hardy made in 1906 was reproduced in the *Times Literary Supplement*, London, October 23, 1937, p. 777.

[6] 'Had You Wept', from *Satires of Circumstance*, 1914, p. 167.

[7] From *Selected Poems* (1916), p. 31; reprinted in *Moments of Vision*, 1917.

[8] *Satires of Circumstance, Lyrics, and Reveries*, 1914.

[9] *Later Years*, p. 164.

[10] Edmund Blunden, *Thomas Hardy*, English Men of Letters Series, London, Macmillan, 1941, p. 137.

Notes and References

[11] H. C. Duffin, *Thomas Hardy*, Manchester University Press, 3rd edition, 1937 (reprinted 1962), pp. 291–3.
[12] Arthur McDowall, *Thomas Hardy, a Critical Study*, London, Faber and Faber, 1931, p. 235.
[13] Samuel C. Chew, *Thomas Hardy, Poet and Novelist*, New York, Alfred A. Knopf, 1929, p. 78.
[14] 'The Poetry of Thomas Hardy' by J. E. Barton, in *The Art of Thomas Hardy* by Lionel Johnson, New York, Dodd, Mead and Company, 1923, p. 275.
[15] Douglas Brown, *Thomas Hardy*, London, Longmans, revised edition 1961, p. 171.
[16] *Hardy's Love Poems*, edited with an Introduction on 'Hardy's Cornish Romance' by Carl J. Weber, London, Macmillan, 1963.

XXII. 'LET ME ENJOY THE EARTH NO LESS' (*pages 261–269*)

[1] Published in *Satires, Lyrics and Reveries* in 1914, but written some years earlier.
[2] We shall have more to say about this and other dramatizations in the next chapter.
[3] *Hardy and the Lady from Madison Square* by Weber, p. 169.
[4] Published in *Late Lyrics*, 1922.
[5] *Hardy and the Lady from Madison Square*, p. 171.
[6] *Hardy and the Lady from Madison Square*, p. 192.
[7] J. Middleton Murry, *The Problem of Style*, Oxford University Press, 1921, p. 146.
[8] Published in *Satires, Lyrics and Reveries*, 1914.
[9] Published in *The Times*, London, May 22, 1909.
[10] Siegfried Sassoon, *Siegfried's Journey*, New York, Viking Press, 1946, pp. 221–3.
[11] *Later Years*, pp. 192–3.

XXIII. 'THROBBINGS OF NOONTIDE' (*pages 270–282*)

[1] *Letters of Thomas Hardy*, ed. Weber, Waterville, Colby College Press, 1954, p. 87.
[2] Gertrude Bugler, *Personal Recollections of Thomas Hardy*, Dorchester, Dorset Natural History and Archaeological Society, 2nd edition, 1964, p. 5.
[3] The Hardy Players did manage to enact some 'Wessex Scenes from *The Dynasts*' on December 6 and 7, 1916; and on January 31, 1918, they presented a somewhat revised version of *The Mellstock Quire*. This brought to an end A. H. Evans's ten-year association with the Hardy dramatizations.
[4] Gertrude Bugler, *Personal Recollections*, 1964, p. 6.
[5] 'The Oxen'.
[6] *The Famous Tragedy* was published by Macmillan in November 1923. The play was enacted by the Hardy Players at Dorchester on November 28, 29, and 30, 1923, and was repeated in King George's Hall in London on February 21, 1924. It was again performed in Bournemouth, April 25, 1924, and at Glastonbury, in connection with the August Festival there.
[7] Gertrude Bugler, *Personal Recollections*, 1964, p. 9.
[8] Published in *Late Lyrics*, 1922.

XXIV. 'AFTERWARDS' (*pages 283–295*)

[1] *Later Years*, p. 221.
[2] *Later Years*, p. 222.
[3] Weber, *Hardy and the Lady from Madison Square*, p. 163.
[4] *Letters of Thomas Hardy*, ed. Weber, Colby College Press, 1954, p. 96.

Notes and References

[5] This was the story Hardy contributed to *Longman's Magazine*, January 1890. It became 'Dame the Eighth' in *A Group of Noble Dames*.

[6] L. Abercrombie, *Thomas Hardy*, London, Martin Secker, 1912.

[7] Weber, *Hardy and the Lady from Madison Square*, p. 158.

[8] *Encyclopaedia Britannica*, 14th ed., 1929: XI, 193. This subtle reference to *The Early Life of Thomas Hardy* was missed by Professor Richard Little Purdy when (in the London *Times Literary Supplement* for December 20, 1960) he claimed that he had made 'the first disclosure of Hardy's authorship of *The Early Life*'. Quite apart from Abercrombie's disclosure in the 1929 *Britannica*, twenty-five years before the publication of Professor Purdy's book, Hardy had also admitted at least one other individual to his secret. Cyril Clemens, Mark Twain's nephew, had called at Max Gate one 'October day in the year 1925' and had learned from Hardy's lips about the autobiographical device he was then making use of: 'I slant my memoirs as though my wife were writing them herself' (Cyril Clemens, *My Chat with Thomas Hardy*, 1944, p. 26). One notices that Clemens uses the same word, 'memoirs', that Abercrombie had used in his *Britannica* article, and one wonders whether that is not what Hardy had called his work.

[9] *Later Years*, p. 217.

[10] *Later Years*, p. 8.

[11] *Early Life*, p. 172–173.

[12] When Hardy's library was sold at auction on May 26, 1938, the Rabelais Club *Recreations* were a part of Lot No. 23.

[13] *Dearest Emmie*, Hardy's Letters to his First Wife, 1963, p. 76.

[14] *Times Literary Supplement*, London, January 19, 1928, pp. 33–34.

[15] The last poem in *Moments of Vision*.

[16] *Music and Letters*, London, April, July, and October 1940, and July 1941.

[17] It may be appropriate to remark here that a similar special Hardy Number had appeared in Paris twelve years previously, when the *Revue Nouvelle* published its February 1928 issue as 'Homage à Thomas Hardy'. It contained articles by Pierre D'Exideuil, Marcel Proust, and others.

[18] Hardy's novels have been translated into

Bengali	French	Norwegian
Bohemian	German	Polish
Bulgarian	Hungarian	Russian
Chinese	Icelandic	Slovak
Danish	Italian	Spanish
Dutch	Japanese	Swedish
Finnish	Lettish	Tamil (Madras, India)

Index

Index

Index

Index

Index

Index

Index

Index

Index

Index

Index